A FIELD-MARSHAL
IN THE FAMILY

Montgomery of Alamein
F.M.
17-11-67

A FIELD-MARSHAL
IN THE FAMILY

BRIAN MONTGOMERY

CONSTABLE
LONDON

First published in Great Britain 1973
by Constable and Company Limited
10 Orange Street London WC2H 7EG
Copyright © 1973 by Brian Montgomery
All rights reserved

ISBN 0 09 459560 7

Set in Monotype Plantin

Printed in Great Britain by
Ebenezer Baylis & Son Limited
The Trinity Press, Worcester, and London

TO
MY WIFE

CONTENTS

ILLUSTRATIONS

FOREWORD

In my Introduction I have described how the project for this book arose and my reasons for writing it, but that does not reveal how grateful I am to many people for their assistance and advice.

My first and foremost debt is to my wife, who read each passage in draft as it was finished and provided much stimulating comment. I shall always be particularly grateful to my stepson Tom Mac-Neece, now a journalist, who, one Sunday morning at our cottage in Saltwood, skilfully outlined a structure and sequence for a story of this kind. My grateful thanks are due to my sister-in-law, Margaret Montgomery, for the useful material she provided, and to my nephew James Montgomery in Vancouver who sent me fresh details of the family in Canada.

I was most fortunate in having the wise counsel and guidance of Field-Marshal Sir Gerald Templer, Major-General Sir Francis de Guingand, Major-General Sir Miles Graham, Air Chief Marshal Sir Hugh Constantine and the late Lieutenant-General Sir George Cole. The help of these officers was invaluable, especially the time I spent in company with Sir Francis at a vital point in the preparation of the book. I was also fortunate in having the advice of Lieutenant-Colonel C. P. (Kit) Dawnay who was my brother's Military Assistant during the 1939-45 war from OVERLORD onwards. I am equally grateful to the Warden of Rhodes Trust, Mr. E. T. (Bill) Williams, for the time and trouble he took to advise me on the more controversial issues which arose during my brother's desert campaign, and afterwards during the fighting in Italy and in North-West Europe. I have also to thank Major-General W. D. E. Brown for the useful information he gave me, as well as Mr. John Henderson, who was my brother's ADC for so long. My grateful thanks are due to Mr. T. E. B. Howarth, High Master of St. Paul's, for all his assistance, including the help given me by his library staff during my search in the school's archives, and to Dr. J. M. Rae, Headmaster of Westminster, for kindly allowing me access to 17 Dean's Yard. I have also to thank Lord Dulverton for information on the OVERLORD Embroidery. Last year it was my good fortune to meet Mrs. Tommy Macdonald, née Betty Anderson, who at one stage played so important a part in my brother's life. I am most grateful for what she told me.

I could not have completed the research which a project of this kind entails without access to, and assistance in searching for, particular papers stored in the Public Record Office. I am therefore very grateful to Mr. E. K. Timings and his staff, notably his Research Assistants, Mr. N. E. Evans, Mr. J. L. Walford and Mr. A. R. Ford, for kindly guiding my footsteps in that maze of historic documentation. Equally I could not have done without the resources of the London Library where the Deputy Librarian, Mr. Douglas Mathews, kindly gave me much useful information. My thanks are also due to the Librarians and Staff of the old War Office Library in the Ministry of Defence for helping me with my inquiries. I should add that this book could certainly never have appeared without the skill and expertise of Sheena Barber and Julia Hanbury, who spent long hours unravelling my handwriting to produce the typescript on time. Finally I have to thank my publishers, and particularly Mr. John Jolliffe, for their expert guidance and advice during all stages in the preparation of the book.

Chelsea 1973   BRIAN MONTGOMERY

ACKNOWLEDGEMENTS

I am grateful to the following authors and publishers for permission to quote from the books shown below:

Frederick W. Farrar, *St Winifred's or The World of School*, A. and C. Black, Edinburgh.

Frederick W. Farrar, *Julian Home*, A. and C. Black, Edinburgh.

Reginald Farrar, *F. W. Farrar, Dean of Canterbury*, James Nisbet & Co. Ltd. – 1904.

Professor L. E. Henry, BA, MRCP, *Napoleon's War Maxims*, Gale & Polden Ltd.

Field-Marshal Montgomery, *The Memoirs of Field-Marshal Montgomery*, Wm. Collins.

Robert Jackson, *Thirty Seconds at Quetta*, Evans Bros. Ltd.

Field-Marshal Montgomery, *A History of Warfare*, Wm. Collins.

Sir Arthur Bryant, *The Turn of the Tide*, Wm. Collins.

Sir Arthur Bryant, *Triumph in the West*, Wm. Collins.

Sir F. de Guingand, *Operation Victory*, Hodder and Stoughton.

Sir F. de Guingand, *Generals at War*, Hodder and Stoughton.

Correlli Barnett, *The Desert Generals*, William Kimber.

Sir Basil Liddell Hart, *History of the Second World War*, Cassell & Co. Ltd.

Alan Moorehead, *Montgomery*, Hamish Hamilton Ltd.

Lord Tedder, *With Prejudice*, Cassell & Co. Ltd.

Bosworth Smith, *The Life of Lord Lawrence*, Thomas Nelson & Sons.

Maud Montgomery, *Bishop Montgomery, A Memoir*, Society for Propagation of the Gospel.

Charles Lethbridge Kingsford (published 1921), *The Story of the Royal Warwickshire Regiment*, Country Life Ltd – also by George Newnes Ltd.

Kay Summersby (1948), *Eisenhower was my Boss*, Prentice-Hall, Inc., New York.

Ronald Lewin, *Montgomery, as a Military Commander*, B. T. Batsford Ltd.

Dwight D. Eisenhower, *Crusade in Europe*, W. H. Heinemann Ltd.

Major-General R. J. Collins, *Lord Wavell*, Hodder and Stoughton, Ltd.

INTRODUCTION

It was a late summer evening in 1933. My father, formerly Bishop of Tasmania, had died the previous winter, so as many as possible of the family had arranged to come home that year. Quite a number of us therefore had been able to join our mother in the family home at Moville in Co. Donegal. My eldest sister was there with her husband on leave from Cairo; he was in the Egyptian Civil Service and they lived in a house-boat moored to the bank of the Nile opposite the Gezira Sporting Club. One other sister married to an army officer was present, and also one of my sisters-in-law, whose husband, my brother Colin, was a clergyman. These two were later to spend long years in Canada, amongst the Eskimo community, when Colin was appointed Canon in the Arctic. My brother Bernard, with his wife Betty and their young son David, then aged five, completed the party. Bernard was on leave from Alexandria where he was commanding his regiment, and they were both shortly due to return there as the battalion was under orders to move to India.

It had been an unusually fine and hot summer and as the family gathered in the drawing-room I remember my mother remarked to Bernard, 'I suppose you will be staying in London before you fly back to Alexandria, so that Betty can get the clothes she will need in India.' The reply was instant: 'Certainly not, there is no reason to stay in London. Betty doesn't need any extra clothing. All she needs, all any woman needs, is one serviceable gown and a waterproof hat – finish!' My mother well understood that her daughter-in-law wished to do some shopping in London, go to the theatre, etc. and she wanted to help her. No one could say my mother was not experienced in bringing up a family for she had had nine children in the space of twenty-one years. There were six boys: Harold, Donald, Bernard, Desmond, Colin and Brian; and three

girls: Sibyl, Una and Winsome. Our mother was probably one of
the first of her generation to become a 'working mother'. In addition to rearing her large family (in Tasmania she never employed a
nurse) she found time to cope, not only with the many and exacting
duties of a bishop's wife, but also, later on, to work daily as
organiser of the Mother's Union in London.

Nowadays large families, of say five or more children, are seldom
encountered, but for my parents' generation, which knew nothing
of family planning, children came from God and must be seen as
His blessing. I have therefore always found it intriguing, as a member of a very large family, one of whom reached the pinnacle of
fame, to reflect on the influence, if any, we exerted on each other.
Furthermore it is interesting to consider how much of the Field-
Marshal's personality and character, with all its determination and
tenacity, and complete dedication to his profession, should be attributed to heredity. Did he inherit all that immense confidence in
his own opinions and ability, which his detractors, and there are
plenty of them, have never been slow to regard as arrogance and
conceit? Like begets like, be it man or woman, so our forebears
both male and female are equally relevant where heredity is
concerned. We come from an old Irish family the roots of which are
wide-spread and whose history is long.

My grandfather Sir Robert Montgomery, a Lieutenant-Governor
of the Punjab, had inherited extensive records of the family, mainly
manuscript documents. To these he had added his own personal
papers and diaries, written during his long service in India before
and after the Mutiny. Bishop Montgomery collated and added
greatly to these records, all of which I remember were kept at home
in the loft over the stables, in a midshipman's sea chest. This chest
belonged to an uncle who began his career in the Royal Navy but
later forsook the sea and became a parson in India in the Bengal
Chaplaincy Service. We boys and girls could never be bothered to
look at old papers, and after our home was sold (it is now a hotel)
they vanished as far as I was concerned. I was therefore somewhat
surprised when I received the following letter from my brother
Bernard:

FROM: FIELD-MARSHAL THE VISCOUNT MONTGOMERY OF ALAMEIN,
K.G., G.C.B., D.S.O.

ISINGTON MILL,
ALTON,
HANTS.
TEL. BENTLEY 3126.

10-9-70

Dear Brian

You may recall that I have here all father's diaries, written in his own handwriting. They were in one of my caravans. I have now brought them into the house and have had a look at them.

I suggest you now take them over. You could write a book and make a lot of money — if you know how to write !!

You can come and collect them whenever you like.

Yrs ever
Bernard

In the late summer of 1970 my wife and I went to the Mill and collected all these records. On examination I found they were in fact all the papers which used to be kept in the loft at our Irish home, and not only father's diaries. I have found them all most revealing, and I have readily accepted my brother's challenge. But the book I have written in the end is not a mammoth family history based on those documents, interesting though that might be to some. It is first of all an explanation of how heredity and environment together produced a Field-Marshal who never lost a campaign. To this I have added the story of his whole life, though not a detailed account of his battles and campaigns which has already been written both by himself and others. I have included a number of more or less personal and generally unknown facts which I believe can only be supplied by one of his own blood, who has known him for over half a century.

Brian Montgomery

Chapter 1

NORMANDY TO DONEGAL

Until the eleventh century, some 900 years ago, the surname Montgomery was unknown outside France. The first person of that name to appear in England was Sir Roger de Montgomeri, Count of Montgomeri in Normandy. From his line are descended all the numerous Montgomery families in England, Wales, Scotland and Ireland, whether their name is spelt Montgomerie, as in Scotland, or Montgomery elsewhere. Sir Roger's family had been long established in Normandy where they owned large estates in the region of Caen, Falaise and Argentan. It may be of interest to recall that this was the very area in which, in the summer of 1944, the British and American armies under the command of my brother, Field-Marshal Montgomery, trapped and destroyed the German armies under Field-Marshal Rommel. In Montgomery's own words, 'I ordered the right flank of 12 Army Group, two American armies, to swing north to Argentan, at the southern end of the trap, and intensified the British and Canadian armies' thrust southwards to the capture of Falaise at the northern end.' Falaise fell to the Canadian army on 16th August, whilst on the same day American forces reached Argentan.

Sir Roger de Montgomeri was also a distinguished and successful soldier. He was one of the most powerful and influential nobles at the court of William, Duke of Normandy, later William I King of England, whose kinsman he was. He commanded the vanguard

of the Norman army at the battle of Hastings in 1066, and also contributed sixty ships to Duke William's fleet. After the Conquest
King William divided large areas of England between his chosen
companions. Sir Roger was particularly fortunate, being rewarded
by advancement to the earldoms of Chichester, Arundel and
Shrewsbury. His main possessions, however, lay on the Welsh
border, and his life in England was by no means peaceful since it
was generally spent defending his estates against perpetual incur-
sions by fierce tribesmen from Wales. In the event he was successful enough for he gained much Welsh land and property and,
incidentally, built the castle at Shrewsbury. The town and county
of Montgomery derive their name from his. All the records show
him to have been a man of many parts. Even in his last years he
astounded the population by entering the church and becoming a
monk of the Benedictine order at the Abbey of St Peter and St
Paul in Shrewsbury, which he had founded himself. He died
there on 1st August 1095 and was buried in the Abbey, where his
tomb can be seen, surmounted by a knight in chain armour, with
an inscription giving an account of his life.

Sir Roger left all his vast possessions intact to his descendant, but
unfortunately his sons, except for the youngest, inherited little of
their father's prudence and sagacity. They intrigued unsuccessfully against Henry I, King of England, who drove them all out of
the country. Since that time no descendant of the name has ever
possessed any of the large territories in England and Wales first
owned by Roger Montgomeri. The exception was Arnold, the
youngest son, who married Lafracotte daughter of the King of
Munster in Ireland. Arnold's son crossed into Scotland early in the
twelfth century and became ancestor of all the Montgomerie families in Scotland, including the branches of Ardrossan, Eaglesham,
Eglinton and Lainshaw. Centuries later there followed the Protestant plantation of the nine counties of Ulster begun by King James
I in 1603. This brought into Ireland all the many Irish Montgomery families, including our own branch in Co. Donegal. Some
of these families, including ours, have as their family motto 'Gardez
Bien' which is very similar to the Eglinton motto, 'Garde Bien', or
Take Good Care. My brother kept this motto when he was raised

to the peerage, and I have often thought how entirely appropriate
it is that he should have it. His first thought throughout his military
career has always been 'to take good care' in all matters for which
he was responsible. Sometimes this led to accusations of undue
caution and over-insurance, but that did not deter him. His most
obvious example of following his motto was the care he always took
for the welfare of his troops. In his desert campaign in Egypt and
Libya, having made his plan and given instructions to his Chief of
Staff, he would leave his Tactical Headquarters and motor many
miles to the rear. He did this in order to see for himself how the
troops were faring on the long communication lines. He knew full
well that units in such areas, employed on vital but little publicised
tasks, can become liable to think themselves forgotten. He therefore went off to find and see them, travelling in his jeep with only
a liaison officer and ADC, and an escort vehicle. It was his custom
to stop frequently on the desert road and have a friendly word with
the men employed at petrol and supply points, or in small working
parties, far from the front line. He would identify himself, though
they all recognised the two badges on his beret, and then tell them
to gather round whilst he briefly described the battle situation and
how he intended it should develop. Before leaving he would hand
out cigarettes and ask if any of them would like him to have a message sent, by himself, to their wives or girl friends. The effect of
course was immediate and most striking as probably no army
commander had been known, let alone seen, to make such personal
contacts before. It was his own particular way to take good care of
morale, and few commanders in military history, at the highest
level, have left their headquarters in this fashion, for such a purpose and for so long. The dividends it paid were enormous, and it
is tempting to see a natural and instinctive connection between
motto and man, rather than mere coincidence.

Another link with our past history, providing evidence of our
French ancestry, is the crest we share with some of the other
Montgomery families in Ireland. This crest shows an arm em-
bowed in armour, the hand grasping a broken tilting spear. The
story of this device stems from the exploits of Count Gabriel
Montgomery at the ceremonies attending the marriage of King

Henry II of France in the sixteenth century. Count Gabriel was a
noted swordsman renowned for his skill at arms. He was a direct
descendant of Sir Roger de Montgomeri, whose family had retained
their titles and estates in Normandy. Unfortunately Gabriel's reputation led to a dreadful catastrophe and near disaster for himself.
When Henry II succeeded to the throne he appointed a Tournament to be held at Paris. After he had shivered many of his
opponents' lances the King proposed, on the third day of the
Tournament, to tilt with the accomplished Montgomery who, not
relishing such a ticklish compliment, did all in his power to decline
the honour. The King however, unhappily for himself, would take
no excuse. Montgomery, whose lance broke in the first shock of
their encounter, omitted in the agitation of the moment to throw
away the broken fragment which struck the King, in the next
charge, through the vizor. The blow was delivered with such force
that the broken lance entered one of the King's eyes and unhorsed
him, and he died in the course of a few days. Henry generously
acquitted Montgomery of any intention to hurt him, and enjoined
positively, that no prosecution should take place after his death.
Yet Gabriel Montgomery did not escape a tragic end. After many
adventures, during which he crossed to Scotland to see his family
relatives and was there converted to the Protestant faith, he was
captured in France, charged with the killing of King Henry II,
tortured, and then publicly beheaded in Paris. My brother bears
this crest of a broken lance on his coat of arms, to which he added,
as supporters, on the one side a private soldier in khaki battle dress,
and on the other a knight in chain armour with his hand resting on
his drawn sword. The symbolic connection of this with his own
family history, past and present, is easy to see.

There are no records to show precisely when our family came to
Donegal from Scotland. It is certain only that they were a Scots
Protestant family who arrived in Ireland in the seventeenth cen-
tury, probably early during the reign of Charles I, in about 1628.
They were settled on an estate, which they farmed, in south west
Donegal between the villages of Killybegs and Killaghtee some
thirty miles from Donegal Town. That they were 'settled' means,
it has to be said, that they obtained their property at the expense of

A MONTGOMERY FAMILY TREE

Catharine Montgomery of Killaghtee — Living 1700 — No record of marriage

John Montgomery — Living 1722 — No record of marriage

David Montgomery — Living 1732 — Mary Law, sister of Rev. Samuel Law of Cumber, Co. Donegal

Samuel Montgomery *b.* 1726 *d.* 1803 — 1750 Ann, daughter of Marino Porter, surveyor, of Greencastle

Rev. Samuel Law Montgomery *b.* 1768 *d.* 1832 — 1803 Susan Maria McClintock, widow of Rev. Mounsey Alexander

Sir Robert Montgomery, GCSI, KCB *b.* 1809 *d.* 1887 — 1845 2nd wife Ellen Jane Lambert, of Woodmansterne, Surrey

Rt Rev. Bishop Montgomery, KCMG, DD *b.* 1847 *d.* 1932 — 1881 Maud, daughter of Dean Farrar

Field Marshal Viscount Montgomery, KG, GCB, DSO *b.* 1887 — 1927 Betty Carver, *née* Hobart

The Hon. David Montgomery *b.* 1928 — 1953 1st wife Mary Connell, daughter of Sir Charles Connell, and has issue living, one s. one d. Marriage dissolved 1967 — 1970 2nd wife Tessa Zulueta, daughter of Lt Gen. Sir Frederick Browning

Frances Thomason = 1834 1st wife Died 1842

Sibyl Harold Donald Una Winsome Desmond Colin Brian

Henry David *b.* 1954

Arabella Clare *b.* 1956

the unfortunate Roman Catholic owners who were forcibly dis-
possessed. This policy was widespread throughout the nine counties and is recognised, in history, as the basic cause of all the trouble
and bloodshed which followed, and is with us still today. There is
no blinking this fact, which certainly no historian would seek to
deny, if only on account of its root causes, namely, deprivation of
property with suppression of religious rights and power. Nevertheless not all the results were bad. One positive and creative thing
was the wholesale introduction of fresh blood into Ireland, coupled
with the intrusion of a new mentality. This has produced the
'Anglo-Irishman' with all his Irish intelligence and humour,
backed by Scots logic and industry. In this context it is surely significant that in the 1939–45 war six officers of the British Army
were promoted to the rank of Field-Marshal, and that all six were
Anglo-Irish, with their family roots in Ireland. Three, my brother,
Sir John Dill and Lord Gort, came from what is now the Republic,
and the other three, Lord Alexander, Lord Alanbrooke and Sir
Claude Auchinleck, came from the six counties. These facts speak
for themselves.

The first recorded member of our family to own and live on the
property at Killaghtee was one Catharine Montgomery who was
certainly resident there about 1700. Unfortunately we have no
reliable records before then because all legal documents in the land
registry were burnt by King James II's soldiers when they retreated
from Londonderry after lifting the siege in 1689. Derry city had
held out for one hundred and five days till it was relieved by King
William III's fleet which burst the boom that the Irish had thrown
across the river Foyle and brought food to the starving garrison. It
was just before Christmas of 1688 when the prentice boys of the
city had shut the gates in the very face of their Roman Catholic
enemy. There had been a traitor in the town, a Protestant Colonel
Robert Lundy, who sought to admit the Irish, and to this day his
effigy is publicly burned on each anniversary of the shutting of the
gates. There is thus a gap in our knowledge until we come to
Samuel Montgomery. The latter was born in 1726 and from then
onwards the record is clear. Family trees, other than one's own, are
generally tedious to read. But on page 9 there is a table showing in

outline our family descent, with special reference to my brother's place in it, and the family that comes after him. The Montgomery wives bred prolifically, as was the custom in the eighteenth and nineteenth centuries. Samuel had eight children and so did Sir Robert, whilst Samuel Law's wife had her last baby (a son) when she was fifty-three years of age; this must be quite a record!

The Family Home

Samuel Montgomery was a wholesale and retail wine merchant in the city of Londonderry. He had left West Donegal and acquired the business in Derry at the early age of twenty-four, about 1750. He inherited the Kilaghtee property in 1768 but never lived there for any length of time, because, in the same year, he bought from the Marquess of Donegal about one thousand acres of farm and mountain land in Inishowen. He liked this northern part of Donegal and built our family home there, having first married a girl who lived near his new property, and who became the great-great-grandmother of the Field-Marshal.

The peninsula of Inishowen lies between Lough Foyle on the east and Lough Swilly on the west. Its sea coast faces the Atlantic and includes Malin Head, the most northerly point of all Ireland. Moville, where we lived, is now a small town on the Donegal shore of Lough Foyle, though when Samuel settled there, two hundred years ago, the place did not exist. Up to 1820 there were only some fifty people living in the area which was still known by its ancient Irish name, spelt *magh-bhile*, 'the place at the mouth of the Foyle'. It is not difficult to see how as time passed both pronunciation and spelling became adapted to the easier, anglicised, version of Moville. The country for miles around is predominantly a land of mountains and hills covered with heather and ling, and in places with bracken and lichens. There is also much bog land from which turf is still dug for burning as household fuel, whilst the rough pastures are generally suitable only for sheep and goats. Communications have always been poor and even today the roads and farms are confined mainly to the regions bordering the shores of the two loughs (the Foyle and the Swilly). Until recent years metalled

highways were few and far between and the nearest railway to
Moville is twenty miles away at Londonderry. There has thus been
very little urban and industrial development and electric light and
power did not reach Moville until 1931. The countryside is therefore still wild and very beautiful, particularly in the mountains on
the North coast where great cliffs sink down some four hundred
feet into the Atlantic. At their base the surf ceaselessly churns itself
into foam among the rocks below and on a clear day the Mull of
Kintyre, on the Argyllshire coast, with the mountains of Islay and
Jura are clearly visible. This is the country in which we boys and
girls grew up and where we spent as much time as possible. There
is a great deal of rain but it is never really cold, as England can be,
and there is seldom any snow except on the hill tops. My mother
was a great believer in exercise for young people, and every day,
winter or summer, we had to leave the house for an outdoor expe-
dition of some kind. We loved walking over the hills, and in summer we bicycled to one of the few beaches below the cliffs and
bathed in the sea – oh! how dreadfully cold it was! Looking back
there is no doubt it was this kind of upbringing which, in later
years, so influenced the Field-Marshal and gave him the reputation
of being a fanatic for physical training. We were not encouraged to
go sailing as the numerous cross currents and strong tides on Lough
Foyle make it a hazardous pastime, except for very experienced
people such as the local fishermen. The danger is mainly caused by
the very narrow entrance to the lough, through which the tide runs
like a mill race. The stories of Bernard sailing boats in rough seas
on Lough Foyle are not accurate. There was also of course a social
side, and we used to bicycle or walk to tennis parties or dances – if
necessary up to ten or fifteen miles and in the rain.

The people of Donegal have always been, and still are, predominantly Roman Catholic. Inishowen however, though so close to the
six counties, has always been relatively free from political and
religious troubles, mainly because, physically, the peninsula is
virtually cut off by the conjunction of the Foyle and the Swilly
from the rest of Donegal. This remote situation has meant that the
people, and their habits and way of life generally, have not changed
a great deal since the time when New Park was built and com-

pleted in 1773. In Samuel's day smuggling was one of the main attractions. The whole population of Inishowen was engaged in illicit trade including distillation and marketing of home brewed Irish whiskey, or potheen. A market for this was regularly held in Moville to which purchasers came daily from the counties of Derry and Antrim. I dare say Samuel Montgomery was probably no exception to the rule where smuggling was concerned for after all he was professionally interested in the sale of alcohol. The family records state that: 'he was the only merchant of Derry at that time who was above suspicion', but I have often wondered if this could really be true.

Even today smuggling is still very prevalent and it increased greatly after the border with Northern Ireland was formed, little more than fifty years ago. Londonderry has always been the market town for Inishowen, as indeed it is and always will be for all Northern Donegal. Derry city is still the only place where sophisticated goods of every kind, clothing, books and the like, can be obtained. Equally it provides a ready market for products made in the Republic. Everybody takes full advantage of this, and, in her day, my mother was certainly not averse to following suit, particularly in her old age when she could no longer drive her car to Londonderry. Instead she used to go by bus from which all the passengers were ordered to disembark at the border for customs declaration and search for dutiable goods. But she always refused to stir, saying, 'I am a great-grandmother and if you want me to leave, you will have to carry me.' As an additional safeguard she generally carried a basket in which she protested she had her cat which would run back over the border if the basket were opened. On one occasion the customs officer insisted on opening it and sure enough a cat jumped out and ran back over the border. My mother immediately followed and after some delay returned with the cat. Her basket was never searched again and she often told us she found this most convenient. My father, the bishop, would have no part in such matters and preferred not to comment.

Soon after acquiring his business in Londonderry Samuel Montgomery met a girl from Greencastle, the small village at the mouth of Lough Foyle. She was Ann, daughter of Marino Porter, surveyor of Greencastle, by his wife Mary Carey of Inishowen Head. Green-castle village with its fourteenth-century castle, now in ruins, and Martello Tower, faces the sands of Magilligan Point across half a mile of water. Magilligan, which is in the six counties, is now well known as one of the special internment camps set up by the Northern Ireland Government in 1971. Samuel must have ridden frequently from Londonderry along the shore of the lough to Greencastle, and on the way he would have passed the site of his future family estate and home. There is a miniature showing him as a strongly built fresh-coloured man of about thirty-two, not tall, but vigorous, with a very prominent nose and full mouth. This Montgomery nose has appeared frequently in his descendants, both male and female, and particularly in the Field-Marshal whose nose has always featured so large in cartoon drawings. He married Ann about 1750 but went on with his wine business and eventually became Chamberlain of the City of Londonderry until his death in 1803. Some years after his marriage he completed his permanent family home for which he had selected a demesne of sixty acres on the shore of Lough Foyle and running up into the Donegal hills. He made a good choice for the site of his house, New Park, for it had a south aspect and faced the mountain Ben Evenagh on the other side of the Lough, some six miles wide at this point.

Samuel built New Park of grey stone, taken from a quarry near-by, with a slate roof, and using local labour. He was his own architect and clerk of works though his father-in-law, the sur-veyor, gave him professional advice. It was not a very large building and certainly had none of the architectural beauty normally looked for in mid-Georgian country houses. But the windows appear typical of the time with bow-fronts in the drawing room and on the first floor. Inside, the rooms were spacious with a wide hall and a shallow curving staircase to the first floor. Altogether Samuel allowed for ten bedrooms which he certainly needed with his large family of eight children. He also built the out-houses, including a gardener's cottage, stables for horses with a coach house (still referred to as the 'coach house' right up to the time the property was sold), a hay loft, cowshed and dairy. The view from the house was and still is superb. In Samuel's day the garden was in front of the house, from the top windows of which you look out over the Lough with its ever changing shadows and colours to the view of Ben Evenagh and the hills of Co. Londonderry. A later generation moved the garden to a walled site behind the house where flowers grew in profusion, and I remember especially the wealth of sweet peas and the roses which flourished year after year. Fuchsias grow in abundance in all parts of Ireland, and at New Park there were great banks of that flowering shrub, red, purple and pink, which in places grew to form a veritable hedge up to ten feet high. From the garden the hills rise up gently to a great black bog, the scene of many an exciting afternoon among the snipe. Beyond, the heather begins to cover the slopes until, at the height of some thousand feet or more, you reach the summit to see before you wave after wave of purple mountains with scarcely a house in sight. This mountain land is wonderful country for game birds, especially grouse, snipe, wild duck, and in some places golden plover. But by the time the Field-Marshal, as a young man, went out with his gun the local poachers had already taken their toll and large game bags were the exception. However, records show what a wonderful sporting country Inishowen used to be. Partridges were common up to a century or so ago, also otters, and, very remarkable, a hoopoe was shot near Greencastle about 1928. Salmon were astonishingly plentiful in Lough Foyle, and many seals followed them through the narrow entrance at its mouth. At Carse Hall, on the opposite shore of the Lough the servants felt compelled to request that they should not be fed on salmon for more than half of each week.

This then was the land and home where my father and mother, and their family after them, whenever possible spent their holidays, and which they always knew was their home – no matter where they were living. Some years ago my brother sent me an account of the social life at New Park during the summer holidays, about the time he left Sandhurst. This is what he said.

28-10-68

Dear Brian,
    Enclosed booklet was sent me by Eric Warrington, who wrote from Jersey, and asked me if I would visit him and his mother

at the Dorchester Hotel, Park Lane, for lunch or 'drinks' on
October 31. Presumably she wrote the booklet.

She says she danced with me at a ball at New Park in honour
of my having 'passed out' of Sandhurst. I certainly don't recall
it, and, as you know, I was nearly pushed out instead of 'passing
out'! I declined the invitation.

Yrs. ever,
Bernard

Below is an extract from the booklet which described life generally
in Inishowen in the early years of this century. Bernard's reference
to being 'pushed out' refers to the unusual circumstances in which
he left Sandhurst, and which figure in a later chapter of this
story.

'From 1905 onwards, our chief friends, apart from our cousins at
Malin Hall, were the Montgomerys of New Park, Moville.
Bishop and Lady Montgomery, father and mother of our now
famous Field Marshal were living there. In the Montgomery
family there were nine young people, and a very lively lot they
were too; up to every prank that could be thought of. We all met
several times a week either on picnics, shooting parties, or dancing, and played cricket, "Culdaff vs. Moville". On one occasion we drove the eight miles to Moville in sidecars, to a ball
at New Park in honour of "Bernard" having passed out of
Sandhurst.

'This ball was a very grand affair, with a band from Derry
with all its trimmings. My cousin Amy Stuart (afterwards
my sister in law) and myself were put up by two old ladies,
the Miss Galways. The others stayed in New Park, or in
places near Moville. I mention Miss Galway, as being the
writer of the words of that well known song "Londonderry
Air". . . .

'At New Park we danced until 4 a.m. or longer, and then
played a game called "Prisoner's Base"; all over the house even
on the roof. After that, as light dawned we departed to the shore,
and continued dancing and playing around in boats.

'The bishop of course had retired to his study soon after we arrived at the ball; he spent hours there trying to find out how the Israelites really did cross the Red Sea. Lady Montgomery stayed with the dancers till after supper at midnight. Supper was very well done; lots of marvellous sandwiches and dishes. I remember dancing the supper dances with Bernard, but found him rather stiff, and rather looking down on such a young girl. The others were more amusing, and I was a great friend of his youngest sister called "Winsome". She was fun.

'At about 12 noon next day, we found our sidecars and horses, and started for Culdaff, stopping at Termone to let some of the boys off to go shooting. Their party consisted of Bernard Montgomery and his brother, Jim Harvey a cousin, and my eldest brother Robin. No girls were allowed to share this sport.'

In 1921 my parents finally retired, and after 1932, when the Bishop died at the age of eighty-five, my mother continued to live alone at New Park. She died in 1949 and the house was then sold to become a hotel, though the village still remains as the family property. There is no doubt that New Park, with its atmosphere and the memories we all retain of it will have profoundly influenced the whole family. During the Great War of 1914–18 Bernard came, whenever he could, to spend his periodical seven days' leave from the battlefront in France, at New Park; in spite of the fact that in those days, when there was no air travel, the journey to Moville took the best part of two days each way. But it was worth it to him. Curiously none of us ever went to Killaghtee, where what remained of the land the family had owned there was sold after my father's death.

Samuel Montgomery, the wine merchant, died at New Park on 20th August 1803. Of his large family of eight children, four sons and four daughters, only two were married; the remaining six either died very young or did not marry. His youngest son inherited the Killaghtee and Moville properties but not the wine business in Londonderry which was sold after Samuel died. This youngest son, my great-grandfather, was born in 1768. He was given two Christian names, Samuel after his father, and Law, which was the maiden

name of his maternal grandmother. Since then the name Samuel
has appeared twice more in our family; one great uncle was called
Samuel and so also was Sir Robert's eldest son. My parents however dropped the name but called their fourth child Bernard Law;
he became the Field Marshal.

Samuel Law, our great grandfather, was evidently a very different character from Samuel the wine merchant. He went to school
at Foyle College in Londonderry and then took his BA degree at
Trinity College, Dublin, after which he was ordained deacon in
the Protestant Church of Ireland at the early age of twenty. A letter
he wrote to his mother at New Park in 1786, whilst an undergraduate at Trinity College is I believe worth quoting for it shows the
great care young people took of their clothes just under two hundred years ago – how very different from the trend of today. In this
letter Samuel Law wrote: 'I send by the bearer an old coat and
waistcoat which you will be so good as to give to Thos Mitchell
and desire him to make me a waistcoat from the skirts of the old
coat. He will get lining from the old waistcoat and he must have it
ready to return by the bearer in the course of the next week.' He
was not apparently averse to giving instructions, and he certainly
knew how to make a 'master plan'! After he was ordained Samuel
Law became a curate at various parishes in Co. Donegal, where for
ten years or more his stipend remained at £50 per annum, until
finally he was appointed rector of Moville, his home parish, where
he stayed for many years. He married a widow, née Susan McClintock, in the year his father died, her first husband having preceded
him as Rector of Moville in earlier years. His six children, three
sons and three daughters, were all born at Moville where he died
in 1832. His portrait hangs in the dining room of my brother's
home in Hampshire.

In our family Samuel Law is remembered as the man who began
that very close connection with the Church, which so influenced
life at New Park for three generations after him. He was fervently
religious and had only two interests in life, his faith and an absolute
passion for his family home. The following extract from a letter he
wrote to his second son, afterwards Sir Robert Montgomery, before
the latter went out to India as a young man, clearly shows his

character and outlook on life. It was quite usual in those days for members of a family, when they wished to converse on serious topics, to write to each other though they were all living in the same house at the time. Imagine, for instance, the astonishment of a son of any present-day family if, whilst at home, he were handed a letter written by his father in the following terms:

'As the time approaches which must separate us for many many years, suffer your attached father to give you some hints for the guidance of your future conduct. . . . Remember your Creator in the days of your youth . . . never lie down at night without asking forgiveness for the errors of the preceding day . . . never go in debt, never play or gamble . . . be sure always to associate with persons of the best character and conduct . . . never have dealings with the idle or vicious. Finally I beg you not to be careless, nor to put off whatever might be done now. Procrastination is the thief of time.'

Samuel Law made many improvements at New Park and in his time also Moville began to develop and grow. In his will he left legacies to his wife and children, but unwisely, as it turned out, directed that the money should be found by mortgaging all his freehold properties in Co. Donegal. His complete obsession with his religion was certainly inherited by his descendants, as it was my father and mother who eventually converted one of the bedrooms at New Park into a chapel, where services were held daily. This chapel figures prominently in the story of the terrible day when Bernard was caught smoking. It was at New Park in 1902, when the family were all at home for the summer holidays, and Bernard was just three months short of his fifteenth birthday. After he had been found smoking a cigarette he was taken by my father into the chapel where he confessed his sin. They both knelt and the Bishop prayed to the Almighty for his forgiveness. This account has been told by others, but what has not been published so far is the sequel. Bernard emerged from the chapel thankful, if not chastened, that all was over and forgiven. But he was wrong. At the door he was confronted by my mother, with a cane, who straight away gave him

six of the best! At that time she was in her middle thirties and a
slender beautiful women, who possessed a very strong character
as we all had good cause to know.

When Samuel Law died he left New Park and his Donegal properties to his eldest son, Samuel, who was always referred to in the
family as 'Uncle Montgomery'. He was a quite extraordinary
character and, like his father, a clergyman with the same interests,
religion and his home and family. Strangely, in spite of these two
absorbing passions, he spent very little time at New Park, although
he was the landlord of Moville from 1832 to 1874, presumably
because his work as a parish priest was always in Co. Londonderry.
Uncle Montgomery merits a reference in this story because he was
so completely different to any other members of the family, past,
present and, I hope, future. Unfortunately for him he was never
strong; he had a spinal defect and he was somewhat humpbacked.
As a result he never played games, he never shot or fished and so,
presumably because of this, my generation tended to regard him as
rather a joke. It is perhaps not surprising that he was entirely
ignorant of the ways of the world. He only travelled in a railway
train two or three times in his life, and only once left Ireland, to go
to London. But though he was so ignorant of worldly matters he
was a great student and scholar and he was always reading. He
could probably best be described as a kind and gentle soul who was
greatly loved by his parishioners, for he truly lived among, and for,
his people. Nevertheless it is difficult to think of him as a great
uncle, and therefore a near relative, of any of my brothers and
sisters.

Uncle Montgomery's family record however will always be
remembered for two quite different reasons, his attempt to get
married and his unfortunate financial adventures. About 1843 he
proposed to a handsome, dark-eyed, vivacious girl, a Miss Julia
Dysart who lived in Moville. She accepted him, so he must have
had some attractions. Then fear overtook him and he backed out.
For a parson of his generation this was a most serious matter and
eventually, in order to avoid legal action for breach of promise, he
had to pay the Dysarts £1,200, a very large sum in his day. He was
already burdened with heavy mortgage charges so he borrowed the

money from his younger brother, Robert, who, sad to say, never saw any of it again. Finally he spent thousands of pounds on developing Moville which he hoped one day would emerge as a flourishing seaside town or spa. He built houses, roads, a school, the family church in the grounds of New Park, and a wharf for a steamer service on Lough Foyle. He even had a survey completed for the construction of a railway from Londonderry to Moville. All this cost much money and, like his father, he resorted to mortgage. As a result when Sir Robert inherited the property he had to accept charges on the estate amounting, in all, to more than £13,000; a century ago this was a very heavy commitment. However in one way Uncle Montgomery was before his time, for Moville did grow though not entirely in the way he wanted. By the time New Park was sold the village had become a small market town, and, incidentally, it had, and still has, twenty-nine public houses, though Uncle Montgomery certainly had no part in that kind of development. The Field-Marshal did not care for him. He had a portrait of Uncle Montgomery which, some years ago, he gave to me saying, 'I won't have it hung in my house; the picture frame is the only part of it which I like.' My wife and I duly hung it on the wall of the staircase in our house in Chelsea, but one night it fell down and its frame is certainly no longer the best, or any part, of it. Uncle Montgomery died on 16th May 1874 and was buried at Ballynascreen in Co. Londonderry where he had been the Rector for over thirty years. He left his properties to his younger brother Robert who was a very different character.

Robert Montgomery was brought up at New Park from where he was sent to school at Foyle College in 1817, just before his eighth birthday. He was preceded there by three boys with whom in after years he had a life-long and honoured connection in India. They were the sons of the Lawrence family of Coleraine who were also the product of the Protestant plantation of Ulster. All four were at school together and all became famous in the history of British rule in India. Probably no school of its size, not more than one hundred attended, ever contained within its walls at the same time a greater number of boys who were destined to become so distinguished in their generation. Among them were Sir George

2

Lawrence, Sir Henry Lawrence, Lord Lawrence and Sir Robert
Montgomery; the last three of these were destined to rule the Punjab
together and to play a foremost part in the Indian Mutiny. Robert
always used to say it was the tough upbringing he had at Foyle
College which enabled him to survive so well in his subsequent
career of thirty-seven years in India. For life was indeed tough at
Foyle College in those days. The Headmaster was the Rev. Doctor
Knox, a complete martinet whose main instrument of discipline
was the cane. Flogging was a daily occurrence and Lord Lawrence
is on record as saying that he was flogged every day of his life at
school except once, and then he was flogged twice! The boys had
few luxuries, they hardly ever tasted meat except on Sundays and
were inured to every kind of climate. In winter the dormitories
were so cold that the water used to freeze hard in the basins, for
every room was open to a fierce draught; the window frames were
made of stone with only an iron bar across the centre to prevent
exit or entry. There was also keen rivalry and much fighting
between the day boys, drawn from the wealthy merchants of Derry
city, and the boarders who were mainly the sons of the clergy and
gentry of the adjoining counties. Robert, even when he was still
under ten, played a great part in these battles which took place in
summer or winter and generally after dark.

   Like most other boys it was the school holidays at his home
which Robert looked forward to most of all. No place in the world
was more beloved by him than New Park, where he liked wander-
ing about with his gun, an old bell-mouthed blunderbuss. At an
early age also events showed that he was very fearless and generally
regardless of danger. He often used to ride the horses bare-backed
down to the village to water them in the Moville river. On one
occasion the horse he was riding bolted and galloped, with Robert
not in control, straight for an open door into the back yard at New
Park, not the stable yard. This door was set in a high brick wall
with just enough height for a horse to pass through. Instead of
throwing himself off Robert flung himself flat on the horse's neck
and withers so that, mercifully, the top of the door only, but nevertheless completely, ripped off the back side of his trousers; another
quarter of an inch and his spine would have been shattered.

Robert's main concern, and amusement, was the astonishment with which the servants saw him dismount, 'bare-bottomed' as he described it later. Otherwise his education, both at school and home, was conducted in a strong religious setting which undoubtedly influenced his future life. It taught him, so he said in later years, never to fear to do what he thought was right.

In 1824, when he was fourteen years of age, Robert obtained a cadetship at the military college at Addiscombe, the forerunner of our present academy at Sandhurst. In the event he was never commissioned in the army but on leaving Addiscombe was given a writership in the service of the East India Company. This would appear strange as normally the candidates for administrative posts in India went to the East India Company training school at Haileybury, and not to Addiscombe. One is tempted to wonder if perhaps he was compulsorily diverted from a military career because of some misdemeanour or shortcoming, thus providing a precedent for his grandson, the future Field-Marshal who, two generations later, was very nearly refused a commission! Furthermore the family papers give no reason why Robert did not join the army from Addiscombe, except, curiously, a letter from his aunt which states that 'If Robert passes his next examination at Addiscombe he can accept the writership without taking any civil examination.' He did pass. There is no record otherwise of how Robert fared as a military cadet, except a story told later by himself. On one occasion when returning to Addiscombe from Moville he was given a large bundle of letters to be posted in London in order to save expense. At the beginning of the nineteenth century postage from Ireland often amounted to 2s or more per letter. When he arrived at Addiscombe his plain clothes were taken from him and his uniform issued instead. At the end of that term of about five months his plain clothes were returned to him. In the pocket he found all the letters which he had been urged to be very careful to post as some of them were very important! Robert said he was so frightened that he straightaway threw them all into the fire. Strange to say no enquiries about them were ever made, and he himself told no one what he had done.

My grandfather left Addiscombe for Moville just before Christmas 1827. He had orders to sail for India, to join the Honourable The East India Company's service, as a writer, in the spring of 1828.

Chapter 2

SIR ROBERT MONTGOMERY

Robert Montgomery set out for Calcutta, in an East Indiaman via the Cape of Good Hope, at the end of May 1828. In the days of sailing ships, long before the Suez Canal was built, the voyage might take anything up to nine months and Robert did not in fact reach Calcutta until the following November. On 10th August, whilst at sea, he wrote to his parents and sent the letter by a small schooner which passed them homeward bound. They had just crossed the Equator and Robert wrote:

'As it is a Sunday the captain will not allow the sailors to perform the customary shaving, and other pastimes, for newcomers crossing the Line; they are very upset about it but I should not wonder if tomorrow we shall have some fun. We were introduced to the ladies a few days ago, but only I believe because of our not having laughed at the ridiculous ways in which they went on at first. Some of the passengers have cut the ladies, or at least have little to say to them, though the latter appear to wish to be very civil.'

Apparently he took full advantage of this and enjoyed himself immensely. When Robert first arrived in Calcutta he was still only eighteen, inexperienced in every way and certainly unfamiliar with the conventions of social life in India at that period. He was not at all well off, and, having been invited to a fancy dress ball at Government House, he thought the cheapest dress to go in would be that of a chimney sweep. He therefore went disguised as such, complete with blackened face and brooms, which turned out to be most unwise. Apparently his disguise was so very realistic that despite his protestations he was refused admittance. This naturally upset him a great deal and he ran home overcome with shame and mortification.

Looking back at young Robert Montgomery, newly arrived in India to join the civil administration nearly a century and a half ago, it is possible to see the influence of heredity beginning to appear in him. He was the product of a vigorous and strongly marked type of character, evolved from the inhabitants of the Northern Irish counties, by a sturdy mixture of Scots and Irish blood. The men and women of this product possessed all the rich humour, affections and generosity of the typical Irishman, coupled with the patience, morality and determination of the typical Scotsman. Above all, they were brave and resourceful fighters with a deep vein of religious feeling for their Protestant faith. Robert's family before him, the Montgomery men and their wives, were all from this stock, in either Co. Donegal or Londonderry. As yet however there had been no leavening of their blood by the advent of wives from England, of purely English origin. These came later. The effect they had, coupled with a wider environment for all, was very great.

My grandfather's first appointment was to Azamgarh, in what is now the province of Utar Pradesh. In this he was most fortunate as he came under the influence of one of the finest administrators of his time. This was Mr James Thomason who subsequently became Lieutenant-Governor of the then North West Provinces. The first twenty years of Robert's service were professionally uneventful, except for the wonderful training and experience he obtained, from which he greatly benefited. After leaving Azamgarh he went first as Magistrate and Collector to Allahabad and Mirzapore in 1839, and from there to Cawnpore, in the same capacity, in 1846. But undoubtedly the main events of his life during those twenty years were his first marriage, his three years' furlough in the United Kingdom (1843–5) and his second marriage. People had begun to call my grandfather 'Monty' soon after he first arrived in India. Thereafter, and perhaps strangely, this nickname does not appear again in our family until my own generation of which the six brothers have been generally known to our friends as 'Monty'.

Robert's first marriage, in 1834, was to Frances Mary, the sister of James Thomason, his Chief Commissioner. Apparently she was a very simple and retiring girl with a placid nature, very pious and humble, and much opposed to publicity of any kind. There were three children by this marriage, a son and two daughters, but they were all comparatively short-lived. The boy died when he was sixteen and about to go to Addiscombe, and of the girls one died two years before the Mutiny and the other three years after it. Mortality in India in those days was very great compared with today. There were no means then of destroying the anopheles, the malaria-bearing mosquito, and dysentery was rife. In brief, tropical medicine was in its infancy and life expectancy accordingly short. Robert's first wife died in 1842, after only eight years of marriage, and was buried at Allahabad.

After his first wife's death my grandfather took the only home furlough he enjoyed in thirty-seven years' service in India. He had a wonderful leave, travelled extensively in England, Scotland, Ireland and on the Continent, and eventually got married again, on 2nd May 1845, to Miss Ellen Jane Lambert. She was utterly different in every way to Robert's first wife, being a strong, very determined girl, and not shy in any way at all. She was beautiful, with dark brown hair, a high intelligent forehead and full mouth, large grey eyes and wonderful colouring. She inherited her good looks from her maternal grandmother. The latter was one of three sisters, the Misses Le-Grand, who were all famous beauties in their day. The Lamberts were an English family who had been settled in Woodmansterne in Surrey for centuries, and were still living there when my grandfather married their daughter. There can be no doubt about my grandmother's influence on Robert and on her children, including my father. She was what can best be described as a very powerful character, full of common sense – and no nonsense. She brought to Robert that breadth of view which is, frequently I fear, so lacking in many a Protestant Ulsterman to this day. Fortunately she was no stranger to India as her father had been a merchant in Calcutta, and she herself was born at Arrah, in Bihar, in 1824.

Early in 1849 Robert Montgomery left Cawnpore for the Punjab on appointment as Commissioner of Lahore; in success terms this was undoubtedly the turning point of his career. He had already completed twenty years' service in India and was now regarded as a competent and highly professional administrator. Men of this type were urgently needed in Northern India where the second Sikh war had just ended, and the vast new province of Punjab had been created. It was finally annexed, under British rule, by Sir Henry Elliott. The size of the new province was staggering to contemplate. It covered the entire area of what is now East and West Punjab, including the whole of the existing North West Frontier Province, with a population of up to twenty millions and an extent of hundreds of thousands of square miles. It is no part of this story to recapitulate the size and shape of British possessions in India. But a glance at the map on page 35 will show the immensity of the Punjab, covering the five rivers (the Sutlej, Ravi, Chenab, Jhelum and the mighty Indus) and extending through Peshawar right up to the Khyber pass at the frontier of Afghanistan. This was the new territory to which Robert was summoned, in laconic terms, by a letter from Sir Henry Elliott, then Secretary to Lord Dalhousie the Governor-General, to James Thomason, Robert's Chief Commissioner: 'Dear Thomason, will you order up Montgomery immediately? He will be a Commissioner of some sort on Rupees 2,500 a month. The Board of Administration will consist of the Lawrences and Mansel.'

The Board of Administration of the Punjab was to be the machinery of government, proposed by Lord Dalhousie, for the Civil Government of the new province. Since 1845 there had been two campaigns against the Sikhs, preceded by the disastrous first Afghan war. The cumulative effect in terms of bloodshed, loss of life, hardship and disruption generally was very great. The Governor-General had therefore to prove to the East India Company in London that the new territory could be well governed under a

civil administration, and become a financially and politically profit-
able acquisition. Sir Henry Lawrence was Chairman of the Board,
with his brother Sir John as Deputy Chairman. Mansel, the other
member, was not a success and so a little later Robert was nomi-
nated to take his place. Thus began the memorable period of
government of the Punjab by three old boys of Foyle College,
Henry and John Lawrence and Robert Montgomery. Their rule
lasted virtually from the moment of arrival of Robert at Lahore in
1849, until the transfer of Henry Lawrence as Resident in Rajpu-
tana early in 1853. Subsequently the Provincial Constitution was
regularised and Sir John was made Chief Commissioner, with
Robert appointed as Judicial Commissioner and his Deputy. The
next four years were crucial for all India, as they were the prelude
to the Indian Mutiny. For Robert Montgomery in particular the
period was very strenuous, because he was not just the Chief
Judge of Appeal and Assize in all the Punjab. He was also the head
of a police force of more than fifteen thousand men, horse and foot,
Superintendent of Roads, Controller of Local and Municipal
Funds, and above all, responsible for education. Robert paid special
attention to this last subject, having seen for himself the awful
problem it presented in Utar Pradesh. Meanwhile dacoity, or robbery in gangs, was rife everywhere and, worse still, '*thuggee*' and
infanticide were frequent occurrences. The 'thugs' of the Punjab
belonged mainly to the *Muzbi* or sweeper caste and were followers
of Kali, the Hindu goddess of destruction. They were motivated by
cruelty, and much addicted to strangling their victims before hacking their bodies to pieces. That two such evils, dacoity and thuggee,
were virtually eliminated in the Punjab before the Mutiny began
is greatly to the credit of John Lawrence's administration. In all
these circumstances it is perhaps not surprising that few British
officers, civil or military, were sufficiently aware that all was not
well with the armed forces on which they relied so much. In
London also no undue alarm was felt. England was too preoccupied
with the dangers and hazards of the Crimean War to worry over-
much about India; in any case it could take up to a year to get an
answer to a letter originated in London. Besides the British in
India had just conquered the warlike Sikhs, whose army had been

defeated and disbanded, with very heavy losses admittedly on both
sides. The dynasty of Ranjit Singh, who was the ruler of the Punjab
as an independent country until 1845, had been deposed, and,
especially gratifying, all the crown property and jewels of the
reigning house were now in British hands. The treasure included
the peerless diamond Koh-i-noor, or 'Mountain of Light', which
to this day is set in the royal crown worn by the reigning sovereign
of our country on important state occasions. This fabulous gem
came into the possession of the Punjab Board and by them was
nearly lost, in circumstances which are vouched for by Bosworth
Smith in his book *The Life of Lord Lawrence*. The incident is worth
retelling, if only because of the awful result which might have
ensued.

The exact origin of this diamond is unknown. It was in the possession of the first Muslim invaders of India who, led by Mahmoud
of Ghuzni, poured over the Himalayan passes in the twelfth century. From them it passed to the Mogul emperors and was in the
eye of the peacock throne in the imperial capital of Delhi. Centuries later it was possessed by the Afghan conqueror Ahmed Shah,
and eventually fell into the hands of Ranjit Singh about the time of
the first Afghan war. Now the British had it. At one of the early
meetings of the Board the jewel had been formally received by the
Punjab Government, and committed to the care and custody of Sir
John Lawrence in his capacity as Deputy Chairman. John Lawrence was always an extremely busy man and had innumerable
problems to consider, including the welfare of the millions of
people in this vast new territory. Without thinking he had put the
jewel, wrapped in cloth, in a small box which he placed in his
waistcoat pocket – and then forgot about it. He changed for dinner
the evening of the same day and threw the waistcoat on a chair, as
was his custom, well knowing that his bearer would put his clothes
away. Some six weeks later, at a subsequent board meeting, Sir
Henry Lawrence said he had received a message from Lord Dalhousie saying that H.M. Queen Victoria wished the jewel to be sent
to her at once. Immediately Sir John said 'Send for it now,' to
which Sir Henry replied 'Why? you've got it.' Of course John
Lawrence was horrified at the realisation of the trouble he was now

in, and what could happen as a result of his lack of care. However he managed to give no sign of his extreme apprehension and merely said 'Oh yes, of course; I forgot I had it'; after which the business of the meeting continued as if all were well. But immediately the proceedings were over he quickly returned to his house and sent for his bearer, an old and trusted Muslim retainer who had been with him for many years and would have given his life for 'Jan Larens Sahib'. John now said to him 'Abdul Khan, have you got a small box which I think I left, wrapped up, in my waistcoat pocket some time ago?' 'Yes Sahib,' the old bearer replied, 'I found the *dibiya* (Urdu word for it) and put it away in one of your old boxes.' 'Bring it to me at once,' said Sir John. The old bearer then went to a battered tin box (of the kind so well known to generations of British officers who have served in India) and from inside it produced the little box. 'Open it,' said John Lawrence, 'and see what is inside.' He then anxiously watched the bearer remove the cloth wrappings until, to his immense relief, the Koh-i-noor appeared safe and sound. The servant appeared quite unaware of what had occurred, or of the great treasure he had unconsciously preserved. 'There is nothing here, Sahib,' he said, 'but a bit of glass'!

When my grandfather first went to Lahore as Commissioner, in 1849, he had a house built for himself and his family. He called it New Park.

The Indian Mutiny

Much has been written about the causes of the Indian Mutiny of 1857. Many people probably still believe it began as a direct result of the grease with which the new cartridges issued to the sepoys of the Indian army were lubricated. The new cartridge had to be provided for the Lee Enfield rifle which was replacing the obsolete 'Brown Bess'. It was said that the grease came either from the fat of the cow, the sacred animal of Hindus, or of the pig, the unclean animal of Muslims. This rumour, or rather distortion of truth, for the cartridges were never in fact so greased, may well have been the final spark which ignited the flame, but it was by no means the cause of the Mutiny. The truth is that broadly speaking the uprising was long in growth. It was the protest of the Indian races against the flood of Western civilisation into their subcontinent, injuring, so they thought, their customs, thoughts, civilisation, religion and way of life generally. To the great mass of the people, who were virtually uneducated by western standards at that stage, it all seemed a conspiracy – by their British conquerors. For everything the British were introducing, railways, the telegraph, law courts, public health, even canals and irrigation, and humane measures such as strict prohibition of *suttee* (the burning alive of widows) and of *thuggee* appeared, or could be made to appear, as a violation of religious practice; and especially of the rigid caste system. It is therefore not difficult to see how influences such as these had their dire effect on the sepoys of the Bengal army. Fortunately the mutiny had no great effect on the armies of the other two Presidencies, Madras and Bombay. But in the Bengal army the men were largely Hindus from the Ganges valley, including many Brahmins, though there were also many thousands of Muslims. It was possibly the sheer size of the army, the native forces in India numbered two hundred and thirty-three thousand men, with only forty-five thousand British troops, which prevented the British from sighting the storm that was brewing; until it became too late. For there had indeed been signs of trouble ahead which unfortunately went unheeded. There was talk in the bazaars of the cities and in the villages, and even in the cantonments, of the imminence of a *Jehad*, or Holy War, in the name of God and of the Prophet. After all, there was a page in the Koran which promised Paradise to those who met death in the attempt to slay the unbelievers. This spread like wildfire through the Muslim population. Mysterious *chupatties*, pancakes of flour and water, containing secret messages for all Hindus were passed from village to village, and district to district, over thousands of miles. There had even been sporadic outbreaks of mutiny, as early as March of this fateful year. The sepoys of two Indian regiments, the 19th and 34th Bengal Native Infantry, had refused to obey their British officers. The adjutant of the 34th had his horse shot under him and the guard refused to arrest the men concerned. Severe punishments were meted out, and both regiments were disbanded. But this added if anything to the dangers, which even the Commander-in-Chief in India, General The Hon. George Anson, did not seem to appreciate.

Meanwhile in the Punjab peace reigned, or so everyone thought, and Sir John Lawrence, the Chief Commissioner, was contemplating an official visit to Kashmir. He was in bad health at the time and the hot weather in Lahore, where the shade temperature can be well over one hundred degrees Fahrenheit, is no place for a sick person. On 12th May he and Lady Lawrence were at Rawalpindi and about to leave there for the hill station at Murree, when a telegram (electric telegraph it was called in those days) reached him from Delhi. This reported that on Sunday 10th May the garrison at Meerut, near Delhi, had mutinied, set their barracks on fire, and then murdered their officers and as many British men and women as they could find. The uprising took place when the British element of the garrison were at church parade, and were therefore taken by surprise. The following day the mutineers marched on Delhi where they committed the most dreadful atrocities, as a result of which only a handful of the European, Eurasian and Indian Christians in the city survived. In short the Indian Mutiny had begun, and Delhi, the seat of the Great Mogul and the historic capital of India, was in the hands of the mutineers.

At Lahore, the capital of the Punjab, Robert Montgomery, in the absence of Sir John Lawrence, was in sole charge. Under him were the Financial Commissioner and the Military Secretary. The troops of the Bengal army quartered in the Punjab amounted to some sixty-three thousand men, composed as follows:

Regular army (Hindustanis)	39,900
British army	10,326
Irregular Punjabis (mainly Sikhs)	13,450

Fortunately all the artillery units were British with the exception of some heavy elephant batteries. There was also a large force of highly organised police many thousands strong, both horse and foot, including armed police battalions, of all of whom Robert was formally in charge.

The absence of the Chief Commissioner from Lahore placed the responsibility for action of every kind fairly and squarely on the shoulders of Robert Montgomery. His chief was at Rawalpindi, more than two hundred miles distant, and unfortunately, when the news from Delhi arrived, all telegraphic communications from Lahore northwards were disrupted. Sir John had got his telegram by a different route. So Robert alone had to decide what should be done, with special reference to the great arsenals of gunpowder, ammunition and arms of all kinds at Ferozepore and Phillour, and the need to seize and hold the ferries and crossings of the Punjab rivers; these virtually dictated all large-scale movements in the Province. But, above all, swift action was necessary on account of the large garrison of native troops at Lahore itself. For whatever might happen in the provincial capital would be sure to have a profound effect on the native garrisons elsewhere in the Punjab; and indeed throughout the rest of India in view of the great importance of Lahore as a political and military centre.

In one respect Robert Montgomery was fortunate in that his Chief Commissioner was a life-long friend who trusted him implicitly. They had been at school together and their wives were close friends of each other. It was in this setting that Robert clearly took the right decision, and thereafter planned and successfully executed the required action. That this is so can probably best be shown by quoting from a passage in Bosworth Smith's *Life of Lord Lawrence* dealing with the events in Lahore immediately following the outbreak of the Mutiny.

> 'If there is any one act in the long roll of the brilliant achievements of the lieutenants of John Lawrence during the mutiny, which may be singled out from the rest as having been done at the time, at the place, and in the manner in which it ought to have been done – as having been planned with caution as well as courage, and carried out with triumphant success, and so, as having given, at the very beginning of the struggle, an omen of the ultimate result – that act was taken at Lahore on the morning of May 13th, 1957; and the man to whom by universal consent it was preeminently due was Robert Montgomery.'

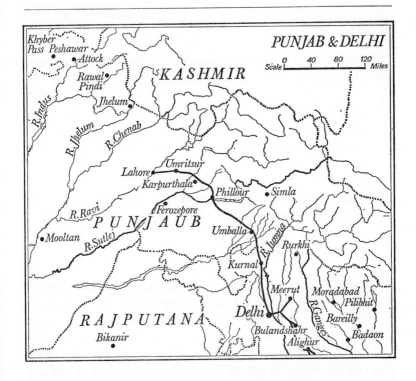

In the mid-1920s when he was a senior officer in his regiment and had already graduated at the staff college, my brother used to give us young subalterns, who I'm afraid often paid scant attention, his own view of the attributes of a good staff officer. He would say, 'To be a success as a staff officer you must at all times have foresight, accuracy and speed. To ensure this you must be able to think two days ahead, and always keep two jumps ahead – of everyone else.' He would then add, with a chuckle, 'and drink two glasses of port'. At that time my brother was very fond of port in moderation, though this may come as a surprise to some people. But a comparison of this anecdote, with the passage quoted from Bosworth Smith, points to the family nature of the source from which the Field Marshal drew so many of his great qualities, particularly his powers of decision and timing. An account of what exactly happened at Lahore on the 12th and 13th May 1857 supports this view and shows clearly that whatever

my grandfather did, he did quickly, with decision and with a
will.

The garrison of Lahore was quartered at Mian Mir, some five or
six miles from the city. The troops consisted of:

> *British Troops*
> The 81st Foot* (Loyal Lincoln Volunteers)   850 strong
> Two troops of Bengal Horse Artillery   12 guns
> *Native Troops*
> 8th Light Cavalry
> Four companies of Bengal Heavy (Foot) Artillery
> 16th Bengal Native Infantry (Grenadiers)
> 26th Bengal Native Infantry
> 49th Bengal Native Infantry

All were under the command of Brigadier-General Stuart Corbett,
who also commanded all the troops in the Punjab in the absence,
on leave, of Major-General Gowan, commanding the Lahore
Division.

The civil lines, where the officers of the provincial administration resided, were at Anarkulli near the race course, about half way
between Mian Mir and the Fort in Lahore City. New Park, the
house where Robert Montgomery lived with his wife and three
young children, was rather isolated as it was some distance from
Anarkulli. The British in India generally lived in bungalows in
which it was unusual to have any rooms above ground-floor level as
there was never any lack of space. New Park was a large and pleasant residence, as befitted the status of the officer who was second
in the hierarchy of the provincial government, with wide deep
verandas and a big garden. There were lawns and flower beds,
bright with cannas, poinsettia and bougainvillea, and the colourful
jacaranda and flame tree. As it was the Judicial Commissioner's
residence there was a flagstaff at the entrance with a sentry from an
armed guard of Sikh constables of the Punjab police force. Naturally, in such a setting, my grandfather and grandmother led a con-

---

* After the Cardwell Reforms in 1875 this regiment became 'The
Loyals' (Loyal North Lancashire Regiment).

siderable social life, typical of the kind to be found, then and since, in any large civil and military station in India, with much entertaining to do. Riding, hunting and polo were very popular, indeed there were few British officers who did not own several horses, and the social round generally was made easier by the availability of native servants.

The morning of Tuesday 12th May was particularly hot. When Robert Montgomery arrived back at New Park from his before-breakfast ride he was looking forward to a bath and change, before breakfasting with his wife and the only remaining child of his first marriage, a young girl, Mary Susan, then aged eighteen. She was about to become engaged to Lieutenant James Crofton of the Bengal Engineers who was seconded for service with the Irrigation Department of the Punjab Government. They were married just after the Mutiny, but she died in Lahore two years later. Two of his sons, the eldest Arthur Samuel and Henry (my father) were already at their preparatory school in England. His two younger sons James and Ferguson, aged eight and five respectively, together with their young sister Lucy, were still with their parents in India. On this particular morning Robert had not intended to go early to his office in the civil lines because it was Lucy's first birthday. She had been born on 12th May 1856 and Robert meant to stay awhile with his wife that morning. When he turned in at the drive he could not have known that this was the last time he would be able to go hacking before breakfast for many a long month; it all seemed so quiet and peaceful. The sentry at the gate presented arms and the *malis* (gardeners) who were still watering the lawns gave him a respectful *salaam*. He particularly liked watching the hoopoes, with their wonderful plumage and tufted crests, strutting about on the grass and there were several there this morning. It was when his *sais* came forward to take his bridle as he was dismounting that Robert saw the orderly with the telegram from Delhi. Having opened it and read it he knew that he must act at once; there was not a moment to lose. News of that kind travels and spreads fast in the Orient. In the East India Company's service there was no book cipher for the telegraph so the text of this telegram would by this time be known to many. Later, during the Mutiny, when the secrecy of the written word became so essential, some commanders used to write to their British subordinates in Greek, if they knew that the recipient, like the originator, was proficient in the classics – as many of that generation were. Robert now told the *sais* to keep his horse saddled and be ready in five minutes to escort him to the *daftar* (office). He thereupon went straight to his wife and told her he could not wait, but must go immediately to Anarkulli. He would be back in the evening. He then galloped for the civil lines where he at once summoned his five chief officers to a council, *viz.* Donald McLeod the Financial Commissioner; Mr Arthur Roberts, Commissioner of Lahore Division; Major Edward Ommanney, Chief Engineer; Colonel Duncan Macpherson, Military Secretary; and Captain Richard Lawrence, Commissioner of Police, Lahore. The latter was the younger brother of Sir John Lawrence and the fifth member of his family, all brothers, to serve with distinction in India during the Mutiny. Alexander and George Lawrence had begun their career in the Indian cavalry, Henry went first to the artillery, and John Lawrence to the Indian civil service – a considerable record for one generation of an Ulster family.

When my grandfather reached his office he received secret information, supplied through Richard Lawrence, that all the native regiments at Mian Mir were prepared to follow the example of the regiments at Meerut and Delhi, whatever that might be. As a trusted Brahmin clerk, who was the informer, said to him, 'Sahib, they will do some bad thing, very very bad, Sahib.' That decided Robert and he at once proposed to the Council that all the native regiments at Mian Mir must be disarmed forthwith. This was unanimously agreed. But the Civil Council had no authority in such a matter so the Judicial Commissioner, with his Military Secretary, rode to Mian Mir to urge the absolute necessity for such action on the Military Commander, General Corbett. Both Macpherson and Corbett were in a very difficult position as they were Indian army officers, the great majority of whom had implicit trust in the loyalty of their men; mutiny in their own regiment was not something that was possible, in the opinion of almost all the British officers. It might conceivably happen in someone else's regiment but never in one's own. That they were later to be proved so wrong was tragic, with dreadful consequences, for many British officers and their families were murdered by their own sepoys. At Mian Mir General Corbett's problem was especially troublesome as his own regiment the 16th N.I. (Grenadiers) were involved and, to make matters worse, he was their regimental colonel. However, although he was at first perturbed at the boldness of the proposal put to him by Robert Montgomery, it is greatly to Corbett's credit that he soon appreciated the grave danger they were all in, and accepted the need for drastic action. It was he who had to give all the necessary orders for the plan they decided on, and who later took command of the actual scene of the disarmament. For all this he must be given very great credit. The military responsibility was his alone.

It so happened that a ball was to be held at Anarkulli that very night, 12th May. It was being given by the officers of the garrison to the officers of the 81st Foot. The British regiment was due to return to England and the garrison were anxious to show their appreciation of the hospitality so often afforded by the 81st. It was therefore decided, as absolute secrecy for the success of the disarmament plan was essential, not to interrupt the preparations for the dance which should take place as planned. In those days a grand ball and supper was a great occasion, and much preparatory work was necessary. The dance floor had to be polished with care, usually done by the laying down of English canvas, tightly stretched, which was then rubbed with wax candles till it became very strong and slippery. All the ladies in Mian Mir were helping with this work, and none of them, as yet, were aware of the events planned for the following day. About this time also ice was being issued for the hot weather, and was particularly needed for the dance that night. Of course there was no electric power available so ice was always made throughout the winter in specially designed pots, and the supply lasted, in good years, up to September.

Towards the close of the evening of the 12th May the majority of the British officers in the garrison were told, in outline, of the plans for the following day. They had to be so told, and it says much for their discretion and that of their wives who had also to be kept informed, that no word of the plans leaked out to the native lines. Robert returned to New Park at dusk and then he and my grandmother drove by carriage to the ball in the cantonments. He had already arranged for the armed guard on the house to be doubled with effect from dawn on the 13th. The dance appeared a great success, and the night passed very pleasantly after the fashion of the ball on the eve of Waterloo, forty-two years earlier. But, as an eye witness later wrote, 'It was a sham of smiles over tears. The ladies bravely tried to disguise their anxiety, while the officers had to try to give, and maintain, the impression that nothing was wrong.' They were no doubt assisted in doing this by the magnificent spectacle of the scene at the ball. All the officers in Lahore, both civil and military, with their wives and families, were present in uniform; and the variegated colours of the mess dress, in many hues of scarlet, green and blue and gold, presented a wonderful picture. Of course it was terribly hot. The little *pankha* boys had to work hard pulling the great fans of cloth suspended from the ceiling, which was the only way to keep the air circulating. All the British officers had been warned that no one should leave the dance, to go home, any earlier than they would normally do in case it aroused any undue curiosity on the part of their servants. Few of those present therefore got more than one hour's sleep that night, if they could sleep at all.

At New Park my grandfather was up early, well before five o'clock. He wore a grey frock coat and jodhpurs, with his customary high black stock, and for headdress a white *topi*. He had a revolver under his coat and a cavalry sabre, buckled to a sword belt, round his waist. The revolver was loaded; he was taking no chances. Both the revolver, with its six chambers, and the sword, always used to be in Bishop Montgomery's study at New Park in Ireland; but they vanished after the house was sold and I have not seen them again. It was still quite dark when my grandfather's staff arrived, all mounted, and consisting of the officers of his Council with whom he had conferred at Anarkulli the previous morning; but not the Financial Commissioner who was to remain in charge of the provincial headquarters in the civil lines. My grandmother was up to see the party leave for Mian Mir and her feelings, like those of other British officers' wives who knew what was afoot, can well be imagined. The sun had not yet risen when they moved off, so nobody saw them go except the police constables of the guard. At that hour it was still comparatively cool, but Robert felt it was going to be a very hot day.

Sunrise on the 13th May was at five minutes past five, but long before then, just after the ball had ended, three companies of the 81st Foot fell in, fully armed, and marched off to the fort at Lahore. On the afternoon of the previous day Richard Lawrence's men had intercepted certain letters, destined for the native troops at Mian Mir. These disclosed a plot whereby it was intended to seize control of the fort on the very morning of the 13th, overpower the small British element of its garrison, and then release all the prisoners from the central gaol, some two thousand five hundred in all. Control of the fort would give the mutineers possession of the large armoury of weapons, the extensive magazines, and, equally important, all the vast treasure (many hundreds of thousands of rupees) which was held there. While this was going on the remainder of the native regiments were to rise and massacre all the Europeans, women and children included, at Mian Mir and Anarkulli. It was indeed fortunate that this villainous plot was nipped in the bud. For by six o'clock on the morning of the 13th the three companies of the 81st had entered the fort, where a detachment from the British battalion was in any case due for relief, surprised and overpowered the native garrison, and disarmed them all completely.

At Mian Mir a general parade of all troops in the garrison had been ordered for six o'clock on the morning of 13th May. This was a quite usual occurrence if only on account of the great heat later in the day at that time of year. On this occasion however, the remainder of the 81st Foot paraded at four o'clock, fully equipped with their arms, and with live ammunition. The colours and the band and drums of the regiment were also on parade. Leaving their barrack guards doubled, six companies marched to the garrison parade ground on the *maidan*. There they were joined by the two troops of the (British) horse artillery, also fully armed and equipped; their gun limbers were full, with each echelon containing

grape-shot as well as ball ammunition. By six o'clock the four
native regiments had arrived on parade and the whole garrison was
formed up in mass, in two lines facing each other as shown in the
diagram below. This formation was customary for an occasion
when the General Officer wished to address all his troops on
parade. Apparently the sepoy regiments were still completely unaware that any unusual preparations had been made for that morning. It was also not unusual for the Chief Commissioner, or his
deputy the Judicial Commissioner, to attend a garrison parade,
mounted, on important occasions.

8th Cavalry	16th N.I.	26th N.I.	49th N.I.	Bengal Foot Artillery

G.O.C. and Staff
mounted

Horse Artillery   81st Foot

Judicial Commissioner and Staff
mounted

The distance between the British and sepoy regiments was about
one hundred yards.

After General Corbett had been received with a general salute he
sent staff officers to address each native unit, except his own regiment of grenadiers, the 16th Native Infantry, which he addressed
himself. Each address was in similar terms and began by a reading
aloud of the Governor-General's orders for disbandment of the
19th and 34th Native Infantry at Barrackpore. There followed a
recital of the battle honours won by each regiment of the Lahore
garrison, and of the trust and confidence in which each was held by
General Corbett. He could not believe that regiments such as they,
which had fought with distinction for the *sirkar* (Government) in
so many hard-won battles, would follow the bad example of
Barrackpore. However an evil spirit seemed to be active in the
Indian army, and he now thought it advisable to save the troops
under his command from its despicable influence. He was going to
instruct them to show their true loyalty by laying down their arms

when ordered to do so. While the sepoys were being addressed in this fashion, their attention was diverted from the fact that the horse artillery were quietly taking up action stations, and that the 81st Foot were forming into line. Staff officers then rode in turn to the front of each native regiment and informed its commanding officer, 'The General wishes you to order your regiment to pile arms immediately.' At the same time the following orders to the British troops rang out and could be clearly heard: 'Horse artillery, all guns: grape shot, load.' '81st, load.' There followed the ringing sound of the ramrods as the charges were rammed home. The gun numbers of the horse artillery stood with their portfires lighted, and were seen by all. It was a tense and dreadful moment for the commanding officer and officers in each sepoy regiment. Would their men obey orders to lay down their arms? If they did not they faced immediate and certain death from grape shot and rifle fire at very close range, and so did their British officers. The orders were then issued in turn by seniority of units, beginning with General Corbett's regiment, and in the terms of the drill manual of those days. 'Grenadiers, shoulder arms. Ground arms.' 'Pile arms.' There was a moment's hesitation; a few sepoys began to pile their weapons; then eyes glanced at the black artillery muzzles, so menacing, so close, and aimed directly at them. It was enough and it was decisive. All piled their arms. 'Stand from your arms.' 'Right about face.' 'Quick march.'

After this the 26th and 49th followed suit in turn, the 8th Cavalry dropped their swords, whilst the foot artillery stood from their guns and laid down their side arms. Soon there were some seven hundred sabres and two thousand five hundred muskets piled on the ground, with the bayonets glittering in the early morning sunshine. Amongst them, in places, could be seen the swords and spurs of some of the British officers, who refused to dissociate themselves from the visible evidence of their regiment's obedience to orders. The tragedy of this misplaced trust was yet to come. Finally a company of the 81st fell out, packed all the weapons in carts, and escorted them back to their barracks. The native regiments, deprived of their arms, then marched back to their Lines, with the bands playing and colours flying. It was all over, or so it seemed. In fact it was not so, it was not even the beginning of the end for everyone present on that memorable parade. My uncle, James Alexander Lawrence Montgomery, Robert's son, then just eight years old, remembered the strained atmosphere at New Park, and how very anxious my grandmother appeared, until the party returned from Mian Mir. He recalled that my grandfather and his staff came back looking very pleased, and that they all ate a very good breakfast.

Sir John Lawrence, at Rawalpindi, was of course quite unaware of the events of 13th May at Lahore. He was a very different character to Robert, not given to instant decision in spite of all his great vigour and resolution. When he first heard of the disarmament he was inclined, in spite of its success, to question its long-term wisdom. So indeed were some other officers, including very senior staff officers at the headquarters of the commander-in-chief. These were on record as saying: 'Montgomery has done either the wisest or the most foolish thing in the world.' In fact this was fair comment. A fearful risk had been taken, for what might not have happened if the sepoys had refused to lay down their arms? Presumably hundreds would have been killed and the rest would have scattered, to set ablaze all the Punjab and thereby increase immeasurably the scale and dangers of the rebellion. But Robert Montgomery was convinced he was right to attempt what he had done, and events were to prove him right, including his actions immediately before and after the disarmament parade. On 12th May he had sent trusted messengers to warn the commanders of the great arsenals at Ferozepore and Phillour, and the important garrisons at Mooltan and Kangra. On the 13th, a short while after the parade, a company of the 81st was on its way, in hastily collected native carts, to relieve the Indian garrisons at Amritsar and Govindghur. Then, on his own authority, my grandfather sent orders to all deputy commissioners and other civil officers, telling them to seize the ferries and river crossings, intercept letters if need be, keep a strict watch on travellers, especially all *faqirs*, and to guard all treasure with special care. His instructions ended with the following admonition: 'Make over all mutineers you come across to the police authorities. Should they resist you will of course be prepared to fire on them, and destroy them to a man if possible.'

There have been, and always will be, strong critics of the punishment imposed by the British in India on the sepoys who mutinied in 1857. These punishments were severe indeed, but their nature and scale should surely not be judged except in the context of their time. Mutiny was then a capital offence, and when coupled with murder, looting and robbery the sentence could only be execution. Above all, every responsible British authority knew full well that unless the extreme penalty was enforced on convicted mutineers, there would be no end to the rebellion. For this reason the history of the mutiny includes frequent reports of mutineers hanged, shot or blown from guns. My grandfather was certainly no exception in this respect. In one of his papers, dated shortly after the Mutiny began, is a letter from an assistant commissioner. This officer had written to Lahore asking for advice as to the sentence he should properly impose on a native officer and seven sepoys, all convicted mutineers who had murdered their British officers. This letter is endorsed by my grandfather: 'I have ordered them all to be hanged. *R.M.*' Later Sir John Lawrence had added 'All right. *J.L.*' A similar fate befell the 26th Native Infantry, one of the regiments disarmed at Mian Mir on 13th May. All these units had remained in their cantonments but some of them became progressively disaffected as rumours and counter-rumours reached them. Eventually the 26th murdered their commanding officer and then broke out. My grandfather pursued them with armed police but could not catch them. Eventually on 30th July some five to six hundred were caught attempting to cross the river Ravi. They were all either shot or drowned in the river. Finally the frightful atrocities perpetrated on the British in India, men, women and children, by the mutineers has to be remembered. *The Times* of 17th March 1858 recapitulates the official list of all British subjects killed or missing in India since 11th May 1857. The military personnel are grouped by regiments, and it does not make cheerful reading. One entry reads: '26th Native Infantry – Lahore (totally destroyed)'.

Against a background of such terrifying events, it is refreshing to read how British people managed to keep their sense of humour in spite of it all. An officer of the Bengal Engineers, Lieutenant A. M. Lang, who was on the staff of Mian Mir Headquarters, recorded in his diary for Monday 18th May:

'Yesterday was Sunday, but no holiday for me. I had represented to the Brigadier that I had upwards of 30,000 rupees Government treasure, and a guard of one Havildar and 8 sepoys armed with nothing, except bayonets. "What should I do about it?" He said "Get it away as best you can"! So I got two elephants, took a counterpane off my bed, put 15,000 rupees just anyhow into it and flung the bundle carelessly on one elephant. A carpet off the floor held another 15,000 on the other elephant, and off I went at 9 a.m. Mr Alpin and I followed in a tonga [a light two-wheeled vehicle]. I called on Mr Montgomery in the Civil Lines and he referred me to the Commissioner, who told me "to take the stuff to the Fort". So I took off my two elephants to the Fort and lodged my money safely there. Mr Montgomery told me that the Commander-in-Chief, General Anson, had written to say he was afraid to move from Ambala because of the mutinous spirit of the 5th and 60th N.I. Just fancy! 9th Lancers, 75th Queens, 1st and 2nd Fusiliers, and Horse Artillery – all at Ambala, and all British, and he funks it! Mr Montgomery had written to urge him very strongly, and without delay, to have both regiments paraded and then order them to march into the Gaol, and, if they refuse, instanter to blow them to pieces!!'

There seems to have been no doubt about Mr Montgomery's capacity for immediate action. Perhaps he remembered his father's written instructions just before he had sailed for India, which ended with the admonition 'Procrastination is the thief of time'.

It is not difficult to see in my grandfather, at that time, the same iron will and implacable determination, with absolute conviction in the soundness of his own plans, that, two generations later was so clearly seen in my brother. What might have happened if the Field-

Marshal had listened seriously to suggestions that Egypt was untenable and must be abandoned? or given way under pressure to advance the date of El Alamein before he was properly ready? or changed his fundamental strategy after the Normandy landings by agreeing to a proposal that he should mount a major offensive on his left (the British) flank instead of on the American Front?

The months that followed, from May until Delhi was recaptured from the mutineers at the end of September, were a nightmare period for the British population in Northern India. My grandfather had to cope with many and varied problems; and generally in the absence of Sir John Lawrence who was preoccupied with making his province the means of retaking Delhi. Because of this Sir John was not often in Lahore and, as he said himself, 'I made Montgomery my *locum tenens*'. After the disarmament parade on 13th May there was of course a long period of very grave physical danger in the area. To guard against this the families, nurses, visiting friends, etc., of the British officers of the civil administration were all evacuated from their bungalows in Anarkulli and given accommodation in Lahore fort; the latter was garrisoned by British troops. The conditions in the fort were naturally very uncomfortable, overcrowded and very hot. The families in the cantonments at Mian Mir were concentrated in buildings with large compounds, under British guards and equally uncomfortable. But my grandfather and grandmother, with their daughter aged eighteen and their three younger children, remained at their house New Park, some distance from Anarkulli. Of course they continued to have comfortable conditions in their home, and Lieutenant Lang writing again in his diary on the 14th May recorded: 'The Montgomery's [sic] alone stand firm in their isolated place, and quite right they are too, I think. I wonder whether their guests will go there tomorrow night. I will (DV).'

Apparently he did go, for on 16th May he wrote: 'I dined last night at the Montgomery's [sic]. . . . All Anarkulli ladies are in the Fort.' There is another parallel here with the thinking of my brother on the subject of personal comfort – of which he is certainly enamoured. When he first arrived at Headquarters Eighth Army he did not care for its physical conditions; he found no mess tent, a few trucks only, and the work done mostly in the open air under the hot sun, with flies everywhere. He promptly moved Head-quarters to a site near the sea, cancelled the order forbidding the use of tents and mess furniture and said: 'Let us all be as comfort-able as possible.'

Early in 1858, after the pacification of the Punjab, Robert Mont-gomery issued his official report on the Mutiny entitled *Punjab Military Report*. It is a long printed document, of nearly two hundred pages, and covers in detail all the events in the province from 12th May to 31st December of 1857. It includes recommen-dations for suitable recognition of gallant and distinguished service, to be made to many named officers. The last paragraph of this long report is interesting, because it appears so unusual an ending to any official document, not only now but then too. In it my grand-father wrote:

> But it was not policy, or soldiers, or officers that saved the Indian Empire to England, and saved England to India. The Lord our God, He it was who went before us and gave us the victory over our enemies, when they had well nigh overwhelmed us. To Him who holds all events in His own hand, and has so wondrously over-ruled all to our success, and to His own glory, do I desire on behalf of myself and all whom I represent to express my devout and heartfelt thanksgiving.
>
> > *Robert Montgomery*
> > *Judicial Commissioner*

Looking at the background of my grandfather it ought not to be a cause for surprise that he wrote in this fashion. He had been brought up in the strict religious atmosphere of an Ulster Protes-tant family, against which he never rebelled; on the contrary he accepted it as his own way of life from which he never deviated. On Christmas Day 1942 the Field-Marshal issued the following message to the Eighth Army in Tripolitania, following their spec-tacular and successful campaign after El Alamein, during which they had advanced twelve hundred miles.

'It is wonderful what has been achieved since the 23rd October, when we started the Battle of Alamein. Before the battle began I sent you a message in which I said: Let us pray that the Lord mighty in Battle will give us the victory. He has done so and I know you will agree with me when I say that we must not forget to thank him for his great mercies.'

The similarity of address, allowing for change in style and phraseology during almost a century, is striking. Both men were motivated by their belief in the rightness of their cause and in God's will to bring it to a successful conclusion. The Field-Marshal had had the same strict religious upbringing as his grandfather, but, unlike the latter, there was a short period before his marriage, when he repudiated all belief. This was a cause of much concern to my parents, who appear later on in this story.

The insight into the events of the Indian Mutiny provided by my grandfather's voluminous papers, seems to bring to life the characters and lives of many of the famous men involved and is very fascinating. There is much for instance, *inter alia*, on Brigadier John Nicholson, that astounding man who, at the relief of Delhi, was killed sword in hand as he led the final bloody assault on the Lahore gate. Who but Nicholson, long before the mutiny began and when attacked by a Pathan armed with a sword and intent on decapitating him, could first have seized a musket, shot him dead, and then have written immediately to Sir John Lawrence:

Sir,
    I have the honour to inform you that I have just shot a man who came to kill me.

> *Your obedient servant,*
> *John Nicholson*

He did not add that the musket ball had passed into the man's heart through a copy of the Koran, which was turned down – so it was said – at a page which promised paradise to those who fell in the attempt to slay unbelievers. The material in these records is far beyond the scope of the present book. Therefore as far as the

Mutiny is concerned with this story, and it played a vital part in the making of a field-marshal, it will suffice to conclude with some reference to my grandfather's service at Lucknow. He had remained at Lahore, still living with his family in their large bungalow at Anarkulli, until he was appointed Chief Commissioner of Oudh in 1858.

At Lucknow, the capital of Oudh, Robert Montgomery took over from Sir James Outram. In the province as a whole the mutiny was very far from being subdued. Lucknow itself had been retaken. But the population was still disaffected mainly because, apart from the two historic sieges and the battle for Lucknow city in which Sir Henry Lawrence was killed, there had been no large-scale encounters with the mutineers, as in the Punjab. Law and order were conspicuous by their absence and the *talukdars* (landowners) had come to behave like the robber barons of Europe in an earlier age. The country people were mostly Hindu Rajputs, a very fine race of fighting stock from the Ganges valley. They were a farming and peasant community which supplied three-fifths of the Bengal army of the East India Company. However there had been much trouble with the native regiments, who had greatly outnumbered the British troops, and murder and pillage were rife throughout the province. The following account of the fate of a detachment of the Bengal army, under British officers, will serve to show the state of the country both before and after my grandfather's arrival at Lucknow. It also shows the regard of the British officers for their sepoys, including their pensioners, ex-soldiers who had served in the regiment and whose welfare remained the care of the British administration.

During the height of the hot weather season, at the end of May when the humidity in the Ganges valley is really terrible, a military detachment set out from Lucknow to visit Fategarh where the pensioners were clamouring to be paid. The small force consisted of two troops of the 7th Light Cavalry with two companies of the 48th Bengal Native Infantry; in all some 500 men with six British officers and a political agent, Lieutenant Hutchinson. The commander was Major Marriott, Pension Paymaster. They marched through the by-roads of Oudh towards the Ganges, which they were to cross at a ferry about forty miles north west of Cawnpore. The size of the force was dictated by the need to safeguard the treasure, many thousands of rupees, which they were conveying to Fategarh; without an adequate escort the money would certainly have been looted within a short distance of Lucknow. In those days the conditions for troops on the march through the plains of the Ganges valley, during the hottest time of the year, must have been extremely arduous, and especially for European personnel. Khaki drill uniform was not yet in use so officers wore cloth tunics with high collars, heavy leather belts and cartridge pouches, and were encumbered with their swords and pistols; a *topi* (tropical helmet) and long boots, for all British officers were mounted, completed the equipment. Flies were everywhere, and prickly heat, for abundant perspiration was inevitable and continuous, did not help matters. Because of these conditions Reveille was always sounded early before dawn. The column then made a morning march to avoid the intense heat at midday, and, having made camp well before noon, resumed their journey in the late afternoon. During the day they generally made camp near a village where they could water the horses and find some shade, even if it was only from banana or date palm trees. At night they camped in the open to avoid the danger of being surprised. The British officers had tents and were accompanied by their bearers, cooks and mess servants, all of whom were included in the motley collection of camp followers which marched with the force.

When the detachment reached the ferry crossing over the Ganges the political agent (P.A.) was told that their sepoys meant to murder all the British officers that very night, seize the treasure and make for Delhi. The P.A. thereupon urged Major Marriott not to attempt to cross the river but to return to Lucknow with all speed. Crossing the river would be dangerous in any case. It would mean dividing the detachment, including the British officers, as the ferry boats were scarce and the troops would have to cross over in small batches, with their horses swimming the river. A most unfortunate scene followed. Major Marriott sided with the P.A. but the other officers refused absolutely to accept any statement which cast doubt on the loyalty of their men; mutiny was impossible, in their view, in either the 7th Light Cavalry or 48th N.I. Eventually they all did cross the river except the P.A. who refused to go. When they had all reached the other bank the first signs of trouble appeared. The native officers, cavalry and infantry, came forward and said they would not return to Lucknow; they would go to Delhi; but not to Lucknow or Cawnpore. Major Marriott then urged all British officers to leave their men and recross the river in order to save their lives whilst there was time; it was already after midday. All however refused to leave their posts, whereupon Major Marriott handed over command of the detachment to Captain Staples of the 7th Cavalry – including all the treasure intended for the pensioners at Fategarh! – and rode for the river. This he crossed safely to rejoin the political agent. There is no record of what eventually happened to Major Marriott, or whether he managed to justify his conduct. What happened after he left is known.

In the early afternoon fifty of the *sowars* in the Cavalry detachment, and seven of the sepoys from the 48th N.I., openly broke away, recrossed the river, and marched towards Delhi. At four o'clock the British officers dined, as was their custom, and the tents were struck in readiness for the evening march. All the officers were seated under the trees with their baggage ready packed and their weapons handy. The detachment was drawn up on parade ready to move off. Setting aside the departure of the disaffected sowars and sepoys all seemed well, or as well as it could be, and Captain Staples called for his horse. But suddenly a sowar of the 7th Cavalry, Nawab Din, who was apparently the ringleader, fired his musket at Captain Staples. He missed him, but massacre followed. Four of the officers, Captain Staples and Lieutenant Martin both 7th Cavalry, with Captain Bumester and Lieutenant Farquharson of the 48th N.I., were shot immediately. Their heads were then cut off, wrapped in cloths, and taken away by sweepers to Bithur, where they were again seen and recognised by the officers' servants. Meanwhile the mutineers marched off to Delhi. One officer did get away. Captain Boulton, 7th Cavalry, had his horse saddled and handy. When the firing started he swiftly mounted and made off across country to escape.

When Robert and his wife, and the members of his family who

Sir Robert Montgomery,
from a bust in the India
Office

Lady Montgomery
in India, 1854 (aged 30)

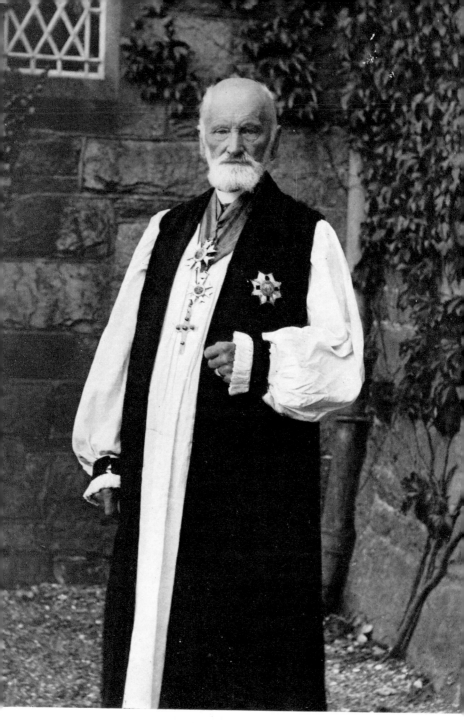

Bishop Montgomery

were with him at Lahore, arrived at Lucknow in March 1858 they found they could not live at the Residency, or Government House as it was called later. The building had been very badly damaged in the siege of the city the previous year, and very little of it remained intact, except the room where Sir Henry Lawrence had died. So a large bungalow on the outskirts of the city was taken for the new Residency, and even the walls of this building were pitted with bullet holes and other evidence of the severe fighting in the area. It was my grandfather's first experience of appointment as the executive head of a very large province. His word was now law, in letter and in fact, and his rule virtually absolute. In these circumstances it was perhaps typical of the man that almost his first act was to write to the Central Government at Calcutta, then the capital of India, and ask that a British chaplain should be sent at once to Lucknow, to minister to the sick and the dying. The field hospital was full to overflowing with soldiers and civilians, either wounded or sick, all under the care of a surgeon major of the East India Company service, who had never before had charge of Europeans, and some very young surgeons. This young chaplain took many days to reach Lucknow from Calcutta, and was not likely ever to forget the experiences he met on the journey. Of course he knew that travelling at such a time would be very dangerous; that the whole country was infested with bands of rebels who burned and pillaged all they could lay their hands on, and robbed and then murdered all travellers who were not escorted by troops. In spite of this he was allowed to set off, alone from Calcutta, travelling by carriage *dak* which was the counterpart, in India, of the British mail coach of that time. There however the comparison ended for the *dak* was a heavy, lumbering, though not altogether uncomfortable, conveyance, rather similar to a bathing machine. Inside it was arranged like a bed, travelling being done chiefly at night, on account of the great heat. The shade temperature by day was already approaching one hundred and eight degrees. At the head and foot, as well as the sides, of the carriage there were shelves and pockets. The luggage, often very varied and very heavy, was carried outside on the roof, and donkeys and goats were sometimes included in the load.

3

When this young man set off on his journey, dressed in the con-
ventional black of a parson, complete with stiff collar and feeling
horribly conspicuous, he was naturally full of apprehension –
though glad to be leaving Calcutta which he had found dreary and
uninteresting. All went well until he reached Shergotti on the
border of what was to become the United Provinces. There he was
informed by the local magistrate that he could not proceed as the
rebel cavalry were in the neighbourhood. The day before they had
shot Major Fanshaw who was on his way, also travelling alone by
carriage *dak*, to join his regiment at Cawnpore. In spite of the state
of the country it seemed that British men, and women too, insisted
on maintaining the pretence of normal conditions, including communications. When the rebels had sighted Major Fanshaw's *dak*
they had started to intercept it. The Major at once left the carriage
and climbed a tree on the roadside, which was a most unfortunate
choice. He was soon spotted by the mutineers who at once set
about using him as target practice for their carbines, until he was
shot out of the tree and finished off with sabres. The young parson
was now faced with an awkward predicament. What was he to do
next? His decision, and what came of it, is best told in his own
words.

'This was unpleasant news, but I had orders to proceed, and
I was anxious to be at my post. The kind Magistrate remon-
strated, and did all he could to dissuade me, and said at last that
if I went I did so on my own responsibility, and against his
warning. Late in the evening I started, after hearing many
stories of planters' bungalows and factories having been burnt,
and of Europeans outraged and killed. Most of them I hoped,
were untrue or exaggerated. I tried in vain to sleep in the lumbering, jolting, springless vehicle, but at intervals my coachman,
to keep up his pluck and frighten away the wild beasts, would
blow a wild and most unmusical blast on his horn.

'The first incident was the unmistakeable and not very distant
roar of a tiger, and the remark of the coachman "that this was a
very bad place for tigers, as a man had been killed by one the
night before", did not do much towards removing my alarm. I

saw no tiger, but something very much worse. Before the sun had risen a dust cloud was visible, and soon a troop of the enemy's cavalry crossed the road at full gallop. They seemed not to notice my *dak*. Prompted by the instinct of self-preservation I opened all the windows, threatened my coachman with death if he blew his horn to attract attention, or did not drive straight on. Then I lay down quite flat out of sight to give the appearance of an empty carriage. Fortunately I escaped, and without further incident completed my journey to Cawnpore.

'The sight of the town at that time I shall never forget. Some of the houses which had been thatched were burnt, and all were gutted. The compounds were strewn with torn and broken articles of all kinds showing the madness of the infuriated rebels. With trembling steps I bent my way to the scene of the massacre. There, still visible on the walls, were clotted blood and hair. The children, it is said, were brained by dashing them against the wall. That place is now the site of a beautiful garden and a monument representing an Angel of Mercy, or Grief, with folded hands, looking, as it were, into the well where so many of our countrymen and countrywomen were thrown by order of the Nana Sahib – a man who had been feted in England, and who lived on most friendly terms with our people. The date 27th June 1857, when two hundred British women and children were hacked to death and cast into the well, is one that will never be forgotten.'

When the chaplain reached Cawnpore his troubles were by no means over. Smallpox had broken out and he was more afraid of it than of any other infectious disease. Fortunately for him, or so it seemed, he ordered the *dak* to take him to the bungalow of the resident chaplain, who he discovered, to his delight, had been a fellow curate with him at Manchester. This chaplain came to the door, and said: 'I hope you are not afraid of smallpox, for that brave fellow, Sir William Peel, has just died of it here.' Hurriedly declining the hospitality offered him, the young parson continued his journey the same night, this time in the mail cart, hoping soon to reach Lucknow. But this midnight journey of forty miles was one of his worst experiences. The road, such as it was, had been cut up by the passage of artillery into a succession of potholes and ruts, into and out of which the cart bumped in the most unpleasant and bone-shaking manner. Added to this the driver drove at full gallop all the way, though the springs of the two-wheeled *gari* were apparently non-existent and the horse too small for the shafts. The effect was that of a constant see-saw which threatened to cut him in two, especially as the seat was as hard as iron and the only rest for the back another iron bar. Fortunately he had taken the precaution of tying himself in by a rope and placed a pillow behind his back; but it was altogether a nightmare journey. At length, more dead than alive, he arrived at the Residency of the Chief Commissioner, Mr Robert Montgomery, who had kindly invited him to be his guest.

The new Residency was large and imposing and reflected the high status and ceremony which was an inevitable accompaniment in the life of a provincial governor. The gatehouse was a plain thatched cottage outside which six or seven natives were generally to be found waiting. These men were *chuprassies*, so called from the *chuprass*, or broad plate of brass embroidered with the badge of their employer, which each wears on his belt. *Chuprassies* are very important people as they carry messages, deliver papers, etc., and, rightly or wrongly depending on their employer's character, are often thought to have 'the ear of their master'. They wear a grand uniform, frequently a red tunic with a scarlet or white *pagri* which also carries their master's badge. They generally act as door keepers and are adept at exacting an appropriate toll from all who wish to have access to the '*burra Sahib*'. To this day a good *chuprassi*, such is the charm of his badge, will scarcely ever fail to arrange things so that every errand on which he may be sent will produce some appropriate reward for himself. Beyond the gatehouse is 'the compound', or walled enclosure, through which there is a drive of about one hundred yards, bordered by a flower garden planted with trees, until you come to the Residency; beyond this building the drive continues to another gatehouse at the other side of the enclosure. There is a guard with two sentries, and sentry boxes, outside the front door of the Residency; and often nearby there is a palanquin on the ground, with its bearers in livery, showing that a native of rank has an audience with the Chief Commissioner. Under the trees on the lawn there is likely to be the '*shoottee sowar*', or armed camelman, perched high up on his gaily padded camel. He is waiting in the shade for some dispatch which he may have to carry to its destination probably fifty or sixty miles without a halt. He is a soldier and carries a carbine, *tulwar* or sword, and a pistol, for his protection on his solitary and generally dangerous errand.

This then was the setting in which the young chaplain came to stay with the Chief Commissioner, and he obviously much enjoyed the comfort and social life he found there. But it was not all easy going and at one stage he found himself in much trouble. His own diary gives the best account of what occurred.

'As April wore on, and the heat became more intense, the deaths from sunstroke, or heat apoplexy, increased in the Hospital as well as in the field, and Sir Robert was much distressed on more than one occasion at the account I gave him of the mortality from these causes. Several times I had spoken myself to the Surgeon about the want of *punkahs*, *tatties*, doors, and windows, as well as coolies to keep off the flies, whose name was legion, but of course in vain. At last Sir Robert volunteered to go with me, and one morning we rode off, he on his hill pony, smiling all over, the picture of health and happiness – arrived at the hot, dirty, and neglected place, where hundreds of our men lay suffering intense pain from heat and lack of almost every comfort. There was no need of a word; he went away looking as angry as he could. Directly he arrived at the Residency he sent a note, officially called a memo, directing attention to the state of the Hospital, and desiring that the necessary furniture should be supplied without delay. Days and weeks passed and nothing was done; the heat increased, and the deaths were more frequent. One day, being rather late for dinner, Sir Robert looked up in his merry way through his spectacles, and said, "Well, Padre (the name given to all clergy in India), where have you been to today, and what makes you so late?" I then told him that I had

had several funerals, and the deaths were increasing at a fearful rate. After dinner he took me aside, and said, "I wish you, as chaplain, would write me a short report of the number and causes of the deaths that have occurred, adding any remarks that you like," which accordingly I did with right good will.

'One Sunday, about ten days after this conversation with Sir Robert, I saw my old friend Dr Douglas standing on the steps of the Mosque where we had service, and going up to him he said, "What is this you have been doing? All the doctors are mad at you." I did not at first comprehend what he meant, but I soon learned that my report, sent with a strong letter from Sir Robert to the Commander-in-Chief, had brought down from head-quarters a tremendous "wigging". They were very indignant, and even my medical friends fought shy of me as a dangerous person for a long time. It is but fair to state that the cause of the neglect, besides the incapacity of the principal medical officer (who knew nothing of European Hospitals), was the inefficient character of the executive engineer. About a fortnight after this carpenters and joiners were busy, and soon the Hospital began to look as it ought.

'Then fell the following shell; one morning Sir Robert sent into my room a long official document, in which were presented in two columns, "Mr B — —'s Charges and the Doctor's Refutations." It was a terrible indictment, and besides denying all my statements, and adding that the Hospital was supplied with all necessary appliances, it wound up magnificently by saying that it would be better for a Chaplain, who must necessarily be ignorant of the duties of another profession, to keep to his own. I was very angry, and meditated a long and crushing reply, but Sir Robert, who saw me on the subject soon after, cooled me down by saying, "My dear fellow, take no notice of it. You have done a public service by bringing these abuses to light, and you forced them into doing their duty, and now they have to make the best of it."

'And so ended my first official row.'

It is interesting to see how 'official rows', of the kind experienced by this young chaplain in India, especially when welfare is concerned, still appear to produce very similar results, even after the lapse of nearly a century. In 1945 my sister-in-law, Mrs Colin Montgomery, was a Red Cross welfare officer at a D.P.s' (Displaced Persons') camp in Western Germany. It was some months after the V.E. surrender day and in camps, such as Belsen, it was very difficult indeed to maintain adequate medical and welfare standards. Perhaps rather unwisely she decided to take advantage of her relationship by writing direct to the Commander-in-Chief, Field-Marshal Montgomery. In her letter she complained strongly about what she saw as bad conditions which ought to be put right. Of course a direct letter to the Commander-in-Chief, from a comparatively junior welfare officer, was not only most unusual but also, in the eyes of the staff, highly improper and most reprehensible! Nevertheless apparently it worked; for in due course it was as if history repeated itself when the young chaplain wrote: 'soon the hospital began to look as it ought'.

The pacification and rule of a province, in which these varied conditions prevailed, now fell to the lot of Robert Montgomery. He at once saw the first priority; the raising, training and maintenance of an efficient police service. In due course, and by the time he was posted back to Lahore as Lieutenant-Governor of the Punjab in 1859, he had completed this task. But it was not only pacification and law and order that was needed. Robert saw very clearly, and in this he was the forerunner of the long line of British administrators who followed him after the Mutiny, that what was required, in all India, was a sound government machinery to replace that of the defunct Mogul empire. It was Robert, and men like him, who evolved and eventually produced a system which resulted in one loyalty – to the British *raj* – irrespective of race, language, class and creed. None of the other conquerors of India, only the British, were able to achieve this. It was the magnanimity and understanding of the British administration that enabled Hindu and Muslim to work, live and fight together, forgetting or ignoring all the prejudices of religious and racial animosity, for many a long year. The prime cause of this success, particularly in the early days after the Mutiny, was the foundation of trust created

by benefits and well being, and general economic advantage.
Schools, hospitals, communications, canals and irrigation, hygiene
and child welfare, a fair tax system, all played their part in bringing
peace to the land. That all this apparently collapsed, with awful
loss and suffering, when the British withdrew from the Indo-
subcontinent twenty-six years ago, is an altogether different
story.

Robert Montgomery will appear again later in this book, but not
until he has become well known and very distinguished as Sir
Robert Montgomery, GCSI, KCB, LLD, with a large district of
the Punjab, and its capital town, named 'Montgomery' after him;
both are still so called. In Lahore itself the native princes and
people of the Punjab built 'Montgomery Hall', in the public park
of the city, where the portraits of all the governors of the Province
are now hung. Finally on the 14th April 1859 he became the recipient of a most unusual honour. In London on that day the Parliament of the United Kingdom at Westminster resolved, '*nemine
dissentiente*', that the thanks of both the House of Lords and of the
House of Commons should be conveyed to him, in recognition of
his services 'for the re-establishment of Peace in Her Majesty's
Indian Dominions'. The original documents issued for this occasion, written and sealed on vellum, are now in the possession of
James Montgomery, senior member of the Canadian branch of our
family which has been settled in Vancouver City in British Columbia for the past sixty-five years.

Meanwhile in Lucknow in 1858 it was said of my grandfather
that his energy was remarkable. He never spared himself, and he
required his subordinate officers to follow his example to the full.
It is again easy to see these characteristics in the Field-Marshal two
generations later. Sir John Lawrence however made one comment
on my grandfather which I can by no means reconcile with my
brother. When Robert left the Punjab to go to Lucknow Sir John
wrote:

'When the insurrection broke out I was at Rawalpindi. It was
mainly Robert Montgomery's moral courage and coolness, and
decision, which kept things straight at Lahore. But for him the

Hindustani troops would not have been disarmed, in which case God only knows what would have happened. He is a fine fellow, brave as a lion, and gentle as a lamb.'

I doubt if anyone has ever likened my brother to a gentle lamb.

Chapter 3

DEAN FARRAR

Our mother's father, The Very Reverend Dean Farrar, DD, FRS, MA, to give him his formal title, was in every way completely unlike my paternal grandfather, Sir Robert Montgomery, except perhaps in his degree of distinction. Both were of the same generation and both were famous and well known in their different ways. But if distinction were to depend only on personal reputation and the extent to which name and attainments are widely known, then undoubtedly Dean Farrar, in his day, would have outshone Sir Robert.

Frederic William Farrar, born 7th August 1831, earned a worldwide reputation for many reasons. He was famous as a scholar, particularly in the field of philology, history, theology and classical literature. He was also a great educationalist, renowned as an orator, and above all a most distinguished and able writer. During forty-two years he wrote thirty-six books and essays, including fiction, and historical, religious and philosophical studies, all of which were published in numerous editions. Probably his most famous publications were, first, *Eric or Little by Little*, which ran to more than fifty editions, thirty-six of which appeared in his lifetime, and later his *Life of Christ*, published in 1874. This book finally established his reputation as a popular writer. It was published in thirty editions in the author's lifetime and translated into all the European languages, and Japanese as well; it had a huge sale in America. Whenever he preached in Westminster Abbey, which he did frequently, the notice 'Abbey Full' was invariably needed, after all available standing room had been filled, and many people had to be turned away. He was a Canon, and Archdeacon, of Westminster, a Fellow of Trinity College, Cambridge and of Kings College. London, and a Chaplain-in-Ordinary to H.M. The Queen and to the House of Commons. Undoubtedly his greatest claim to fame lay in his public reputation as a brilliant man of letters, and a headmaster of exceptional merit and strength of character. Because of this he undoubtedly exerted a great influence on the religious feeling and culture, and the thoughts and opinions of the men and women of his generation, especially the middle classes, for fully forty years. With the passing of time however, and the immense changes in human standards and values brought about by two world wars, his name is no longer remembered, except perhaps by some of the older generation. His books are long out of print and unknown to all but a few. A street in Westminster, Dean Farrar Street, is named after him, and there is a plaque in his memory in Canterbury Cathedral, where he was buried, and also in St Margaret's Westminster.

When we were boys my brothers and I, six of us in all, certainly did not appreciate Dean Farrar's books. Indeed we frankly loathed them! It was a strict rule of my mother that on Sundays her children should only read books classed by herself as 'good' books, and preferably one of her father's stories. The reason for our attitude is therefore not far to seek, though I cannot speak for my sisters in the matter. In a letter to myself about the family, written in 1961, my brother Bernard wrote: 'I do not care for the Farrar blood; it does not interest me'! Again, when talking about the men of the family including near relatives, he would frequently say about one or the other: 'He is a Farrar, not a Montgomery.'

As this story unfolds the reader will be able to see the extent to which the characteristics and strong personality of the Dean, and of his wife who was an equally strong character, were inherited by his grandchildren.

Frederic Farrar was born in the fort at Bombay, the second son of Charles Pinhorn Farrar, chaplain of the Church Missionary

Society. The first three years of his life were spent at Nasik in India, after which he was sent to England to a preparatory school, under the guardianship of two maiden aunts. At a very early age he developed a voracious appetite for books and read everything he could lay his hands on. His parents were always extremely hard up, so his resources for travel or expenditure of any kind, beyond virtually subsistence level, were strictly limited. When he was eight years old his father and mother returned from India for their three years' furlough, and took a house in the Isle of Man. This led to Frederic being sent to school at King William's College, as a boarder, and was the foundation of his scholastic and literary life.

King William's College, Isle of Man, where Farrar remained for more than eight years, was a very great change from the comparatively sheltered life of a small village preparatory school. The conditions were tough at all English public schools in the mid-nineteenth century, and the standard of teaching also had little to commend it. At King William's College the boys had to, and did, live a spartan life, especially in terms of bare creature comforts and food. Two or three boys generally had to share the same study, a very small room in which there was barely enough space for the chairs, a table, and a small coal box. The latter was filled once a week only so there was never enough fuel for even the smallest fire except in the evening; yet all their work out of the classroom had to be done there. The food, by present-day standards, was virtually non-existent. For breakfast and tea the boys got only thick pieces of buttered bread, though there was little enough butter. Dinner consisted of one very scanty helping of meat with either boiled rice or swedes, never both, and no potatoes or bread. On Sundays there was pudding and on Thursdays treacle roll, but no second course on other days. At all meals silence was strictly enforced. If a boy was caught even whispering to his neighbour he had to 'stand down' and lost the remainder of his meal. Of course the boys used to get up from their meals almost as hungry as when they sat down to them. As at all public schools of that time there was much fagging done by the junior boys, with a great deal of bullying also to be endured, amounting sometimes to near torture. It was considered 'fun' by some of the seniors to make a new boy bend over a chair, with dire threats of what would happen if he moved, and then drive pins into his behind up to the head. Notorious bullies made a speciality of kicking, and would sometimes send for a new boy to come to their study. The wretched victim was then systematically kicked in cold blood, the kicker having first put on his football boots.

There is no doubt it was conditions such as these that profoundly influenced Farrar's school and university life, and which later led him to such eminence in the teaching profession, particularly in the field of school and educational reform. He felt passionately that no schoolboy or undergraduate could possibly assimilate, and benefit by, instruction unless two pre-conditions were satisfied. First, the physical conditions must be amenable, and secondly the standard of teaching must match the requirement, namely the absolute need for education. It was these aims, put simply in these terms, which he made his life-long ambition and determination to achieve. His method of doing so was by writing, teaching, exhortation and example, coupled with his intense religious fervour. The measure of his success was evident in the really astonishing demand, on the part of the general public, to obtain and read his books, and to listen to what he had to say. His knowledge was immense and he was fortunate in being able to impart that knowledge in a simple manner, so that his audience, in colloquial terms, shouted for more. He was never at a loss in satisfying that demand. In all this he was fortunate again in his possession of a commanding height and appearance, a stately manner and, most important, a strong oratorical voice. People looked for and grew accustomed to the sight of him, with his clear cut features, well-opened eyes, broad forehead and fine wavy hair.

Of all Dean Farrar's works of fiction, probably the best known and most widely read were his three books on school and university life, namely, *Eric, or Little by Little*, *St Winifred's or The World of School*, and *Julian Home*. The first named was really autobiographical and reflected, truthfully, his experiences at King William's College, Isle of Man. Probably no writer today of schoolboy fiction would regard such work as having any research value, and no schoolboy would ever think of reading it, even if he were told about it. Every chapter had its lesson with special emphasis on the 'good' versus the 'bad' in terms of manly conduct and example. In short it would bore any modern reader, especially a boy. But it did reflect Farrar's ardent temperament and unselfish idealism, and, to give the story its proper due, it survived, and equalled, contemporary publication with that other best-seller *Tom Brown's School Days*. Tom Hughes who wrote the latter and published it in 1857 was a great friend of Farrar's. *Eric* was published a year later. Both books provided a most fruitful field for comparative review, frequently, and, perhaps naturally, *Eric* suffered in the ensuing comparison. For *Tom Brown's School Days* gave a picture of the average public school boy of those times, and indeed of later generations also, healthy and very active, keen on games and responsive to discipline and *esprit de corps*. *Eric* on the other hand, written solely for a moral and educational purpose, undoubtedly achieved its aim. Because of this, comparison of the two stories was probably irrelevant. The fact however is, and remains, that people of today are more likely to have heard of, and will possibly have read, *Tom Brown's School Days*, but not *Eric or Little by Little*. Finally it may not come amiss to bring Rudyard Kipling into this context. In *Stalky and Co* the chief character is wont to jeer at Eric! Certainly the boys of my generation, including my brothers and myself, rather enjoyed that.

St Winifred's or The World of School was first published anonymously in 1863, because, as Farrar then said, 'I did not wish attention to be diverted from other work in which I was then engaged.' The authorship was however immediately recognised and the book published, with Farrar's name, in 1868. The twenty-sixth edition was printed in 1903, and a final edition, with illustrations in colour, as late as 1909. The story reflected the author's experiences as a master at both Marlborough and Harrow, but was less open to the type of criticism often levelled at *Eric*. Nevertheless the tone and language of the book were still fashioned in a manner which would appear wholly alien to and would find little response in, the generations which grew up after the 1914–18 war. For instance in the plot the hero, whose name is Walter and who, by any standards, could not fail to be looked upon as a dreadful prig, breaks open and ransacks the desk of his classics master for whom he has scant regard. Walter then proceeds to burn to ashes not only the master's punishment book, but also his commentary on the Hebrew Text of the Four Greater Prophets, the work of a lifetime. Subsequently Walter, overcome by shame and remorse, confesses to the master, Mr Paton, what he has done. But the master reacts in an unpredictable way, and says to Walter:

> 'Yes, Walter, this occurrence may do us both good, miserable as it is. I will say no more about it now, only that I have quite forgiven it. Man is far too mean a creature to be justified in withholding forgiveness for any personal wrong. It is far more hard to forgive oneself when one has done wrong. I have determined to bury the whole matter in oblivion and to inflict no punishment on you for this folly and sin. I will try henceforth to be your friend.'

Walter then bursts into tears and is led away sobbing by Mr Paton. But Walter is an athlete and later, at the annual school sports, he wins the high jump in front of all the assembled pupils, their fathers mothers, daughters and girl friends. His victory however is greeted by his colleagues in dead silence, in which he could not fail to hear a pretty young blonde say to her brother, 'Why don't they cheer him as well as the others? He looks such a nice boy.' To Walter's mortification the reply was: 'Because he did a very shabby thing not long ago.'

Julian Home appeared in 1859 and was a story of university life. The local colour for this tale was derived from Farrar's experiences at Trinity College, Cambridge, from where he graduated with honours in 1854, in both the classical and mathematical tripos. He was already a graduate of King's College London, also with honours, and with classical and theological scholarships and prizes for divinity and English literature. Indeed he won so many scholarships, at both London and Cambridge, that throughout his university career he was able to pay personally for all the expenses of his education. This was a great relief for his father, who during that time was Curate-in-Charge of St James', Clerkenwell, with scarcely enough for himself and his wife to live on. Nevertheless the time he spent at university was certainly a financial struggle for Farrar. He is on record as saying that at Cambridge he could not afford tea or coffee for breakfast and drank only water. With it all, this astonishing man found time to prepare himself for entry into the Church, no light task in those days. He was ordained deacon in 1854 and priest in 1857.

The story of *Julian Home* highlighted, *inter alia*, the moral theme of unlawfully obtaining prior knowledge of examination papers. Kennedy, an undergraduate, by chance obtains improper access to a manuscript copy of his forthcoming examination paper. Every question is printed indelibly on his memory, but then doubt assails him. The only honourable thing to do, surely, would be to go at once to his tutor, inform him that he had accidentally read this particular examination paper and presume it would be changed. On the other hand if he did no such thing he would assuredly pass with honours, and in a subject in which he knew he was weak. But, meanwhile, had anyone seen him while he was reading the manuscript? If not, he was safe; but there had been someone else in the same room at the same time. He is sorely tempted. In the event he gives way to temptation, with the result that he obtained first place in the examination, having passed with flying colours well ahead of all other candidates. For this he does not escape the penalty of conscience or remorse, and is soon taunted by a colleague with the remark: 'You did so well in that examination, Kennedy, you couldn't have done the paper better if you had seen it beforehand.' Of course then Kennedy blushes furiously and the colleague he is with tells him, 'I saw you coolly read over the whole examination paper, you know, which wasn't the most honourable thing in the world to do – but cheer up, man, I'm not going to tell on you.' And he never did! though Kennedy carried the scar of guilt for all time.

The theme in each of these three books of fiction clearly carried its own moral, though doubtless nowadays quite outmoded. Most Kennedys of today, or even of my generation, being more opportunistic, would presumably seize the chance presented and profit accordingly, without too many qualms. A minox camera, instant photography, and I'm all right, Jack, would be a more likely reaction today.

When Farrar left Cambridge in 1854 he was already, at the age of twenty-three, the recipient of much academic honour and merit, and a clergyman. He had read widely, and had been much influenced by his reading; so it suited him well to accept a mastership at Marlborough College. He left there after a year to join the staff at Harrow School, first under the headmastership of the celebrated Dr Vaughan, and later under the equally famous Dr H. M. Butler. He very soon became a house-master and remained at Harrow for sixteen years. This was the main formative period of his life in which he devoted all his leisure hours to literary work, a practice he followed all his life. He had scarcely ever played any games, though there is a record of his playing football whilst at Harrow. But he certainly did not play cricket and he never fished, or handled a shot-gun. He did not play golf and he could not ride a horse. Nowadays it may seem strange that a schoolmaster at a great public school should appear almost entirely divorced from all contact with games and sport of every kind. If so it is all the more testimony that he became so outstandingly successful; though perhaps this aloofness from outdoor activities was also the reason that so often he does not seem to have been in any way concerned with the important political, military and constitutional developments of his time. Great events in our history such as the Crimean War, the Indian Mutiny, or the exploration and political acquisition of British Africa, find no mention in his papers. Only once does he mention such an event. This was the Boxer Rising in China of 1900 when the Allied troops marched on, and entered Peking. Farrar's second son, Cyril Lytton Farrar, had been commissioned in the Marines and was a subaltern in the Royal Marine Light Infantry. He was killed in the Boxer Rebellion.

It was while he was at Harrow that Farrar married his wife, by whom he had a large family of five sons and five daughters. She was Lucy Mary, third daughter of Frederick Cardew, a judge in India, and she married my grandfather in 1860. The Cardews were an old family long settled at Truro in Cornwall. Curiously enough, we

Montgomerys have become distantly related, by the marriage of
Dean Farrar with a Cardew, to the infamous Russian spy and
traitor 'Kim' Philby. It has happened in this way. H. St J. B.
Philby, the famous explorer and Arabist, and the first European to
cross Arabia from north to south via the Hadhramaut, was Kim's
father. His (maternal) great-grandfather was Henry Clare Cardew
whose sister was Mrs Farrar, my grandmother. Because of this
Jack Philby wrote in his autobiography, *Arabian Days*, 'At West-
minster I was encouraged to think that my childish delight in
Greek verbs was but an echo of my kinship with the great Dean
Farrar himself.' It was thus through my grandmother that the
Philby family became known to my parents though Jack Philby
never came to New Park. He was however well acquainted with my
Field-Marshal brother when they both served together in India,
Jack in the Indian Civil Service and my brother with his regiment.
In his *Arabian Days* the explorer wrote, 'In September (1910) I
took ten days leave to get married at Murree with the support, as
best man, of my cousin, Lieutenant Bernard Montgomery of the
Warwicks.' After this marriage Kim, the traitor, was born in 1912.
In this connection his father, friend of T. E. Lawrence and of the
famous King of Saudi-Arabia, Abdul Aziz ibn Saud, had very
early on showed signs of being a rebel against the establishment,
which he certainly was. As long ago as 1908, in his last term at
Cambridge, he was already a left-wing socialist. As he said himself,
'I was probably the first socialist to enter the Indian civil service,
and I suppose I scandalised most of my friends by proclaiming
from the beginning my adhesion to the ideal of Indian independence.' Later he became a firm supporter of the Labour party.
But in the early part of the 1939–45 war he fell foul of the British
authorities on account of his extreme views, which he voiced to all
and sundry, and was imprisoned for some months under the
Defence of the Realm Regulations. Looking back, with all the
advantage of hindsight, it is perhaps permissible to wonder why, at
the time, more thought was not given to the possible effects of
heredity and environment, with special reference to the father's
record, before admitting the son to the inner counsels of the
British Secret Service. Be that as it may, in the late 1960s, Lord

Wigg, then Paymaster General, and the Minister in the Cabinet responsible for security matters, saw fit to enquire about an alleged relationship between the traitor, Kim Philby, and Field-Marshal Viscount Montgomery! This naturally caused no small stir and being then in the Diplomatic Service I was summoned, at a high official level, to explain matters precisely, including the fact that the Field-Marshal had been best man to Kim's father. I heard no more about it!

My grandmother, Lucy Farrar, was a young and lovely girl of nineteen when she was married to the Reverend Frederic Farrar, as he was then. Their house at Harrow, called The Park, was large and beautiful and was built on the side of Harrow Hill. It stood in its own grounds of thirty-six acres with fields and a home farm in the midst of them. It was a far cry from the days of the young university undergraduate and comparative poverty, when Farrar looked upon girls, or anything to do with them, as a dreadful waste of time. Work was then his only leisure and he resented any interruption, especially frivolous conversation. When reminded of this by his family during his Harrow days (eight of his ten children were born at the school) he replied without the slightest hesitation by quoting Shakespeare in *Much Ado about Nothing* where in Act II, Scene 3, Benedick says, 'When I said I would die a bachelor, I did not think I should live till I were married.' His knowledge of poetry was phenomenal and he was able to stimulate and enthuse his pupils, both at Harrow and Marlborough, with a love for English literature, and especially for English poetry. Above all he had the capacity to simplify every lesson so that all could understand, even in the complications and idioms of the classical languages. He composed a simple card of 'Greek grammar rules', which was printed in twenty-two editions. In short he was a reformer and evolutionist in the science of languages; so much so that he became a friend of Darwin, on whose nomination he was elected a fellow of the Royal Society in 1866, in recognition of his work as a philologist. In 1870 Farrar was moved to Marlborough College as Headmaster, and there began perhaps the happiest period of his life, where he could give full reign to his desires and aspirations in the whole field of teaching, scholarship and literature.

It was here he wrote his greatest work of all, *The Life of Christ*, by which his name became known to the world of his time, and for which he prepared by a long visit to Palestine. The book is most unusual in the sense that it is in no way what one would expect of a biblical theme. It is as if the author had set out to write a 'popular' story in simple terms, and primarily for unlearned people, not scholars and theologians. If this was his real aim he certainly succeeded, especially in his truly vivid descriptions, which are still remarkable. Of course the wording of English prose in those days, a century ago, and its construction, differed somewhat from the fashion of our own time. But it is still possible to see how attractive Farrar's method of writing, on serious issues, must have appeared to the Victorians in particular, with their normally stereotyped approach to any religious subject. Farrar, above all, made everything appear so simple to understand, for people of every class and social background. Much later this was seen to be true also of his grandson, the Field-Marshal, who indeed has sometimes been accused of over-simplifying great issues. However on one occasion it has been said that the Field-Marshal, at a crucial moment, did not make everything as clear and simple as it should have been. It was at his briefing conference in the Egyptian desert, just before the battle of El Alamein, when he outlined his plan to all officers of the rank of lieutenant-colonel or above. At the end of the meeting, as they were dispersing, a brigadier of the New Zealand division is said to have remarked to a companion, 'The army commander always makes everything so clear and simple, but this time there was one important matter on which he did leave some doubt in the plan.' 'What was that?' said his companion, 'I thought it was all entirely straightforward.' 'Not entirely,' said the brigadier. 'He did not say if the Lord, Mighty in Battle, was in support or under command.'!

My mother was only six years old when the Farrar family moved to The Lodge, the Master of Marlborough's residence. But she well remembered the house, which, with its large garden, many flower beds, tennis court and a woodland tract, was as charming a home as children could possibly have enjoyed anywhere. There were ponies to ride, and the river Kennet flowed at the bottom of the garden. It was in this beautiful setting, in which he was in his element as headmaster of a great public school, that Farrar developed to the full his belief, and confidence, in the schoolboys of his time. He loved their companionship whether in class, or at The Lodge where many were invited, or during the long walks he took with them. His teaching was, for so many, strangely fresh and inspiring and this was probably the secret of his success; the more remarkable when one remembers he could not find any meeting point with public schoolboys in games or athletics. But that they, for their part, accepted him as their leader and friend is without question. He was often to be seen pacing up and down the garden with his arm on a boy's shoulder, or sitting with him on the lawn correcting his prose. Heredity must have been at work again two generations later, for in the same way and in a similar kind of setting, nothing pleased my brother more, particularly after he had given up active employment, than the company of young people at his Hampshire home. In June 1961 he invited the entire cast of *Oliver*, the well-known musical play that ran for so long in the West End of London, to visit him at the Mill. They all arrived one fine sunny afternoon and had a wonderful time, swimming in the river, exploring the famous caravans, and of course eating an enormous tea.

In 1876, after six years as Master of Marlborough, Farrar accepted a canonry of Westminster Abbey combined with the appointment of Rector of St Margaret's, Westminster. In some ways it was a bold step to take because, although Farrar had been ordained twenty-two years earlier, he had so far had no experience whatever of parish work. However he was fortunate in having two curates, one of whom was my father, who were both very experienced in every aspect of the work. These two at once appreciated that the Canon had not been brought to Westminister for the parish work, but for the sake of the Abbey and of St Margaret's pulpit, both considerable factors in the religious life of London. As a result the curates made themselves responsible for nearly all the routine tasks, thus leaving the Rector free to continue his many literary and scholastic activities, including his preaching both at the Abbey and in the parish church. Farrar remained at Westminster for nearly twenty years during which time, until 1895, many, for him, momentous events occurred, or were originated and developed later.

Of our grandfather's ten children, five sons and five daughters, the five sisters all married clergymen of the Church of England, and three of the sons also became parsons, one of whom was for a time his father's curate at St Margaret's. That eight of the ten children should have chosen to follow the same way of life was natural enough in the circumstances of their upbringing and background. They lived in the middle and late Victorian era, with its strict religious taboos and conventions, when so much of the realities of life, and especially of the facts of life, could not be mentioned; at any rate not in the strict evangelical circles in which they moved. Kind and loving to all their children as the Farrar parents were, there is no doubt that, in today's terms, their sons were forced to lead a very repressed life, especially in matters of sex. In those days sexual austerity, outside marriage, was generally taken for granted in any person of good family, particularly if he happened to be a cleric or the son of a cleric. On the other hand all the sons were well read and educated, and they certainly had much freedom of reading at their university and later. They had also been well grounded in, and had learnt to appreciate, the arts, music, painting, sculpture and the beauties of nature. Furthermore it was the age of Oscar Wilde and Freud in literature, and of painters such as Gustave Moreau in France, and of Rossetti and Burne-Jones in England. These and many others contributed, each in his own field and particularly on the continent, to what has sometimes been called the age of decadence at the end of the nineteenth century; others may call it the age of awakening. Be that as it may the art and literature of the time not infrequently carried their homosexual implications and the Farrar sons, who in their under-graduate days had travelled on the continent, certainly could not have failed to draw a comparison with their own more sheltered lives. They had all studied Greek literature with its emphasis on youth and male beauty and they had read *Eric or Little by Little* with its veiled hint at homosexuality. Against this background it was perhaps only to be expected, or at any rate not surprising, that three of the Farrar sons broke the then generally accepted rules. One, who moreover had been appointed a chaplain to the reigning sovereign, was caught *in flagrante delicto* with one of his own choir-boys, and had to leave the country immediately. Another was also found to be a homosexual. A third was charged, in the courts, with suggesting to his young girl secretary that her wages should be paid, in part, by co-habitating with himself. In those far-off days such conduct, especially by a clergyman, was regarded not only as highly improper but also as constituting an attempt at assault, particularly if the plaintiff gave evidence to that effect. It was treated as a very serious matter. My mother therefore went to the hearing of the case in order to see what could be done to mitigate any sentence which might be passed on her brother, if he were found guilty. In the event he was advised to plead to that effect, and, rather dramatically, he was carried into court on a stretcher with a crucifix clasped in his hands. Before then he had fallen ill with anxiety. My mother's intervention was evidently successful as no sentence was passed. Of course these events, especially as they involved, at different times, three clergymen, all sons of the great Dean Farrar, had all the seeds of a considerable scandal. But today, scores of years later, the result might well have been nothing more than a recommendation for psychiatric treatment. Another event, deeply disturbing in those days for orthodox Church of England people, was the conversion of one of the Farrar daughters, after her marriage, to the Church of Rome. One of her sons became a monk.

My grandfather himself created no small stir, and aroused a storm of criticism, about a year after he came to Westminster. He saw fit to challenge the doctrine of eternal punishment, by preaching that the penalty of hell-fire, foretold for all sinners, was a chimera, a myth and an unsound doctrine; though without prejudice to the need for repentance of sins. He published these views in a volume of sermons under the title *Eternal Hope*, and as a result drew upon himself much wrath from ecclesiastical and other authorities. It was probably the influence of that distinguished Professor, Frederick Denison Maurice, who had been Farrar's tutor at King's College London, which impelled my grandfather to adopt this line. Maurice, who was ordained into the Church of England, had been Professor of History and Literature and his lectures were designed to deal rather with the overall meaning and philosophy of history, than with the facts and details which could be acquired from text books. In his day he became an important and influential figure in the whole field of theology and philosophy, and in what he himself described as Christian socialism. On the evidence of what it had brought about on the Continent, 'socialism' was not popular in mid-Victorian England! so much so that eventually the London University authorities 'got rid' of Maurice, after he had published a theological essay which cast doubt on the inevitability of everlasting punishment for all wrongdoers. It says much for his influence on my grandfather that the latter should have published his own sermons, with a very similar theme, some twenty-five years later. It was this, in those days, unusually broad outlook that for long hindered and postponed Farrar's preferment to high rank in the Church. To many people it will seem strange that a clergyman should hanker after promotion in secular terms. However my grandfather certainly did so and his letters make it quite clear that he held himself in high esteem, or, to put it more frankly, was exceedingly conceited about himself and his performance. He had become very fond of my father, who was his curate, and he confided in him on all matters, including his inability to pay him a stipend of more than £100 a year (it seems little enough now). In the late 1870s he wrote to my father:

'I must be content with what I am enabled to do. I never saw a more overwhelming congregation at the Abbey than when I preached there yesterday. Men standing down both gangways, right to the door and not a seat vacant. They had to put up "Abbey Full" and everyone was most impressed. I think people liked my sermon very much.'

Later, in another letter to my father he voiced his extreme exasperation at the delay in making him a dean, which he blamed entirely on Gladstone, then Prime Minister.

Aug. 21st 1881

My dear Henry,

I am struggling hard to find resignation and peace – by the blessed help of work – and to throw off the depression which is sometimes caused by a sense of Gladstone's obstinate injustice in resisting the almost universal wish that I should have this reward which assuredly, in a worldly sense, I have fairly earned. What has pained me is not the fact that I am passed over determinedly in the offer of the Deanery and that he has probably persuaded the Queen against me in spite of both Archbishops, and the Dean of Windsor, favouring me – but the fact that if now he resists so much urging in my favour it is clear that in any other post, where there will be a vacancy, I am the last man he will think of. He will be succeeded by Salisbury who would appoint the humblest deacon before he would appoint me. So, humanly speaking, I am likely to be left till death in a sphere to make my heart sink deeper every time I return to it.

Yours very affectionately
F. W. Farrar

In the event he had to wait another fourteen years to get the promotion he so ardently wanted. For it was not until 1895, on the recommendation of Lord Rosebery, who became Prime Minister in the previous year, that my grandfather became Dean of Canterbury.

Notwithstanding his frustration Farrar's name will also be long remembered at St Margaret's for all the hard work and energy he put into the restoration of that ancient and historic church. He thoroughly reorganised its interior, putting in many stained-glass windows under the guidance of Sir Gilbert Scott and a distinguished committee. Above all he was instrumental in restoring the church's beautiful fifteenth-century east window, originally presented to Henry VII to commemorate the marriage of his son, Arthur, with Catherine of Aragon. It contains the only surviving portrait of Prince Arthur. At Westminster also Farrar continued his prolific output of books. He wrote there, *inter alia*, two works of fiction: *Darkness and Dawn*, an account of the days of Nero and the struggle of the early Christians against pagan practices, and *Gathering Clouds*, which described the decadence of the early Byzantine empire, after its establishment at Constantinople. But of all the happenings at Westminster in Farrar's time the most important, for him, were the marriages of his children; and in particular that of his third daughter Maud to his favourite curate.

There were frequent visitors at the Canon's residence, (which was also the rectory), at 17 Dean's Yard in those days. The building is still there and is very much as it was in my grandfather's time. It is a beautiful early Georgian house – part of it very much older – with the lovely long windows typical of the period. At the entrance, on each side of the front door under the porch, are the cast iron sconces in which the link-boys of the coaches and sedan chairs of the eighteenth and early nineteenth centuries used to extinguish their torches, whilst waiting for their masters to emerge. Inside there is a wide and spacious hall with the long dining room, now used as the common room for the masters of Westminster School, opening out of it. The upper floors, reached by a wide and shallow staircase, with a delicate balustrade, constitute the residence of the Headmaster. The long drawing-room, with the adjoining study, are beautiful rooms looking out on the lawn of Dean's Yard and ideal for entertaining. Here came many distinguished writers and poets to see and consult with Doctor Farrar whose reputation as a scholar and man of letters was already widespread. My mother and the other young daughters of the family were often thrilled to meet men with such famous names as Tom Hughes, author of *Tom Brown's School Days*, Lewis Carroll, the painter Sir Edward Burne-Jones with his wife, and Matthew Arnold, the poet, besides many others. On one occasion there was a dinner party at 17 Dean's Yard when Tennyson, the Brownings, and Matthew Arnold were all present. In those days young people did not dine with their parents and the Farrar children were not allowed into the drawing room until after dinner. On this occasion, when the men had joined them, Tennyson read some of his poetry aloud. His reading of 'The Revenge' with his deep voice declaiming 'At Flores in the Azores' made a great impression on them all. Another time Gladstone, then Prime Minister, came to dine and, standing with his back to the fireplace, waved his hand and said 'All you people have come here to admire me.' This was of course long before Canon Farrar had occasion to change his opinion of Gladstone!

At Dean's Yard in particular Farrar showed to many his wonderful capacity to absorb himself in his work, in spite of so many children, and other diversions, always around him. At Westminster many of his best books and famous sermons were written in a study that was separated only by folding doors from a drawing room, where his five daughters practised on the piano in succession. This power of absolute concentration enabled him, not only to maintain his theme against all distraction, but also to endure, and ignore, what would have driven so many men to despair. This talent for concentration of time, energy and thought was to appear later, to his great advantage, in Bernard Montgomery.

Of all the many men who came to 17 Dean's Yard Maud Farrar, still only a very young girl, had eyes for one only – Henry Montgomery, her father's curate and seventeen years older than herself. Henry was a frequent visitor to Dean's Yard for he very soon came to the notice of the Dean of Westminster, Dean Stanley, who appointed him his secretary; this meant Henry had to spend much of his time at the Deanery nearby. He was a tall, impressive and very good-looking man of thirty-one when, early in 1879, he became engaged to our mother Maud Farrar, then only fourteen years old. At first, owing to her youth, she was told to keep her engagement secret and not even to tell her sisters of it. When one of them heard that 'Mr Montgomery was engaged to be married' she asked Maud, 'Who is the girl?' Also, owing to her extreme youth, Maud was not allowed to wear any engagement ring, and even had to go on with her school lessons until a few days before she was married – interrupted only by shopping with her mother for the trousseau. Finally, later in the year, when Henry was appointed as vicar to the parish of St Mark's, Kennington, he gave her a gold bangle, which she had converted into the ring she was to wear for the rest of her life. Our mother was a brunette, beautiful and very slender, with a high forehead and a determined chin. She was vivacious and high-spirited and a great tomboy, but not clever. Of course my father very soon took his fiancée to meet her future in-laws, Sir Robert and Lady Montgomery, who at that stage were living at No. 7 Cornwall Gardens at the corner of Gloucester Road. This large house is still there but has now been converted into flats. Sir Robert had come home from India in 1865 expecting to lead the customary life of a retired proconsul. Normally this involved acceptance of relative obscurity, compared with a previous life in office, and not being consulted any more except in rare instances. In his case the contrast would have been great indeed. After being accustomed to ruling many millions of people, travelling in state with an escort, able to carry out administrative reforms of many kinds, and with a large salary and retinue of servants, the change might well have been hard to bear. But he was fortunate beyond his expectations, for not long after his return he was appointed a member and Deputy Chairman of the Council of India at the India office. In effect this meant he never did retire, but continued to live a full official life in Whitehall, with corresponding social activities in his house in Cornwall Gardens. Now, in 1879, he was still in active work and continued to be so until his death in 1887; in all therefore his official career covered fifty-eight years. It is interesting to compare, and see the similarity between, this record and that of the Field-Marshal, who went out to India on his first commission in 1908. As these words are written he is still on the active list of the British army, in which he is the senior field-marshal, after a service of sixty-five years.

Although the Farrar family must have met and known Sir Robert, and his wife and children, extremely well, there is, strangely, very little record of the correspondence which will assuredly have passed between them. It is certain that Dean Farrar made what, in those days, would be regarded as a sufficient marriage settlement on my mother. But, all in all, it seems likely that the Dean did not get on very well with Sir Robert. They could have had very little in common in the circumstances of their very different careers. Dean Stanley took the greatest interest in the approaching marriage of the young couple, and insisted they should be married in Westminster Abbey by himself. Unfortunately he died a week before the wedding and they were married in the Abbey in King Henry VII's Chapel, by Archbishop Tait on

28th July 1881. The bride was not yet seventeen. She was married in a white satin dress and a veil that had been worn by her mother at her wedding. They had been engaged for two years and their marriage ended a difficult period for both of them. Although in their day and age for a young girl to become engaged at fourteen did not excite the comment it might do now, they had not been able to enjoy the freedom they both wanted. My father was not allowed to come and see his fiancée more than twice a week during the greater part of their engagement, which obviously imposed a great strain on them both. But family discipline, on each side, was extremely strict so that disobedience, and even criticism of any parental edict, was unthinkable. As was the case in their parents' generation, this form of authority stemmed directly from their deeply held religious beliefs which nothing could shake.

For their honeymoon the young Montgomerys, our parents, were to visit Sir Robert and Lady Montgomery in their Irish home.

Before he became Dean of Canterbury my grandfather paid a long visit to Canada and the United States, lasting three months. During this tour he preached in all the principal cities including Montreal, Toronto, Philadelphia, New York, Boston, Washington and Chicago. He was received everywhere with extraordinary warmth and enthusiasm, and people flocked to hear him lecture on any subject he chose. This was perhaps due in some measure to the memory of his outstanding eulogy on General Ulysses Grant, Commander-in-Chief of the Federal army in the American Civil War and later President of the United States, which he delivered in Westminster Abbey in August 1885. His sense of timing on that occasion was superb. Grant had just died and he knew that he himself was leaving for the United States a few weeks later and that his oratory, on such a subject, would bring him considerable dividends – which it certainly did! The tour also showed his possession of a keen sense of humour, which until that time his papers do not show. He had chosen to give lectures on his favourite poets, Dante, Milton, Coleridge and Robert Browning, and he was evidently much amused at one comment by a Chicago citizen who remarked that 'Dante was a mugwump, and the father of mugwumps'; this was followed by another remark: 'Oh, yeah! it is all very well, but Dante is a dead issue.'! Finally came a hint for himself, 'Not to talk quite so much about "that Dant" '! However probably the foremost result of his tour, as far as the Americans were concerned, was the popularisation of Browning's work which was virtually unknown in either Canada or America, until he gave his memorable lecture on the poet and his life. Afterwards Robert Browning said how grateful he was to our grandfather for so greatly promoting the sale of his writings in America. This was very necessary because until then some of the reviews in current literary journals were dismissive in the briefest possible terms. For example '*Bells and Pomegranates* by Robert Browning: Balderdash' had actually appeared in one leading journal.

As a result of his visit our grandfather formed an immense admiration for the United States and the Americans. Of American audiences he said: 'the stillness is absolute and the attention is perfect'. His last engagement of the tour, an address entitled 'Farewell thoughts on America' and delivered to large audiences in Boston, Philadelphia and New York, showed him as in advance of his time in his thinking on great political and economic issues. The occasion synchronised with a period which saw the summit of British imperial power and grandeur, which few Englishmen would venture to admit as likely one day to be surpassed. Yet Farrar did, as this extract from the address clearly shows.

'I have stood astonished before the growth, the power, the irresistible advance, the Niagara rush of sweeping energy, the magnificent apparent destiny of the nation, wondering whereunto it would grow. In numbers you are, or soon will inevitably be, the greatest; in strength, the most overwhelming; in wealth the most affluent, of all the great nations of the world. I do not believe that America will turn her back upon the ideal of her fathers. I believe that she will lead us on in a triumphant path to a legislation that shall fearlessly smite the head of every abuse, to a religion that shall be free from fetish worship.'

The events of the next century were to prove how right he was.

Looking back I have always found it rather unfortunate, no doubt in common with many others, that the Field-Marshal has never really seen eye to eye, professionally, with his American colleagues. But that time comes later in this story.

The last eight years of Dean Farrar's life, spent in the beautiful surroundings of Canterbury Cathedral, were a very happy period for himself and his wife. Canterbury is the premier deanery of England and the new dean, the thirty-first since the Reformation, took over the rule of the great Cathedral, imbued with a profound sense of the value to the Church of England of all its history and associations. The fabric of the building had fallen into disrepair, due to lack of funds, and much money was needed to save the whole structure from near ruin. As at St Margaret's Farrar achieved the near impossible within a few years, so that the roof and walls were repaired, and the ancient ceiling of the Chapter House once more glowed with its former beauty of blue and scarlet and gold. Finally the Crypt, dating from Henry VIII and the largest in Europe, was restored to its fine and proper proportions. Americans in particular came to see the work of the great Dean of whom so much had been heard during his tour of North America.

The Deanery building also benefited immensely from our grand-father's unremitting care and attention. The structure dates, in its earliest part, from the thirteenth century, whilst much of the remainder is of fifteenth-century origin. The reception rooms are beautiful and well proportioned and there is a lovely walled garden. With such a setting the joint taste of Dean Farrar and our grand-mother could not fail to make it a very beautiful home. One important feature of this Deanery is a very valuable collection of portraits of all the Deans of Canterbury since the Reformation. Our grand-father was naturally very proud to be the custodian of a collection of this kind, to which his own portrait was later added. He loved art, especially paintings with a sacred motif; so the walls of most of the rooms in the Deanery were hung with beautiful and interesting pictures, which the Dean had gradually collected. He was not a connoisseur of technique or style; he just loved paintings and their prints and could not contemplate walls bare of pictures. It may seem strange, but it is true, that though the Dean was our grandfather, none of us nine Montgomery children possess any real taste or talent for aesthetic art.

It goes without saying that Farrar continued his literary work right up to the eve of his death on 22nd March 1903, when he was preparing the lesson which he was accustomed to give on Sundays to the boys of the Cathedral choir. One of his happiest recollections of the period was in 1897, when his son-in-law, my father, then Bishop of Tasmania, brought all his large family home for nearly a year for the Lambeth Conference of Bishops. The family, in addition to my parents, consisted of my two elder sisters, then very young girls, and four boys whose ages varied from thirteen to one year. There was no room in the Deanery for so many family guests, two grown-ups with their six children, so a large empty house in the Cathedral Close was taken for them, where they all spent a very happy time. The three elder boys, Harold, Donald and Bernard all went for the summer term to the junior wing of the famous King's School, Canterbury, in which the Dean had always taken such an interest. For this reason the King's School generally claims the Field-Marshal as an old boy, though his time there was so short. There are no records that I can find of how he got on at that school; he was nine years of age.

By far the most important event for the whole family that year was their summer holiday which they spent in Ireland. New Park was revisited and, for the six children, experienced for the first time. The eldest of them was only five years old when they sailed for Tasmania in 1889, so Ireland was completely new to all the children. On this occasion, when they arrived at Moville, they were greatly surprised by their reception for they were met by a committee from the village with an address of welcome. Our father was much amused at the terms of this address which referred to him as 'The Bishop of Tasmania, the Lord of the soil', and, much later, he wrote:

'This address was presented to me on the wharf at Moville on our landing there in the summer of 1897. We had been in Tasmania for eight years, and I believe people thought we had come to retire, and with a large income. Hence the address, presented

Family group at New Park, Moville. *Seated*, Sir Robert and Mrs Montgomery (holding two daughters). *Standing*, Bishop Montgomery (holding Harold), Lady Montgomery, and Col. James Montgomery with three children

Sir Robert Montgomery's camel-carriage, 1864

New Park, built by Sir Robert Montgomery at Lahore

by our own Church of Ireland clergyman and the Roman Catholic parish priest. When we finally returned for good to England in 1902 no notice whatever was taken of our arrival. They thought that we were poor!'

But the ceremony of their arrival in that summer of 1897 was the future Field-Marshal's earliest recollection of our Irish home.

Chapter 4

TWO UNUSUAL PARENTS

The wedding ceremony of my parents, in King Henry VII's Chapel in Westminster Abbey, had not been the big affair it was planned to be, on account of Dean Stanley's death the previous week. Our mother was to have had seven bridesmaids, but in the event there were none at all, and only near relations were present in the Abbey. But a very large number of friends and acquaintances, of both the Montgomery and Farrar families, had been invited to attend the reception, following the marriage service, at 17 Dean's Yard. It was the last week in July, the end of the London Season, and many of the leading personalities of the day in the artistic, literary and social life of the capital, including Sir Robert's many colleagues in Whitehall, had gathered to greet my father and his very young bride. The reception was held in the long dining room, the windows of which looked out on to the green lawn of Westminster School, and had been a somewhat tiring affair. Henry and Maud Montgomery were therefore very glad they had chosen to make their honeymoon journey to Moville by easy stages, taking some five or six days on the way. Meanwhile Sir Robert and his wife had gone straight back to New Park to await the arrival of the young couple.

My parents spent the first night of their married life at Cambridge, which had left such a deep impression on my father from his undergraduate days, but which my mother had never seen.

They stayed at the Bull hotel in the High Street, which is no longer there, and, years later long after my father died, she said frankly that she did not exactly enjoy that first night. Looking back, at her strict upbringing, extreme youth and the restraints of the religious atmosphere in which she lived, it is difficult to see how her experience could have been otherwise. At that date she scarcely understood the facts of life and had had only one or two embryo love affairs. She was still of an age when, sitting on the drawing-room sofa in the evenings, after dinner at Dean's Yard, her father used to put his arm round her waist, and found her fiancé's arm there too! She was then only fourteen. On the other hand my mother said she had thoroughly enjoyed the wedding reception. She added that, later on, she could not help contrasting that occasion with the altogether unusual, and quite extraordinary, arrangements made by her Field-Marshal son for his own wedding some forty-five years afterwards. From Cambridge Henry and Maud Montgomery went to York, where Maud saw the beautiful York Minster for the first time, and then to Edinburgh. From there they journeyed on to Glasgow in order to cross by sea to Ireland.

Until the coming of air travel there were numerous direct routes between England and Ulster by vessels carrying both passengers and cargo. In addition to the large mail steamers which, as now, crossed from Liverpool or Heysham to Belfast, there were smaller ships, of under 1,000 tons, which made regular voyages between Liverpool, Fleetwood and Glasgow direct to Londonderry. General cargo was carried to the Irish ports and cattle, sheep and pigs on the return voyage. These sea trips generally occupied about sixteen hours and in fine weather the passage could be very pleasant. But when the sea was rough, which was frequently the case, the voyage was anything but pleasant and woe betide the wretched passenger who was not a good sailor. In these small vessels of 800 tons or so, with coal-fired, single-screw, reciprocating steam engines, conditions could, and did, become dreadful. The smell of cattle and other livestock was never entirely absent, added to which a rough sea was nearly always encountered during the passage between Fair Head, on the Irish coast, and the Mull of Kintyre; between these two points the Irish Sea is only thirteen miles wide, and the tides and cross currents meet and run extremely fast. My parents chose one of these short sea routes, from Glasgow to Londonderry, for their journey to New Park where they were to spend their honeymoon. To the present generation it will seem very odd that a young married couple should elect to spend such a time with the parents of either; also to travel by a notoriously uncomfortable route, with considerable risk of sea sickness. But the crossing by those small steamers was very much cheaper than by the larger mail boats and, as the vicar of a parish in South London, Henry was not at all well off. His wife had not yet visited his Irish home and his parents were insistent that he should bring his young bride to see New Park and meet their friends in Donegal. It was therefore something of a thrill for Maud to undertake this sea voyage, at the start of her journey to her husband's home, and only five days after her wedding; it was also the first time she had ever left the shores of England.

Moville is three miles from the narrow entrance to Lough Foyle and some twenty miles from the port of Londonderry at its head. A small paddle steamer connected Moville with Derry, but it was possible to disembark from the cross-channel ship at Moville, provided you were prepared to climb down a wooden ladder, let down from the side of the ship, into a sailing boat which came out to bring the passengers ashore. The vessel did not stop but a line was thrown to the boat, which tied up to the lee side of the ship and was then towed by the latter, until all the work of unloading the passengers and their baggage was completed. Needless to say this could be quite a hazardous business, especially at night or in a gale with a high sea running, and even more so when it took place at the end of a rough crossing from Glasgow, Fleetwood or Liverpool. Similar arrangements were made in the reverse direction, for passengers returning from Moville to England or Scotland, though people generally found the climb up the side of the steamer more disconcerting than the disembarkation. In the 1880s the female passengers, encumbered as they were by skirts and bustles with hooped petticoats, cannot exactly have looked forward to such an ending to their journey.

Fortunately for Henry and Maud, when they disembarked in this fashion from the Glasgow steamer early on the morning of 2nd August 1881, the weather had been fine and their crossing uneventful. They landed at the Moville wharf, a wooden structure built by Uncle Montgomery some twelve years or so earlier, at about six o'clock. The sun had risen and in the early morning light the scene was very beautiful, creating a memory which the young bride especially could never forget. The great cliffs of Ben Evenagh on the opposite shore of the Lough were still shrouded in darkness, as were the dark forests of trees which climb half way up the mountain. On the Donegal side the sun had already lit the tops of the hills behind the little town, showing the broad line of purple heather; lower down the light was beginning to reach the farm lands with their fields of emerald-green grass and grey stone walls. In Inishowen at that time there were very few hedgerows, as seen in England, so this Irish country scene was entirely new to Maud whose holidays (she had left school only a week earlier) had been spent mainly in Southern England. Finally the view of Lough Foyle delighted her. There is almost always a cormorant to be seen standing on the buoy which marks the ship channel opposite the Moville lighthouse. Then, looking south, you can see all the way to the mouth of the river Foyle which flows into the head of the Lough five miles downstream from Londonderry. In the other direction you can just see the narrow entrance at Greencastle. On the morning when Maud landed there was no wind at all, and therefore not a ripple on the surface of the water over which great flocks of gulls and other sea birds were flighting in the early morning sunlight. Perhaps the most remarkable thing, to anyone fresh from London, was the utter stillness of everything and the complete absence of noise. On a fine clear day such as this, you could easily pick out the farms and houses on the Derry side of the Lough which is nine miles across at its widest point.

There were few people about when the young Montgomerys were met at the wharf by the carriage from New Park, with coachman and footman, and drove up through the village to the house. New Park stands about half a mile from Moville, on the Greencastle road, and is approached by an avenue of trees. As the carriage came up the drive Maud Montgomery had somewhat mixed feelings about her reception and how she should conduct herself at her husband's home. She had of course seen much of her parents-in-law in London and she was very fond of Sir Robert who she regarded as a charming old gentleman. But she was terribiy in awe of her mother-in-law, Lady Montgomery. The latter is on record as saying that 'she could do nothing with Henry's young bride who, in her view, was so proud and stiff'. The truth however was that young Maud was consumed with shyness in the presence of her mother-in-law. After all she was wholly inexperienced and had scarcely attended any social functions; she was far too young to have been a debutante at the London season which had just ended. It is therefore not surprising that she felt somewhat apprehensive on her first arrival at New Park with her newly wed husband. Both were rather tired as on the steamer they had been called at five o'clock. The manner of their reception at New Park is best told in her own words, written many years later.

'Williams the butler received us solemnly at the front door and ushered us into the dining room where tea and bread and butter were ready for us. No one else appeared. We were then shown up into the best spare room and went to bed. Porridge, not tea, was brought up to every bedroom at 8 a.m. with little jugs of milk which were filled over night so that there was a coating of cream on the top. The men of the house party all went down to the sea to bathe (it was much too cold for me) after porridge. The ladies had baths in their rooms. There was no bathroom at New Park in those days and no hot water supply. All the hot water was heated in a huge copper which hung over the fireplace in the room which we now call the Nursery, but was then the Servants' Hall. From there it was carried by the house maids to each bedroom in use, where every guest had a hot bath in her room every morning. Breakfast was at nine o'clock and I came down overcome with shyness to meet my dreaded mother-in-law, and a house full of guests. On that first morning I was wearing a very pretty pink dress, part of my trousseau which I had kept for this occasion. However my feelings were much hurt when my mother-in-law said to me: "Did your mother tell you to put on that pink dress the first morning?" The post always arrived while we were at breakfast. The postman was seen walking up the drive, but there was no scramble for the letters as there was at Dean's Yard. They were brought solemnly into the room by the footman and handed round by the butler. I often recall the formality of lunch and dinner at New Park which were great functions in those days; I remember being impressed by the large plum cake which was always handed round after lunch. Personally this suited me because at afternoon tea in the drawing room, always laid on the table in the bow window, you were not supposed to eat much! I don't think my mother-in-law could have approved of me in those days because I loved to tramp over the hills, with Henry, in short skirts and thick boots and I refused to wear gloves. Above all I hated to be taken out in the afternoons to pay formal calls. The carriage used to go out every afternoon with Lady Montgomery sitting in it in solemn state – as I expect she did in India. Of course I had to return the calls which were made on me and I shocked her by coming into the drawing room one day and saying: "Isn't it splendid? We have paid six calls and five of them were out!" The evenings were very formal; I do not remember that we ever had a fire and there was no music, but games were allowed and I was first taught to play whist there. I played very badly and would not give my attention to it, preferring to laugh and talk. I think my mother-in-law must have compared me most unfavourably with Henry's sister, Lucy, who was then twenty-five and as yet unmarried. I remember Lucy took no part in any games and when the bell rang for evening prayers she always went and sat demurely by her mother on the sofa with drooping head and folded hands. Everyone in the house, including the servants, had to assemble for family prayers in the drawing room twice daily – before breakfast at nine o'clock and again before dinner. Another custom which, as a young girl, I found very strange was the fact that every night I was always solemnly escorted to my bedroom by my mother-in-law and Lucy. The men always came to bed later.'

This account shows clearly some of the difficulties my mother must have encountered on her first visit to the Montgomery family home. She was a bride of only a week, approaching her seventeenth birthday, childish and immature and oppressed by what appeared to her as the grandeur and style of New Park as it then was. But she loved Ireland and the Irish and early conceived a passion for Lough Foyle and the Donegal hills. The best part of the day for her, so she said, often began at sunset when she and Henry went out pollock-fishing on the lough with the local boatmen. This had the added advantage that they escaped the solemn late dinner at New Park, and were able to bribe the butler to give them something to eat on their return. For Maud also these summer months of her honeymoon were the prelude to her own assumption of family responsibilities. Family planning in any form, except abstinence, was quite unknown in those days. Besides, for young couples like Henry and Maud children came from God and contraception would be a violation of their religious principles. My mother had her first baby one month after her eighteenth birthday, and there-after children arrived at two-year intervals until after her fifth was born. There was then a gap of six years after which she had four more children.

In the years that followed her first visit to Moville Maud came to know her mother-in-law very well and they eventually became great friends. She also made many friends locally with people in all walks of life. These varied from the tenants on the Montgomery property to other families, like our own, who had houses along the shores of the Foyle and the Swilly. There were many such families with well remembered names like Cochrane, Mac Neece, Hazlett, Gosselin, Young, Crosby and Harvey, all of whom contributed to a lively social life and whose children grew up with the Montgomery children. Today none of these families remain except the Youngs, the Montgomerys, Mac Neeces and Harveys, all of whom still own property in Inishowen. But the most colourful character my mother ever met in Ireland was Sir Robert's game keeper called 'Jimmie the De'il' who lived in a remote cabin on the mountain side and whose sayings were famous. On the first occasion he met my mother he said to her: 'Her Leddyship's got a bush hanging on

the end of her tail.' She convulsed the men servants and scandalised Lady Montgomery by saying at lunch one day that 'she had
been out with Jimmie the De'il'. In later years a delightful description of Moville in the 1880's appeared in the *Londonderry Sentinel*
and is worth reproducing in full. It concerned the time when
Prince George (later King George V) was a lieutenant in the Royal
Navy and commanding officer of a torpedo boat. During naval
manoeuvres off the Inishowen coast, when there was a severe storm
and heavy seas, the Prince came across a disabled coaster. With
immense labour he towed the little ship into Lough Foyle and
dropped anchor off Moville; but his small crew was completely
exhausted so except for the anchor watch all hands were sent
below. This accounted for the apparent delay in reporting to his
senior officer, as alleged in the following account.

INTERESTING ANECDOTE OF
KING GEORGE

An Incident of his Visit to Lough
Foyle as Duke of York

His Royal Highness the King — at that time Duke of York* —
was in command of a torpedo boat, and driven by stress of weather
off the Inishowen coast took safe anchorage in the beautiful bay of
Moville, on Lough Foyle. The Prince was delighted with his surroundings. On one bank of the lough's broad bosom nestled the
sweetly pretty watering-place Moville, with its quaintly irregular
but comfortable houses, its lovely church, and New Park, the seat
of Sir Robert Montgomery, formerly Governor of the Punjaub; the
residences of Colonel Lyle, Mr Haslett, the Hon. Ernest Cochrane,
and others stretching towards Greencastle, with its world-famed
ruined castle, all backed by the beautiful range of the Inishowen
mountains. Opposite were the mountain ranges of Londonderry of
rich and varied hues, conspicuous among them the clear-cut profile
of Ben Evenagh. Two stately liners and many vessels of lesser size

* Prince George was not in fact created Duke of York until 1892, some
seven years later.

4*

dotted the surface of the water. The sun was near his setting, and the lough was like molten gold. Altogether the scene was one which must have had a peculiar charm for such a lover of nature as our present Gracious Sovereign.

His Royal Highness gave orders for the anchor to be lowered just opposite some white buildings. Now, these chanced to be the Coastguard station, and Captain N—, the Commander of the Coastguard, happened to be living there at the time, the Admiralty house being under repair. The Captain was sitting down to a homely repast, prepared by the chief officer's wife, when the arrival of the torpedo boat was notified to him. Rightly conjecturing that this was one of the vessels belonging to the portion of His Majesty's Fleet then on warlike manoeuvres, Captain N— despatched a boat to the little craft, ordering her commander to 'Come ashore and report himself to his senior officer, immediately'.

Soon the boat was seen returning with a young officer in the stern. When he landed and saluted, Captain N— spoke rather severely to him on his neglect of duty in not reporting himself at once to his senior officer. The commander of the torpedo boat received the reprimand with due deference, but with a slight twinkle in his blue eyes, and made his apologies, which were rather stiffly accepted. He then asked as a favour that he might be allowed to write and send three telegrams.

The requested favour granted, the young commander sat down and rapidly wrote his messages, and, again saluting, handed them to Captain N— for despatch. What was Captain N—'s surprise and dismay when he read the first, which ran somewhat thus – 'Have come for shelter into Lough Foyle and anchored in Moville Bay. The scenery a fair picture. Have made the acquaintance of Captain N—, who is very kind. – George.' The telegram was addressed 'To Her Majesty the Queen, Windsor Castle'. The two other telegrams were in somewhat similar terms, and respectively addressed to His Royal Highness the Prince of Wales and the Lords of H.M. Board of Admiralty.

Captain N— hastened to explain, but the Prince, with that charm of manner which all the Royal Family possess, at once set him at ease, and ended by accepting an invitation to supper, to which he did full justice, carrying away as a welcome souvenir one of the excellent loaves baked by the coastguard's wife, much to the good woman's delight, and expressing in no measured terms his admiration of Lough Foyle, Moville and its lovely scenery.

When I began to write this chapter, and devised its title, I asked myself: 'But were my parents really unusual?' That they both undoubtedly exercised a very great influence on their children is unquestionable, but that is not unusual; neither is the fact that, except in one respect, the character and personality of each differed a great deal. In his youth my father was a noted athlete, and, professionally, he became a great missionary and administrator. In addition, perhaps strangely, he was also a seer, a mystic, a visionary as it were. But where his family were concerned, to use a colloquialism, 'he never wore the trousers'. His wife did! At its finish I saw no need to change this chapter's title.

Our father Henry Hutchinson Montgomery was born in India on 3rd October 1847 at Cawnpore, where Sir Robert was then the Collector and Magistrate. It was just one and a half years before the latter was transferred to Lahore. The name Hutchinson derived from Sir Robert's close association with his first Chief Commissioner James Thomason. The latter had two sisters, one of whom became Robert's first wife; the other became Mrs Eliza Hutchinson and was a very warm friend of all the Montgomerys in after years. My father's very earliest recollection, and this has been told in bare outline by others, was the occasion when he fell off an elephant. It happened at Lahore when he was only about four years old. In British India in those days, and particularly in the Indian states for generations after the Mutiny, both camels and elephants were in frequent use for transportation, especially in the Ganges valley. Camels were employed both for riding and as draught animals, and some of the camel carriages looked very curious, though elegant enough in their appearance. The *Illustrated London News* of 21st May 1864 carried a photograph with the caption 'Camel Carriage used by the Lieutenant Governor of the Punjaub'. This shows Sir Robert seated in the carriage with his ADC,

Captain Alick Heyland of the Indian army who was his relative by marriage. The camel carriage looks to be an ordinary victoria, a low light four-wheeled vehicle with seats for two, and a folding top. It is drawn by four camels, each ridden by a cameleer; two outriders sit on the box at the front of the vehicle, so altogether there are six retainers, all dressed in livery with the cameleers wearing long black riding boots. Behind comes a waggonette, with fixed top drawn by two camels, each again ridden by its cameleer. Inside this vehicle, which has facing side seats, a *khidmatgar* can be seen, and no doubt he has ready the cold refreshment which the Lieutenant-Governor will certainly need! The whole retinue consisted of nine servants, six camels and two camel carriages, which was considered appropriate for the governor of an Indian province. The armed escort would normally have been seated in the waggonette but are not seen in the photograph, which was taken outside the porch of Government House, Lahore; to complete the picture there is a grey pony, saddled and waiting with his *sais*, at the entrance. Elephants were not normally ridden, except on ceremonial occasions by people of high rank and status with their escorts, by the artillerymen of the elephant batteries, for *shikar*, and in the forest service where they were used extensively. Otherwise these large beasts were invaluable for very heavy load carrying, and, even more so for such arduous tasks as clearing the jungle, by dragging away all the tangled mass created by fallen trees, heavy cut timber, and the like.

When Father fell off the elephant the family were at New Park, their house at Anarkulli outside Lahore, some four years before the Mutiny began. He was on the lawn in front of the bungalow with the *ayah* deputed to look after him. It so happened that that morning a full-grown bull elephant had been brought into the compound in connection with some jungle clearing business by the Forest Service. The Indian elephant is a domesticated animal by comparison with his African counterpart—except during his *musth* (disturbed) periods, when he is very dangerous—and is generally quite tame by the time he is in work, especially when employed by the Forest Department. Young Henry, who was very high spirited, ran to see the elephant which was led by his *mahout* but had no *howdah* (seat with a canopy) as he was not a riding animal. Of course Henry was extremely interested and, after feeding the elephant with *chupattis*, insisted on being put up on his back. Unfortunately the *mahout* did as he was requested, he did not dare to refuse, and the boy promptly fell to the ground to the consternation of the *ayah* who started to weep and wail – through fear of what might happen to her for her lack of care. The Indian elephant stands about nine feet high at the shoulder, so her fears were probably justified. Hearing all the hubbub that had broken out in the compound, strangely the Indian elephant rather enjoys getting frightened and was now starting to trumpet with the *mahout* trying to lead him away, Sir Robert rushed from the house to find a scene that is not difficult to imagine. Henry was lying on the ground motionless and quite silent. Years later Henry wrote, 'My father feared I was killed. He picked me up entirely enveloped by dust, hardly a feature visible. As they all looked at me in consternation a little hole appeared in the dust, followed by a tremendous roar! and so all anxiety was banished.'

The year before the Indian Mutiny, and soon after his eighth birthday, Henry Montgomery was sent home, to go to his preparatory school. The journey by sea round the Cape still took anything up to four months, and sometimes even more, and so for such a long journey he was placed in charge of a Colonel Martyn. This man was a bachelor, not over strong and evidently very strict, with pronounced views as to how young boys should behave in all circumstances. He was also, according to my father, a very godly man and a devoted mission worker. However his judgement in agreeing to take charge of a boy of eight on a journey from Lahore to London was probably at fault. They travelled first by *dak-gari* to join a river steamer on the Ganges, where for the first time Henry saw a steam engine. A few days later he saw his first railway train, some sixty miles from Calcutta where they joined the mail steamer for England and the long sea voyage began. My father's chief recollections of the voyage were his daily talks in Urdu with the Lascar seamen of the ship's crew, and the great worry he evidently caused to Colonel Martyn. The latter, at all times a staid and serious man, strongly disapproved of any young boy roaming at will all over the ship and forbade Henry to do so. One day he tied him with reins, like a horse, and led him about the deck. Once he thrashed him severely with a cane for running about the ship contrary to orders. Finally towards the end of the voyage he made the boy go to every lady on the ship and apologise to each for being rude or noisy or in some way a nuisance. My father recalled their astonishment, mixed with pity for his temporary guardian who was regarded as a crank. His one consolation, from what he could only regard as tyranny, was the company of his Muslim servant Hussein for whom he had a great affection. Sir Robert had sent Hussein to England in order that he could remain there as servant to one of Henry's maternal uncles. Later Henry recalled the astonishment of his uncle's domestic staff at the apparently very strange cries which issued so regularly from Hussein's bedroom. They did not realise that the latter, a devout Muslim, was saying his daily prayers. In due course Hussein returned to Lahore but appeared again a couple of years later when he accompanied Henry's two younger brothers, James and Ferguson, on their journey to their preparatory school in England. By that time the Indian Mutiny had occurred with all the events which made Sir Robert Montgomery so famous. Henry however did not see his father from the time he left Lahore until, nine years later when he was seventeen, he met Sir Robert in London on the latter's return from India in 1865.

The preparatory school to which Father was sent was Miss Baker's, at Brighton. Apparently the teaching was governed by the strictest evangelical principles, and aimed chiefly at ensuring the boys learnt their bible and the great truths of Revelation; there was not a great deal of scholastic work. However Henry recognised this was an abiding influence on his life, though at the same time he could not resist writing, at a later stage, 'I think I may say I was brought up on almost undiluted hell fire. On the whole such diet has done me immense good for it has left behind in me an awful sense of the Holy Will of God. The thunders of Sinai should not be forgotten by any Christian.' This stern philosophy and way of life generally was widespread throughout the Protestant people of Ulster from whom our family had come. For Sir Robert and his generation the natural order of things included man's obedience to

God, and children's obedience to their parents. So even if Henry
had not gone to this particular preparatory school his character and
upbringing would probably not have been otherwise affected. He
was already fervently religious, like his parents. It was much later,
when both he and my mother expected all their children to accept
a similar doctrine and way of life that they met with a very
different reception; this had a considerable effect, especially on
Bernard.

The generations of British men and women who for so long
formed the core of the Indian services, both civil and military,
whenever possible had their sons educated in the United Kingdom.
Following this custom Sir Robert and his wife decided their sons
should go to one of the great public schools, and for this purpose
they chose Harrow. My father went there when he was thirteen,
and left five and a half years later in 1866. His elder brother,
Arthur Samuel Law Montgomery, was already at the school when
he arrived there, and the two were together in the same house,
Rendall's. They were devoted to each other and my father felt it
very deeply when Arthur died of consumption – in those days a
killer disease – at the early age of twenty. Arthur however was later
described by Father as having a jealous disposition, very proud by
nature, and perhaps cynical, which appears very little in keeping
with the character of Sir Robert. It seems likely he took after our
grandmother, Lady Montgomery, who, according to my Field-
Marshal brother was 'a very formidable woman, not to be trifled
with at any time or in any circumstances'; clearly our mother had
taken a similar view!

The years he spent at Harrow, his formative years, evidently had
a very great influence on Henry. He loved it all, and years later
wrote a long account of his time there, which he had printed for the
benefit of his children; I would never have seen this if the Field-
Marshal had not given me the family records and challenged me,
as he said, 'to get on with it'! The account shows clearly that the
public schools of the 1860s, their curriculum, instruction, customs,
discipline, games, had changed not at all since the times of which
Dean Farrar wrote in his books of schoolboy fiction. Indeed the
theme and setting of some of the passages in my father's account

seem to fit exactly into the general pattern of the story portrayed in *St Winifred's And The World of School*. Presumably the great changes did not come until the end of the Victorian era and the beginning of the Edwardian period. For the rest, Father was a scholar, who believed firmly in the value of a classical education. But games and athletics were his strong points. He became head of his house, captain of football, and played in the Harrow cricket eleven for three seasons. He also won all the school races, hurdles and flat, up to the quarter mile inclusive, and all the prizes there were for cricketing standards. He never captained the Harrow cricket team, as has been recorded, though when he left school he was rated as a fieldsman at point second only to the famous Doctor Grace; finally he won the first prize for fencing. In this unusually successful and varied athletic record it is not difficult to see from where Bernard inherited his own distinguished athletic prowess, both at school and later. Reading Father's account, written just before his father-in-law was appointed to Canterbury, it is noticeable that he makes no mention at all of Dean Farrar, in spite of the fact that the latter was a house-master at Harrow during the whole of his own time there; neither is there any mention of Farrar's school stories, which had been published and attracted much notice. But *Tom Brown's School Days* was clearly the book which Father loved most of all. In his account of Harrow days he evidently cannot resist letting his mind turn back to that famous story, for he wrote thus – for the benefit of his family.

'Read *Tom Brown's School Days*. Turn to that page where Tom comes back to Rugby, lets himself into the school chapel, and allows his thoughts to recreate the past, memories sad and sweet. He sat in the place where the influence of his great Head Master had flowed into his life, where the unconscious seed had been sown which, he felt now, had borne fruit.'

Henry had the greatest respect and admiration for his own Head Master at Harrow, the celebrated Doctor H. M. Butler, who later became Master of Trinity College, Cambridge, and a close personal friend of his.

Father's story of his Harrow days also brings to light his coura-
geous temperament and incurable optimism. These were the characteristics which he undoubtedly drew from his Irish forebears, an
indescribable charm and humour that endeared him to so many
people. He did not take life too seriously, as when, at Harrow, he
first won the quarter-mile flat race. A wealthy tradesman in the
town had given a cup for it to the school, and, one hour before the
event, during the midday dinner, Henry was asked if he had
entered for it. 'No,' he said, 'but I will for the fun of the thing; I
have never practised for the quarter in my life.' He said this as he
was eating an enormous apple dumpling! This particular race was
run in public on the Pinner road, not on a track, and there were so
many competitors that the runners had to form up in a double line
one behind the other. Henry willingly went into the rear rank and
ran in his socks! He won easily.

The Field-Marshal clearly inherited his own strong sense of
humour from Bishop Montgomery. His favourite Irish story, about
himself and the cow he had killed at New Park is not known to
many. It was in the 1920s, before his marriage, when he had come
home on leave during the summer holiday to join the customary
house party of relatives and friends which mother organised each
year. My mother, who had a strict eye for economy, always made
her own butter and cream, though it has to be said that Johnnie the
Gardener, who milked the cows and lived with his wife and children in the cottage in the stable yard, seldom washed out the milk
churns and pans in the dairy; it was also unfortunately clear that
the byre, where the cows were housed, received scant attention
where cleanliness was concerned. For Johnnie was an Irishman
born and bred in Inishowen, and a Roman Catholic. I doubt if he
had ever been further from Moville than Londonderry. However
he loved the place and the garden and looked after it with great
care; he and his family were like old friends of us all.

At that time tuberculosis was still a dreaded and common
disease in Ireland and the veterinary authorities, including those
in Inishowen, were particularly anxious to detect and isolate all
cows and heifers which might be suspect of infection. This was
known to Bernard, who took the danger seriously as he could in no

way reconcile what he thought was an avoidable risk with the conditions in our cowshed and dairy. Mother on the other hand would have none of it; nobody was going to criticise, let alone interfere, with her conduct and management of domestic affairs at New Park. It was entirely her business what went on in the dairy, and elsewhere, and most definitely none of her own children were to interfere. All of us, family and guests, were quite happy about it (the milk, butter and cream tasted excellent, the sun shone and life was good, so why worry?), except Bernard. He did worry and was determined to intervene, and for one other reason also. When Samuel Montgomery, the wine merchant, built New Park he included a 'privy' close by the wall of the stable yard. This outside lavatory (always reserved for the men of the house for it was a dark and gloomy place and never warm) was a stone hut backing on the garden wall and had been built over an underground stream which, running fast, emerged from beneath the garden at that point. Presumably the builders of two centuries or so ago had seized on this natural means of sewage disposal, and were thankful for it. But what worried Bernard was that the stream flowed on into the yard, where it appeared to pass through an open well. This well was always used by the gardener and his family for both drinking and washing, though none of them had ever been known to suffer any ill affects from the practice. My brother however, accustomed to the strict standards of military hygiene, determined to act.

One cow in particular looked in poor shape so, without telling anyone at New Park, Bernard went down to the village and consulted the local veterinary surgeon. The latter advised that the first essential step was to take the cow's temperature, and explained how it was done. 'Sure, Major,' he said, 'It's no trouble at all ye'll be having. Just insert the thermometer now, as I said, and forby don't forget to take the time by your watch.' Sustained by this advice Bernard waited until mother was taking her afternoon nap when everyone, with the exception of father, had to be out of the house between two and four o'clock. He then advanced on the cow from behind. Lifting her tail as instructed (Phase I) he prepared for Phase II (thermometer and timing) but was immediately faced with a problem requiring instant decision. The vet had not made it clear that there were two 'places'; in fact he had only mentioned one, and now, which did he mean? At that moment the cow turned her head and looked at him, as if to say, 'Here, what's going on?'! Determined to complete Phase II with all speed Bernard selected his target, hoping it was the right one, and inserted the thermometer! The result was surprising. Suddenly the cow, with a low moo, kicked up both her hind legs and Bernard, unfortunately, let go of the thermometer which immediately disappeared inside the cow—and was never seen again. In my brother's view there was now only one course left open to him; the animal must be destroyed, and at once. Returning swiftly to the vet he arranged for the necessary destruction to take place that day, and it was done. Of course the row with mother that followed was very great, though, according to Bernard, he had achieved his aim by ensuring the removal of one source of infection. And who was to say he was wrong? After all, Father's eldest brother had died of tuberculosis at the age of twenty, and my youngest sister had been troubled by consumption for a considerable time, before she finally got rid of it.

Father went up to Trinity College, Cambridge, in the autumn of 1866. His three university years evidently meant a great deal to him for he wrote 'Cambridge has been to me another golden memory.' For the first time he was not short of money. Sir Robert gave him an allowance of two hundred pounds a year which he apparently found ample, not only for the university terms but also for the vacations when he stayed with friends in country houses to play cricket and shoot. He became captain of Trinity College eleven in his second year but, to his great disappointment, he never became a Cambridge cricket 'blue', though he played in almost every match for the university—but not against Oxford. M. H. Stow, another old Harrovian and a close personal friend, was captain of the university eleven and had to tell him that he was not chosen to play against Oxford at Lords. But father accepted this for he wrote, 'I can see now how it was that I never actually got my "blue". I never used to practise. So any cricketer would understand why I was not in the eleven. I was content with the entry in *Lillywhite's Cricket Manual* that "it is sufficient proof of the excellence of the Cambridge eleven in 1869 that Mr Montgomery was left out of it". But I don't regret it. I went to Cambridge to work at my studies not just to play cricket!' In this he was clearly right for eventually he graduated with a Second Class Honours degree in the Moral Sciences Tripos, being bracketed in eighth place with his contemporary, the future Prime Minister, A. J. Balfour.

Looking at accounts of university life in England of one hundred years or more ago, there does not appear to have been any very great change in the relevant importance of games, athletics and studies; the same applies to the incidence of university 'rags', student hoaxes and the like. Father revelled in them all. He became very famous as one of the few men, perhaps ever, who, at a single bound, has jumped up the flight of steps leading from the old court into the hall of Trinity College. There were eight steps covering ten feet, and rising to a height of four feet. But he did this, by any standards a tremendous leap, 'for the fun of the thing' and without any preparation, as was his custom at Harrow. In 1905 he was dining at the high table at Pembroke College when he overheard some undergraduate say: 'Who is that old codger up there?' The reply pleased him greatly: 'Don't you know? That's Montgomery, who jumped up the steps in Trinity.' Shining through all accounts of father's life, from first to last, is the evidence of his tremendous sense of humour. He always succeeded in seeing the funny side of events, or even in contriving them, frequently against himself, and this no doubt was an element in the popularity he achieved at all levels, in both his professional and social life.

Father left Cambridge at Christmas 1869, and spent the greater part of the following year in London preparing for holy orders under Doctor Vaughan, Master of the Temple. He had always intended to go into the church, no other course had ever occurred to him, and his parents thoroughly approved of his choice. He was ordained in January 1871 and was at once appointed to his first parish, as curate to Canon Borrer at Hurstpierpoint in Sussex. He was twenty-three years of age and in a responsible job for the first time, a turning point in his life. From that day he became dedicated to his calling, with an utter determination from which he would allow no distraction to turn him, for the rest of his long life. This is important to the theme of this story as, basically in one way or another, the influence of heredity on children of human beings is not in question; but environment, the surroundings which we as individuals create, or in which we have to live, can be largely controlled or managed, for better or for worse, if we are so minded. Henry's environment, during the first five years after his ordination, definitely set the pace and course for his future life, with the conditions of endless hard work as the governing factor. For him, as a curate, there was no question of 'hours of work', for his vicar expected him always to be on call. Above all, as he wrote later, 'I was altogether without experience and had to train myself in the art of the priesthood. Apart from the conduct of the church services, including the preparation of sermons, I had to learn how to teach in the schools, to visit the sick and poverty-stricken or those in need for any reason, how to cope with the dying and the aged, and to bring hope and encouragement in place of despair.' Looking forward, it is interesting to see how self-training, and the need for it, occupied so large a part of Father's early professional life.

Those first five years for Henry were divided almost equally between the beautiful country parish in Sussex and, for the last two years, the parish of Christ Church, Blackfriars Road in London. In between these two assignments his father, Sir Robert, with wisdom and foresight and presumably aware of the conditions in the slums and dense London streets around Blackfriars, said to him, 'Go and travel now. Here are one hundred and fifty pounds. Go where you like and come back when you have spent it.' To this Henry added one hundred pounds, a legacy from his godfather General Hutchinson, which enabled him to travel in Egypt, Palestine, the Levant States and Turkey. He came back in May 1874, with precisely ten shillings left out of his two hundred and fifty pounds, and went at once to his next curacy in Blackfriars. Here he had to work so hard that his health nearly broke down. It was a far cry from the carefree days of Trinity College, for the day started with giving swimming lessons in Lambeth Baths at a quarter to seven in the morning, and ended with visiting in the back streets till ten o'clock at night or even later. What enabled him to survive, he said, were the annual holidays, summer and winter, spent at New Park, and his custom whenever weather and duty permitted of going to Wimbledon Common every Monday afternoon. This was an unfailing cure for the awful fatigue that generally assailed him on Mondays after the arduous Sunday duties. It was there he learnt, by study and bird watching, to become a competent ornithologist. A century or so ago the Common was virtually uninhabited and it was his custom in the summer months to take a rug and, as he said, 'Insert myself into a furze bush and go to sleep, often being woken up by a sheep poking her nose into me. On winter evenings when returning from a walk on the Common I have at times put up a pheasant, partridges, a woodcock, and, unusually, a snipe.'

After his experiences in Blackfriars the three years Father spent at St Margaret's, Westminster, were a wonderful and refreshing time for him. Intellectually, because of his close association with Doctor Farrar, it was like being in a forcing house where he met continually a whole range of prominent literary Englishmen. Several times he went with Dean Stanley to visit Thomas Carlyle, and once he accompanied the Dean on a tour to the Pyrenees, Northern Spain and the Cevennes. In Westminster he lived at No. 17 Great College Street overlooking the Abbey gardens and here, as has been told, he first met, and eventually married, our mother. Long afterwards he was fond of pointing out that his life, and frequently that of many others, moved in cycles. In 1851 he fell off the elephant and very nearly came to an early and untimely end. In 1861 his mother, Lady Montgomery, returned to England for the summer (Sir Robert as Lieutenant-Governor could not leave Lahore) and took Henry, then a schoolboy of thirteen, to New Park for the first time. In 1871 he was ordained and took on his first appointment as a curate. In 1881 he was married and came with his wife to New Park for their honeymoon. This was the great event of his life, so far. The events attending the later, similar period, cycles turned out to be equally momentous, and so proved his general theory. Meanwhile he had in front of him the ten years (1879–89) when he was vicar of St Mark's, Kennington, in South London. He was thirty-one and, as he put it, 'I now had my first independent command.' It was certainly a strenuous time for he had a parish population of over fourteen thousand with, to assist him, three curates, two hundred and fifty church workers and one hundred and twenty-five Sunday school teachers, with one thousand five hundred children. With it all he had to, and did, find time for home life. For his young wife, only just seventeen years of age, had not yet completed her education. She still loved children's parties and playing hide-and-seek in the garden. After her married life began some of the many callers, from all walks of life, at St Mark's Vicarage were scandalised to see their vicar's wife come pelting down the stairs, pursued by her brothers, to greet them in the hall. But Mother very soon grew up, in every way, for she early started a family. Five of her nine children were born at Kennington vicarage, of whom Bernard was the fourth.

It was during these ten years that Father began his literary career and became, in due time, a considerable author. In all he published twenty-five books, mainly on theological subjects and the work of foreign missions, but including some on cricket and also five biographies. His first book, now long out of print, was a history of Kennington; this was well illustrated with descriptions of cricket at the Oval and an interesting account of Vauxhall Gardens from Charles II's time until their closure in 1859. He also wrote on ornithology and contributed an article to the *Ibis*, in 1898, on the habits of the mutton-bird of the islands in Bass Strait which lies between Tasmania and Australia. He had spent a whole night on a large rookery, with watch and pocket-book, watching these extraordinary petrels. Their young are fed by receiving oil poured into their throats by their parents, who then themselves proceed to eat gravel. Father's style was clear and simple, easy to understand and not scholarly, but he had the ability to make his readers see with great clarity, in the mind's eye, the place or action he was describing. In his papers he recorded his view that no biography was complete which did not record the history of ancestors and forefathers. He held it to be the duty of each generation to write down the memories of their early days, and acknowledge the debt they owed to those who trained and inspired them. 'Family histories create traditions,' he said and added, 'and I hope traditions of honourable life.' He certainly set out his own record for he filled nine large tomes with papers, either typed or hand-written in ink, with newspaper cuttings and photographs by the hundred. Finally he kept, and had bound in several volumes, almost every letter he had received from Sir Robert in India, and from Dean Farrar after he became engaged to mother. Certain it is that this story could not have been told without this material; though perhaps it may not come amiss to enter here a mild protest at the predilection of the Victorians for so much cross-writing in their letters, and for seldom including the year in any date, only the day and the month.

My parents were always extremely busy and active during their years at Kennington and time sped swiftly by. Every Saturday they dined with Sir Robert and his wife at Cornwall Gardens, and every Sunday evening they went to Dean's Yard to be with Dean Farrar and his family. Of course they spent every holiday they could get at New Park where Father renewed his strength among his beloved Donegal hills. Then one day, just before New Year 1888, Sir Robert died at 7 Cornwall Gardens which had been his London home for twenty years or so after leaving India. His time there had been a very happy one with frequent visitors, and dinner parties at which he was often able to entertain his many friends from the Punjab. He used frequently to see Lord Lawrence who, as Sir John Lawrence, had been his chief in the Punjab and who lived close by in Queen's Gate. After Sir Robert died father was told that Lord Cross, then Secretary of State for India, had recommended to the Prime Minister (Lord Salisbury) that the Queen should be advised to confer a baronetcy on Sir Robert. However the latter died before further action could proceed. There are memorials to him in the cathedrals at Lahore and Londonderry, in our family church at Moville, and at Foyle College, Londonderry. The latter commemorates the names of four famous old boys of Foyle College, Sir George Lawrence, Sir Henry Lawrence, Lord Lawrence and Sir Robert Montgomery, and was unveiled by my father in 1930. In London a plaque, in the form of a medallion portrait of Sir Robert, was put up in the crypt of St Paul's Cathedral in the chapel where his great friend Lord Napier of Magdala is buried. The portrait was the work of Bruce Joy, as also was a marble bust of grandfather which was placed in a main corridor of the India Office. This bust stands there to this day, on the first floor of the King Charles Street building of the Foreign and Commonwealth Office. Whenever my duties took me there I always took off my hat as I passed Sir Robert, to the considerable surprise of anyone who saw me.

Early one spring morning, at nine o'clock, Father was having his weekly conference with the curates at Kennington vicarage when Doctor Farrar was announced. He had come unofficially from the Archbishop of Canterbury to ask if Henry Montgomery would go to Tasmania as bishop. If he did go he would have to stay there, as long as health permitted; there had apparently been too many cases of Australian bishops resigning their sees after their initial experience of the country and its conditions. Father accepted immediately; he would obey orders. His first step was to go at once to the Athenaeum, of which by now he had been elected a member, to find out exactly where Tasmania was! He had heard of it, under the name of Van Diemen's Land, as an island in the antipodes where convicts used to be sent, and where the forests were so dense that escape through them was impossible. He was consecrated in Westminster Abbey on 1st May 1889 and sailed for Hobart with his wife and family of five children a few months later. Little did he know at that stage that he and his wife were destined to return to London, with seven children, thirteen years later. He also could not have known that he would be coming back to an appointment which eventually would make him famous in the Church of England, and in the Anglican Church throughout the world, as The Right Reverend Henry Hutchinson Montgomery, KCMG, DD, DCL, MA, Prelate of the Order of St Michael and St George, and Prebendary of St Paul's Cathedral. Meanwhile he was preoccupied with many matters, including the fact that he had only just succeeded his father in his Irish property, which now he would not see again for many a long day, if ever. Furthermore the estate was still burdened with mortgage charges to the tune of nearly twelve thousand pounds – a disturbing thought. In the event the charges on the property were not fully paid off for another sixty years.

The time the family were to spend in Tasmania was momentous for them all, both parents and children. For the elder children in particular it meant growing up, the end of childhood and the beginning of their education. Above all they learned to know and understand their parents. Looking back there is no doubt that all we children, very early in our separate lives, grew to appreciate the great and wonderful man that Father was. More important we loved him, all of us in equal measure without difference of any kind, to an extent that could be called worship. Mother, adored him with a fierce and passionate devotion that knew no bounds. It was in her nature always to be the boss, as indeed her father Dean Farrar himself would have liked to be, and it was this that made her want to wear the trousers where her husband was concerned, and similarly of course to 'command' her children. Her difficulty however was that she had literally moved from the schoolroom to her marriage, and all the manifold duties and activities of a vicar's wife in a busy London parish, without any intervening period. She had had neither time nor opportunity to make any of those close friendships, with either boys or girls, in her own age group after leaving school, which can be so valuable in after life. Virtually her only girl friends were her two elder sisters, one of whom also married another of her father's curates. She therefore began her married life with only the experience of a schoolgirl who had never left her home, and knew nothing of social life generally. Against this background it is small wonder that she wrote of herself:

'To be frank, I must say I was not very happy at first in our married life. My husband loved me devotedly, but he took our love too much for granted. I was young and foolish and I wanted to be told that I was loved. Also, I came from a very large family and I was often very lonely at Kennington in early days. My husband was out every evening, and I can remember sitting in the drawing room and crying bitterly because I had nothing to do and felt so lonely. But all that was changed when our first child, Sibyl, was born. Harold, Donald, Bernard and Una were also born at Kennington, and we had charge as well of three small boys, Rivaz by name, cousins of my husband, whose parents were in India. So I soon had my hands full, with so many children and with parish work.'

Our mother therefore, long before she was twenty-four, had charge altogether of eight children, apart from her many parish activities. It is surely natural to ask, how did she do it all? and to conclude that she did not have sufficient time to cope with everything, except by imposing a strict discipline and routine, both of which resembled the experience of her own quite recent girlhood. Furthermore her available time, far from increasing, if anything became less in Tasmania as her family increased in number (Winsome, Desmond and Colin were all born there) and they all began to grow up. Of course some of the children did not take kindly to her notion of parental authority, as practised by herself, though the girls were never any trouble. The future Field-Marshal however, very early in his life, earned, and merited, the reputation not only of being a very naughty boy but actually a rebellious one. In short he defied his mother's authority when his wishes or actions ran contrary to her own ideas for himself, and this inevitably led to trouble. But situations of this kind are by no means unique, especially in very large families, and Bernard was not the only one to upset his parents. I myself, in a fit of ungovernable rage, once threw a knife at my brother Colin (it missed him) and on another occasion, when ordered into solitary confinement in my room for some grave misdemeanour, removed the sheets from my bed and proceeded to cut them into small pieces! Meanwhile Bernard did not grow up in an atmosphere of fear – of mother – or develop any inward-looking, withdrawn characteristic because of her. If this had been so it would inevitably have affected his immense sense of humour which was never impaired. The simple truth is that he inherited from her an indomitable will which frequently clashed with her own inflexible purpose. This situation continued and developed, and became unfortunately plain to see, but in the first place only up to the time that Bernard was commissioned in the army. Thereafter their relationship was placid and generally pleasant (except for incidents such as the death of the unfortunate cow at New Park). It was only after Bernard became famous that the fierce and sometimes very bitter disagreements again occurred. and, curious though it may seem, these were governed and dictated solely by Mother's intense pride and admiration for what he had accomplished for the nation, for himself and for our family name. I have written at some length in this fashion lest uninformed comment should, rather naturally, tend to overlay and obscure the truth of the matter. Finally the facts need to be seen, briefly, against the reality of Mother herself.

When she was a young woman in Tasmania Mother was sometimes described as a typical Irish beauty. Beautiful she certainly became, with her high forehead, large wide spaced eyes, dark hair and wonderful skin and complexion. She had a slender figure and looked very well in a riding habit. But Irish she certainly was not, being pure English by birth, though like many English women who marry into Irish families she eventually became, by adoption and inclination, more 'Irish' than the Irish. She very quickly accepted those standards of domestic cleanliness which, though customary in many an Irish country house, would certainly never find favour in an English counterpart. New Park was no exception to this condition which derived largely from the fact that the servants were generally, if not frequently, young Irish girls who, after leaving school, went straight to jobs in houses such as ours. Many of these girls came from cottages in the hills where there was then no electric light, or power, no piped water supply or bathroom, and probably no staircase. Unless therefore there was very strict supervision one was not surprised sometimes to find traces of a bygone egg lingering in the potato dish. After all the young house-maid might well never before have seen a bathroom. But otherwise mother had developed a passion for order and method, all governed by a strict routine and subject always to the absolute priority of religious practice and a strict morality. In other, more material, matters her life was generally conditioned by the need for stringent economy. The Bishop's salary in Tasmania was only one thousand pounds per annum, which, even in those far-off days, was little enough for the upbringing and education of six boys and three girls. In her thinking and regard for the position of women in life she was well in advance of her time as she longed to organise and control both people and events. In London, on return from Tasmania, she became a full-time working mother long before the 1914–18 war.

Tasmania Days

The family sailed for Hobart early in September of 1889 in the Shaw Saville liner the *S.S. Tainui*. She was a small four-masted vessel of about six thousand tons, with one tall smoke stack, and took six weeks to complete the voyage of some twelve thousand miles, round the Cape of Good Hope, to Tasmania. The children had to do lessons every morning in the saloon with their mother – except Bernard, who was then not yet two years of age, and Una, still a baby in arms. When the *Tainui* cast anchor in the beautiful harbour of Hobart, on the twenty-third of October, a new venture for them all began. At first it was a tremendous shock, especially for the Bishop and his young wife, as everything was so completely different from the life, and the people, they had known in London or in Ireland. There was only one choice open to the whole family, they decided. This was, as far as possible, to forget completely everything about their past life, and become 'Colonials' (now a long-outmoded word) and Tasmanian, in thought and outlook. But there was to be one very strong exception to this policy. None of them were to be allowed, under any circumstances, to adopt a Tasmanian accent. It was Mother who insisted absolutely on observance of this rule, and swift retribution awaited any member of the family who broke it – especially if the breaking was deliberate mimicry or otherwise mischievous! She attained her object apparently for no member of the family has ever shown evidence, by accent, of having lived long in Australia.

It goes also almost without saying that Mother continued to impose a strict routine on all the children. She had begun this at Kennington, and maintained it on the long voyage to Hobart, so it became the natural order of things to include it in the new era which now began. It was the type of routine to which we all became accustomed and which, broadly, remained in force, even for adults, in every house of which mother was the mistress, throughout her life. The day began, and ended, with family prayers as it had at Dean's Yard, and everybody, servants and guests included, had to attend. After breakfast the girls made the beds, the boys cleaned the shoes, and adults were expected to look after themselves, unless

mother had organised something for all. The children had lessons
in the morning with games or exercise of some kind in the afternoon. Later in life, especially in Ireland, she added another very
strict rule. Everybody had to be out of the house between two and
four o'clock in the afternoon, so that she could rest undisturbed by
noise or interruption of any kind. It did not matter where you went
or what you did as long as you were not in the house, though if you
remained in the garden you must make no noise that could reach
her. The Bishop was the only exception to this rule, though he,
very willingly on his part, had to remain in his study. Meanwhile at
Hobart, with her usual organising ability, Mother had arranged for
tutors to come from England and take over the whole job of teaching the children, who were rapidly growing up. The arrival of these
tutors gave her more freedom to devote her attention to the many
and varied activities of a Colonial bishop's wife. Fortunately
Bishopscourt, their home in Hobart, was a large rambling building
with a big garden, well suited to her purpose. She had an additional
room built, outside the house, which served as a school where not
only her own children were taught, but also those of certain close
friends in or near Hobart. One of the boys who came was Andrew
Holden, the son of Doctor Holden who was father's closest friend
in Tasmania. Much later, Andrew married my elder sister Una.

The boys of the school had the charge of the schoolroom, taking
their turn weekly to keep it clean, light the fire, chop the wood and
generally maintain it. Here too they got their own evening meal,
and for this purpose the boy in charge for the week was given half
a crown to spend on 'extras' over and above what the cook provided. One boy would spend the whole sum on cake or biscuits,
whilst another bought tinned salmon and persuaded the cook to
make it up into fish cakes. The future Field-Marshal, on one
occasion when his turn came round, discovered, with due regard
for economy, some cheap eggs. He announced, to the great amusement of his parents but the dismay of his fellows, that he was
providing 'reduced eggs'! Although all the children had to submit
to Mother's routine and sense of order it should not be thought
they were unhappy or discontented in Tasmania. On the contrary
they loved it all, especially the constant outdoor life, the picnics,

riding, fishing and the like. In fact when the time came to return to England the whole family were miserable at the thought of leaving the island, which they had imagined would be their permanent home. Sunday however was never a popular day with the children for it meant very considerable church-going, reading, with Mother, the collect for the day and reciting the Bible or church hymnal, with, overall, a restriction on the games and pastimes that might otherwise be enjoyed, and, of course, the wearing of Sunday clothes.

In Tasmania Father very soon appreciated in what direction his own gifts lay. He did not expect ever to become an eloquent or rhetorical preacher, or a 'platform' man, or a 'citizen' bishop with an eye on the political scene. In his case every fibre of his being responded to what he regarded as his vocation in life, mission work. He determined therefore to concentrate all his efforts and energy on getting to know his diocese, especially the isolated bush districts, the outer islands, with their lonely lighthouses, and the solitary mines where gold was still being dug. In such areas many half-castes, descendants of the indigenous inhabitants (the Tasmanian 'blacks'), were still living, but were largely neglected. This meant a great deal of travelling which the Bishop gladly accepted, and indeed to such an extent that he was generally away from Hobart for one hundred and eighty days in the year, visiting every parish on the island. In this he was fortunate in having, as his dean, a very close friend Dean Kite, who he knew could be relied upon to manage all matters during the Bishop's absence. Tasmania has an area of over twenty-six thousand square miles, not far short of that of Scotland, and much of it, especially on its west coast, is very mountainous with extremely dense forests. In Father's time there were no railways and very few roads, or even tracks, over much of this forest region. The traveller frequently had to walk, and sometimes hack his way through the thick bush, unless the country was suitable for horses which still provided the main form of transportation on the island. Rivers were crossed by boat ferries with the horses swimming, in hand, on long rein. Everything, including tents, had to be carried, either on a pack-horse or as a man load. When travelling food consisted generally of bacon, bread and butter, and fruit, with billy-can tea or thick cocoa. But the mountain scenery was unforgettable with vast forests of the Australian myrtle tree which rises to a very great height and has evergreen leaves with white scented flowers. Even higher are the gigantic gum trees with their completely smooth stems, which do not throw out a single branch till they have risen twenty or thirty feet above all other trees. It was in this woodland setting of high mountains with deep gorges, in which rivers ran some hundred feet below the mountain track, that Father rode for miles accompanied, generally, by one of his bush parsons. Sometimes they spent as much as eleven hours in the saddle in one day, starting at five o'clock in the morning. They were always on the lookout for the fierce and sometimes dangerous 'Tasmanian devil' which lived in the forests but was not often seen. This unusual flesh-eating animal, now extinct, was of the marsupial species, which stood about two feet four inches high with a tail a foot long. It lived in a burrow and fed generally at night, especially on poultry and young lambs. Sometimes the Bishop was accompanied by his wife when he toured the eastern side of the island, the main feature of which lay in its English appearance, due in part to its lanes and hedges with houses built in the English style of the nineteenth century. Once they drove together in a dogcart from one end of the island to the other. Mother was a fine horsewoman and probably at her best when driving horses in harness, frequently in tandem where good hands are more than ever necessary. In addition to his arduous tours in Tasmania Father also travelled widely in Australia and over large areas of the Pacific Ocean. One year he was away from Hobart for seven consecutive months while acting as Bishop of Melanesia, during a vacancy in that see, during which time he visited Fiji and many of the islands including the Solomons.

In his last year in Tasmania Father rode right over the central plateau, over three thousand feet high, during which he spent three weeks in the saddle and had, for him, a memorable experience. With the local bush parson he had come to the top of the ridge, from where the land dropped abruptly two thousand feet to the plains below. The parson said, 'There are half a dozen men up here finishing a culvert on the track, and their contract has to be

The Field-Marshal's mother, aged 18, as Joan of Arc
by George Joy

Lady Montgomery
in later life

The future Field-Marshal

aged 10   aged 15

Shooting at New Park:
Bernard (standing, right)
Harold (seated, right)

completed today. They want to be confirmed but they cannot come down to the church [a day's ride away]. Will you confirm them up here?' Father's reply was instant. 'Of course.' So they got off their horses, Father put on a rochet (bishop's surplice-like vestment), and the men knelt down on the rough track and were confirmed. It was a most glorious autumn day with a view over an immense stretch of country, and afterwards Father said to the men, 'This is the best of cathedrals.' Then they all had lunch together. Later, when leading their horses down the track (it was too steep to ride) they were met by half a dozen women who said: 'Have our husbands been confirmed?' When told 'Yes', the women said: 'Then we will be confirmed too.' Then a problem arose. There were no veils! So handkerchiefs were used instead, and in one case for lack of anything else, a pair of gloves placed cross wise on the woman's head. My father's complete and absolute dedication to his calling enabled him, when necessary, to simplify and virtually dispense with all the trappings of high ecclesiastical office, with no thought for pomp or ceremony, and deal only with essentials. Years later it was not difficult to see this same ability, some would call it genius, appearing in the Field-Marshal who, with similar dedication to his profession, would never allow himself to be diverted, by extraneous detail, from achieving his aim. On the other hand Father's own philosophy of life was clearly quite different, for at this stage, in Tasmania, he wrote:

'All my life I have had the same experience in having passed my contemporaries without anyone realising what was happening, or expecting it. As a curate I was far inferior to my colleagues, but from a worldly point of view I have done best. When I went to Kennington (which was regarded as advancement) I remember the Bishop of London looking at me with curiosity and amusement. It all comes to this; if a man will only do his very best, night and day, and be humble and live in his work, things happen. I have no great gifts or talents; I am neither a scholar, nor a preacher, nor a speaker. There is great hope for a man of fair ability, common sense and industry, in any profession or vocation.'

5

In this statement Father clearly did himself less than justice
where his own mental capabilities were concerned. He omitted to
mention his unusual ability to develop and express his thoughts,
for himself and others, in terms of a deep personal and mystical
experience. He saw the great importance of this as an aid to the
human soul in finding direct communion with God, and bringing
with it enlightenment and revelation. These were the thoughts
that inspired his two books, entitled *Visions*, published in 1910 and
1913. At one stage, after a tour on the continent, Father wrote a
short monograph, based on his study of the portraits of the Meyer
family in Holbein's religious painting of the Madonna, now in
Darmstadt (the so-called Darmstadt Madonna, *c.* 1528). He had
this monograph, with the picture in colour, published by A. R.
Mowbray & Co. Ltd. In it he poses the question in his own mind,
albeit surprised himself why there should be the slightest per-
plexity, as to which of the two children in the portrait is meant to
be the Divine Child. He then relates a notional conversation, by a
supposed couple (a brother and sister) who stand behind him also
gazing at this masterpiece. They discuss this very problem, for
themselves, and eventually dispel all doubt in terms of their absolute conviction that, by the Divine suffering, man can find relief
from his own mental or physical torment. This apocryphal tale, for
so father calls it, was written because, he said, 'If you wish to
understand a picture you must, of course, put yourself into a
receptive state and look and look. After a while the meaning grows,
like a photograph in its developing bath.' I have included this
paragraph as evidence of a quite different side to Father's character, which might not otherwise have been apparent. It seems a
wholly Irish and mystical side, with a depth of spiritual insight
not given to many.

On 6th June 1901 Bishop Montgomery received a cable (it cost
£12, a large sum in those days) signed by the Archbishops of
Canterbury and York and the Bishops of London, Winchester,
Bath and Wells, and Newcastle. That was the committee of six
bishops appointed to select the clergyman of high rank and status
who was to be offered the post, in London, of Secretary to the
Society for Propagation of the Gospel in Foreign Parts (SPG). Our

parents were overwhelmed with dismay at the thought of leaving their home, which they loved so much, their free life and their many friends in the diocese and in Australia. The irony of it all lay in the fact that the Bishop had brought it on himself. His time in Melanesia, and with the Aborigines of Australia, his burning zeal for the cause of missions and his work for the Australian Synod – all this had brought his name prominently before the Church at home. Eventually they agreed to go, after much persuasion, and some pressure, from London. Longmans had asked Father to write a book on Foreign Missions and this was actually written during the long voyage home. The elder children also were very loath to return to London. My eldest brother, Harold, was devoted to riding and hunting and had become a magnificent horseman. He had joined the Mounted Infantry in Tasmania, when still only sixteen years of age, and had won almost every prize for show jumping and point-to-point racing on the island.

The whole family left Melbourne for England in the P & O ship *S.S. Cuzco* in November 1901. This time they travelled via the Suez Canal and arrived at Plymouth, where they disembarked, on a wet and dark Christmas morning. None of them felt in good spirits especially the children who had all been made, by Mother, to put on their very best clothes 'for the occasion of your return to London'. The three boys in particular, aged seventeen to fourteen, were taking a somewhat jaundiced view of life, because their mother had insisted that they should all wear bowler hats on disembarkation, and until they reached London! As the future Field-Marshal said to me years later, 'At Christmas 1901 I returned to England with a bowler hat, and very little else!' I have always wondered where our mother got those bowler hats. They would surely have been an unusual form of head dress for boys in Tasmania in those days. Meanwhile the plight of the family, having disembarked, was not made any easier by the girl in charge of the refreshment room at Plymouth railway station. They had to wait there, as, being Christmas morning, there were no trains to London for some hours. Father had gone to the refreshment room in search of breakfast for the whole family, but had been told, 'Oh no! you can't 'ave it. We only serve *bona fide* travellers.' The Bishop replied, with his customary good manners, 'Madam, we have just come twelve thousand miles!'

My parents will appear again in this story so I shall leave them now as they stood on Plymouth railway station, early one rainy Christmas morning, waiting, with their seven children, but no breakfast, for a train to London.

Chapter 5

PREPARING FOR WAR

When the family arrived in England early in 1902 they rented a large house at Chiswick, with a garden, which became their London home for the next nineteen years. The Bishop and his wife needed plenty of space, not only for themselves and their seven children but also for the cook and other domestic servants; the latter included a sewing maid who was able to relieve our mother from the ever growing task of maintaining all the children's clothing, linen, etc. At that time electric sewing machines, or electrically operated household equipment of any kind, were virtually unknown in England so the manual labour needed with a large family was still very considerable. The house they leased (it was promptly called Bishopsbourne) was at 19 Bolton Road, not far from the river Thames at Mortlake. Although now this whole area is completely built over and urbanised, it was then very much on the outskirts of London, almost in the country in fact, with tree shaded avenues and large areas of market gardens, which lined the river bank and stretched inland from Barnes Bridge for a long way. There was a horse bus which provided a service to connect with the electric tramway at Turnham Green, and thence to Hammersmith, or in the other direction to Kew. Horse trams were still running to Kew Gardens, so evidently the communications in the area were not very well provided for, though fortunately there was a railway station nearby which took one to Vauxhall and Waterloo.

The mid-Victorian houses in Bolton Road were well suited for mother's purpose (it was she who found the house) as, like ours, they generally had thirteen rooms with two bathrooms and three lavatories; of course the kitchen, scullery, pantry, larder, etc. were all in the basement from which a hand operated lift brought the food up to the dining room on the ground floor. The garden had a big lawn bounded by flower beds and four large cherry trees, behind which were the apple trees, gooseberry and currant bushes and the vegetable garden. It was in this setting that Mother continued to operate the same kind of routine for the whole family which had been her custom in Tasmania. This meant appropriating one room for use as a chapel where the family prayers, conducted by the bishop, were held twice daily. To the furniture of this room she added a harmonium, which she played herself for the singing of the hymns that always preceded the prayers, and, to complete the scene, she had a chapel bell, with a cord, suspended over the doorway. This had to be rung vigorously, by one of the younger children, and continued to ring until all the family were present, including the servants and any guests there were, when the short service could begin. Not surprisingly, there was a considerable degree of parental umbrage and sorrow if anyone was 'late for chapel', and I do not recall anyone who failed completely to attend! unless it was for health reasons which had to be very fully evident to become a valid excuse.

Just under two years after the family came to Chiswick Mother's ninth and last child, a son, was born. My parents, somewhat misguidedly I have always thought, chose to give him the Christian names Brian Frederick. The future Field-Marshal, by that time sixteen years old, was under no delusion that this youngest brother might, at some stage, find such initials a cause for embarrassment and advised strongly there should be a change. Our parents however were adamant for they could see no reason at all for disquiet! and in any case I had been born on St Luke's day and some thought had already been given to calling me Luke, but this had not been followed up.

Meanwhile new plans for the elder children's education and future, which it had been thought would lie in Australia, had to be made, especially for Harold the eldest son. Not long after he knew he was returning to London Father had written to Dean Farrar for advice, and said:

'Where shall we live? and about education, what shall we do? What is best to be done about Donald (then aged fifteen)? He is clever and ought with ease to get a scholarship at Cambridge; only I don't want him to go to some school where he may be put back into some old work (as a "Colonial"!) for a year. He would have passed a very strict Matriculation Exam at the end of this year with honours. But there are schools where they are prepared to push boys who are strong. Donald has had plenty of open air life and is strong. Is Tonbridge a good school? Has the Head Master a good reputation? Bernard could go there too. But I want special attention for Donald who is strong in mathematics and has a great love for classics and literature also. But Harold too is a problem. He will dislike England. His magnificent horse-manship will be of no use till he can enter the army in some way, and he is not brilliant at books. I think he ought to make his career in South Africa, and go there to stay. He has all the love of solitude some men gain out there, does not care much for society, is very independent, and as strong as a horse. But I wish you could give us some ideas about Donald and Bernard, something to muse over ere we come home.'

This letter shows how ill prepared the family were for the great upheaval in their lives caused by the decision to return to London. More important it is clear my parents had no inkling, at the time the letter was written in August 1901, that their fourth child possessed any unusual characteristics, let alone had it in him to become the military genius of his time. They were no doubt more impressed with the evidence of his apparent lack of discipline, expressed by his reluctance to accept parental authority, and they regarded this as obstinacy on his part. They could not have been expected to appreciate that the troubles they had had with Bernard in Tasmania were but the early manifestation of his tremendous strength of character, which came to the surface more particularly whenever he was prevented from doing what he thought was right – for himself or others, or for both. This strength of character was to stand him in good stead, in later years, though it also bred a great deal of trouble – for himself and for others. There is no record of the advice which Dean Farrar sent to Father – it would have been unlike the former to remain silent – but in the event matters turned out well for my parents on their return to England. Harold did go into the army and he did go to South Africa, where he remained to begin a career, as Father had hoped, which kept him in Africa for the rest of his life. Evidently Father had friends in Whitehall, family influence still counted a great deal in those days and Sir Robert's name was well remembered, for Harold was granted a commission in the Imperial Yeomanry the day after the family had landed at Plymouth – which sounds like quick work! His regiment had been raised in England early in 1900 as part of the great military reinforcement drive following the disasters which befell the British army in South Africa at the outset of the Boer War. Harold was well suited to join this territorial unit as it was composed almost entirely of men chosen for their skill as horsemen and marksmen, and Harold was both himself. Looking again at father's letter to Dean Farrar it may seem strange, in these days, that any parent should deliberately seek to send his eldest son, not yet eighteen years of age, to take part in one of the most savage and arduous wars of our military history. But the Victorians looked on war in a different light to our present generation; above all it was the professionals who had actually to fight the battle, and the professional soldiers (all volunteers) expected, and the majority wanted, to take part. The era and concept of the nation at war had not yet arrived. So Harold went to war, though a few months after he landed at Cape Town the Boer War ended and his regiment, in which he was a second lieutenant, was due for repatriation. Father was quite right about my eldest brother, who undoubtedly loved Africa and was born with a flair for native administration, obviously inherited from Sir Robert. Rather than return to England Harold resigned his commission, and, the same day, enlisted in the ranks of the British South African police, a mounted force well suited to his liking, which operated over a vast territory as far north as the

Zambezi river. It seems a lot to be able to do in one day; but Harold was essentially a practical person, very popular wherever he went, extremely generous and a very fine bridge player. After five years with the South African police he went north to Kenya where he joined the East African administration, as an assistant district commissioner. He made Africa his life service and died there in 1958, having become Chief Native Commissioner in Kenya and been awarded the CMG. He was always entirely self-sufficient and remained quite unaffected by the influence of others, including any other member of the family, our parents included. His obituary notice, published in a Kenya newspaper, described him admirably, and showed how utterly different he was from the Field-Marshal:

'Montgomery hated paper work; he boasted that he never wrote an unnecessary letter, and his minutes on the Secretariat files were as terse and rare as his letters. If he said what he meant he most certainly meant what he said. He was the straightest and most direct of men. I don't think he had much use for Departmental Officers, he administered directly through his Administrative Officers. He was respected, he was liked, he was obeyed. Though neither suffered fools gladly, our "Monty" was in many ways the direct opposite of his younger brother the Field-Marshal. He was not ascetic: he preferred "the wine that maketh glad the heart of man" to "the water wherewith the wild asses quench their thirst"; he enjoyed a smoke, a bet or a gamble – but in moderation. He was excellent company and under a gruff exterior was the kindest of men. He was the type of Officer who won the respect of the Arabs on the Coast, and indeed of gentlemen of all races throughout the Colony, European, Asian and African. When in later years the history of the Colony comes to be written due tribute will, I hope, be paid to Harold Montgomery and the other strong men who, by courage and force of personality, laid the foundations of our administration.'

In London Mother very soon added a governess, Miss Lawrence, to her ménage. The whole family owe a great debt of gratitude to

5*

Miss Lawrence who not only taught us younger children, and was an immense help in every way, but in order to do so must have journeyed, on foot in all weathers summer and winter, at least five miles a day five days a week. Equally important she freed our parents from much household and domestic responsibility, so that both Father and Mother were able to go daily to their offices in London, weekends excluded, before nine o'clock in the morning and not return until six o'clock, or later, in the evening. During their absence Miss Lawrence, though kindness itself, stood very much *in loco parentis*. She would not tolerate disobedience from any of the family, including the future Field-Marshal if he were present and 'tried it on', or equally the children of nearby friends who also came to the house for instruction; as in Hobart Mother had organised her own local school from neighbouring families. We children always took much interest in one of our neighbours in Bolton Road. This was Mr Barker who owned the famous store of Barkers in Kensington High Street where Mother frequently went shopping. He used to be driven daily to Kensington in his horse-drawn carriage and passed our house each morning punctually at eight-thirty. We were instructed by Mother to wave to the great man, which we certainly did, and he always courteously waved back to us from his carriage window.

St Paul's School

Of the six brothers in our family all five who were still of school age went to St Paul's School at different periods between 1902 and 1921. This great public school, founded by Dean Colet early in the reign of Henry VIII, was then at Hammersmith. It had been built of red brick, in the Gothic style, during the late Victorian era and stood on a site of eighteen acres on the south side of Hammersmith Road just west of Olympia, with extensive playing fields behind it. In 1969–70 however the school was moved and it now stands on a magnificent site of forty-five acres on the south bank of the Thames at Barnes. My parents chose St Paul's for their sons' secondary education for three main reasons. The first was because of the school's close and historic connection with the Church and its outstanding reputation for learning and scholarship. (To this day Winchester, Westminster, St Paul's, Manchester Grammar School and Dulwich are probably the best schools in the United Kingdom for scholarship record to the universities.) Equally important for my parents, the fees were low by comparison with other public schools, the majority of which were boarding schools whilst St Paul's was, and still is, predominantly a day school. With such a large family nearly forty years of their married life had passed before my parents were entirely freed financially from the need to provide for their children's education. Here too they were fortunate for Father's prophecy that Donald, their second son, was clever was correct. He did get a foundation scholarship to St Paul's, which absolved his parents from payment of all school fees, and later also obtained an exhibition to Selwyn College, Cambridge; the other four brothers, including the future Field-Marshal, attempted the scholarship examination but all failed. The other reason was that our mother wished to retain control of her children during their school days, and this, in her view, she could not possibly do if they were not living at home during term time. She insisted that her sons, on returning from the school each evening, should at once set about, and complete, their 'prep'. St Paul's therefore suited her admirably; it was reasonably close to their London home at Chiswick, besides which the house itself was large enough for all their needs, including the servants without whom she could not possibly have coped with her many and varied activities, in London and elsewhere. Our mother also arranged, and no doubt very wisely as it was much appreciated by us all, that whenever possible we should not spend the school holidays at our Chiswick home. Of course the entire family, parents, seven children (less as time went on) and servants invariably went to New Park each summer holiday. The journey there was really quite a business with so much luggage, a dog, the children's bicycles and food for the hours spent in the train; there were so many packages that Mother always hired a bus to take the whole outfit from Chiswick to Euston. Finally there was the sea voyage from Liverpool or Heysham, and the disembarkation into the motor-boat waiting off shore in Lough Foyle. For many years the Liverpool to

Londonderry steamer (Belfast Steam Ship Co.) was the *S.S. Comic* which, with her officers and crews, became well known to us all; she was also, in our view, well named, especially in the rough weather so frequently encountered in the Irish sea. We boys generally spent our Christmas and Easter holidays at the home of one or other of our numerous cousins. As Mother was one of a family of ten children, and Father also came from a large family, there did not appear to be any difficulty, in those more spacious days, in so arranging matters.

Looking back over those school years, with their regular pattern of term time in London, followed by holidays spent always in the country, not in a town, at the home of relations or friends in our own age group, it is likely for two reasons that none of us boys ever realised how fortunate we were. We did not fully appreciate either the benefit we all derived from the variety of this pattern of life provided by our parents, or, equally if not more important, how much we all owed to St Paul's School. This last point appears clearly if one considers the possible effect on my Field-Marshal brother if he had gone to some other public school, not St Paul's. To continue this line of thought it is necessary first to look at the record of how he got on during his five years at the school from January 1902 until December 1906. At the outset however our mother made what can only be described as a most unfortunate mistake. The very first day of the term, on a cold winter morning, when my two eldest brothers, Donald and Bernard, were to go to St Paul's as new boys, she got out those bowler hats which they had worn on their arrival at Plymouth from Tasmania the previous Christmas. It was her idea that they should 'wear their bowler hats so as to be respectably dressed on their first day at school'. She did not however know that at St Paul's in those days the wearing of a bowler hat, together with the carrying of a walking stick, were the symbols of power, reserved only for boys in the Top (VIII) form, and also for those who had been awarded their colours as members of the first XV or first XI or any first, games team. Other boys wore school caps. In these circumstances for a new boy, of all people, to appear on his very first day at the school clad in the paraphernalia reserved for the great ones was an unheard-of event!

Fortunately both brothers escaped any form of retribution, due, it is said, to the alertness of the school porter who spotted the offending headgear and took immediate action. He was a great character, an ex-regular soldier and good disciplinarian, known to everyone as 'Spiky' on account of his long, pointed and waxed, moustaches.

It has been said that Bernard was always very happy at St Paul's. But this is only half true because, clearly, at that stage, he did not care for the compulsion of school lessons and procedure. As he himself said, 'I must admit that I did practically no work at the school. My main preoccupation was games and I thought of little else.' He was therefore only content when playing or organising games, in which he certainly had great success for by the time he left St Paul's he was captain of both football and cricket. He had also become a member of the school swimming VIII, of which Donald was the captain, at the astonishingly early age of fifteen; both brothers had learnt their swimming in Tasmania where their long and varied experience placed them well ahead of their contemporaries in England. The school records show that the future Field-Marshal was a fine cricketer and top of the batting average in his last summer term. His football record is interesting because, in spite of his undoubted prowess it highlights, in near disparaging terms, his unorthodox method of tackling. The report of the characters of the 1st XV, in which he played left centre three-quarter, includes the following assessment: 'B. L. Montgomery. Runs strongly but takes too long to get away. Should tackle lower.' Be that as it may there is no doubt he was regarded as a most redoubtable and fierce opponent on the football field. At St Paul's he was given the nickname 'Monkey' because he was small, tough, wiry and extremely quick in all his movements. The school magazine, run by the boys, had this to say about him.

The Monkey

'This intelligent animal makes its nest in football fields, football vests, or other accessible resorts. It is vivacious, of unflagging energy, and much feared by the neighbouring animals owing to its unfortunate tendency of trying to pull out the top hairs of the head.

This it calls "tackling". To foreign fauna it shows no mercy, stamping on their heads and doing many other inconceivable atrocities, with a view, no doubt, to proving its patriotism. . . . In hunting the monkey the sportsman should first be scalped, so as to avoid being collared.'

As regards his school studies, his report for his penultimate term at St Paul's clearly bears out his own admission that he did practically no work, for it includes the following warning, in July 1906, 'He is rather backward for his age, but has made considerable progress. To have a serious chance for Sandhurst he must give more time for work.'

From that moment he did work. There was however one subject in which he was already highly proficient and that was scripture. It would indeed have been surprising if it had been otherwise, for all the nine Montgomery children had been given, and had had to assimilate, almost daily instruction from their parents in this subject. Nevertheless it was this proficiency which led to the future Field-Marshal being awarded his first sentence of corporal punishment at the school. The form he was in, Army Class C, was having a scripture lesson from the Old Testament dealing with the exploits of King David, including his shame-making intrigue against Uriah the Hittite in order to obtain the latter's wife for himself (Second Book of Samuel Chapter XI). Bernard, who knew the passage well, was bored and wrote the following schoolboy doggerel, which was promptly passed round the class:

> David on his palace roof
> In his night attire
> Saw a lady in her bath
> Her name it was Uriah.
>
> He sent a message to the battle
> If you would be savèd
> Put Uriah in the line of fire
> Yours sincerely, David.

The form master, Captain Bicknell, spotted the offending verse and was much incensed. The culprit must be punished and made an example of by being caned. In those days, and for many years thereafter, form masters at St Paul's had the right to administer summary punishment, by caning, in front of their whole class. Offences of the most serious kind were liable to similar punishment by no less a person than the High Master himself, in the privacy of the latter's study. No one then could have foreseen that this room, which was also the board room of the school governors, was many years later in 1944 to become the personal office of Field-Marshal Montgomery, Commander of the Allied armies for the invasion of Europe.

Against this background of school life at St Paul's, with its admixture of life at home and holidays spent in the country, it is possible to see certain dominant characteristics beginning to develop in the future Field-Marshal. First, his determination to make the army his life career found its expression at St Paul's. As has been often told he registered this wish on his first day at the school, and was promptly sent to the army class, from which time his dedication to master the art of war can be said to have begun. It was not this choice that so upset his parents when he informed them of it. What worried them more was that not one of their three elder sons had shown any inclination to take holy orders. Their fear now was in case the remaining three boys should all show the same disinclination when their time came to choose a career; in the event only one of the six, my brother Colin, was ordained, in 1927. It was the school games at St Paul's in which the seeds of leadership and authority born in the future Field-Marshal began to appear and grow; added to which were the signs of unorthodoxy, the new approach and the inclination not always to accept as permanent what had been done before. Bernard's conception of the rugby tackle was clearly most effective and had earned him a fearsome reputation. His parents thought him obstinate, and they were indeed right. He always had in him this streak of obstinacy which in the event has stood him in good stead – whenever he was right and he generally was. Yet, when he knew he was wrong, reason came to the rescue, so that he accepted the need for change and acted accordingly. There is much evidence of this, beginning with his realisation, in his last term at St Paul's, that he must accept what was in his school report and 'give more time for work' if he was to have a serious chance of entering Sandhurst. He did so. Finally, and in some ways perhaps unusually, Bernard did not make any very close friendships amongst his fellow pupils at St Paul's, at any rate none with whom he maintained long term contact after his school days were over. Until last year his senior surviving contemporary at the school was probably Doctor 'Tubby' Clayton (The Rev. P. T. B. Clayton, CH, MC, DD, of TOC H fame) who died just before Christmas 1972, and there are now not likely to be any great number of his fellow pupils alive today. For the majority of the masters who taught at the school when he was there he had respect and regard, as I believe all Paulines in any generation have done; it was they who insisted on maintaining the standards and values, in every field, which they thought it proper for St Paul's to have. Setting aside the humorous nature of the episode, the future Field-Marshal never forgot the scripture lesson about King David and Uriah the Hittite, with the action taken by Captain Bicknell; its memory has remained with him. For the rest, long before he left school he had joined the company of the comparative few who were entitled to wear the bowler hat which, all unwittingly, he had put on for his first day as a new boy.

We can now consider the possible effect on the Field-Marshal if he had gone to a public school other than St Paul's, as might have been the case. Few will dispute the influence of education and upbringing on any boy, perhaps more particularly if his formative years, from say fourteen to eighteen, are conditioned largely by the standards and practices of the English public school system, though it would almost certainly be unwise to generalise about this as the schools themselves vary so much. St Paul's for example always has been, and still is, an essentially middle-class school, or, to put it another way, it is a school which has never had any social pretensions. Would therefore the Field-Marshal's attitude and outlook generally have been substantially changed if he had gone, say, to Harrow which was Father's old school? There the pattern of his life would have been quite different, there would have been no specific army class, only the classical and modern sides, and the majority of his fellow pupils would have been cast in broadly the same upper class mould. Would this necessarily have affected his approach, in later years, to the human problems he had to face, especially after he became a high-ranking general? It would be difficult, if not impossible, to give any direct answer to such a query. There is perhaps however a guide line, no more, in that the Field-Marshal has always been essentially an individualist, with his thought processes influenced at all stages, in his early career and thereafter, by his own intensive reading and study of his profession. In conclusion, in this context, one is probably on much surer ground by recalling that St Paul's is predominantly a day school. This postulates the condition that the home influence, its atmosphere, conditions, everything that affects the family environment, must at all times be reasonably equable, not disruptive, in order that the school life can achieve its desired aim. Our Chiswick home fulfilled this condition.

Bernard went to Sandhurst in January 1907 when he was just over nineteen. Although in the competitive examination for the military college he had passed quite satisfactorily (he was placed seventy-second in a list of one hundred and seventy successful candidates) he was older than the majority of his contemporaries as he had stayed longer at school than most boys generally do. The reason for this, as he himself, later on, was the first to admit, was his delay in doing any really serious work at St Paul's until virtually his last two terms there. But there is no doubt he loved his time at the R.M.C. It was his first experience of real independence, freed from all day to day parental influence and restraint, and at first all went very well for him. His proficiency and energy at games helped a good deal, and counted for much in a curriculum which consisted of little else but instruction in military subjects with a great deal of drill, physical training and equitation. In those far off days there was no Royal Army Educational Corps and military history with military geography (the strategic and economic influence of a nation's topography and natural resources) were the main items in a limited field of non-military instruction. Bernard always had a good eye for a ball and at Sandhurst he soon added hockey to his other sporting achievements, whilst at football he found no difficulty in becoming a member of the college first fifteen. Even for an infantry officer riding was an almost essential accomplishment (all commanders of companies and above were officially mounted officers) and hunting, particularly for junior officers, was regarded as a considerable military advantage because it 'gave you an eye for country'. This cult of the horse was traditional in the army and remained so, as a strong professional and social asset, for many years to come. In the Indian army in particular to be 'good on a horse' was a distinct advantage; in fact, right up to 1939 the regulations for the Staff College at Quetta required that every student, on joining, should bring his horse with him. This was because a staff officer was officially a mounted officer and could not properly carry out his duties unless he was capable, and seen to be capable, of riding across country. Bernard was never a skilled horseman but he was certainly not an indifferent one, as has been averred by others. He had been riding horses since he was a boy in Tasmania, so equitation was never a problem for him. However he never had sufficient money to buy his own horses, until he became a senior officer, and even if his financial resources had been large he would not have spent money on riding; he utterly rejected the notion that hunting was good for soldiering.

So Bernard started very well at Sandhurst due in large measure to his success at games. He was very soon promoted to the rank of lance-corporal, which, for a junior cadet, signified a very good start and generally led eventually to further promotion to sergeant, or even to the coveted highest cadet rank of colour-sergeant. This initial success however was also his downfall, for in due time he forfeited his lance-corporal's stripe and was reduced to the ranks, as a plain gentleman cadet, for a serious disciplinary offence. The circumstances which gave rise to this most unfortunate incident have often been told, though there has been speculation as to its underlying cause, for everything had been going well for the future Field-Marshal. Not only did he enjoy cadet life but between terms also he was fortunate as, whenever he was not at New Park, he was able to follow the same custom as he had done during his school holidays, by staying at the country homes of our numerous family friends and relations. He used to go often to Halse, near Taunton, to the home of the Rev. Ferguson Montgomery, father's youngest brother, who had started life in the Royal Navy, and in whose midshipman's sea chest at New Park all those family records, which the Field-Marshal gave me, had lain untouched for so many years. What then could have gone wrong at Sandhurst? The fact is that his promotion, and above all his prowess at games which brought with it popularity and reputation, misled him into thinking that he need not worry about anything. So he stopped working, because, as he wrote in his *Memoirs*, 'I suppose this must have gone to my head.' Worse still he became the leader of a gang of cadets who were noted for their tough tactics, including quite unnecessary and uncalled for violence, in the frequent 'rags', amounting sometimes to gang warfare, which the cadets of his time indulged in, and in which improvised weapons were sometimes employed. The climax came when Bernard was foremost in the ragging of a certain cadet for no better reason, apparently, than that, to use Bernard's own words, 'He was a dreadful chap'! The main building of what was then called the Royal Military College is a mid-Victorian stone structure with wide, uncarpeted and bare corridors and high ceilings, from which rooms including the cadet bedrooms lead off on either side. One evening the unfortunate victim was changing into his blue mess uniform, which the cadets wore for dinner, when suddenly he heard a loud yell (it was Bernard's war cry), the door was thrown open, and a party of some six cadets burst into the room, some of them carrying bayonets. Amidst much laughter from this gang the occupant of the room was seized and his hands and feet pinioned so that he could barely move, whilst another cadet stood in front menacing him with a bayonet in case he attempted to escape. The timing of the attack was excellent as they had caught him at an awkward moment, when he had nothing on except his under-pants and shirt. When he was firmly secured Bernard took a box of matches, went behind him and set fire to his shirt-tails. The dreadful result for this particular cadet can well be imagined! He was very severely burnt, suffered great agony and had to be taken to hospital at once, where, to his undying credit, he refused absolutely and forever to reveal the identity of his chief assailant. But of course at the subsequent court of inquiry into the incident, ordered by the Commandant, Bernard was soon found out and stood convicted, not only as the leader of the gang but also the perpetrator of the act.

It goes without saying that this whole affair was treated very seriously. It was of no avail to claim youthful high spirits, or to attempt to draw a parallel with incidents in *Tom Brown's School Days*, in mitigation of punishment. Cadets were not school boys, they were gentlemen cadets and expected to behave as such. So the inevitable occurred. Bernard was reduced to the ranks, and worse still, consideration was given, in the circumstances of this case, to his fitness to hold a commission in His Majesty's army. Could he ever perhaps become an officer and a gentleman? Had he got the right qualities? Father and Mother were informed of all this, so of course there was a great outcry at Chiswick, where now mother's very great determination and resolve had their effect. At all costs Bernard's career in the army must be saved. Besides there had been enough trouble already and it would be particularly unfortunate if, at this juncture, one of Bishop Montgomery's sons had to be removed from Sandhurst. Father, by this time, had become very well known to a wide circle of people, not only in the Church of England but overseas as well. He had already paid long visits to Canada and the United States, and in London he had been made Prelate of the Order of St Michael and St George. Soon after Bernard went to Sandhurst, there had been a magnificent service of inauguration in St Paul's Cathedral in the presence of the Sovereign of the Order, King Edward VII, and of the Grand Master, H.R.H. The Prince of Wales. Looking back it is probably true to say that Father rather enjoyed all the pomp and ceremony that was inevitable on such occasions. One hundred and eighty Knights Grand Cross, robed in their mantles and wearing their insignia, with one hundred Knight Commanders and many Companions, walked in the Cathedral procession. The Prelate, as the senior officer of the Order and wearing the mantle of a Knight Grand Cross, came last but one in the procession, immediately in front of the Grand Master. Apart from this, Father now invariably left all matters concerning the family entirely in the hands of our mother. He recognised her efficiency, and her passionate desire that all her children should do well in the world, and he was therefore content never to intervene. Furthermore he was entirely happy that she should wear the trousers where he himself was concerned, and therefore gladly allowed her to control all monetary matters, which she did to good effect. Accordingly the Bishop, when in London, was given five shillings a week for his day to day expenses and he was not expected to exceed this sum, though after the 1914–18 war his allowance was increased to ten shillings. Nevertheless he had been known to point out that with pocket money at that level it was difficult enough, even with money values of the Edwardian era, to lunch at the Athenaeum!

When therefore news of the catastrophe which apparently threatened Bernard's career had reached Chiswick Mother immediately got in touch with the Commandant at Sandhurst, Colonel W. B. Capper. She must have impressed him for he at once asked her to come down to Camberley and stay the night with him and his wife, in order that they could jointly discuss matters. She was then forty-three and a very handsome woman with a great look of determination and resolve about her. In the event it appeared most fortunate that she did make the visit, for finally it was decided that Bernard should be given one more chance, though in addition to being reduced to the ranks he would have to stay on at Sandhurst for an additional term of six months. On the face of it this was indeed a severe penalty for it meant that the date of his first commission, which would determine his relative seniority in the army, would be gazetted six months later than that of his contemporaries; in cadet parlance he would have to drop a term which was always regarded as a grave handicap for anyone's future. But why, it may well be asked, should all this happen, or, equally important, why was it allowed to happen? The truth almost certainly lies in a remark by Bernard himself on page 24 of his *Memoirs*, where, in discussing the frequency of near-gang warfare by cadets, with special reference to his own case, he wrote, 'This state of affairs obviously could not continue, even at Sandhurst in 1907, when the officers kept well clear of the activities of the cadets when off duty.' Surely this statement points to a strange lack of communication between the officer instructors on the staff of the Royal Military College and the cadets under their command. Apparently it was the custom, when Bernard was there in 1907, for the officers deliberately not to become involved in cadet activities when the latter were off duty. If this was the case, then they, the officers, might not have been fully aware of the adverse tendencies prevalent amongst certain cadets; or, in any case, they would not have been available to provide that wise counsel and advice, and where necessary correction, which should always be quickly forthcoming if and when danger signals start to appear. The short point is that if the officer instructors were not sufficiently close to their cadets to know and appreciate what was going on, or if they did know, deliberately took no corrective action, then trouble was inevitable. However, this by no means implies condonation of the incident of the burnt shirt-tails and all those who were involved – far from it. Bernard was wholly culpable, of that there can be no doubt. But this time he really learnt his lesson and for good. As he himself said, 'I worked really hard during those last six months at Sandhurst and was determined to pass out high.' No one ever again had cause even to suspect idleness in Bernard. For the rest of his professional life, which is still in being, he has been the embodiment of, to quote his own favourite dictum, 'ceaseless work'.

An impartial observer of this incident of 1907 will see in it, not only the profound effect it had on Bernard's personal conduct thereafter, but also its broader significance in that it probably laid the foundation for his almost fanatical belief, throughout his military career, in the absolute need for a commander to be close to his troops. The evidence of this is particularly clear, and loses nothing by quoting, out of context, from his *Memoirs* where, in his chapter entitled 'My Doctrine of Command' he wrote:

'Bottled up in men are great emotional forces which have got to be given an outlet in a way which is positive and constructive, and which warms the heart and excites the imagination. If the approach to the human factor is cold and impersonal, then you achieve nothing. But if you gain the trust and confidence of your men, and they feel their best interests are safe in your hands, then you have in your possession a priceless asset, and the greatest achievements become possible.'

One more setback however was in store for Bernard before he finally left Sandhurst in July 1908. It had always been assumed that he would join the Indian army and follow the family tradition of service in India where his illustrious grandfather, Sir Robert, had become so famous. There was also another reason for this. In the Indian army the British officers opted to spend their whole professional life in the Far East, and their pay was therefore much better than that of officers of the British army serving in India. Above all Indian army officers got their promotion on a time scale up to the rank of field officer. It took nine years to become a captain and thirteen a major, whereas in the British service regimental promotion was governed by your relative seniority position when vacancies for promotion occurred; as a result there were cases known in some regiments of subalterns having nearly twenty years' officer service. The Indian army therefore had great attractions for a young man, and the competition was so keen that it was essential, in order to join it, to appear in the first thirty names on the Sandhurst passing out list. Bernard only just missed this opportunity as his position on the list was thirty-six. At the time he was bitterly disappointed at the result and so also were my parents and the whole family. It was not until years later that events showed how very fortunate it was that these early setbacks in the life of the Field-Marshal had occurred, and had channelled his career into the path it was to take. There was however one by-product stemming, on the face of it, from his failure to be accepted for the Indian army that left its mark. This is the view, held with reluctance by myself, though presumably there are many who will not share it, that the Field-Marshal appeared to develop some prejudice against the Indian army generally; and that on occasions this possibly found its expression in some reluctance to give proper and sufficient credit, when due, to Indian troops and their officers. His opinion of Field-Marshal Sir Claude Auchinleck's strategic and tactical control of events is well known. Reading between the lines there may even be some who wonder why, on 4th November 1942, at the close of El Alamein, he did not immediately employ the 4th Indian Division, under its very able commander, 'Gertie' Tuker,* in an active pursuit role. Be all that as it may there will certainly be general agreement that even if Bernard had been accepted for the Indian army he would undoubtedly have reached the top of his profession. He, of all men, would not have been numbered with those officers of the Indian army who, as he wrote in his *Memoirs*, 'tended to age rapidly after about forty-five'. In this context it may be more to the point to wonder what would have happened to the Indian army if he had joined it!

So the future Field-Marshal joined the British army and was fortunate in his preference, for he was commissioned in the Royal Warwickshire Regiment† and posted to its 1st Battalion stationed in India. The Royal Warwickshire are one of the famous English county regiments of the infantry of the line, which has fought in many wars throughout British military history and earned battle honours starting with Namur in 1695, continuing through the eighteenth and nineteenth centuries, with the Peninsular and other famous campaigns, and ending with the two world wars of this century. It is also one of the oldest regiments in the army, having been raised in 1674, as one of the English regiments in the Dutch service under William of Orange with seniority as the 6th Regiment of Foot. Bernard joined his battalion at Peshawar late in 1908 when he was just over twenty-one. There is no doubt he loved his regimental service as a subaltern in India. For the first time he had command of men and in conditions in which he was able to give full rein to his intense energy, and interest in everything that came his way, whether it was weapon training, or other regimental duty, or the organised games at which of course he excelled. He even took the time and trouble to learn both Urdu and Pushtu though there was no obligation for officers of the British service to do so. In short the time for ceaseless work had begun, and neither climate nor the diversions of social life were any bar to his endless activity. It has often been said that Bernard took no part in social life in

---

* The late Lt.-Gen. Sir Francis Tuker, KCIE, CB, DSO, OBE, FRGS.
† Now 2nd Battalion The Royal Regiment of Fusiliers.

India, but this is not so and particularly after the battalion moved down to Bombay in 1910. He became a member of the Bombay Yacht Club and was secretary of its sailing committee, all of which inevitably brought its quota of social activity. But by far the most important and significant outcome of his early service in India was the development of his regard for the British private soldier – the Other Ranks. A corollary to this, and equally significant, was his realisation that by contrast the standard of officer efficiency at battalion level (he had not yet had any experience of staff work) was deplorably low. From this fact stemmed his utter determination to make the study of his profession his main concern. As he wrote in his *Memoirs*,

'I had now begun to work and seriously. Looking back I would put this period as the time when it was becoming apparent to me that to succeed one must master one's profession. It was clear that the senior regimental officers were not able to give any help in the matter since their knowledge was confined almost entirely to what went on at battalion level; they had little or no knowledge of other matters. When the battalion arrived at a new station the first question the C.O. would ask was: "How does the General like the attack done?" '

On the face of it such an indictment of his senior brother officers, by a junior lieutenant of under three years' service, would appear difficult to substantiate, but unfortunately there was a very great deal of truth in it. In those halcyon peaceful days, with the Boer campaigns a thing of the past, the entente cordiale with France fully established, and no major war in sight (only a very few far-sighted men thought otherwise) there were not very many keen soldiers in either the British or Indian armies. Regimental rivalry was confined mainly to polo, cricket or football fields, and 'appearance' and turnout counted far more than was necessary or desirable. A senior major in one famous regiment serving in India was wont to tell the newly joined subalterns, 'The only things that really matter are the band and the officers' mess.' In India however there was always the north-west frontier, with its incessant tribal campaigns, to stimulate and foster professional interest and pride, and gallantry and courage were certainly never lacking. A senior lieutenant in Bernard's regiment had won the DSO on the frontier not long before the latter joined his battalion at Peshawar. But in Southern India particularly (in areas irreverently known as the 'sloth belt') there was no such incentive, so that General Sir Charles Napier's description, written some sixty years earlier, of the long service British officer, civil or military, was still sometimes liable to be accurate. Napier was then Commander-in-Chief in India and is on record as saying, 'By an old Indian I mean a man full of curry and bad Hindustani, with a fat liver and no brains, but with a self-sufficient idea that no one can know India except through long experience of brandy, champagne, gram-fed mutton, cheroots, and hookahs.'

By the time Bernard returned to England with his regiment in 1913 he was a Subaltern of near five years' service and a comparatively experienced Infantry Regimental Officer. He had already passed his promotion examination for the rank of captain and had held the appointments of Assistant Adjutant, Quartermaster and Transport Officer. He had certainly made his mark in the battalion for he was known as a serious student of military history, and was studying his profession in a fashion probably never seen before in the Royal Warwickshire Regiment. He was twenty-five, about five feet nine inches tall, tough and wiry, with the customary fairly heavy moustache worn by so many army officers of that time. He had already had his first brush with the Germans, though not on the battlefield, in circumstances most admirably described by Alan Moorehead in his book entitled *Montgomery*. It happened in Bombay in 1911 when the battleship *Gneisenau* of the Imperial German Navy had arrived on a courtesy visit, and the local authorities were anxious to appear as hospitable as possible during what was regarded as an important diplomatic and social occasion. The festivities were to include a public football match between a team from the German man-of-war and the local British infantry regiment – the Royal Warwickshire. Bernard, who was the battalion sports officer, had been given strict instructions that the regimental first eleven should not play in this particular match; it was a notable team, clearly far too good for the sailors to take on, and tact required that a team of lesser calibre should be fielded. However immediately the match began it was abundantly clear that something had gone wrong, for the regimental team proceeded to annihilate the Germans who were eventually defeated by the staggering score of forty goals to nil! Of course Bernard had to account to his commanding officer for what had occurred, and had no option but to confess that he had fielded all his very best players. His excuse was: 'I was not taking any risks with Germans.' It was just three years before he was to meet the Germans again in very different circumstances.

Whilst Bernard was at Sandhurst, and later also during his four and a half years in India, life at Chiswick for our parents had been far from placid. Both Father and Mother went daily to their work in Westminster, the latter to the offices of the Mothers' Union which were then, as now, in Tufton Street a few yards from father's S.P.G. office. Breakfast, preceded of course by the family prayers, was always at eight o'clock; after which the Bishop and his wife caught either the 8.45 or the 9.18 train from Chiswick Station to Vauxhall, from where they walked over the bridge to Westminster. One or other of us younger boys generally went with them to the railway station, and if for any reason there had been a late start and the train was seen approaching the platform before they reached it, Mother would say to one of us: 'Quick, run to the guard and tell him not to start; say to him "the Bishop is just coming, wait for us".' Strangely, in those more undemocratic days, the guard generally did keep the train waiting, if my parents were in sight. But my father never broke into a run so perhaps his general appearance, in his bishop's gaiters and apron, long frock coat and pectoral cross with the wide-brimmed hat with strings on it, was impressive enough; he certainly was an imposing figure as he was six feet tall with a short pointed beard and a moustache. Apart however from the busy routine of their daily life there were other distractions which kept my parents very preoccupied. In 1911 Bernard had come back from Bombay for six months' leave, and that was also the year of the Coronation of King George V. Then in 1906 and 1907 Father had paid long visits to Canada and the

United States, and in 1910 he went to China, Japan, Korea, Hong Kong, Borneo, Malaysia and Burma. Finally in 1913 he visited India, but there he became very ill with dysentery and had to come home after a few months. As if that was not enough, in 1908 he had been appointed Secretary to the Lambeth Conference of some one hundred and fifty bishops, and to its immediately preceding Pan-Anglican Congress; of course Mother became deeply involved in it all and organised the extensive hospitality for the many visitors from overseas. To crown everything our parents suffered a fearful blow when Desmond, their fourth son, the brother whom I can scarcely remember, died of meningitis whilst a schoolboy at St Paul's. He was in his fourteenth year at the time and was described by my mother as a gifted and beautiful boy.

Bernard thoroughly enjoyed his long summer leave. He bought a motor bicycle with a side-car and travelled a lot, and of course came with all the family to New Park for August and September. That was the summer when Mother, motivated no doubt by the memory of meals on the veranda of villas on hot sunny days in the Mediterranean, where she used to go for holidays with Father in their early married life, decided at Chiswick, that 'the family ought really to have breakfast in the garden on most days of the week'. This decision, having once been taken, was not to be lightly set aside so breakfast had to be in the garden unless the weather conditions were quite impossible. But the results were not always all they might have been and I remember Father sitting at the table in his overcoat and bishop's hat, whilst the drizzle persisted, hoping no doubt that his pocket money would suffice for lunch at the Athenaeum that day. Bernard, straight from the hot weather in India, never appeared on such occasions and let it be clearly known that 'he would have no part in such folly'. Father had been fortunate in his trip to Canada for the entire journey was financed, in a spirit of missionary zeal, by the Canadian Pacific Railway. He travelled the country from the Eastern provinces over the Rocky Mountains to the West Coast, where he lost his heart to British Columbia and in particular to Vancouver City and Island. In so doing he was able to arrange for Donald, on leaving Cambridge where he had studied Law, to be articled to a firm of lawyers in

Vancouver City. Graduates from the United Kingdom were much needed in Canada in those early days, particularly in the professions and the public service, because so much of the country was still unsurveyed let alone developed. So in 1908 Donald went to Canada, married a Canadian girl, and prospered exceedingly, becoming a Canadian citizen with a Canadian accent, and eventually became chairman of his firm of lawyers and a Queen's Counsel. In the 1914–18 war he had been commissioned as an infantry officer and served with the Canadian army in France, where he won the MC. He died in 1970 aged eighty-five, leaving two sons to follow in his footsteps; on his gravestone is inscribed: 'His word was his bond'. Like the Field-Marshal Donald was a complete individualist. Except in his great generosity, however, he was otherwise very different. After leaving home he never went to church. Perhaps in his case our parents had overdone it?

Father greatly enjoyed his long visit to the United States in 1907. He took my elder sister, Una, with him on this trip; she was then a beautiful girl of eighteen, and they were both astonished and impressed by the wealth and power of the nation, and especially by the kindness and hospitality of the many people they met, some of whom became our life-long friends. Father in particular found the country most fascinating, particularly the pace at which people moved and the amount of work, or leisure, they contrived to complete in every twenty-four hours. Later he wrote: 'The atmosphere of the USA is very electric and exciting for the Englishman. We lived for days at a time on our nerves in one ceaseless round of activity and excitement. People screamed at us everywhere, overwhelmed us with kindness, and fed us too well with meals, oysters and rich sauces galore.' He was also much impressed by the informality he found at church services. People talked openly and loudly before the service began, but remained utterly silent when a loud yell (it was the war whoop of the American Indian) came from the vestry as a signal that the time for service had arrived. A call to order at a formal conference of bishops would be made in like fashion. My sister Una however was rather horrified at the noise and laughter, discussion of personal and social matters, etc., which went on before church services began. But she probably did not appreciate that the Americans, then as now, were not so stiff or formal as the British. At the time she was a very attractive girl, but with little experience of life outside her own family circle, and I think it likely that she did not always respond to the approaches, and certainly the intentions, of the many American young men she met, with that degree of ardour and enthusiasm which they had perhaps expected or hoped for. So Una did not lose her heart to any American, but five years later she married Andrew Holden, who by then was in the Egyptian civil service, and spent many happy years with him in Cairo where five children were born to them. Throughout her life she remained conditioned and restricted by her strongly religious upbringing and background, which influenced her outlook and also I think affected her sense of humour. She was utterly different from any of the rest of us. We all had an immense liking and admiration for her husband,★ and they were devoted to each other. Father travelled back from the USA in the Cunard liner *Astoria*, then on her last voyage before going to the shipbreaker's yard, and was astonished to discover she was in fact the ex-Shaw Saville vessel the *Tainui* in which the family had gone out to Tasmania many years before; she had been much changed and now had two masts instead of four. On this her last voyage there were only five passengers in the first class so father had the run of the ship and of the bridge, and saw much of the Captain and Chief Engineer. Of the latter, a Scotsman, he wrote, 'They are extraordinary people, these Scotch. I told him the story of the Irish butler whose master had just died, and who, when asked about the date of the sad event, said, "If he'd lived till tomorrow he'd have been dead a fortnight." But he only looked on me with a solemn face, thinking I was mad.'

As prelate of an order, father was commanded to be present at the Coronation of King George V in Westminster Abbey, and, as (technically) a member of the King's Household, to take part in the King's Procession. Of course he wrote a long account of the whole proceedings, and kept it in his papers, from which these few brief extracts are worth repeating.

★ Andrew Holden died in his ninetieth year on 31 May 1973.

'When the Queen's Procession passed it was delightful to see the whole mass of Peeresses drop their curtsey together as the Queen went by. It was equally delightful to see five hundred pairs of white arms flash up, when the Queen was crowned, to put on coronets. It was done amazingly quickly.

'We five officers of the Order marched two and two, with myself as senior officer in the rear, for the sixth officer, the Chancellor of the Order (the Duke of Argyll) was not present as he held some other place in the Procession as well. For us this was perhaps just as well for His Grace has such a strange temperament that he is really not of the slightest use. He does not concentrate, he cannot keep his place in a procession, he is generally forgetful of all his surroundings. I cannot imagine how he manages his properties or keeps accounts. Probably he is allowed 1s a day, like myself!

'So in due time the great service ended, the most wonderful and solemn I remember, equal at least to one's own consecration as bishop in feeling. I was near Lady Mary Trefusis in the Annexe, and was told the names of all the great people. I also learnt that the King and Queen were angry at any one supposing they would go, or care to go, to balls during this week. I found Maud in Dean's Yard rather blown about. In the Abbey her place had been among city Aldermen who had passed whisky flasks round which she did not care for.'

Years earlier our mother had signed the Pledge, and ever since had developed an absolute horror of 'liquor', as she called it, in any form.

When that fateful year 1914 began Bernard had been back in England with his regiment, at Shorncliffe near Folkestone in East Kent, for over six months. He had attended the infantry officers' course at the School of Musketry at Hythe, nearby, and had obtained first place in the passing out list; he had also played hockey for the army. It was a pleasant time in England for people in his circumstances during the years 1913 and 1914, and the regular officers of the garrison towns in England made the best use of it. At Shorncliffe during the autumn and winter months there was hunting with the East Kent Foxhounds or with packs further afield, and in the summer there was much social activity combined with tennis and cricket. In those days polo was still played on the Leas at Folkestone, and it made a wonderful setting for polo on a fine summer afternoon, with the view from the Leas cliff looking over the English Channel to the coast of France little more than twenty miles away. Bernard meanwhile had bought a motor car which gave him the mobility he wanted; not many officers in his regiment had cars and it showed his determination to move with the times that he preferred to use his slender income for a car, rather than anything else. He was still living on his pay, with the aid of an allowance of one hundred pounds a year from our parents. No subaltern officer in the regular army could live on his pay, and maintain himself and his equipment, including full dress uniform, the undress frock coat, and regimental mess dress, without some form of private means. But in addition Bernard was continuing hard to study his profession, and in this he was fortunate in having with him in his battalion at Shorncliffe an officer who had just graduated from the Staff College at Camberley. This officer, Captain Lefroy, was killed in the 1914–18 war but Bernard fully appreciated his worth and the value of his advice and assistance, and later, in his *Memoirs*, wrote this of the influence Lefroy had exerted on himself: 'He was a bachelor and I used to have long talks with him about the army, and what was wrong with it, and especially how one could get to real grips with the military art. He helped me tremendously with advice about what books to read and how to study.'

In Ireland however, in 1914, matters were not going at all well. The British Government in London, under Mr Asquith, was seeking to pass a Home Rule Bill which would give Ireland an independent legislature while retaining representatives for her at Westminster also. Looking back it is interesting to note that this is precisely what the British did for the six counties of Ulster in 1922. However in 1914 Asquith's proposal brought a crisis which threatened civil war within the realm. The Protestant Unionists of Ulster would have none of it and avowed their determination to resist, by force, any attempt to subject them to a Dublin parliament.

Bernard, *right*, Brigade-Major, in France, 1915,
and *left*, Brig. Sandilands

Bernard, GSO 2, 9th Army Corps, France, 1917

Accordingly they formed the Ulster Volunteers, an orthodox military organisation covering the nine counties, armed with rifles and small arms and largely organised and trained by ex-British army officers. This force was really the ancestor of the famous B Specials which were raised as part of the Royal Ulster Constabulary after Northern Ireland's independence. Of course in 1914 there was a great deal of illegal gun running into Ireland, particularly in Ulster, and much ingenuity was employed to outwit the British authorities. At one of the ports a party of mourners went to the dock to meet the Liverpool steamer which had brought back to Ireland the coffin of an Irish lady who had died in England, but in her will had expressed a wish to be buried in her own home land. The coffin was handled with all due care and reverence: the mourners took their places, and as the sad procession left the ship and made its way to the waiting hearse, everyone took off their hat to the deceased on her last journey on this earth. But they took them off to a consignment of rifles as the real coffin came a few days later. One of the heads of the police, living near Belfast, had ordered a piano from England. In due time an invoice reached him and a message arrived from the nearby railway station that the piano was there. Everyone would be wanting to help the head of the police. However, strangely, another message came to say that his piano was at the next station, not the one first mentioned; there must have been some mistake. So the police chief went to both stations the next morning but the same answer was given to him by the station master at each station: 'Piano, yer Honour? Sure now, your men fetched it yesterday; that's right now.' To both he answered: 'I know nothing about it.' His own piano came two days later.

In Moville the Nationalist (all Roman Catholic) Volunteers, about two hundred of them, were numerically much stronger than our own small Ulster Volunteer detachment of some forty men; though at that time the former were largely made up of ignorant illiterate mountain farmers (many of them Father's tenants) whose only ideas about Home Rule were no rents and possession of all the Protestant houses and farms. Of course both sides knew each other well and both were gun running. The Bishop had signed the

Ulster Covenant, the document embossed with the red hand of
Ulster, in which each signatory pledged himself to 'use all means
which may be found necessary to defeat the present conspiracy to
set up a Home Rule Parliament in Ireland'. It seems however that
in that summer of 1914 Father became rather embarrassed by a
request from Major X, of our local Ulster Volunteers, to include
some weapons and ammunition in the family luggage when we all
set off for New Park, in late July, for the summer holidays. It was
arranged that a Morris tube (it was part of a land-mine device)
should be delivered by the Army and Navy Stores to our Chiswick
home. The tube was enclosed in a hollowed-out bamboo walking
stick, completely sealed up and very cleverly done so there was no
sign of it. In any case as Major X, an Irishman, said: 'No one will
be searching *your* luggage, Bishop'! Also to be conveyed by our
party was a consignment of one thousand rounds of ammunition;
('No one will be noticing it split up among you all.') In the event
Father appears to have planned matters rather well for himself,
because, he wrote, 'It all arrived at Chiswick too late, twenty
minutes after we had left for New Park. So it was brought over, all
quite safely, by Aubrey Farrar, Ralph Kite and some other young
people, boys and girls, who were joining us at Moville some days
later.' Aubrey Farrar was another grandson of Dean Farrar, the
son of Doctor Reginald Farrar the Dean's eldest son, and Ralph
Kite was the son of Dean Kite who had been Dean of Hobart when
Father was Bishop of Tasmania. It is not difficult to conjure up the
scene the party must have presented as they set out on their journey to Ireland with their concealed, and very illegal cargo. Aubrey,
a grandson of the great Dean, was in command, and was carrying
the loaded bamboo walking stick, presumably on his arm. Ralph
Kite, a dean's son, was in charge of the ammunition consignment
which was split up amongst their suitcases, including those of some
other boys, and girls, in the party. It was a good plan for they must
all have looked very much what in fact they were – a group of young
people starting out on their summer holiday, with the men (who
were then at their university) wearing the straw 'boaters' and
blazers customary in their day, and the girls in their pretty summer
frocks. Few would have suspected the presence of anything illegal

in their personal luggage, though it would have been decidedly embarrassing if there had been any baggage search, for at that time the authorities at the sea ports were very much on the look out for gun runners. But an equal, and possibly greater, risk was incurred during their sea voyage, when the whole party had to disembark from the *S.S. Comic* (the Liverpool steamer) into Lafferty's fishing boat waiting off shore at Moville, especially if the sea was at all rough. That climb down the side of the *Comic* always had some hazards, for both the passengers and their luggage, and it might have been very awkward to have to account for the contents of a suitcase which, on bursting open accidentally, was clearly seen to include a lot of rifle ammunition, especially if the case belonged to a charming girl. Worse still perhaps, it would have been dreadful to lose the whole consignment, or any part of it, and have to report the loss to Major X! Looking again at this episode, on a more serious note, it surely reflects the outlook at New Park in those days, to which we were all so accustomed that we did not realise its existence. It was a blend of conviction and determination to do and to achieve what we all thought was right and if necessary to accept conflict in the process. It was the way in which the future Field-Marshal was brought up, and it applied equally to our neighbours in Inishowen.

I can just remember the Moville detachment of the Ulster Volunteers drilling in the field below New Park, but always after dark. I expect they had that Morris tube, and the ammunition. But it was a curious time, for outwardly everything appeared very peaceful. When the Nationalist Volunteers were marching in or near Moville and met my father, or the local rector, they saluted and of course the salute was returned. Nevertheless it did look then as if a civil war (with three sides participating) was about to begin in Ireland and probably it would actually have happened, until suddenly the Irish question vanished, at any rate temporarily, when Asquith's government suspended operation of the Home Rule Bill, though it had been passed a few days previously, and deferred any kind of settlement till the Great War should be over. For the sands of time were running out that summer of 1914, with its wonderful weather and the happy time we were all having at New Park, where Mother

had gathered her usual large house party for August and September. By this time a squash rackets court had been added to the
house and we all spent many hours playing endlessly. It was very
much an amateur construction, open to the sky, with two sides
formed by one wall of the house and the dairy wall, and a wooden
gallery for spectators; but we all got marvellous exercise and much
enjoyment out of it. So none of us were concerned about the world
situation and certainly few of us bothered to read the newspapers
which in any case always came very late. You got yesterday's paper
at tea time today. It was therefore very much a surprise to us all
when suddenly we woke up to the fact that something very serious
was going on in Europe. German troops were actually marching
across the frontiers of Belgium and Luxembourg and heading for
France. This state of blissful ignorance was generally widespread
throughout the population of Great Britain and Ireland during
those summer months. Only a comparatively few people, in the
Whitehall ministries and the governments of British possessions
overseas who had to be kept informed, had a proper appreciation of
the threat to world peace posed by the German nation, highly
organised, ambitious and hard working, armed to the teeth and
directed by a powerful military oligarchy. Indeed few people in any
country realised that the lights were going out over Europe and
would not be relit for more than four years.

Bernard had planned to come over to New Park that summer
early in August but of course at the end of July all that had to be
cancelled. The 10th (Shorncliffe) Infantry Brigade was in the 4th
Division of the planned British Expeditionary Force, and consisted
of four regiments, one English, one Scots, and two Irish, under the
command of Brigadier General Haldane. The regiments were: the
1st Bn Royal Warwickshire Regiment, the 1st Bn Royal Irish
Fusiliers, the 2nd Bn Royal Dublin Fusiliers, and the 2nd Bn
Seaforth Highlanders. These were all famous regiments which had
fought in many campaigns including the Boer War. Bernard was a
platoon commander in C Company (under Captain Day) and his
battalion was commanded by Lieutenant-Colonel J. F. Elkington.
The latter had no inkling then of the dreadful disaster in store for
him, when, little more than a month later, his conduct led to his

being cashiered after trial by court martial. Meanwhile in Shorn-cliffe Camp Bernard's battalion was quartered in Napier Barracks, which, with those of the other units of the garrison, were built round an open grassy plain named after Sir John Moore who had trained his famous light infantry there during the Napoleonic wars. It was in these barracks that the regiment received the orders for general mobilisation of the British army, at the start of the war with Germany which began on 4th August 1914. As in most regiments the war came as an immense surprise to all ranks, but in Bernard's case it was no such thing. He had studied the newspapers and read widely and was aware of the dangers that had been steadily growing in Europe for a long time past. The lack of preknowledge however could do nothing to mar the smooth and rapid process of mobilisa-tion, in any unit of the army wherever it might be in the world. This technical readiness for war, in terms of the availability of military manpower, equipment and stores of all kinds, and trans-portation, was one of the great assets of the nation without which we should have been hard pressed indeed, then and since. The extent of the work and effort that mobilisation entailed, at all levels, can well be imagined, if not seen clearly shining, by a glance at the laconic statements in the record of the *War Diary* of Bernard's battalion during the early days of the 1914–18 war. War diaries, kept by all units and formations, were written up daily with meti-culous care and in all circumstances, whatever and wherever they might be, during times of engagement with the enemy or otherwise. The entries which follow below show that in 1914 the extensive use of military abbreviations, to save time and paper, had not yet come. Nor was the twenty-four hour clock yet in use.

		WAR DIARY	Army Form C. 21
1914			
SHORNCLIFFE		1st Bn R. WAR. R.	
29th July	11.30 pm	Precautionary period	
30th July	12.40 am	Officers recalled from leave	
4th August	7.5 pm	Orders to mobilise	
		* Reservists sent for	
5th August	9.15 pm	* Reservists began to join	
(1st day of			
mobilisation)			

6th August	All day	* Reservists continue to join
7th August (swords and bayonets sharpened)	7.45 pm	Orders to hold in readiness to move
	9.30 pm	Orders to move in 2 trains to York
8th August	3.30 am	1st train left Sandgate for Hythe junction and York

* The results of intensive care and preparation underly these entries. Orders to rejoin, with railway warrants, had to be sent to every reservist in the UK. It says much for efficiency that they began to arrive just twenty-four hours after recall orders had been issued. All had then to be fully equipped with uniform and weapons, etc.

YORK

9th August	Lt Col. Elkington took over command of Flying Column of Dublin Fusiliers and R. War. R.
10th August	At Knavesmire. Route Marching
11th–13th August	Route Marching
14th August	Marched to Strensall Camp
15th–17th August	March and Attack drill
18th August	Left Strensall by rail and arrived at Harrow

HARROW

19th–21st August	Brigade Assembly area
22nd August	Arrived Southampton. Embarkation in *SS Caledonia*
23rd August	Arrived Boulogne and camped on hill above the Town. Orders to move tonight. Left 11.30 p.m. in one train. Tpt and horses loaded without mishap. Destination not known.

So Lieutenant Bernard Montgomery of the 1st Bn Royal War-wickshire Regiment, then aged twenty-six, went to the war for which he had been preparing ever since he had joined the army class at St Paul's School twelve years earlier. His peace-time uniforms of scarlet and gold, with blue facings, had all been packed away and he was dressed in drab khaki. He was wearing his sword, duly sharpened by the regimental armourer, and just before mid-night on 23rd August 1914 left Boulogne with his battalion, all in one troop train, horses and transport included, for an unknown destination. It must all have seemed very strange to the men. Many of them had never been in France before and could not speak French; and they probably did not find the French rolling stock much to their liking, particularly as it was a very fine and hot summer's night. Barely forty-eight hours later they were to come under enemy fire for the first time.

Chapter 6

THE SHAPE OF THINGS TO COME

The unknown destination for which the 1st Royal Warwickshire had entrained at Boulogne on 23rd August 1914 turned out to be Le Cateau. By the time the battalion arrived there on 24th the battle of Mons had already been fought and lost, and the British army had begun its famous Retreat from Mons, which was to take them over a hundred miles south until the whole force had withdrawn behind the River Marne. However the first task given to the battalion, as part of the Shorncliffe brigade, was to march forward to St Python to assist in covering the retirement of the 3rd and 5th Divisions which formed the 2nd Corps under General Sir Horace Smith-Dorrien. In battle a forced retreat is always most unpleasant, and is generally accompanied by a failure of communications as Bernard's battalion very soon found to their cost, for, by 25th August, there was no sign of the retreating British though heavy firing was heard to the east about Solesmes. More ominous however was the growing evidence of the approach of the enemy shown by the crowds of refugees who crowded the roads and hampered movement; the proverbial fog of war had descended. The *War Diary* of the battalion for 25th August included the following entry: 'Sighted troops, evidently retiring, far to our right. No contact. Rained a good deal. No rations arrived.'

When that night the Shorncliffe brigade was ordered to begin a withdrawal southward the circumstances were therefore not of the best. It was in these conditions that the 1st Royal Warwickshire were very nearly trapped, at close range, between a large force of German cavalry and a regiment of German infantry, and were lucky to avoid a night encounter against a far superior force. The area round Le Cateau was then open but cultivated country, inter-mingled with small copses, and, as it was late August, the corn was standing high in the fields waiting for the harvest which the war had very largely prevented. Fortunately it was a dark night with a good deal of cloud, and only a half moon. Bernard's battalion was avoiding the roads and marching across country by compass, in a south-westerly direction, in order to cross the main Cambrai-Le Cateau highway and take up a position between Haucourt and Ligny. This was part of the plan of Sir Horace Smith-Dorrien who had decided he would not retreat, but would turn and fight the Germans between Cambrai and Le Cateau. The Royal Warwick-shire had safely passed the Cambrai road and were nearing the village of Caudry, moving through fields of standing corn, when suddenly the moon shone out, between a gap in the clouds. To their astonishment, away on their left and clearly visible in the moonlight moving along a route apparently parallel with them-selves, was what appeared to be a large force of Uhlans (Lancer regiments of the German cavalry). The horses and lances of the men, with their traditional head dress, were clearly visible. At the same moment a regiment of German infantry was spotted on their right marching along another parallel route. Almost instinctively the order was passed to halt and lie flat in the corn, so that by some strange good fortune the British troops went unnoticed. When the moon had gone in again, and the enemy were no longer visible, the march was resumed though it now looked as if something had gone very wrong with the plan to stand and fight on the Cambrai – Le Cateau line; evidently it had, as events soon showed on the follow-ing morning, 26th August.

At about six o'clock the regiment was resting in a cornfield. During the night the brigade had reached its objective and was now in bivouac in the fields near Haucourt with one battalion deployed forward on a ridge covering the remainder of the brigade. The long-awaited unit transport had turned up and the men were

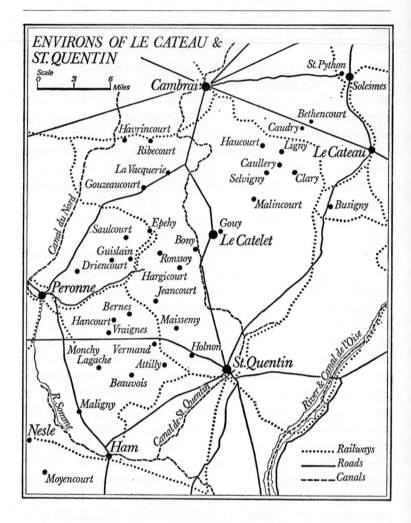

having breakfast. Suddenly the forward battalion came under very heavy and accurate fire from the enemy, who had mounted a very successful surprise attack, with the result that the British battalion was quickly driven off the ridge in some disorder, and suffered heavy casualties. Colonel Elkington immediately mounted his horse, galloped to the two forward companies of the Royal Warwickshire, which included C Company, and ordered both company commanders to 'attack and recapture the ridge in front immediately'. No further orders were given, there was no mention of any plan for the attack, of the need for prior reconnaissance, or measures for supporting fire and their timing, or any administrative instructions. So the two infantry companies, under Major Christie with Bernard commanding a platoon of C Company, dashed forward to attack the hill but without any clear idea as to how to do so, yet automatically forming into extended order. Bernard's own account of this attack, told years later, is well worth reading:

> 'Waving my sword I ran forward in front of my platoon, but unfortunately I had only gone six paces when I tripped over my scabbard, the sword fell from my hand (I hadn't wound that sword strap round my wrist in the approved fashion!) and I fell flat on my face on very hard ground. By the time I had picked myself up and rushed after my men I found that most of them had been killed.'

The official account of the action said that a thick hedgerow marked the top of the ridge but few men reached it as both companies met very heavy rifle and machine-gun fire and were forced to retreat to the line of the road from where they had started. In so doing they suffered unusually severe casualties as seven officers were wounded and forty men either killed or wounded; this was indeed a serious loss and made worse as the day drew to its close by an addition to the wounded list of one more officer and fourteen men. Captain Day, Bernard's Company Commander, had been hit by machine-gun fire in their first attack on the ridge and left on the hillside with a badly wounded leg. Bernard, with two men from C company, therefore went back to bring him in. But they had no stretcher and could not manage to carry him, so there was no alternative but to leave him, together with other badly wounded men who could not be moved, in a nearby church where the local priest promised to look after them. In the event all this wounded party were later taken prisoner by the advancing Germans and spent the next four years in a prisoner-of-war camp. The battalion *War Diary* recorded of this day: 'Held our position under heavy fire for the remainder of the day. Ordered to retire south as night fell, but in the darkness the battalion got split up into three parts, each with no definite information as to whereabouts of other troops.'

Thus ended a most unfortunate day and one which, for Bernard in particular, drove home the reality of the British army's lack of training for modern war. For the experiences of the Royal Warwickshire were by no means limited to their own battalion, as throughout the days of the retreat that followed other units of all arms suffered a similar fate, became equally split up, and lost all contact with their parent formations. It was only the high standard of individual training of the British soldier, combined with the courage and tenacity of all ranks, which was never impaired, that probably saved the British Expeditionary Force from disaster in those late summer days of 1914. Meanwhile on the following day, 27th August, there occurred the dreadful catastrophe that befell the Commanding Officer of Bernard's battalion, Lt Col. Elkington. Towards evening he had arrived at St Quentin with a party of men from his battalion, all of whom were by this time utterly exhausted and urgently in need of food and rest. What happened then is now part of history often told, but the brief extract from the official *War Diary* of the battalion, recording the events, makes significant reading, as much for what it says as for what it leaves unsaid:

'*27th August.* Party under Col. Elkington arrived at St Quentin where Col. Elkington surrendered at the Mayor's request on a German threat to bombard the town. This surrender he later withdrew, and then left the town, alone. The men, under Lt Cooper, found their way to Ham where they discovered their 1st Line Tpt.'

Reading between the lines it is easy to discern the torture and agony of mind which this most unfortunate commanding officer must have suffered when the full significance of what he had done burst upon him, and he walked out into the night, alone. The Mayor had pressed him to sign an agreement to surrender if the enemy attacked the town whilst his regiment were there. Mindful of the condition of his men, and equally of the loss of civilian life and damage to this town of fifty thousand people, if subjected to artillery bombardment, he unwisely signed the agreement. For this he was later court martialled and cashiered; this meant he was deprived of his commission and dismissed, by implication with ignominy, from the service. Ironically the Germans never did attack, let alone occupy, St Quentin, which could only have increased his suffering. However, and again this is part of history, Elkington later made full restitution for his conduct in 1914. He enlisted as a Légionnaire in the ranks of the French Foreign Legion where he saw much active service and was seriously wounded, as a result of which he was awarded both the coveted Médaille Militaire and the Croix de Guerre. Finally, after the war, his gallant conduct was brought to the notice of King George V, following which he was restored to his rank and position in the British army, and awarded the DSO. His portrait was hung in the Royal Academy.

While the events at St Quentin were taking place the main part of Bernard's battalion, including his C Company, were retiring southward as best they could; they had no transport and were hampered with many of their walking wounded casualties. When darkness fell on 26th August it had been abundantly clear that they were alone and cut off from other British troops, except for some men from the Dublin Fusiliers and other elements of the brigade, who had joined them after losing touch with their own units. Major Poole was the senior officer of the battalion present and he now took charge of the whole party. In his *Memoirs* the Field Marshal wrote this about Major Poole: 'In command of our party was a first class regimental officer Major A. J. Poole, and it was due entirely to him that we finally got back to the British Expeditionary Force and joined up with our battalion.' But their journey was extremely hazardous until they finally reached the River Somme at Voyennes, just in time to cross over before the bridge was blown up by sappers of the French army. For nearly a week they could only move by night in order to remain concealed by day in the woods and copses, from where they watched Von Kluck's 1st Army now moving, very fortunately for them, in a south-easterly direction. Their chief danger was from the German cavalry detachments who were intent on rounding up as many stragglers from the British army as they could find. Their one stroke of good luck was finding some country carts on which to convey their wounded men; also at Hargicourt, early on during their march, they had been able to buy food in the village. Bernard was thankful he had had the good sense to take with him from England ten pounds in golden sovereigns and half sovereigns which proved invaluable.

At length, after reaching the Marne, the retreat of the British Expeditionary Force came to an end, and on 5th September Major Poole was able to reform his battalion as its commanding officer. Better still on 6th September the army resumed the offensive and once again marched north to recross the Marne. Later Bernard's battalion, with the rest of their brigade, was moved north to St Omer as part of the effort to save the Channel ports from the advancing German armies. Here on 12th October Brigadier-General Haldane received orders to attack the enemy at Meteren and on the following day the brigade went into action accordingly. It was shortly before ten o'clock when the Royal Warwickshire moved off as the leading battalion of the brigade, with an advance guard formed by its A and C Companies, preceded by the Divisional Cyclist Company and a detachment of cavalry. The Germans were holding the high ground in front of Meteren but as A and C Companies advanced the enemy withdrew to the village. From then on the battle for Meteren raged all day, and, as has often been told, Bernard was shot through the chest whilst leading his platoon, sword in hand, in a bayonet charge to clear the enemy from the village. This happened at one o'clock in the afternoon, and from then until nine o'clock in the evening he was left out in the pouring rain unable to move. Very fortunately for him, a soldier of his platoon who ran to him in order to apply a field dressing was killed and fell across him; so that when an enemy sniper continued to fire at him (they knew he was an officer) many bullets intended for Bernard hit the dead British soldier instead. The Germans had recognised him as a British officer because, just before he was shot, he had been fighting them hand to hand and, in the process, had immobilised, and taken prisoner, a large German corporal by, as he said later, 'kicking my opponent as hard as I could in the lower part of the stomach at a very tender spot'! Nevertheless during the course of that afternoon Bernard was shot again, this time in the knee. Eventually, after the Germans had been finally driven from the village, the stretcher bearers discovered him. But only quite by chance was he seen to be still alive and sent to the field hospital; otherwise he was about to be buried on the spot. The day's fighting was summarised in laconic terms in the battalion *War Diary*, the final entry of which for 13th October listed the very heavy casualties incurred, including Major Christie who had so gallantly led the first ill-fated assault by the battalion on 26th August:

> 'Our casualities 13th October 42 killed and 85 wounded. Maj. Christie and Lt Gilliat killed. Lt Montgomery badly wounded twice. Lts Young, Brindley and Thornton wounded. Very wet all day. A perfect advance by companies concerned with dash and spirit shown by all ranks.'

Thus ended a most eventful day. When Bernard finally regained full consciousness he was in the Herbert Hospital at Woolwich, having been promoted in the field and awarded a decoration. He was just short of twenty-seven, and had become Captain B. L. Montgomery, DSO. For his regiment the day's events were momentous indeed, in that they had finally restored the good name and reputation, and hence the morale, of the battalion. When a commanding officer is cashiered for his personal conduct in battle it inevitably reflects in some measure on the unit under his command. All that had now been put right by the results of the regiment's first major engagement since that day at St Quentin.

One of the wounds that Bernard had incurred at Meteren turned out to be extremely serious. A rifle bullet had struck him full in the chest, and had then passed completely through his body to make its exit on his right-hand side. It was really very fortunate that it had been fired at close range and, striking him with maximum velocity, did not remain inside him; otherwise a major operation to remove the bullet would have been necessary. But its passage through his chest had permanently damaged his right lung, so that ever since he has only had one and a half lungs. However his strength and constitution were always formidable, and known to be so in our family, and I do not think any of us were surprised to hear that he had made what appeared to be a miraculous and virtually complete recovery. The injury from the bullet which struck him on his knee fortunately did no damage. However it was naturally some months before he was sufficiently recovered to leave hospital but when he did, in February 1915, he found he had been made a Staff Officer and appointed as Brigade-Major of the 91st Infantry Brigade. This brigade, commanded by Brigadier-General Mackenzie, was one of the new (volunteer) brigades recently formed in the United Kingdom as part of what, in those early years of the war, was known as Lord Kitchener's Army. Conscription into the armed forces had not yet been thought necessary, the German submarine campaign had not yet begun to take its toll of British shipping, and the Zeppelin airship raids on Great Britain had not started. So life generally in England, including social life in London, had not changed very much, though many thousands of young men were daily enlisting as volunteers in the ranks of the new citizen army. This meant that regular officers, professional soldiers, especially if they already had recent battle experience in France, were invaluable for the raising and training of the new battalions. Bernard therefore found himself very much in demand, and directed all his immense drive and energy into the task of producing trained soldiers, in the shortest possible time, from the virtually raw recruits who filled the ranks of the 91st Infantry Brigade. In this difficult job he was in his element for there was a great shortage of senior officers and he was literally given a free hand to decide and carry out the methods and practice he thought best. His brigade commander was a 'dug-out', that is a retired regular officer who had been called back to the active list to help in raising the new armies. Bernard was fortunate as from the outset General Mackenzie, who was a wise and tolerant man, full of common sense, fully appreciated his brigade major's worth and gave him all the support he needed, without stint of any kind. It was just twelve months later, early in 1916, when Captain Montgomery was posted back to France to be the Brigade Major of 104th Infantry Brigade.

During this twelve months in England Bernard took occasional leave which he generally spent at our home, either at Chiswick or in Ireland depending on where the family was at the time. On one of his visits to London my sister Winsome, who was then a young and attractive girl, aged twenty and decidedly fond of young men, was also at home. When the war came she had at once joined up as a nurse with the V.A.D., and so was also given leave periodically. On this particular occasion, it was the summer of 1915, Bernard had decided that it was time Winsome had a new hat. She was naturally fond of clothes and Bernard, on seeing her dressed for some social occasion, had concluded 'that her turn-out was all right, except for the hat'. With his customary speed of thought he made his appreciation which included a plan to obtain a new hat for Winsome that very morning. He would do it himself and would get the hat at Gorringe's which was then a large, and in his view fashionable, store in Buckingham Palace Road opposite the Royal Mews. Some years ago Gorringe's went out of business and no longer exists. That same morning about noon Bishop Montgomery and his wife were walking from Westminster to Victoria and had chosen to go via Bird Cage Walk and Buckingham Palace. When they came opposite Gorringe's mother noticed that more people than usual seemed to be stationary on the pavement, apparently attracted by someone walking about just inside one of the large ground-floor windows, where goods for sale were displayed. The Bishop would not have taken any notice but Mother insisted they should both go and look, and they were both certainly astonished at what they saw. It was Bernard, who was walking about among the ladies' hats advertised for sale behind the plate-glass window, pointing with his stick to this or that exhibit and apparently giving instructions to the girl assistant behind him. There might well have been nothing unusual in this except that it looked rather odd when the man concerned was clearly an army officer in uniform, wearing service dress and with the red tabs and red hat band which showed him to be a staff officer. (In those days all officers holding appointments on the staff, no matter what their grade, wore the distinguishing red tabs and red hat. Rank badges were then worn on the cuff, not on the shoulder, in khaki service dress, with which it was also *de rigueur* to wear brown leather gloves and carry a short stick or regimental cane.) Bernard was thus equipped and with his ribbon of the DSO quite unmistakable for what he was. He was determined to buy a good hat for his sister, but had probably underestimated the variety and range, with so much scope for difference in colour and design, let alone price. Few other men will have dared to emulate such a venture, but setting aside its humorous aspect, it underlines the fact that he has always liked to help people, whenever in his view they needed assistance, and it was in his power to provide it. There are many who will testify in like fashion.

The 104th Infantry Brigade, commanded by Brigadier-General Sandilands and to which Bernard was appointed as Brigade-Major in January 1916, was in the 35th (Bantam) Division. The nickname derived from a decision by the War Office no longer to insist on a minimum-height standard for army recruits; instead some divisions were formed composed mainly of men of short stature. Events soon proved what a very wise decision this was, for divisions such as the 35th were recruited chiefly from Lancashire and Yorkshire and other northern counties of England including the mining regions, so that the other ranks in all its brigades were short, wiry and very tough young men whose average height was a positive advantage in the trenches. For by now, regrettably, the Western Front had crystallised into the static conditions of lineal trench warfare, which stretched without a break from the North Sea coast at Nieuport in Flanders right through France to the frontier of Switzerland. In the main this was due to the rapid growth of fire power, especially by machine gun and artillery bombardment, which meant that a man standing or even lying on the ground, or behind any kind of shelter at ground level, was liable to be shot at, directly or indirectly, from a variety of ranges and by a variety of weapons. The only limit to the constant use, by day or night, of this astonishing and novel volume of fire was the supply of the weapons and ammunition needed to maintain it, and the training and skill of the gun crews, including the machine gunners. When the 1st Royal Warwickshire went to war in August 1914 there were two machine guns in the battalion. Later whole regiments were converted into

Vickers machine-gun battalions, each armed and equipped with forty-eight machine guns. The cumulative effect on the battlefield of all these weapons, when produced *en masse* by the mobilised effort of highly industrialised nations, could only have one result, which was, in simple terms, that all mobility was brought to an end. Furthermore as there were no flanks to be turned for over three hundred miles, the soldier sought the only kind of protection he could find from an extremely high risk; he dug trenches, erected miles of barbed-wire defences, and went underground. This was the situation that caused the awful carnage of the war of 1914–18 on the Western Front, as the opposing armies sought to assault each other across the no-man's-land between the forward trench lines, which sometimes were less than one hundred yards apart. Each attack was inevitably preceded by very heavy bombardment followed by an infantry assault on the opposing trench lines, ending not infrequently with a hand to hand engagement in which prisoners were taken largely in order to obtain intelligence; otherwise little quarter was given. In these circumstances it was not surprising that the casualties lists on both sides grew and grew, and it was certainly this that made Bernard write the following opening sentences of his chapter on the 1914–18 war in his last book, *A History of Warfare*:

'The conflict which began in August 1914 in Europe developed into the bloodiest war in history. The only impressive results were the casualties – and these had a profound influence on my military thinking. A large number of those killed had no known grave; in some cases corpses formed part of trenches, and were devoured by rats.'

These conditions continued to prevail, even after the introduction of yet another novel weapon (poison gas) until eventually human ingenuity restored mobility by production of the armoured fighting vehicle – the tank. Even then mobility was long in coming and trench warfare loomed large in Bernard's experience throughout his years of fighting in France, until the Armistice in November 1918. In the writing of this book my research took me a great deal to look at the fascinating papers held in the Public Record Office. The war Diaries of battalions were almost always written up by hand in pencil, and so sometimes were those of brigade headquarters, depending on the operational conditions, whilst a typewritten record was generally possible at divisional headquarters and above. Leafing through many hundreds of documents and papers while writing this book it was exciting for me to come across the familiar handwriting of the future Field-Marshal on the cover of the *War Diary* of his brigade for June 1916. One could find no difficulty in reading between the lines of an entry signed by him, where it recorded a visit by his general and himself to the forward trenches. This entry read:

CHIMPANZEE   June
TRENCH   25th

   The GOC and Brigade Major visited the line held by the 17th Lan. Fus. on the east of ANGLE WOOD at 5 a.m. The enemy were extremely nervous and evidently feared another attack. Intermittent barrages of great intensity were kept up by the enemy on the valleys and slopes round ANGLE WOOD. This made progress very difficult and very exciting. However the outward and return journeys were successfully accomplished through the barrages.

   Visits of this kind must have included periods of great danger and intense anxiety. It would have been dark when they started but quite light when they reached Chimpanzee trench; the journey 'through the barrages' speaks for itself.
   Another entry in the *War Diary* of the 104th Brigade for the same month includes the following entry which shows the need there was then to improvise, in order to maintain reliable communications in the days when there were no W/T facilities at unit level, let alone R/T; often even a field telephone line could not reach battalion headquarters, and, as a result the casualties amongst orderlies and runners were very high:

   'A telephone line was laid to within 800 yards of Battn HQ;

the remaining distance being covered by orderlies. Messages were dispatched from the front line by pigeon and received at Bde HQ in 35 minutes.'

After he had been a year in France as a Brigade-Major Bernard was appointed to a higher-grade staff appointment as GSO2 of the 33rd Infantry Division, with the rank of major. He was still only twenty-nine and very young to have become a field officer. It was now 1917, and the worst year of the war for the Western Allies on land and sea; the year which saw, with other ordeals, the awful slaughter of the third battle of Ypres and Passchendaele Ridge, which cost the British army the staggering total of two hundred and forty thousand casualties. It was during the early days of his six months with the 33rd Division that an incident occurred which finally convinced Bernard, and led to his complete determination, that the peculiar carnage of trench warfare, as practised on the Western Front, must never be allowed to happen again. This incident was not connected with any special raid, or battle encounter; it was the deep impression that something was very wrong, borne in upon him by the last sentence in the final paragraph of an instruction issued by higher authority to divisions, including the 33rd Division. This document, entitled 'Offensive Policy of XV Corps', ended with the admonition: 'The value of patrol work, wiring, and raids, in raising the confidence of our infantry, and giving them a feeling of superiority over the enemy cannot be too strongly emphasised; *casualties in carrying out these duties must be accepted.*' It was this statement 'casualties must be accepted' (the italics are mine) which crystallised Bernard's determination. Every soldier knows, none better, that in battle casualties will occur and are generally inevitable to a greater or lesser degree. But that is not to say in written orders, bluntly, and in so many words without qualification of any kind, that casualties are a secondary consideration. The time was the prelude to this third battle of Ypres which raged for four long months from July to October. Small wonder then that in writing of the events of 1917, in his final book *A History of Warfare*, Bernard said, 'It was normal for orders to be given that attacks were to be delivered regardless of loss.' A

determination to keep casualties to the minimum possible remained with him throughout his career.

About this time Bernard was transferred as GSO2 to Headquarters IX Corps under General Herbert Plumer, where he
remained for twelve months. It was during his service on the staff
in France that he was wounded again, for the third time in three
years, but on this occasion not seriously and he was not off duty on
account of it. It happened, as he described it, 'When I was running
about in Bourlon Wood, but it was only a flesh wound in the left
hand, caused by a shell splinter, and I was not impeded by it.'

Meanwhile in the middle of the First World War Father made
another of his long visits to the United States and Canada. He
went in September 1916, this time taking Winsome with him, and
did not return until over two months later. On this tour he did not
see my brother Donald, who had joined the Canadian army and
was then serving in France, in the front line at Arras with the 29th
Battalion of Canadian Infantry, where he met Bernard who was
then a brigade-major; the two brothers had not seen each other
since they were schoolboys at St Paul's. Travel by sea in 1916 was
becoming very hazardous; but the convoy system had still not
become compulsory and passenger ships, each armed with one
gun manned by naval ratings, generally sailed singly, relying for
their protection against submarine attack mainly by keeping a
zigzag course, with abrupt and constant changes. However Father's
outward voyage was uneventful and on arrival in the United States
he was able to resume the friendships he had made during his
previous visit there in 1907, particularly with the Russells at
Edgerstoune whose kindness and hospitality were boundless.
'Cloud Capped', the house of the Randalls at Baltimore, became
almost another home for him. It was while Father was in New
York that he had, for someone living in London at that time, an unusual experience. He had been preaching at the Cathedral, to a very
large congregation, and had taken the opportunity to speak his
mind about Germany and the need for American participation with
the Allies. The United States had not yet declared war, though she
was close to it at that stage. As Father, still wearing his cassock,
was walking in the cathedral after the service, among crowds of

people who had come to hear an English bishop preach, he suddenly felt his hand seized from behind. Turning round he saw it was a big, handsome, well dressed man who had got hold of his right hand and was clearly in no mood to let go of it. This person was also apparently very angry, and said loudly that Father had 'desecrated the House of God' by speaking from the pulpit as he had done, was unworthy of his position and office and should be ashamed of himself. He spoke perfect English but finally gave the reason for his outburst when he declared himself to be a German, and added that no country had the right to crush another country! Coming from a 'Hun', as all Germans were described in the time of that war, this was a bit much for the Bishop! Of course to make a scene in a cathedral in which he had just been preaching would have been discourteous to his American hosts, to say the least of it. But Father, although he was then sixty-nine, had certainly not lost his strength of wrist, derived from his skill at bowling in his cricketing days. He was by now very close up to this Hun, so, twisting his wrist with all his force he savagely wrenched his hand away; however it happened that, in doing so, his fist collided with a very important part of the Hun's anatomy. The Bishop said afterwards that he was always very glad his hand had accidentally come in contact with the man, who apparently then disappeared in the crowd and was not seen again.

Father returned to England in the Cunard steamer *Carpathia*, leaving Winsome behind to stay with the Randalls until Christmas, as Una had done when she had accompanied him to the United States nine years earlier. It was November 1916 and the last days of the great British offensive at the battle of the Somme in France, where the casualties on each side were very great. At sea one morning, after reading the news received by wireless, father recorded the following:

'I have spent a couple of hours with the skipper (Capt. Prothero) smoking in his cabin, a charming apartment. He showed me the wireless news, amazingly good, our great offensive, 7,000 prisoners, two battalions of Germans annihilated. . . .'

Those who read these words may think it somewhat strange that a bishop of the Church of England should glory in such destruction of human life. But in the protracted nightmare of the First World War there were very few, on either side, who did not subscribe to this philosophy.

During his return voyage across the Atlantic Father thought much on all these matters; and perhaps because the chance of destruction from submarine attack was so obviously never far distant, his mind turned back and ranged a great deal over the past, particularly about New Park and our own family. With his great sense of vision, and his passionate belief in a life to come, he wrote: 'I think silent musings always bring the unseen nearer to us, and almost lift the curtain which divides us from a life so unreal to some, so real and near to others.' On this journey, which during that war took fourteen days from New York to Liverpool, he developed these thoughts and wrote a paper, for his family, which he entitled 'Our Garden'. In it he described his experiences one Easter morning at New Park, many years earlier, in 1907, when he had come over from Chiswick by himself in order, as he said, to have time to think, after a period of very hard work. He began his paper with these words: 'So I found myself alone in the old home for a few days, breathing its memories, dwelling upon the past, looking once more upon the portraits and possessions of past generations.' He then went on to tell how he went into the garden, and there he suddenly came upon groups of people who seemed to love the place and this deprived him of any sense of fear or of wonder; clearly he had a tie with them. Soon he saw the group included one, dressed in a coat of a past age, with knee breeches and a high cravat, who it seemed to him must be our great-great-grandfather, Samuel Montgomery, who built our home, with his wife Ann. These two left the garden and came to the front door where they stopped before the long line of names cut on the bark of one of the trees. 'And I planted those trees,' he said. Then he counted the names. 'Nine children, Ann: and we have had eight.' Next Father saw one who was surely his own grandfather Samuel Law Montgomery, Rector of Moville, and he found he was actually able to converse with him, about the home which he had loved so well and the family church which did not exist in his day. At length the old Rector of Moville asked: 'And what is your own work?' 'I am a Bishop.' Upon that the old Rector made a full and courtly bow and passed on along the terrace. Finally he saw his father, Sir Robert, walking on the terrace, in his well-remembered dress, the grey suit, with high white collar, Inverness cape and grey hat; but then a veil, a mist, grew, and father wrote: 'I dared not stay, nor look any longer. It was holy ground. . . . I awoke, and lo! I had been dreaming. But I was happy and I hoped that such a dream, mingled with the memories of home and ancestry, might give me strength for the tasks which had still to be accomplished.'

In his book *The Path to Leadership* (there are many who will agree this is the best of his writings) the Field-Marshal named his final chapter 'The Epilogue – In My Garden'. In this he describes an experience, written round the time, one fine and hot summer afternoon, when he was alone in his garden at the Mill – the house he created after the 1939–45 war was over and which he loves so well. The afternoon sun was hot and it was difficult to keep awake. Suddenly he saw the Bishop, standing on the bank of the mill stream, and dressed in the clothes he always wore when tramping over the hills in Donegal, or fishing the mountain streams – a grey Norfolk jacket and trousers and carrying a shepherd's staff. The Bishop saw Bernard in the garden and smiled; but Bernard wrote, 'I did not approach closer, it was holy ground.' Then Father spoke: 'You have a lovely garden; it is different from ours in the old Irish home, better kept and tidier. But you were always neat and tidy in your habits and in your thinking, and that has helped you in your military life. I have watched your career as a soldier. You chose well and you reached the top of your profession.' Then Bernard wrote: 'And I awoke, and lo! I had been dreaming. But I was happy, and I hoped that such a dream, mingled with memories of the father I had so worshipped in his lifetime, might give me strength for the remaining years of my life.' The theme and the setting of both experiences, one in 1907 and the other well over half a century later, are very similar. An experienced reader, a cynic maybe, might at once give credit for author's licence. Others, perhaps the type referred to by Dean Farrar as his 'gentle reader', may take pleasure in a strange coincidence with evidence to justify the saying 'like father like son'.

In July 1918 Bernard was appointed as GSO1 of the 47th Infantry Division with the rank of Lieutenant-Colonel. There were just four months before the First World War was to end and promotion for the future Field-Marshal had been rapid indeed. He had begun the war as a subaltern; when it ended four years later he was a Lieutenant-Colonel and the senior staff officer in an infantry division. Many regular officers in the British army will probably agree that of all staff appointments that of GSO1 of a division is probably the most rewarding. For an infantry division is a relatively small and compact formation in which the GSO1 in particular will have to deal, and cope personally, with the employment of virtually every weapon in the armament of the British soldier. Furthermore, because of the compact nature of his formation, he still retains that vital and direct contact with troops which at higher staff levels tends to become lost. For Bernard therefore his final appointment of the war was all that he could have wished for, and he made full use of it. The 47th was a London division composed of London-based regiments, including battalions of that famous regiment the Royal Fusiliers, and in these last four months of the fighting in France the future Field-Marshal soon recognised their sterling value. Good fighting troops were particularly needed in this final phase because the course of the war, on the Western Front, had finally turned in favour of the Allies. Above all mobility had returned to the battlefield, due almost entirely to the intelligent employment of tanks in co-operation with other arms, especially the infantry. The March 1918 offensive of the Germans, mounted by Ludendorff without the use of tanks against General Sir Hubert Gough's Fifth Army, had failed and, from July onwards, the enemy was on the run. For Bernard in particular this was a most testing time, and especially for his own ideas which he proceeded to develop in his own way, with, as it turned out, astonishingly good results, the final dividends of which did not appear until the 1939–1945 war. He never forgot his experiences as a Platoon Commander, at the battle of Le Cateau four years earlier, when his battalion was completely cut off from its Brigade Headquarters and could receive no orders of any kind from higher authority. As a Brigade-Major he had been much impressed by the great difficulty of keeping contact with forward battalions, and the need, incredible as it seemed to him, to have to resort to carrier pigeons as a means of maintaining vital communications. Something, he decided, must be done about this and the ideal opportunity presented itself in the 47th (London) Division, especially with the return of mobility and the end of perpetual trench warfare. In those days the radio telephone (R/T) had not yet been invented, but wireless communications (W/T) had begun to appear in the armed forces and wireless sets, heavy and cumbersome by comparison with their counterpart of our times, were being issued to Formation Headquarters. Bernard seized this heaven-sent opportunity to supersede the out-of-date, slow, and expensive systems of communicating with forward units by runner or mounted orderly, or by ground telephone line which was equally liable to disruption. The method he introduced in the 47th Division is best told in his own words, quoted from his *Memoirs:*

'We finally devised a system of sending officers with wireless sets up to the headquarters of the leading battalions, and they sent messages back by wireless. The difficulty in those days was to get reliable sets which could be carried by a man and would give the required range. . . . This was the germ of the system I developed in the 1939–45 war, and which finally produced the team of liaison officers in jeeps operating from my Advanced Tactical Headquarters. In 1918 in the 47th Division we were groping in the dark and trying to evolve ideas which would give increased efficiency to our operations.'

Looking back it is interesting to reflect that the idea and impetus underlying the formation of the Field-Marshal's famous team of liaison officers, who operated so successfully in the 1939–45 war did not have their origin in the 1940s. It had all begun in France and was, literally, sparked off by the GSO1 of the 47th London Division about a quarter of a century earlier.

For my brother the First World War ended at La Tombe, near Tournai, when he personally made the following brief entry in the *War Diary* of the 47th (London) Division:

> *11.11.18* Early in the morning news was received from Corps HQ that hostilities were to cease at 1100. This was communicated to the troops. Divisional HQ moved to La Tombe in the morning opening at 10.30.
>
> The Divisional Commander will hold a conference at 10.00 on 12th Nov., for all C.O.s, on the Duties of Commanding Officers during the Armistice.
>
> (sd)   B L Montgomery
Lt Col. G.S.
47th Division

In Germany, soon after the Armistice, Bernard was given his first experience of real independent command. A commanding officer was urgently needed for the 17th Battalion Royal Fusiliers near Cologne, and Bernard was given the appointment. There are some who think that of all the tasks in the army probably that of a battalion commander is the most difficult to make a real success of, for several main reasons. In the first place everything depends on you and you alone; you must have your men's trust and respect, including their respect for your professional knowledge and ability, and you must be known personally to them all. But if, in the process, you fall for the temptation also to exercise direct command over all the companies, as well as being commanding officer, you will merely stifle all initiative and you will be a failure because you took away from your subordinates the responsibility that should be theirs. Finally it is quite certain that if you are rated a failure as a regimental commanding officer you will get no further in your profession. But none of these risks presented any problem for the future Field-Marshal. As he said, 'I had already seen so many examples of how not to command a battalion'! But it was not in fact an easy assignment because, as in all the many battalions raised during the war, the great majority of the other ranks were now conscripts eager for disbandment; they had had enough of soldiering and wanted to forget it all as soon as possible. This was just the sort of problem which brought out all the energy and inspiration of the new commanding officer of the 17th Royal Fusiliers, and he decided there was only one way to solve it: 'The men must be kept interested, and that means sound training, but not just routine stuff day after day; there must be variety of every kind, including discussions and advice about their return to civilian life.' This was his directive to the company commanders – and it worked. Meanwhile in April 1919 he had been posted back to a staff appointment as GSO2 at Cologne with the Headquarters of the Army of the Rhine. As always happens after a major war when the process of demobilisation begins and armies are drastically reduced in size, it meant dropping a rank, with of course its pay, and Bernard became a Major again. But that did not worry him so much as the fact that he was convinced he must obtain a nomination for the Staff College at Camberley. The competitive examination for entry to the college had not yet been re-introduced, following the end of the war, and instead there were to be two courses, in 1919 and 1920, with admission to each dependent solely on nomination by the War Office. Much to Bernard's chagrin his name had not appeared in the final list for admission to the 1919 course. It was now nearly half way through that year and the candidates for the 1920 course would by this time have been selected; or at any rate have been reduced to a short list from among the very large number of officers recommended by army commanders both at home and overseas. This was Bernard's thinking on the matter, and he decided that action was urgent and imperative, more particularly as he knew many of his contemporaries were attending the 1919 course. If he missed the following one it would indeed be a serious setback in his view.

The story of how Bernard obtained his nomination to Camberley has often been told. How he made a personal approach to his own army commander, General Sir William Robertson, during a tennis party at the latter's house near Cologne, and persuaded him that he, Bernard, must attend the 1920 course. It was of course a very bold way to set about it and full of dire risks. He might so easily have been snubbed and told that it was for higher authority, certainly not a second-grade staff officer, to decide such matters. But in the event he had gone to the right man for his general, later to become Field-Marshal Sir William Robertson, Bt, GCB, GCMG, GCVO, DSO, had begun life in the army by enlisting as a trooper in a British cavalry regiment. Subsequently, by a combination of persistence, courage, sheer merit and professional ability, he had risen through all the ranks to become CIGS, and finally emerged at the summit of his profession. Furthermore he had done all this without the advantages of social standing or financial wealth, both of which, in those far off days, were still important assets in any walk of life. With this background it is perhaps not surprising that Sir William should have agreed to help a major on his staff who had the courage, and above all the self-confidence, to ask him to intervene personally at the War Office in order to obtain a nomination for the Staff College. So it worked and Bernard went to Camberley in January 1920. Looking back, with this in mind, I have always felt some surprise that many years later Field-Marshal Robertson's eldest son, now General Lord Robertson of Oakridge, GCB, GBE, KCMG, KCVO, DSO, MC, was not fully supported by Bernard when the time came to select a very senior officer for the highest appointment in the army – that of CIGS and the professional head of the service. Lord Robertson was an extremely able Sapper officer. He had been a student under Bernard at the Staff College and head of his administration in the Eighth Army, from where he had become Chief Administrative Officer of 15 Army Group under Field-Marshal Earl Alexander in Italy. Later on he returned to Bernard as his deputy in the military Government of Western Germany and then himself became Commander-in-Chief of the British zone. Finally he was Commander-in-Chief in the Middle East from 1950–53, when Bernard was with NATO in Paris. On the face of it it would appear hard to find an officer with a more distinguished military career, but when it came to choosing the next CIGS Bernard visited London to advise that Robertson should not be given the post. He told me, 'Robertson was not the right man for the job. He was a first-class administrator, quite outstanding in that field and probably the best administrative staff officer there has ever been. However I was determined he should not become CIGS.' One may perhaps be permitted to wonder what precise reasons he had for this judgement. When I tackled him on the issue he only smiled, and said, 'All Sappers are mentally constipated'! But was he not perhaps right after all? For Lord Robertson went on to become Chairman of the British Transport Commission, where he remained for a long time with very great benefit for industry generally, and for the people of his country who owe him a great deal.

As a student at the Staff College Bernard soon drew the attention of the directing staff (the DS) to himself. This was not however on account of his professional knowledge and qualifications, which might well have been presumed, but because, with a group of other like-minded students, he was, in the DS view, in the category of officers sometimes described as a 'bloody menace'! For Bernard was the leader of a group who were convinced that insufficient thought and practice was being given to the need for a radical change in virtually all military matters; in their view there must be no return by the army to what they regarded as the conservatism and complacency of pre-1914. The Commandant of the Staff College at that time was Major-General W. H. Anderson,* CB, DSO, who had been an infantry officer in the Cheshire Regiment. The Directing Staff included two men who later became very famous. One of these was an Irishman, the late Sir John Dill, who had begun his army life in the Leinster Regiment and was eventually made a Field-Marshal and CIGS before his untimely death in Washington during the 1939–45 war. The other was a Sapper officer who had already won the VC at Neuve Chapelle in December 1914; this was Lieutenant-General Sir Philip Neame, KBE, CB, DSO who became a Corps Commander in the last war, and added to his distinction by winning a gold medal for rifle shooting in the Olympic Games. The students on the course included a future VCIGS and Army Commander, Lieutenant-General Sir Robert Haining, and that very famous Commander-in-Chief of the 1939–45 war, General Sir Bernard Paget. Another of the students

* Later General Sir Hastings Anderson, KCB, DSO.

was a close personal friend of Bernard, Arthur Grasett, a Sapper officer, who became a Lieutenant-General and a Corps Commander. Also there was Captain Victor Fortune,★ an officer of the Black Watch who would assuredly have gone very far in his profession had he not been taken prisoner in Normandy at the disaster of St Valéry-en-Caux on 13th June 1940. It seems right to give these details now because my brother, in his *Memoirs*, rather tends to disparage the level of professional ability of his fellow students at the Staff College in 1920. As he told me later, 'Very few of them were any good.' But this was manifestly unfair and inaccurate, as events showed. However, to do him justice, he did add in his *Memoirs* about himself at that time, 'I must admit that I was critical and intolerant; I had yet to learn that uninformed criticism is valueless.'

During his year at Camberley Bernard invited me to stay with him there for two nights. I cannot remember why this occurred though I suspect my parents had a hand in it. I was then a schoolboy at St Paul's, and it was the half-term holiday when no doubt Father and Mother were extremely busy (as they always were) and were reluctant to have additional commitments at that particular moment. It was the winter term and my thoughts were concentrated on rugby football to the virtual exclusion of everything else. Nevertheless certain memories of that visit have remained permanently etched on my mind. Of course I loved all the meals in the officers' mess, after the comparative restrictions of food rationing during the war just ended, and I was impressed and overawed by the glitter of the uniforms, and the silver and other appointments all round me. But what I recall most vividly was the apparent very strong influence that Bernard had on his fellow students, including his infectious sense of humour. Unlike the custom in some regimental messes, where 'shop' was not mentioned at meals or in the ante-room, the students frequently discussed their work and the various exercises set for them by their instructors. I remember Bernard being asked so often 'What about that paper we were given last week? Do you think it's difficult?

★ The late Major-General Sir Victor Fortune, KBE, CB, DSO, Commander 51st Highland Division.

What do you make of it? It looks pretty tricky to me', or words to that effect. Bernard's reply would be 'Oh! that one. I've done it and jolly good it is too! In any case the DS have got it all wrong. They just don't know the answers!'

Soon after graduating from the Staff College in December 1920 Bernard was appointed as Brigade-Major of the 17th Infantry Brigade at Cork in Southern Ireland. This was a key appointment as, in strength, the brigade with its nine battalions, all under the command of Colonel-Commandant H. W. Higginson, CB, DSO, was in reality a division with a correspondingly large area of operational control over many counties in the South. Ever since the execution by the British of Sir Roger Casement in 1916, there had been revolt, with much violence, all over Ireland. The Sinn Fein movement was pressing Lloyd George's Government at Westminster for a political decision on the future of Ireland, and the Southern Irish, as so often before, and since, were resorting to arson and murder in an attempt to blackmail the British Government and people. They thought that Great Britain, weary of war after the ordeal of 1914–18, might well give in to such pressure, if it was exerted strongly enough in terms of assassination, robbery and destruction of property, including the killing or maiming of innocent women and children. But the Government at Westminster had not given in and martial law had been declared in areas where it was thought essential to suspend civil rule. However, early in 1922 Lloyd George's Government made history by creating the independent Irish Free State of twenty-six counties, in which a Provisional Government was formed and martial law brought to an end. But this by no means brought peace to the land as the Irish Republican Army remained in virtual control of the South, and British troops were still needed there in large numbers. This was the overall situation, in broad terms, when Bernard arrived as Brigade-Major at Cork early in 1921. He remained there almost one and a half years. What happened during that period is best described in an extract from a letter he wrote to Father early in 1922:

17th Inf. Brigade
Cork
1.3.22

My dear Father,

It is very difficult to find out how long they intend to keep us here in the south of Ireland. The situation is really impossible; we have had two officers murdered in the last fortnight; ambulances and lorries are held up almost daily by armed men and the vehicles stolen; the result is we now send armed escorts with every vehicle or body of men that leaves barracks, just as we did when the war was at its height. It is really more dangerous now than it was then, as we are now powerless; then we had martial law behind us and could do what we liked. The Provisional Government have no authority of any sort or description here; the south is entirely ruled by the Irish Republican Army who publicly state by proclamation in the local papers that they owe no allegiance to the Provisional Government, and that they adhere to the Republic. We have to be very careful as a false step would be a match that would set the whole country ablaze again. Our policy is that we do not care what any one does, or what happens, so long as the troops are left alone and are not interfered with; any civilian, or Republican soldier or policeman, who interferes with any officer or soldier *is shot at once*. The result is we are now left alone. Three armed civilians held up one of our closed cars the other day; they thought it was empty but for the chauffeur, and that they would be able to steal it. Unluckily for them there were three British officers inside it; they opened fire at once through the windows with revolvers; two of the civilians were killed, but the third escaped. It was a good lesson for them and they will think twice in future before they try similar hold-ups.

The I.R.A. get no pay; there is no money to pay them with. They are now living in all the barracks in out-stations vacated by us. When they want money they go round the town and forcibly collect 5/- a head from every resident; this happens once a week.

It really is most degrading for us soldiers having to stay on here; and I shall be heartily glad to see the last of the people and of the place. Our presence here undoubtedly acts as a deterrent on the more extreme of the I.R.A., and I am sorry for the loyalists and others when we are gone. They get persecuted now but it is nothing to what will happen later. I fancy the elections will go against Griffiths & Co, and then there will be a nice mess.

Bolshevism is really the trouble here. No man wants to work when he can live for nothing in the I.R.A., and go round with a revolver when he wants money.

Have you heard the nonsense being rumoured about the burning of Cork? It is complete nonsense. Cork was burnt by K Coy of the Auxiliaries,* and by no one else. A bomb was thrown into a party of them near Cork Barracks one night, wounding 14 of them. They broke out of barracks that night, and by the aid of petrol, etc., set fire to the City Hall and half the shops in Patrick Street.

I hope to get away about 7th April for a month's leave. The Army Golf Championships are on 24th April at Deal, and I want to get in some good practice before then. I shall go and stay at Camberley and practice there. Will you be in Town about 8th April?

Your affectionate son
Bernard.

Surely no one who reads this letter by Bernard, written in Ireland over fifty years ago, can fail to see depicted, a situation which is almost identical with the tragic happenings in the six counties of Ulster that began in 1969. In 1922 the British troops, did not wait to be shot at by the IRA; they fired first and evidently the results of this policy had a most salutary effect. One is tempted therefore to wonder if, notwithstanding all the political involvement, the same results might not have been achieved in 1969, had the British Government of that day been bold enough to act, at once, in a similar way. For Bernard in particular a bold policy was very

---

* The Auxiliaries were a para-military police force, raised by the British Government after the 1914–18 war, and known in Ireland as the 'Black and Tans'. They were famous for their tough and ruthless policy and much hated by the civilian population generally.

satisfying because some six months earlier, in Dublin on another
so-called 'bloody Sunday' (for which the IRA were solely responsible), our first cousin Lieutenant-Colonel Hugh Montgomery,
CMG, DSO, had been brutally murdered. Hugh was the son of
Father's younger brother, the Rev. Ferguson Montgomery, and a
regular officer in the Royal Marines, who was serving as a GSO1
with the Irish Command in Dublin. One Sunday morning the
IRA assassins came to his flat and rang the bell. When Hugh's wife
opened the door they burst in, shot and wounded her, and then
shot her husband; he died shortly afterwards in hospital.

During that summer of 1922 the IRA, as expected, were active
in Inishowen, including Moville. By then our own small Protestant
community had shrunk to become a very small proportion of the
overwhelmingly Roman Catholic majority in Inishowen; there was
no question now of any Protestant Ulster Volunteer Force being
able to exist in Moville. The operation of the Irish Land Acts was
also having its effect on the estates of Protestant land owners in
Ireland, and much of our mountain land had been taken out of
Father's possession, though the Moville Town land was still his
and remains to this day in our family ownership. Culdaff House,
the home of our friends the Youngs, some eight miles from Moville,
had been burnt to ashes by the IRA, who then turned their attention to New Park. Father was in England, and of the family only
Mother was present when late one summer night the IRA came up
the drive, hammered on the front door and demanded entrance.
At the time there was normally only one shotgun in the house, it
belonged to my brother Colin, and it had already been sent down
to the local bank following a warning we had had of what might
happen. Mother duly opened the front door and in came eight
men, none of them local people, who said they wanted arms and
must have them. Although there were no modern firearms then at
New Park there were quite a lot of old muskets and pistols, chiefly
muzzle-loading flintlocks, which Sir Robert had captured in India
and brought back to New Park when he finally retired. These,
with a collection of native *tulwars* (swords) and shields were hung
on the walls of the hall and the main staircase. There were also
some bows and arrows and ferocious-looking wooden clubs, with

iron spikes in them, which father had brought back from the Pacific Ocean Islands; finally Harold had added to this collection a number of African tribal spears and daggers. Altogether therefore there was a quite an armoury in the house, though all of it entirely obsolescent and certainly, as far as the firearms were concerned, very dangerous for any user if he were so foolish as to attempt to fire them. Having searched the house and found no guns the IRA proceeded to help themselves from this motley collection of ancient weapons which, even at that time, were really museum pieces. They also took away mattresses and blankets from the beds, but nothing more. Mother was apparently quite unmoved by all these happenings. Like so many English women who marry into Irish families she had by this time become more Irish than the Irish, and so she now proceeded to make tea for the raiders! Finally she was given a receipt for all that the men had taken signed 'in the name of the Irish Republican Army'.

Later that summer the IRA came again to Moville and occupied the wharf of the Moville Steamship Company (founded by our family) whose three paddle steamers maintained a daily ferry service to and from Londonderry. The unarmed detachment of the Civic Guard (the police force of the Irish Free State) could do nothing to stop the armed raiders when they boarded the paddle steamer (*S.S. Lady Clare*) as she tied up at the wharf at six o'clock one evening. In addition to taking as much of the vessel's cargo as they wished the IRA men carefully searched all the passengers and confiscated anything they thought would be of value to them. Father had gone to Londonderry that day by the morning boat and was returning in the *Lady Clare* when this incident took place. Strangely, when his turn came to disembark by the gangway the raiders stood back and let him pass unsearched. 'It's all right now, Bishop,' they said. 'Pass along please.' Whether it was just respect for the Church, or father's impressive appearance (he always wore his gaiters and bishop's hat whenever he visited Derry), or a combination of both, which made them leave him alone we never knew.

At the end of May 1922, much to his delight, Bernard was transferred to Plymouth as the brigade major of the Plymouth

Brigade in the 3rd Division. The brigade commander was Brigadier S. E. Hollond, a professional soldier for whom Bernard had much respect and regard, and who, above all else, recognised that in Bernard he had a staff officer of exceptional talent and professional knowledge. Hollond now let his Brigade-Major have his own way in matters generally, and particularly with the policy for training and practice in all units of the brigade. Although the Kaiser's War, as Bernard called the 1914–18 conflict, had ended four years previously this was his first opportunity to apply his own ideas and methods to the training of troops, in England in peace time, in preparation for the next war. His time in Ireland with the Cork Brigade was all spent under virtually active service conditions and he had not been able to apply there the instructional methods he had learnt, or equally questioned, at the Staff College. It was not that he challenged the principles of war as laid down in the *War Office Manual of Field Service Regulations*; but that, as a result of his own study and experience, and particularly his intensive reading of military history and the conduct of war in the past, he had developed very definite ideas about the conduct of any future war. Increasingly he felt that sound training policy and methods, in peace time and to meet all circumstances, were the first essential steps to be taken after the ending of any great war. In his view the army lacked a sound policy for training, and at Plymouth he began his own campaign to achieve one. Above all, he thought, training must always be conducted with sound leadership at the higher levels, and in such a way that both officers and men become interested in what they are told to do; in short they needed inspiration. This was the doctrine which the future Field-Marshal began to put across, as a Brigade-Major at Plymouth, just fifty years ago.

Early in the summer of 1923 Bernard left Plymouth on appointment as GSO2 of the 49th (West Riding) Division with Headquarters at York. This formation was a territorial army division where, as in all TA formations in peace time, the main emphasis was on the training of officers and men of all arms. This suited Bernard very well as a corollary to his efforts at Plymouth, and furthermore, as there was no GSO1 on the TA establishment he was the senior General Staff Officer at the divisional headquarters.

As a bachelor officer he was accustomed to mess life and he therefore asked to be given quarters in the officers' mess of a famous
regiment, the West Yorkshire Regiment, the depot of which was
at York. As so often in life small and purely fortuitous beginnings
turn out to be the forerunner of great and important events. For it
was here that he became acquainted, for the first time, with the
regular army officer who, much later, was to become his Chief of
Staff from the time he took command of the Eighth Army until he
accepted the final surrender of all the German armed forces in
Northern Europe in 1945. Lieutenant F. de Guingand, The West
Yorkshire Regiment, had been posted for a tour of duty at his
regimental depot late in 1922, and had already been there some
months when Bernard came to live in the same mess. Although two
years later each went his separate way and they only met intermit-
tently until the war began, it is true to say that the unique partnership of Bernard and de Guingand had its origin at York in the
officers' mess of the depot of The West Yorkshire Regiment in the
summer of 1923. For each undoubtedly impressed the other in a
way that neither forgot. Bernard, because he has the capacity, so
essential in sound leadership, first of never failing to recognise real
talent, and secondly of being able to isolate it to his own advantage; de Guingand, because he fell under Bernard's spell at York
and, in his turn, had the capacity to recognise genius when he saw
it.

I could not, incidentally, have written this had I not been present
in York during the time in question. That summer I was a cadet in
my last term at Sandhurst and while waiting for the passing-out
results, which determined your regiment and place in the army,
Bernard had invited me to stay with him at York for a few days. It
was his view that I should benefit by 'getting the feel of a good
regiment' before joining the regiment of my choice, the Royal
Warwickshire—there had been no question of my joining any
other. The visit must have made a deep impression on me for even
after this long lapse of time I so well remember the details of it.
Chiefly I recall how de Guingand, although only a subaltern officer
in those days, stood out from the other officers in the mess. When
he was present he dominated discussion, and it was fascinating to

see how he and Bernard took charge, without conscious effort, of the conversation. At the time de Guingand, as an officer of the Depot staff, was concerned with the introduction in local territorial battalions of what was then termed the 'weapon-training cadre'. This project involved the formation of a small team of especially selected and trained officers and non-commissioned officers, who, as specialists and preferably having graduated from the small arms school, would become responsible for the training of NCO instructors in each company or sub-unit. De Guingand was very keen on this and was constantly asking for advice about it, and it was very noticeable how Bernard always responded. He had the gift not only of simplifying a subject but also of making it appear very interesting, however boring it might be to those who had no reason to see the point of it. In this case he was able, as it were, to paint on canvas a picture of the use of infantry weapons, and their employment in minor tactics, in such a way that his audience saw it all developing with increasing interest. Better still, he always managed to find a humorous side to every task, and very few of their discussions did not end without great bursts of laughter. As always he was at his best when helping young officers.

It goes without saying that as a cadet, not yet commissioned, I sat silent and spellbound during those discussions in the officers' mess of the West Yorkshire Regiment. I was equally entertained when I accompanied Bernard on the golf course with de Guingand and others. Looking back at the course of the next war, it is interesting to consider what might or might not have happened if the Montgomery–de Guingand partnership had not been available. Of these two imponderables it seems to me logical, against the background of recorded events, to see at least one particularly unfortunate result which might well have occurred, at a crucial time for the Western Alliance. Bernard was no easy chief to serve, as has so often been told; he could be obstinate to the point of bigotry, particularly if he was convinced he was right but found his views obstructed. Such a time came in Europe at the end of December 1944 when the last major German offensive, under Von Rundstedt in the Ardennes, was being successfully contained. Bernard, not for the first time, had made a direct and personal approach to

Eisenhower with a proposal that full operational direction, control and co-ordination of operations by both the Allied army groups, British and American, should be vested in the Commander-in-Chief 21 Army Group, i.e. in himself. However right and desirable the proposal appeared in the strategic sense, and presumably historians of a future generation should judge finally on this issue, it was clearly one which on political grounds alone was quite unacceptable. With the great preponderance of American forces in Europe the combined Chiefs of Staff (CCS) in Washington, let alone the United States Government, could never have agreed. Furthermore, apparently Eisenhower was about to signal General Marshall, Chairman of the CCS, that, exasperated by Bernard's continued insistence on the need for one Land Forces Commander, he did not feel able to work with Bernard any longer. So the issue now was crystal clear: either Bernard withdrew his proposal, or surely another Commander for 21 Army Group would need to be found. What followed has been most admirably, though far too modestly, described by de Guingand in his book *Generals at War*. Appreciating the urgency and magnitude of the crisis he had flown immediately to SHAEF Headquarters to see Eisenhower, with whom he was on most friendly terms, in order to cool down what was by now a red-hot situation, and so avert the danger. In this he was successful, and it was due to this tactful intervention, followed by his equally tactful handling of Bernard on the issue, that the latter remained in command of 21 Army Group. The particularly unfortunate effect on our armies everywhere, if the British Field-Marshal and Commander-in-Chief had been withdrawn at that time, is so clear that very great credit is due to the Chief of Staff who was able to avert this catastrophe. To do so must have required patience and tolerance, combined with a very strong personality, and great ability to speak clearly and concisely. In all this he was much helped by his personal friendship with General Bedell Smith, Eisenhower's Chief of Staff. The latter's influence probably counted for much as at first neither Eisenhower nor his deputy, Air Marshal Tedder,* were inclined to accept de Guingand's request to defer dispatch of the signal to Washington for

---

* The late Marshal of the Royal Air Force Lord Tedder, GCB, DCL.

7*

twenty-four hours. This gave de Guingand time to visit Bernard at the latter's tactical headquarters and represent to him the real gravity of the situation.

After the war my brother wrote in his *Memoirs* of this incident, and of the time when de Guingand came to him after seeing Eisenhower, 'I decided at once to pipe down.' This laconic statement carried a wealth of compressed meaning; for he then sent a message to Eisenhower assuring him of his full support and acceptance of his (Eisenhower's) decisions. This message was based on a draft already prepared by de Guingand. It was no doubt happenings such as those described in the preceding paragraph that caused the Field-Marshal also to write about de Guingand in his *Memoirs*, 'He was a brilliant Chief of Staff and I doubt if such a one has ever before existed in the British Army or will ever do so again.' Major-General Sir Francis de Guingand, KBE, CB, DSO, as he later became, will, in the judgement of many, find his place in history as the modern counterpart of that most famous Chief of Staff, Marshal of the French Empire Alexandre Berthier, who served his imperial master Napoleon so well and for so long.

It was in the early part of 1925 that my brother left York, on being posted back to his regiment with which he had not served since he was severely wounded in France over ten years earlier. It has always been the custom for officers to return to their regiments after long periods of duty on the staff. Not only is it extremely good for them to serve again with troops, but it is also very good for their regiments to see, and be able to assess, an officer who may have been absent for a long time; especially if he is in the running for appointment as their commanding officer at a later stage. So Major Montgomery went back to his regiment and joined the 1st Royal Warwickshire at the same garrison station, Shorncliffe, and in the same Napier Barracks, where he had taken part in the mobilisation of the battalion for war in August 1914.

When Bernard re-joined his regiment, the 1st Battalion had only just arrived at Shorncliffe following two years' garrison duty at Chatham. The Commanding Officer was Lieutenant-Colonel C. R. Macdonald, CMG, who was an old friend of Bernard's, and had been Adjutant of the battalion when Bernard joined it at

Peshawar as a Second Lieutenant. Macdonald was a popular and charming man. He had been with the regiment in South Africa during the Boer War, but had not seen any active service in the 1914–18 war, which he had spent wholly in New Zealand. He had been sent there to assist in the raising and training of the Dominion's forces, and now, rather naturally with his war experiences limited and conditioned by the Boer campaigns of over twenty years earlier, he was not very up to date in the professional sense. All the key appointments in the battalion were held by the six or seven senior regimental officers who had been commissioned in the first decade of the century, or a little later, and were still imbued, professionally, with the ideas and practice of those times. This is not to say that their like was not found in other regiments of all arms; it certainly was, and, to give them all their right and proper due, they were second to none in their *esprit de corps*, their regard for their regiment and its good name, and their concern for the men under their command. Indeed it was these aspects which chiefly governed their professional life, for they were not, as they themselves were wont to maintain, 'Staff College minded', behind which statement however there was undoubtedly some degree of bias against the p.s.c. officer. None of them had risen to high rank in the 1914–18 war, and one at least had had the misfortune to spend most of that period in a German prisoner-of-war camp. Another of them was a first-class athlete and represented the army in several games; two were excellent horsemen with their thoughts concentrated chiefly on horses and hunting. The middle-rank officers (the junior captains and senior subalterns) had all joined the regiment during the course of the 1914–18 war, or just after; these included quite a number who had been commissioned after considerable service in the ranks, and therefore had perhaps sixteen or more years' service but were still lieutenants at an age, maybe, of thirty-seven. Finally there were the half a dozen junior officers who had no war service, having all left Sandhurst some time after 1918. The troops (the other ranks) were magnificent, with many experienced non-commissioned officers; the Regimental Sergeant-Major, a wonderful man, had recently transferred to the regiment from the Grenadier Guards on promotion to warrant rank.

In the somewhat special circumstances of the mid-1920s Bernard's return to the battalion had a definite impact on the officers' mess. In his outspoken way he soon made clear to all and sundry his very poor opinion of the standard of military training in the battalion, and that this was entirely due to the lack of professional knowledge of the senior officers, and of interest in their work. Looking back over the years, it is not difficult to see that he was quite right. It must be admitted that far too much interest and effort, in all regiments, was diverted to ensuring proficiency in organised games and sport, for and with the troops. The appalling carnage of the war was over, and a perfectly natural reaction had set in. There was much opposition in the mess to Bernard's attitude, and I recall witnessing some bitter slanging matches, with few holds barred. However, not surprisingly, as the months went by, my brother's influence certainly had an effect in the battalion, though this could not have happened without the firm support and co-operation which Colonel Macdonald wisely gave to Bernard from the outset. In the army manoeuvres which were held on Salisbury Plain that year the battalion acquitted itself very well, and memories of past disagreements soon faded quickly.

Bernard's novel and systematic methods of provoking interest in training, particularly among young officers, always paid him dividends. In the spring of that year he organised a tour of the battlefields of Northern France for subaltern officers in the battalion, an attractive feature of which was that it would be free of all cost to the participants. He had obtained sufficient funds for the tour from the Eastern Command Training Grant, and divided the money equally between the four officers who accompanied him; no one was allowed to spend more money than this – I think it was £15, which in those days was not far short of a month's pay for a second lieutenant. The other condition he stipulated, and this perhaps was not so popular, was that the whole tour had to be conducted on bicycles, and no luggage was allowed except that which could be carried on the bicycle. If an officer did not possess a bicycle then he could have the use of an army one – from the battalion stores. This somewhat daunting condition, particularly if you drew an army 'push-bike' (a really dreadful machine, heavy and cumbersome) was accepted by Lieutenants Morley, Bowlby, Poole and myself. One morning the party of five, with Major Montgomery in the lead, duly bicycled from Shorncliffe to Dover where we embarked on the steamer for Ostend. I remember the first hazard we encountered was the ascent of the steep hill on the Dover road just beyond Folkestone, and that on it we certainly did not keep in any military formation! In those days bicycles were not at all light or convenient machines, besides which each of us had a bulky soldier's pack, filled with the clothing, etc., we needed, strapped on the carrier. Bernard had warned us that the tour would be a spartan one, otherwise the money would not suffice. We went third class on the boat to Ostend and stayed each night in small inns, never in hotels. But of course we fed wonderfully and had a marvellous time; often it was all very amusing, though not for all of us. It was Geoffrey Bowlby who suffered: he had recently returned from Nigeria, after some years' secondment to the West African Frontier Force, where he had become a victim to a malignant form of malaria. Unfortunately for him this tour coincided with an attack of that disease. The climax, for him, came on the day when we were approaching Ypres. It was raining hard, about the only day we had any rain, and poor Geoffrey had clearly almost reached the end of his tether. Pedalling painfully he caught up with Bernard, who as usual was in the lead, and said he thought he would have to fall out. We all stopped, and the future Field-Marshal then, I recall, gave him the biggest dressing down any of us had heard for a long time! He ended by saying that Geoffrey could fall out for ten minutes, after which he was to mount and rejoin us at speed! We four then pedalled away and halted about half a mile on. Strange to say Geoffrey then re-appeared, and after that seemed to be very much better!

As a training exercise this bicycle tour was a huge success. We went first to Le Cateau and then re-traced the route the battalion had taken during the retreat from Mons. We visited the site of the battle on that disastrous day, 26th August 1914, when the battalion had suffered so many casualties to no purpose. At each stage we young officers were told to think out and say if we thought an action could have been fought better, and if so, how. Finally we were required to fight the battle again with the greatly increased fire power and equipment available since 1914. We visited St Quentin, Meteren, Ypres, Lille and finally Nieuport on the Flanders coast and saw many signs and sites of the trench-warfare battles of the First World War. Our cash lasted as planned, including a final journey by rail with our loaded bicycles, third class of course, from Lille to Ostend, for by then we were all a little tired of pedalling! The whole exercise took about ten days. Looking back at those months of 1925 when the future Field-Marshal was with his battalion again, it is clear he did an immense amount of work to the great benefit of all ranks. It has always been his contention that his regiment never produced any officers of real distinction from 1908 onwards – except himself; though this is not really a fair or accurate statement! For instance Geoffrey Evans was a subaltern in the battalion at Shorncliffe in those days. He is now Lieutenant-General Sir Geoffrey Evans, KBE, CB, DSO, having been Commandant of the Staff College at Quetta, a Divisional Commander in the 14th Army in Burma, and finally an Army Commander. Archie Nye (the late Lieutenant-General Sir Archibald Nye, GCSI, GCMG, GCIE, KCB, KBE, MC) was also in the regiment in those days, and became VCIGS. Colonel Macdonald lived to a great age, and his son Major-General Ronald Macdonald, CB, DSO, OBE, is now Colonel of the Regiment.

After serving for just under a year with his battalion my brother was appointed an instructor at the Staff College at Camberley, with the temporary rank of Lieutenant-Colonel. Meanwhile, about this time, he had suffered a traumatic shock in a sphere which was quite new to him. By those outside our family it has always been assumed, beyond doubt, that in all Bernard's life there has only been one woman in whom he ever evinced real interest, namely his wife. But this is quite wrong. It was while he was at York that it became a habit for him to have a golfing holiday in the early spring, at Dinard in Brittany, in company with his old friend Colonel Macdonald and his wife. On one such holiday there, just before he went back to Shorncliffe, Bernard met and proposed to a young and charming girl called Betty Anderson. She was a blonde and extremely attractive, and he fell very much in love with her, though this did not overcome the difficulty that she was so much younger than he was; at that time he was in his thirty-eighth year while she was still only seventeen. Betty Anderson's father was then in the Foreign and Political Department of the Government of India, having started life in the Indian army, and he and his wife had come home on leave. Notwithstanding their considerable difference in age my brother was intent on marrying Betty Anderson, and lost no time in making this clear to her parents, who, very wisely, left the whole matter for Betty to decide. Her mother however appreciated that Bernard was a most unusual and interesting man and told her daughter that she must give him a chance and try to get to know him. Some time later when I was at Shorncliffe, and quite by accident, I met Betty Anderson at a dinner party in Folkestone to which we had both been invited. I knew about my brother's infatuation for her but I had no details and she now told me about it. When they first met, she was more interested in music and dancing than in getting married, though she soon realised that Bernard was becoming increasingly attached to her. He had asked her mother if he and Betty could go for walks together in order that he could get to know how she felt about him. Listening to her account of those days showed me once again how dedicated my brother was to his profession, even to the extent of shaping his method of approach in pressing his suit on the girl he wanted to marry. They used to walk round the walls of St Malo, and then through the pine woods and across the dunes down to the sea shore. There Bernard would draw pictures for her in the sand to illustrate his ideas for the employment of armoured fighting vehicles in war. He showed her how he would position his tanks (at that stage still very much a novelty in the British army) to be used in conjunction with infantry and other arms, in order to win the war which he knew, even then, was coming. Against such a background it is perhaps not surprising that Betty Anderson, then aged seventeen, did not accept my brother's proposal. She liked him very much and enjoyed being in his company, and she particularly admired his obviously strong character and personality, including his great ambition amounting to a determination to rise to the top of his profession. But her liking for him was not true love, and she

never could get over the great disparity in their ages, which ruled
out all question of marriage. Knowing this I was not at all surprised, and indeed felt some relief because of the age problem,
when much later at New Park, Mother showed me the letter
Bernard had written to her to say he now knew beyond doubt that
Betty did not love him. His final words were 'It is all over and I
have to accept it.' I feel sure very few people know about this
incident in my brother's life, which is important for three main
reasons. First it shows that, very naturally, he had reached a stage
where he wanted to get married. Secondly, this meant he was now
able to abandon his previous conviction, sincerely held, that to be
really successful in his chosen profession an officer of the regular
army must accept life in a celibate state. So often I have heard him
say, to officers in mess, in his own regiment and elsewhere, 'You
must decide what to do. You cannot marry and be an efficient
officer. If you marry you must realise you will have to give up to
your wife much of the time which you would otherwise need for
the study of your profession; you can't have it both ways.' He used
to add that in any case an army officer should not marry unless and
until he had sufficient financial means to maintain himself, and his
wife, in a manner befitting his profession. Finally, and more important, the fact that he had confided in our mother about this
whole matter, and had written to her at its ending, points to the
growing influence she then had on his life. The days of conflict
with her were over, at any rate for the time being. Meanwhile the
sequel to the events just described was even more important for my
brother.

In January 1926 Bernard went to Switzerland for a skiing holiday, before he joined the Staff College as an instructor, and elected
to stay at the Hotel Wildstrubel at Lenk. He had gone there in the
hope of seeing Betty Anderson once more, in case she had changed
her mind. He knew there were a number of people in the Indian
civil service on leave from India, staying in this hotel, who were all
great friends and had decided to form a joint party for the winter
sports. They included a Mr and Mrs Keane,* Colonel and Mrs
Anderson, Betty Anderson, and a widow, Mrs Betty Carver, with

---

* The late Sir Michael Keane, KCSI, CIE, Governor of Assam.

her two sons then aged eleven and twelve. Bernard was in due course introduced by Betty Anderson to Betty Carver. Looking back at that important stage in my brother's life one cannot help noticing the coincidence of the two 'Bettys' and that the younger introduced the elder. It was many years later in September of last year, 1972, that quite fortuitously I again met Betty Anderson who now lives in London. She reminded me then of those happy carefree days, on the sands at Dinard, when she had been told, but had not really listened to, the future Field-Marshal's plans for winning the next war. Of course she had got married herself about 1930 and spent many happy years in India, where her husband became a sugar planter and where her children grew up.

Late in January 1926 Bernard went back to the Staff College at Camberley, this time as an instructor, and in the summer of 1927 he got married.

Chapter 7

TEN HAPPY YEARS

Not the least of my brother's achievements in the army was the work he did for the Staff Colleges at Camberley and at Quetta in India; it was an unusual distinction to have been an officer on the directing staff of both colleges. When he arrived at Camberley, where he remained for three years until 1929, the Commandant was a Gunner, Major-General Sir William Ironside, later to become a Field-Marshal and Chief of the Imperial General Staff. After about six months Ironside was succeeded by a Sapper officer Major-General Sir Charles Gwynn, who in later years became a great friend of my brother. Looking through the Army List of those days, the late 1920s, one sees the wise manner in which both the directing staff and students had been selected to attend the Staff College. For during his three years at Camberley Bernard found himself working with some of the best officers in the army, of whom at least twenty were to become very famous in the war that followed, and many more were to reach the rank of general officer. The DS included, first and foremost, that remarkable man Alanbrooke. Among the other instructors were not only Paget, Haining and Grasett (all of whom had been students with Bernard) but also that very famous officer of the Cameronians, General Sir Richard O'Connor, besides men like General Sir Henry Pownall, General Sir George Giffard and General Sir Wilfred Lindsell; the last named became a great administrative expert in the 1939–45

war. The list of the students is very interesting too, for it included
so many who were destined to achieve high rank and distinction,
some of them as army or corps commanders under Bernard. Their
names, with the ranks they held when students at Camberley will
surely be recognised even after this long lapse of time.

Major The Hon. H. R. L. Alexander	Field-Marshal Earl Alexander
Captain Miles Dempsey	GOC 2nd Army, 21 Army Group
Captain E. E. Dorman-Smith	DCGS to Auchinleck
Captain A. J. F. Harding	Field-Marshal Lord Harding
Captain Oliver Leese	GOC 8th Army after Montgomery
Major R. L. McCreery	Chief of Staff to Alexander
Major C. W. M. Norrie	Commander 30 Corps
Captain Archie Nye	VCIGS
Captain J. G. des R. Swayne	GOC South Eastern Command after Montgomery
Lieutenant W. G. Templer	Field-Marshal Sir Gerald Templer
Captain D. N. Wimberley	Commander 51st Highland Division

Indian Army

Captain F. W. Messervey	Corps and Army Commander
Captain R. A. Savory	Army Commander
Captain Gertie Tuker	Commander 4th Indian Division

I have listed the Indian army students separately, as it is sometimes
forgotten that the British officers of the old Indian army were
eligible to attend the staff colleges at Quetta or Camberley, as
indeed were the British army officers.

Having colleagues of this calibre, either on the DS or as students,
suited my brother very well because it made it easier for him to put

across his own ideas on the conduct of the next world war, for which he thought it essential his country should prepare. Equally important he was able, at Camberley, to give full rein to his undoubted ability as a teacher. There must be few of the students who were at the Staff College when Bernard was their instructor, and later also at Quetta, who did not acclaim his reputation as a teacher; particularly his ability to impart knowledge to others in a simple way, which was not only interesting but also easy to understand. When I had recorded these words I remembered I had already written in almost identical fashion about our grandfather Dean Farrar. I saw that early in Chapter 3 I had written about the great Dean: 'His knowledge was immense and he was fortunate in being able to impart that knowledge in a simple manner, so that his audience, in colloquial terms, shouted for more. He was never at a loss in satisfying that demand.' It is easy therefore to see from where Bernard got his teaching ability. It derived chiefly from his Farrar blood, of that there can be no doubt. Standing back, as it were, and looking at my brother in the year 1926, the picture that emerges is worth more than a glance. He is in his thirty-ninth year and a professional soldier with eighteen years' service in the army. Six of these years, if employment in Ireland is included, have been spent mainly on active service, during which he was awarded the DSO and the Croix de Guerre and mentioned six times in dispatches. He was severely wounded but is quite fit again, though half his right lung is non-effective. He has had considerable experience both as a regimental officer and on the staff and has graduated at the Staff College. He is now a member of the directing staff at Camberley, and, as such, becoming well known in the army as an officer of considerable talent and ability, with, if he plays his cards right, a very successful career in store for him. His record includes a reputation for being an ardent reformer, in the sense that he claims much was wrong in our conduct of the 1914–18 war; the mistakes made then, over a wide field, must not in his view be repeated in the next world war, for which there is much need to start preparing now. In his opinions on such matters he shows a definite tendency to be obstinate, and he will not give way in argument to the views of others, even his seniors. On the other hand his own views clearly carry much weight and meet with respect, especially when presented by himself. He is generally very popular, particularly with his subordinates who appreciate his perpetual and infectious sense of humour. He is certainly not well off, but is financially independent and insists on comfortable surroundings for himself and those he works with. At this particular stage he does not go to church and does not appear to have religious convictions or practice, though he is definitely not agnostic. He is a bachelor and, on the face of it to most of the people who know him well, very much a confirmed one and not likely to get married.

From the picture drawn in the preceding paragraph it is clear that, by the time my brother went to Camberley as an instructor, both heredity and environment had already played their full part in the moulding of his character and personality. Only future events, and the influence of new friendships and new experiences, would be likely to have any material effect on his outlook and attitude generally. Over the next eighteen months fate stepped in and confronted him with those very issues, all new to him and in no way military, and required him to make a decision. Briefly this was: should he, or should he not get married, having already had one setback in that connection? He had first met his future wife early in 1926 during that winter sports holiday at Lenk in Switzerland. Betty Carver's first husband, a Sapper, had been killed at Gallipoli in 1915. She had two sons, both then at preparatory school age, and it was probably this in the first place, more than anything else, that brought them close together. Bernard had always liked helping young people and now he spent much time teaching these two boys the rudiments of skating and skiing. This naturally drew their mother's attention to him, particularly as both boys responded readily to his offer to help them. Betty's maiden name was Hobart, her brother being a regular soldier (nickname Hobo)* who later became so well known in the army as an ardent supporter of the role of the armoured fighting vehicle in the modern land battle, including amphibious warfare. He was a genius with an unusual capacity for invention and, fortunately for the British army, very far sighted in his appreciation of how the fruits of his research and

* Major-General Sir Percy Hobart, KBE, CB, DSO, MC.

development could best be given practical application on the battlefield. He was to work very closely with Bernard during the invasion of Europe, for it was the latter, more than anyone else, who realised the full value of his inventions. Betty Carver was about the same age as my brother, but otherwise utterly different from him in every conceivable way, except one. She also was the fortunate possessor of a very keen sense of humour, matching his in its range and scope; in fact she was always laughing, at people, events and life generally, and in a manner which was highly infectious. In appearance she was dark and vivacious, with a high forehead, wide-spaced grey eyes, a large nose and full mouth. Not exactly good looking one would say, but unquestionably a very charming woman and liked by all. Perhaps her greatest attribute was the fact that she could laugh at my brother's eccentricities, and he never minded, because they were devoted to each other. In our family she was universally popular, we all loved her, and our parents thought the world of her. Of her two sons, who became Bernard's step-sons, John Carver, the elder one, resembles his mother in many ways; he also is dark and vivacious with a great sense of humour and prone to laughter. Dick Carver is somewhat different, and in his make-up probably owes more to his father whom none of us knew. He is the quiet clever type but still with much of his mother's great sense of humour, and certainly with all her sense of values.

It may well be asked how two such utterly different people as the future Field-Marshal and Betty Carver ever came to get married. Her father had been in the Indian Civil Service and came from a family with industrial interests in the north of England. Before she met my brother she had never 'lived a military life' and was entirely ignorant of military matters. To make their disparity even wider she was a woman of considerable culture and talent, and well versed in the arts, which Bernard was certainly not, except for the art of war. She was well read in aesthetic art and was herself a painter of some merit, in both oil and water colour; she also painted on ivory and had done some charming miniatures, and was accomplished in sculpture, in wood. In short it would appear difficult to find two people of greater disparity: one a soldier, on the face of it already married irrevocably to his profession and with few, if any, interests outside the military sphere: the other an artist, able to paint portraits, landscapes or other subjects with equal facility, and possessing a highly developed sense of colour. Her first husband had been killed in war, and so rather naturally the profession of arms was repugnant to her. She lived in a charming house on the bank of the Thames at Chiswick Mall, a relatively short distance away from our own old Chiswick home. Her friends and neighbours were mostly painters or writers and people whose tastes and interests matched her own. They included A. P. Herbert who lived nearby in Hammersmith Terrace and whose literary and political reputation became so famous and Dick Shepherd, the famous Rector of St Martin-in-the-Fields. It was into this circle, so alien to my brother in every respect, that he dropped early in 1926. The effect both on himself and them was stupendous and needs little imagination to envisage. But it did not deter him and he pursued his courtship accordingly, assisted, there is no doubt, by men of vision such as A. P. Herbert and Dick Shepherd. These two, with their wives and families, were only too glad to welcome Bernard into the circle of their friends and acquaintances. In the year immediately preceding his marriage a new world began to develop in front of Bernard; a world of people for whom the armed forces counted little, if at all, and yet were clearly intelligent, hard working and highly talented. The memory of this was to stand him in good stead in the years ahead.

As so many men have found in their lives my brother had no difficulty in making his decision to give up his bachelor life. It may have taken him some time to reach that point for he had much to consider, not least professionally, and he never completed any important task without first making an appreciation, in the military sense. In his first two years as an instructor at Camberley his ideas on the conduct of future war, particularly the training of infantry and on vital issues such as the exercise of command and leadership, had not yet become finalised. That stage came later and was given full impetus during his period as Chief Instructor at the Quetta Staff College. With the benefit of hindsight it seems strange, almost unaccountable, that Bernard as late as the early 1930s was a little wary of the efficacy of operating on the battlefield at night. But then those were the days when 'night operations', as they were still described in the official training manuals, were regarded as relatively unusual, a particular technique to be adopted only in special circumstances for limited periods. No doubt it was the aftermath of those long years of trench warfare when the power of the machine gun (able to fire effectively on fixed lines for long periods in conditions of fog or darkness) had so dominated the battlefield that induced and perpetuated this view. But otherwise my brother's thoughts were forming steadily during the period immediately preceding his marriage. In particular he was preaching his doctrine for staff officers of Foresight, Accuracy and Speed. Equally important he was coming to recognise and appreciate the absolute importance of wise and sound decision in the selection of commanders at all levels. So it was not until after a second visit to Lenk in January 1927, when Betty Carver and her two sons were there again, that my brother finally appreciated he had fallen in love, this time irrevocably. For her part Betty Carver was equally in love with Bernard but she loved him, intensely, for what he was as a man and certainly not as a soldier. It was perhaps this fact that, later on after their marriage, so endeared her to the many wives of army officers, particularly those serving under Bernard, whom she met during her married life; they all seemed to love her, just as we all did.

After leaving their preparatory school John and Dick Carver went to Charterhouse, and one summer day in 1927 my brother took Betty there by car from London. It was the annual school speech day and sports meeting so Betty naturally wanted to be there, and so also did Bernard who by this time was much attached to the two boys. Up till now Bernard, in his courtship, had made no mention of marriage, though reticence was not exactly his custom. They got engaged on that day, and I have always remembered Bernard telling me about it later on; his account, so simple and charming, seems to illustrate them both in a delightful manner. It had been a beautiful June day and at the close of the sports meeting, as the evening drew on, the two boys went off to change leaving their mother and Bernard alone together. These two were walking round the school buildings and presently found themselves in the fives courts; there was no one else there and they were both silent for a while, until suddenly Betty said 'I don't think we ought to see each other again.' Bernard's reply was instant: 'Don't be silly, I love you.' Betty then burst into tears, and that, as Bernard said 'finished it, we were engaged'. They motored back to London that evening a very happy couple, as indeed they remained until the day of her tragic death. Of course the news of their engagement, when it was announced in *The Times*, met with a great deal of astonishment and was widely talked about, particularly in army circles and in our own family. De Guingand, whose sense of humour matched my brother's, was then serving with the King's African Rifles, and he probably expressed the thoughts of many in the telegram which, on hearing the news, he sent to Bernard. In his book *Operation Victory* de Guingand wrote as follows about this telegram:

'One of his [Montgomery's] maxims was that "You cannot make a good soldier and a good husband". Some years later when serving in East Africa with another officer in my regiment who was at our Depot during Montgomery's stay, we were shaken to read in *The Times* the announcement of his engagement. We then and there sent him a cable saying: "Which is it to be, the soldier or the husband?" We received no answer, but time showed that he excelled at both.'

The marriage of Lieutenant-Colonel and Mrs B. L. Montgomery took place on 27th July 1927, about a month after the engagement was announced. Their marriage service was held in the beautiful old parish church of Chiswick which stands on the Mall and, with its early fifteenth-century tower, is such a well-known landmark on the riverside. The service was conducted by Father, assisted by my elder brother Colin who by that time had been ordained and was curate of Northfleet near Gravesend. Both Bernard and Betty wanted a quiet wedding, with only the family and a few close friends present, so no formal invitations to attend were issued. Otherwise all the arrangements of every kind were made personally by my brother who was clearly in his element in doing so, and no one else was allowed any say in the matter. The service at the church was to be held at twelve noon but none of those attending it were told where to go for the party, or reception, generally held after such an event. My brother had asked me to be his best man, and when I inquired about this, and other relevant issues, I was told, 'All the arrangements have been completed and will be made clear in due course.' I was also left in no doubt that my duties, as best man, were to be confined strictly to the holding, and proffering, of the wedding ring at the church service. As Bernard told me: 'You will have nothing else to do, and don't make a muck of it; put the ring in your pocket and be very careful not to drop it!' As the date of the wedding drew near I was often asked, as the best man, where the reception was being held, but I could only reply as I had been told, namely that we should all know in due course; I wondered if they really believed me!

On the night before the wedding day there was no question of a customary bachelor dinner party for my brother and some of his old friends. On the contrary Bernard had arranged that he and his bride-to-be should dine together at his club in London, then the Junior United Service in King Charles Street, with myself as best man and his step-sons-to-be, John and Dick Carver. I do not recall much of that evening except I was instructed to report at the Junior United Service, where Bernard was staying, punctually the next morning at eleven o'clock. I therefore duly turned up, at the appointed time, to meet my brother and we both drove down together, in his car, to Betty's house on the Mall just opposite the island of Chiswick Eyot. This pretty little house was later entirely destroyed by bombs during the period of the German blitz on London in 1940. When Bernard and I arrived at this house shortly after eleven o'clock on 27th July we both went inside 'to see that everything was all right'. We met Betty who was thereupon told by her fiancé not to be late at the church, where she was due at twelve noon. We then drove on to Chiswick parish church where I remember Bernard gave me the wedding ring with a repetition of his previous injunction about it. He himself then went first, he said, 'to tip the verger and see that he knows what he's about'; and secondly 'to the vestry to make sure that Father and Colin are there and that they are all ready and know what to do'. Looking back I have often thought it must have been quite an unusual event, even for a bishop of world-wide experience, to be tackled in the vestry by a bridegroom, whom he was about to marry, with a query as to his own ability to conduct the service! I then went into the church and at the steps leading to the choir stalls met Hobo, Betty's brother, who was to give her in marriage. I remember we stood there chatting as the members of the family and close friends, perhaps some twenty-five in all, were arriving. Betty herself came to the church punctually at twelve noon, and the marriage service then proceeded. When it was over we all followed the bride and bridegroom down the aisle to the West door, and beyond the porch into the street outside, where Bernard's car was parked. This was the moment when most of us expected to be told where to go for the reception, including some too who by that time were thinking it was about time they had a drink. Father and Colin had also joined us, still in their robes, so there was now quite a crowd outside the church, opposite that wonderful old inn in the street leading down to the river, when Bernard and Betty got to their car. To our astonishment the bridegroom then turned to our parents and said: 'Goodbye, goodbye, we're going off now, straight to our honeymoon.' I cannot recall if Betty had much more time in which to say a quick farewell! For almost at once Bernard opened the car door and they both drove off — to their honeymoon in Switzerland. There was no reception and none had been planned! But for Betty and Bernard Montgomery there now began an era of complete happiness which was a pleasure for all to see, and which continued without interruption for ten years. While it lasted she was unquestionably one of two great influences in the Field-Marshal's life. Bernard's marriage to Betty also had a considerable effect on the lives of John and Dick Carver. After leaving their public school they went to the 'Shop' (the Royal Military Academy at Woolwich) and to Cambridge, where they took their degree having both been commissioned in the Royal Engineers, as their own father had been.

The year 1927 was an eventful one in our family for more

reasons than the future Field-Marshal's marriage. Father became eighty years of age in October of that year. On his birthday he walked alone to the top of the Cairn, a mountain just over one thousand feet high in the hills behind New Park, involving a journey of some four miles each way. A little while later he was made a KCMG for his long service as Prelate of the Order of St Michael and St George. In that year also two other of my brothers were married. In East Africa Harold married a Mrs Montgomery which at first was liable to cause some confusion, particularly as she was the widow of his first cousin. She was Ursula Johnson, a Canadian born in British Columbia, whose first husband was Neville Montgomery, younger son of father's brother, Ferguson. Harold and Ursula had one son, Gardner (Garry) Montgomery born in 1931, who now owns the family property in Moville town. He lives permanently in the United States where he has business interests, and, *inter alia*, is a director and producer of plays for the Denver city theatre in Colorado. Neville had gone out to Vancouver, where he married Ursula, before the 1914–18 war and had been killed with the Canadian Expeditionary Force in France in 1917. Ursula died in 1937, and some years later, in East Africa, Harold married another widow, Betty Galton-Fenzi, who survives him. My brother Colin had been teaching at Foyle College Londonderry before going to Durham University, from where he was ordained in the Church of England early in 1927. Later in that year he married an Irish girl, Margaret Drennan, whose family lived at Carse Hall on Lough Foyle near Limavady, not far from Londonderry. Not long after Bernard's wedding I went out to East Africa to join the King's African Rifles.

When Bernard and Betty returned from their honeymoon they lived in one of the directing staff married quarters at the Staff College. These were bungalow-type houses on the ridge overlooking the Wish Stream between the Staff College building and the Royal Military College at Sandhurst. There in Bungalow No. 17 their son was born on 18th August 1928. He was called David Bernard. The students on the 1927 Staff College course, and on that in 1928, are on record as saying they did not see any change, outwardly, in my brother after his marriage. He was just as keen a disciplinarian, still very decided in his opinions and convinced that he was always right, on most issues. This was the view of students who included two of his most famous subordinates, Dempsey and Oliver Leese, and also of two future field-marshals, Harding and Templer. But in fact there was a change in him, slow in growth and therefore at first imperceptible, but none the less it was there and it was inevitable. It was a blend of happiness of mind superimposed on a broader life, composed of new responsibilities and occupations with, overall, a wider society in which to live; and all without prejudice to his professional life. Of course his wife was responsible for this and that is why, at first, no change could be seen, except in his own home. She handled him, if that is the right word, simply but cleverly, by gradually introducing him into that very different world, of literary and artistic interests, in which she had lived before their marriage. Soon they were both going, in the high summer of the August holidays, to the Italian Riviera at Portofino. There they stayed with Dick Shepherd and his wife in a castle at the mouth of that beautiful little harbour; and it was there that Bernard first took part in all the picnics, bathing parties and what he would previously have termed 'other idle pursuits' which make up social life on the Riviera during the summer months.

Early in 1929, after his three strenuous years' teaching at the Staff College, my brother returned to his regiment which by that time had moved from Shorncliffe to an equally pleasant station at Woking. This posting however was in reality only a formality as he had been appointed secretary of a War Office Committee charged with the task of revising, which meant rewriting, the official manual entitled *Infantry Training*. This task was of course all he could have wished for. His selection for it was entirely due to the reputation he had gained, particularly during his time as an instructor at Camberley, for new ideas and new thinking generally on the role of infantry in the army. Much has been written, by Bernard himself in his *Memoirs* and by others, about the conflict which arose between the secretary of the committee and its members during the writing of this manual. Bernard wanted to produce a comprehensive volume, not just on infantry tactics, but embracing the whole subject of the role of infantry in war and written specifically for the infantry officer. Perhaps he did not fully appreciate, or was reluctant to accept, that his committee members, all distinguished officers and some of them senior to himself, were from the outset inhibited by a directive from H.M.G., then current. In 1928 the British Government had promulgated, as a policy ruling, a statement that the service manuals of instruction were to be prepared against a background that 'there will be no major war for the next ten years'. Inevitably this unfortunate statement, accurate though it was, had its effect on the military thinking of the time, and not least on the financial departments who frequently saw it as a heaven-sent opportunity to cut back on planned expenditure. Besides, those were the days of great shortages in the army both in equipment and manpower resources. Troops were in such short supply that during army manoeuvres, or other large scale training exercises, it had become necessary to resort to quite strange devices in order to simulate the presence of troops on the ground in strength. Light wooden figure targets were issued which, when carried by one man, enabled him to operate and to be accepted by the umpires, as representing an infantry section at its full strength of one non-commissioned officer and six men. During exercises which included the employment of armoured regiments it was not unusual in the training areas to meet an officer riding a horse quite alone and with no apparent role. When asked what he was doing he would reply 'I am a tank'! Against a background of this kind it is small wonder that my brother, with all his enthusiasm for perfection in training, should have at times found himself at odds with the members of his committee. In the event, as has been told, he got very largely all he wanted, and the *Infantry Training* manual which appeared in the early 1930s was in force when the war years began in 1939. In this connection it is significant that the great military historian, the late Sir Basil Liddell-Hart, published his well-known book *The Future of Infantry* during the 1930s. He and Bernard were by then close friends of long standing and their mutual consultation no doubt had its effect on both works: the official manual, virtually written by the future Field-Marshal, and the standard book on the future of infantry, which any aspirant for the Staff College in those days was very ill-advised not to read, by the great historian.

During his task of rewriting *Infantry Training* Bernard and Betty lived very comfortably for the greater part of two years, in the barracks at Woking. They had a house with a garden and it was a very pleasant setting for the task he had been given. He seldom wore uniform and had virtually no regimental duty to distract him. During the early summer of 1930 he and Betty decided they would like to give a dance, in their house, for the young officers of his regiment and their friends. It was certainly an event which had never happened before in his life, and was clear evidence of Betty's growing influence on him. I happened to be on leave from East Africa at the time and was invited to this dance. I remember we were all 'instructed' to bring our own partners and of course I took Bunty, now my wife, who was then staying nearby at Camberley with our old friends of the Sherwood Foresters, Colonel (he was then a Subaltern) and Mrs Jackson. As far as Bernard was concerned it was to be a 'controlled' dance, and I shall always recall how some of those present found it rather disconcerting when, not infrequently, he climbed on to a table and, in ringing tones, gave everyone orders to 'change partners'. In those days certainly when a Field Officer, who was also your host, gave orders to a Subaltern there was no question of failure to comply with the instruction! Otherwise the whole affair was a great success and made particularly pleasant by Betty's charm of manner and infectious gaiety. It was another example of my brother's interest in helping young officers, not only professionally but in their everyday life, socially or otherwise; and part of his training technique which aimed, frankly, at being all things to all men in such a way that he gained first their interest and loyalty. Thereafter the task of professional training with, equally, the assessment of a subordinate's capacity for leadership was easier to accomplish.

That same summer Mother held her usual house party for friends and relatives at New Park. Quite a lot of us were there including Bernard and Betty, my brother Colin and his wife Margaret, and my sister Winsome with her husband 'Wangy'

Holderness, then a major commanding the depot of his regiment, the Royal Sussex, at Chichester. Dan Broadwood, a cousin in the Royal Marines, and Dorothy Babington, a Tasmanian, with one or two other girls were also in the party. For some reason or other John and Dick Carver were not there, though David Montgomery, then aged two, was making his first visit to New Park. All of us present then will always remember that happy time if only for the way in which Bernard, not long married and for the first time with his wife and son in his family home, decided to take control of the house party 'in a proper military manner'. In his view our holiday activities should be well organised and not just left to drift, with day-to-day *ad hoc* decisions. When therefore we all came down to breakfast after family prayers in the chapel (the influence of marriage had turned the wheel full circle and churchgoing was now imperative in Bernard's life) we generally found a notice pinned to the dining-room door, signed by Bernard, and couched in terms of which the following is a typical example.

PROGRAMME FOR TODAY
– Date –

Time	Event	Remarks
1000	The men will play squash. Girls will go shopping in the village. Orders by Mother	
1100	Bathing	Optional
	Betty will paint	
	Colin will write sermon	
1200	Girls will pick flowers for the house	
1300	Lunch	Don't be late
1430	All to golf course at Greencastle, less Winsome and Wangy who will prepare tea and convey it to Golf course. RV in club house 1700	
1800	Return to New Park	

Looking back, this programme seems to smack of the package tour, so perhaps at New Park in those days we were the forerunner of what is commonplace today!

In January 1931 my brother was promoted substantive Lieutenant-Colonel and appointed to command the 1st Battalion of his regiment, in Palestine. It had taken twenty-three years to reach this so often coveted goal, including a world war, and he was now just forty-three years of age. He was again fortunate in this command for at that time one battalion of British infantry was considered sufficient as the regular element of the garrison for the whole country, and his duties therefore included those of 'OC Troops, Palestine'. Betty was able to join Bernard in Jerusalem and for the nine months or so that they were there they led an idyllic existence. Although there were already distant signs of the Arab-Jewish war, which was to follow later in the same decade, the local situation did not deter them from travelling together throughout the Holy Land, and beyond into the Levant States and Trans-Jordan. At that date H. V. Morton's book *In the Steps of the Master* had not yet been published (it appeared three years later), but Bernard and Betty were able broadly to follow the same pattern of travel described in that great work. In addition to the Holy Places of Palestine they visited the rock city of Petra, and then returned northwards via what is left of the lovely Greek city of Jerash, and then on to Damascus. Finally they went to see the almost matchless wonders of the ruins of Baalbec with their great temples dedicated to the pagan gods of Jupiter and of Bacchus. For Betty in particular, with her artistic bent and talent, this tour must have been an endless delight, and she would have derived especial pleasure in comparing the grandeur of the pagan architecture of Baalbec with all the splendours of the Roman Empire, so evident at Jerusalem and elsewhere. I do not know if they made a final stop in the Lebanon at Djoun, the home of that famous, and yet extraordinary, woman Lady Hester Stanhope, who for nearly thirty years so dominated the Arabs of the Levant; but it would have been in keeping with Betty's inquiring mind to insist on doing so, and her husband would have gladly assented.

8

Late that same year Bernard's battalion was transferred to
Egypt to become the garrison of the great port of Alexandria where
he and Betty, with their young son David, lived in a comfortable
flat overlooking the harbour. It was a very different kind of life
from that which they had led in Palestine. The infantry battalion
at Alexandria was part of the Suez Canal Brigade with its headquarters at Ismailia, then commanded by Brigadier F. A. Pile. The
latter was that renowned artilleryman who was so successful as the
GOC-in-C of the Anti-Aircraft Command during the 1939–45
war and is now General Sir Frederick Pile, Bt, GCB, DSO, MC.
The Commander-in-Chief in Egypt, still at that time with his
Headquarters in Cairo, was General Sir John Burnett-Stuart.
Bernard was now therefore serving very much under the watchful
eye of authority, and in circumstances very different from his
command in Palestine where, as OC Troops, he was virtually left
to his own devices. Both Burnett-Stuart and Pile were wise and
far-sighted men which again was fortunate for my brother as
otherwise, with his passion for innovation, he might have got himself into trouble. The British battalion at Alexandria was expected
to be smart on parade and attentive to ceremonial drill, but neither
of these military duties has ever had any appeal for my brother.
The *Infantry Training* manual which was eventually superseded
by the edition he had written had contained the dictum: 'Drill is
the foundation of military discipline.' But Bernard would have
none of that and never accepted it as a true saying, for he simply
could not equate proficiency in the formalities of the parade ground
with the skills required of the infantryman on the battlefield. It
followed that he might even himself have been superseded but for
the wisdom and foresight of his immediate superiors, Pile and
Burnett-Stuart. These two commanders were not long in appreciating that although the 1st Royal Warwickshire did not perhaps
match up to that standard of drill and smartness on parade which
was normally expected of the battalion in garrison at Alexandria,
nevertheless the regiment was exceedingly well trained, in terms
especially of alertness and battlefield technique, by a commanding
officer who was quite unusual; this adjective applied mainly to my
brother's determination not necessarily to accept as sound what

had always been regarded as such in the past; in short he was the very embodiment of initiative.

It has often been said, and written, that my brother was unpopular in his battalion at Alexandria, particularly among the officers. This is not however accurate and I write these words with the knowledge of an officer of the regiment at the time, though not serving with it. The truth is that he dealt firmly, and equally, with officers or other ranks who in his view partook too liberally of the 'fleshpots of Egypt' to the detriment of their own and the battalion's proficiency. Alexandria at that time was the playground of the wealthy Pashas in Cairo, including a very rich Greek colony, and the standards of luxury and good living, all readily available to healthy young men, were hard to resist. Also of course all the spurious attractions of a large Eastern city and sea port, with the innumerable bars and brothels and cheap goods on sale in the bazaars, including poisonous drinks and drugs and general invitations for self-indulgence on a massive scale, were there for all to see. More sinister were the temptations and often dire results which stemmed from the much advertised offers to take part in pornographic and homosexual activities. In fending off these dangers, which he saw solely as a serious risk to the well-being and efficiency of both officers and other ranks, Bernard employed means which were clearly in advance of his time. He was particularly concerned at the incidence of venereal disease and he adopted preventive measures on the lines of those which, when repeated eight years later in Europe during the early days of the 1939–45 war, got him into serious trouble. He also pioneered the abolition in the army of the formal church parade service on Sundays, with its compulsory attendance (unless leave of absence was obtained) and the ceremonial march past the commanding officer, led by the band and drums and the regimental mascot (the Royal Warwickshire badge was an antelope and, traditionally, a black buck from India was kept by each battalion). It was Bernard's view that the men, on Sundays, should be free to attend church in plain clothes, and not have to spend half Saturday cleaning and preparing their uniform and equipment for a parade they heartily disliked. Although there was a considerable row over this innovation events

have since shown how right he was. None of these incidents however were so important as the impact made on him personally at
this time in Egypt, and reflected in his battalion, by his first
experience in training for war in the Western Desert. Coinciden-
tally with this, also in time and place and equally important, there
was a renewed contact with de Guingand. In those days the latter
was the Adjutant of his battalion at Moascar, near Ismailia, and
quite fortuitously he was acting as Brigade-Major for a training
exercise in the desert, at the same time as the future Field-Marshal
was temporarily acting as the Brigade-Commander. What followed
has been most graphically described by de Guingand in *Operation
Victory*, including the story of how, between them, they completely
outwitted and defeated their opponents for the exercise. The really
important dividend however lay in the fact that victory was only
secured by operating at night. My brother was finally converted to
a belief in the efficacy of 'night operations' (the inverted commas
are mine). Alan Moorehead, summing up this event in his book
Montgomery, hit just the right note when he wrote:

> 'It is hardly likely that either Montgomery or de Guingand
> could have felt the touch of history at that moment. Yet before
> ten years were out the things they learned on this night were
> going to engulf a million men in one of the decisive struggles of
> the world; and all this was to happen in much the same way and
> not fifty miles from that same valley of the desert.'

On 28th July 1931 our parents celebrated their Golden Wedding
at New Park. The facts seemed to justify the Bishop's belief that
his life moved in cycles. In 1881 he had been married and came
with his wife to New Park for their honeymoon. In 1901 he received
the summons to leave Tasmania. In 1921 he retired to his family
home. In 1931 he and his wife kept their Golden Wedding there.
There was of course a special house party at New Park for the
event, covering a week or so, with fifteen people in all staying in
the house not including grandchildren. Five of my brothers and
sisters (Harold, Donald, Una, Winsome and Colin) with their
wives and husbands were present. Only Bernard and I could not be

there; the former was about to move his regiment from Palestine to Egypt and I was Adjutant of my battalion in Kenya. The whole affair was a very joyous occasion, though not entirely so because, as with all large families when brothers and sisters get together with their respective wives and husbands, some very considerable quarrels ensued. Clearly the two Canadian spouses of Harold and Donald did not care for each other and there was a lot of in-fighting as a result, in which, perhaps too rashly, my elder sister intervened with doubtless good intentions but no good effect! However the climax came one day during that week when the whole party, except our parents, were out on the hills. Apparently Mother, intent on some household task, was in the bedroom allotted to Harold and his wife, Ursula, when she came upon a bottle of gin! This discovery brought disaster with it in view of mother's well-known horror of alcohol in any circumstances. It was now clear to her that our eldest brother had secretly brought 'liquor' into the house and thereafter concealed it in order to indulge, with his wife, in clandestine drinking bouts; above all he had chosen to do this in the middle of this most auspicious occasion – the celebration of his parents' Golden Wedding. Could anything be worse? It was in vain that Harold made rejoinder that he was no longer a schoolboy (he was then in fact forty-seven) and that he and his wife enjoyed a drink before dinner – and were determined they should have it. Of course in the end peace was restored. Meanwhile Father had taken no part at all in any such family quarrels. He retreated to his study where he was entirely undisturbed and could continue with his thoughts and his writing. He was then in his eighty-fourth year and had recently received a letter from Lord Stamfordham, Private Secretary to King George V, about the business of his Order (St Michael and St George) which pleased him a great deal, and which had ended: 'His Majesty congratulates you on this the twenty-fifty year of your office as Prelate of the Order, and knows what the whole Order owes to you.'

Looking back at my five brothers and sisters, gathered together at New Park in that summer of 1931, it has become easier for me to see the extent to which, in their character and temperament, they all resembled our Field-Marshal brother. Like him their outlook, particularly their approach to any problem on which they might hold pre-conceived views, was generally inflexible. They did not relish having to give way in argument, as he does not, unless their own opinion was clearly demolished, in which case their sense of humour generally came to the rescue. Also like him they were essentially individualists in character, and because of this they tended never to lack self-confidence, which perhaps gave each one a reputation for being too self-opinionated. At New Park there is a low doorway of wood, crowned by a porch, which leads from the orchard behind the terrace into the churchyard, thus giving us private access to the family church. It is not possible to pass through this gateway without bending low, and one of our forebears inscribed on its porch the following text:

> Humble ye must be if to Heaven ye would go
> The sky is high, but the Door is low.

No doubt our parents fully appreciated the aptness of this wording to all their children, for we were often reminded of it! It followed also that there were inevitably times when my brothers and sisters found themselves in strong disagreement with Bernard, particularly as they grew older with their own family ties and interests. Their common meeting point, always, was their intense love and affection for Father which nothing could ever diminish. In this context my brother Colin was the only one of us who, in his choice of vocation, matched up to my parents' aspirations by becoming ordained.

Colin was never strong and, on account of a weak heart, had had to leave St Paul's before his public-school education was completed. An ardent churchman he was nevertheless fascinated by the armed forces and by a liking for foreign travel, particularly by sea. He had a remarkable gift for organisation and might well have become a most successful administrator, especially as a soldier, had his physique been stronger. After the 1939–45 war, which he spent as a chaplain in hospital ships, he became Vicar of Ladysmith in South Africa. From there he quite startled the family by having himself and his wife transferred, in one move of fifteen thousand

miles, from the hot summer climate of Natal to Aklavik in Western
Canada (more than a hundred miles north of the Arctic Circle)
where the temperature on their arrival was fifty degrees below
zero. It must have required a great deal of determination, let alone
stamina, on the part of Colin and Margaret to undertake volun-
tarily such a great transformation in a short space of time. The
conditions they met in the Arctic, in those days, were still a strange,
and frequently a very bizarre, mixture of the primitive and the
modern world. The local inhabitants of the region, Eskimos and
Loucheux Indians, were quite used to modern ships and aero-
planes of all types, but had never seen a horse, cow, sheep or pig,
or a train or a motor car. Their normal movement was almost
entirely by sledge drawn over the snow by up to ten husky dogs
harnessed in line, with the lead dog controlled only by voice.
Otherwise they communicated, on a house-to-house basis, entirely
by radio telephone or sound broadcast. In these conditions my
brother and his wife had to live a hard and exacting life, particularly during 1949–50 when a severe epidemic of measles, followed
by pneumonia and a sharp rise in the tuberculosis rate, swept
through the region. Whole families collapsed being unable to keep
their stoves alight and so had to be evacuated long distances by
sledge. At such times Margaret had to supervise all the hospital and
relief work until additional medical staff were flown in to Aklavik;
all this she did exceedingly well.

In some ways Colin very much resembled our grandfather Dean
Farrar. He had the same completely sincere and intense religious
zeal, which he combined with a clear and quite candidly expressed
desire for secular advancement in his vocation. He was obviously
very pleased when he was made a Canon on appointment to
Aklavik just as Canon Farrar was overjoyed when appointed to
the Deanery of Canterbury. None of this however was allowed to
interfere with the conduct of his mission, or with his highly
developed sense of humour. His favourite story of the Arctic, told
in his own words, makes this clear:

'Arriving a few years ago a missionary friend of mine had to
make a forced plane landing at a remote Indian camp. It so

happened that there had been no missionary there for some time and at least two couples wanted to get married. The missionary explained that he was not registered to conduct marriages in that province and if he did the weddings would not be valid, but the couples were so disappointed that he decided to take a chance and marry them. He would then inform the authorities, describing the situation and hoping that they would register the marriages. The two couples came to the little church together and the only person who could speak English was the Chief, who acted as interpreter. My friend found somewhat to his astonishment that both the girls were called Rosie, so he said to himself "I must be very careful to marry the right Rosie to the right man." They were very ignorant and did not really know where or how to stand but the Chief said he put them into the right order and both marriages were duly performed. When they went into the little vestry to sign the register, he discovered to his horror that he had married the Rosies to the wrong men. What was he to do? They were married and he could not unmarry them! In addition he had no qualifications to marry any of them at all. So, after a lot of thought he decided to send a radio message to Ottowa the next morning from the local Army Signals Station, informing them of the facts and asking that under the circumstances the marriages should be annulled so that he could marry them correctly. He then made the husbands promise they would not see their wives until the reply came. By this time it was 11 p.m. and he decided not to trouble Army Signals till the next morning, but to sleep on the problem. It was just as well he did, for the next morning the two men came to him early with the Chief, and told him that they had talked it over all night and decided they would be quite happy to keep the "Rosies" they had been married to and there was no need to make any change! The Missionary wired for the marriages to be registered and they were accepted.'

When the time came for Colin and Margaret to leave the Arctic they were both very sad. They had become much loved by both Eskimos and Indians and had themselves sincerely enjoyed working with each community. But they had only volunteered to do three years in the region and did not think it wise to remain longer; there is a saying in the Arctic that if you stay more than four years you become 'bushed' and never want to leave. Besides Colin did not feel spiritually fulfilled in the Arctic. The Eskimo community is plainly Nonconformist and did not match his own ideas of church doctrine and practice. So in 1952 they made the long journey back to South Africa, only this time they returned to Vryberg in Cape Province on the edge of the Kalahari Desert, where my brother became the rector of the parish. Then six years later Colin died of a sudden heart attack, whilst in the act of refereeing a boxing match. He may not have achieved all his secular ambition, but he enjoyed his life to the full in which he was helped and strengthened by Margaret, who has always been so popular with our family.

The year 1932 saw the last of the summer house-parties at New Park with both our parents present. The early part of that year had been a wonderful time for Father in particular. He had published his last book, *Old Age*, and had asked if Queen Mary would accept a copy, which Her Majesty had been graciously pleased to do; in those days the royal acceptance of any such proposal meant a great deal so he was very pleased by this. Father's last service as Prelate of the Order of St Michael and St George, on 24th April, was attended by the Duke and Duchess of York (later King George VI and Queen Elizabeth), and on the following day he received a letter from their Private Secretary, telling him how deeply impressed they had been by his conduct of the service and its beauty. But perhaps more than anything else, he had so enjoyed the three months when he had agreed to have charge of Moville parish during the Rector's absence. His happiest hours had then been spent, on foot, visiting the scattered farms and cottages in the hills which he knew so well. That last house party had been well attended. Father's sister who had married Roger Delison was there, as well as three of my brothers and sisters with four grandchildren, besides John and Dick Carver and also my future wife who was a great friend of my sister Winsome. On 30th August the Bishop's illness of three months began, and, if illness can have

8*

beauty, this was surely an example of it. There was little pain, only great weakness, and he was much cheered one day when he received a telegram from Queen Mary inquiring after him. Then, on Friday 25th November 1932, aged eighty-five, he died and passed peacefully to his long rest. He was buried at Moville church where a small stream divides the cemetery from the grounds of New Park. The Bishop's grave is just beyond this stream and there he lies, looked down on by the hills of Donegal, and facing his family home overlooking Lough Foyle.

Father's death brought much publicity in the press in many countries, and the King and Queen sent a telegram of condolence to Mother at New Park. In London there was a Memorial Service in St Paul's Cathedral, where also, later on, especially carved wooden panels were set up in his memory, on the South wall of the Chapel of his Order of which he had been Prelate for so long. But in our own family, quite simply, what mattered was that a light had gone out in our lives; and for my brother Bernard in particular, and also for myself, this was especially hard to bear, as we had not been able to go to the Golden Wedding party. I so well recall the telegram arriving at Nairobi the day Father died. It had come in the afternoon and afterwards I rode out alone (we seemed to live on ponies in those days) into the Game Reserve. The cantonments are on a hill, overlooking Nairobi Town, from where the Reserve, which in this region is set in a vast plain surrounded by hills, stretches for many miles to the south. This fertile land, then as now, is a haven for many species of African fauna. There have always been herds of zebra and wildebeest roaming the plain, with many other kinds of antelope, including hartebeest and impala, and lions are frequently seen. The game are well aware of the Reserve boundary and have no fear of the human being so long as they are not molested. I remember once, on a dark night when driving to Mbagathi along the boundary track, that we accidentally ran over a lion who was lying out with his fore paws across the path. We were not overturned so we drove off at speed listening to the most terrifying roars! The sun was setting over the Ngong Hills as I rode back that evening and the scene was particularly beautiful. The short rains had just ended so the land was fresh and green.

I thought much of Father on that evening ride, and by the time
I got back to the cantonment was more at peace and not so alone.
I felt very certain, indeed I knew, that when the Bishop crossed
over Jordan, still I am sure with his firm and measured tread (but
with bowed head for the Door is low), 'All the trumpets sounded
on the other side'.

Immediately after Father's death it seemed as if an almost desperate energy, a renewed impetus, had arisen in Mother. For,
alone at New Park, she sat down and within the space of a few
months, wrote and had published by the SPG a memoir of Father,
comprising an account of his whole life. It was not a long book
and not really well written: after all, she had been engaged at fourteen and married at the age of sixteen; but it served its purpose
well by sketching in simple terms the life and work of one of the
most delightful and lovable of men.

Early in 1934 the 1st Royal Warwickshire moved to India to join
the Brigade in garrison at Poona. Soon after the battalion arrived
there Bernard, who still had about a year to do in command, found
himself faced with a considerable problem which might well have
damaged his career, perhaps irretrievably. The trouble was of the
same kind he had met on first arrival at Alexandria, namely the
standard of drill and smartness on the parade ground, and of turn-
out and appearance generally, of the men under his command.
This time however the trouble was doubly intensified for reasons
which very soon became clear to my brother. The history of the
British Empire in India has never lacked evidence to show the
importance which the authorities, both civil and military, have
always attached to ceremony of all kinds, particularly ceremonial
drill. To be good on parade, with smart and clean uniform and a
high standard of arms drill, and with officers well turned out at all
times, was almost a pre-requisite for a commanding officer who
wished his battalion to be well reported on by higher authority.
This requirement was applicable equally to the units of all arms in
both the British and Indian forces serving in the Indo subcontinent. The garrison at Poona in the 1930s certainly did its best to
live up to these standards which, unfortunately for Bernard, were
regarded as particularly important by the brigade commander.

The latter was an officer steeped in all the customs and tradition of an age which was fast coming to an end, and clearly he was not going to report well on any commanding officer whose men, in his view, were neither alert nor well-disciplined; furthermore it was his strongly held opinion that alertness and discipline depended in the first place on parade-ground performance. This therefore was the situation which confronted Bernard on his arrival at Poona, though this time he did not have the safety valve, as he had at Alexandria, in the form of efficient, highly professional and forward-looking superior officers, like Pile and Burnett-Stuart, with whom he could deal. There is a story told about my brother's tenure of command of his regiment at Poona which illustrates very well not only the situation just described but also his method of handling it. Unfortunately I cannot claim the story is true, it is only I fear apocryphal, though worth inclusion for the insight it provides into that very standard of alertness which the garrison commander thought was lacking.

The battalion had not been long at Poona when orders were received that the brigade commander wished to inspect the regiment in barracks. The battalion was to parade in ceremonial order in mass formation with the colours and the band and drums and the regimental transport. On arrival the brigade commander was to be received with a general salute, after which he and his staff would ride round the ranks. He would then return to the saluting base and take the salute as the battalion marched past in column of companies in quick time. Thereafter all companies would proceed to their barrack rooms for a kit inspection by the brigade commander. This order was naturally greeted with some concern in the battalion – that sort of order generally was in any unit! On the appointed day the regiment paraded as ordered with Bernard, and other mounted officers, on horseback. After the initial salute the garrison commander came forward, halted his horse in front of Bernard, and said 'Colonel Montgomery, you are not positioned properly in front of your regiment in mass formation. You are six paces too far to your right. Please take up your correct position now.' Bernard's reaction was instant. Having saluted in acknowledgement of the instruction he gave the following order: 'Royal

Warwickshire. Six Paces Right Close. March.' Of course this order, which involved moving some seven hundred men, band and drums, colours and regimental transport (pack mules and mule-drawn wagons) six paces and then re-dressing the ranks, instead of moving his own position slightly, all took some time to complete. But he had complied with the order – in his own way! My brother has so often said to me, 'I never took on a job which I knew that I personally, for lack of resources or any other reason, could not tackle properly, or complete within a required time limit.' Looking back, this statement, some will say, is the pointer indicating the way to his constant run of success in the years that followed the outbreak of the 1939–45 war. Be that as it may, the remark was certainly in line with his action shortly after his arrival in Poona and his first acquaintance with its brigade commander. Very wisely he applied for leave ex-India in order to visit the Far East and Japan. This was granted, so Betty and Bernard left Poona on a long sea voyage which took them to Singapore and Hong Kong, as well as China and Japan. They enjoyed it all immensely. On reflection it seems likely that the brigade commander at Poona may in his turn have been only too glad to sanction a leave application by one of his commanding officers! This account of my brother's short stay at Poona had an unusual ending. He and Betty were returning to India, after visiting Japan, when the passenger ship they were in called at Hong Kong. Who should embark there, in the same ship, but the garrison commander at Poona who with his wife had been making a similar but shorter tour! Amongst their mail, which Bernard had arranged to have re-directed to the ship at Hong Kong, was a telegram from Army Headquarters India. This informed him that he was to proceed forthwith to Quetta on appointment there as GSO1 and Chief Instructor of the Staff College, and that he would be promoted full Colonel. When Bernard told me of this incident he added: 'I could not resist taking the telegram to Brigadier . . . and asking for his advice as to whether I should accept the appointment'!

The three years, 1934–7, that my brother spent at the Staff College in India were among the happiest times of his life. When he and Betty first got there Quetta was a flourishing town of more than sixty thousand people, not far from the head of the Bolan pass on the trade route to Karachi, and guarding the strategic road and railway communications with Kandahar and South Persia. Before they left however the entire city had been destroyed by an appalling earthquake, in which thirty thousand people lost their lives. Quetta lies at an altitude of nearly six thousand feet and has a wonderful climate, never excessively hot in summer, by comparison with the heat in the plains of India, but very cold and dry in winter. My brother and his wife lived in a pleasant bungalow, with a large garden, on Hanna Road, where they were very comfortable and were able to do all the entertaining expected of a senior officer on the directing staff. For the greater part of the time they were there the Commandant of the College was a Sapper officer, Major-General G. C. (Guy) Williams whose breadth of view and foresight were all that Bernard could have wished for in his superior officer. There were always two Chief Instructors at Quetta, one from the British service and one from the Indian army, and during the last two years my brother was there his I.A. colleague was that controversial figure Tom Corbett.* It is well known that Bernard and Corbett never got on well together professionally; they had no identity of views, no meeting point in that sense, for they were both such entirely different characters. Corbett, an officer of a famous Indian cavalry regiment, the 2nd Lancers, whose record in battle was and still is of the highest order, rose to high rank and became the Commander, in war, of the first armoured division produced by the Indian army, until he was appointed Chief of the General Staff to Auchinleck. He has been much criticised by many writers of the war years, but I am concerned here only to find an explanation for the unfortunate fact that my Field-Marshal brother never saw eye to eye with his fellow Chief Instructor at Quetta. When I discussed this matter with Bernard I added that Corbett, who was still a Chief Instructor at the Staff College when I was there as a student, had always seemed a very nice chap. He was not unpopular with the students and was certainly very good on a horse, and had, incidentally, sold me a most beautifully trained polo pony, called Lancer, for which I was profoundly grateful. My

---

* Lieutenant-General T. W. Corbett, CB, MC.

brother's instant rejoinder, at that time, seems to provide the perfect explanation. 'Yes,' he said, 'that's just the trouble. I am not a nice chap, quite definitely not! I myself sack a commander if I think he is no good.' The same devastating logic once led him to endorse a student's paper with a comment which, no doubt accurate, must have had a most shattering effect. The officer concerned was well below the average of his contemporaries in their professional standards, and there was apparently some doubt of his ability to graduate at the end of his time at the Staff College. The endorsement by his GSO1, made in the red ink reserved for directing staff comment, read: 'A great improvement, thoroughly bad.' *BLM*.

My brother's time as Chief Instructor at Quetta was possibly the most significant period of his professional life between the two world wars. He had already spent three years as an instructor at Camberley after which he had re-written the army's manual on Infantry Training, and then completed three and a half years in command of his regiment in Palestine, Egypt and India. Now, at Quetta, he had time to think out and assess in his own mind, in the light of all his varied past experience, what he saw as the greatest task facing any commander in war. Put simply he defined this as the task of leadership. In this book it is not my purpose to recapitulate all my Field-Marshal brother's thoughts on leadership. Those who wish to study the subject in detail should turn to Chapter 6 of his *Memoirs* and then follow that up by reading his own assessments of great national leaders in his subsequent work, *The Path to Leadership*. Nevertheless it is appropriate to look now at what he wrote and try to extract from it a broad picture of the ingredients in his definition of the requirements of leadership. When we have done this we shall be able to see how these same elements appear time and again in the war years, not only in his own application of them, but also how he used them as his yard stick with which to measure the capacity of his subordinate leaders. My picture of these ingredients follows below, and of course there will be those who will not agree it is a sufficient outline of the original, begun at Quetta so long ago.

Fundamentally, leadership depends on truth and character in the individual.

Next is personality. A leader must have courage, and the confidence born of his own standard of professional knowledge and experience, which he regards as greater than that of his subordinates. He thus has confidence in himself, and he must imbue his troops with the same degree of confidence in him.

He must be able to make a decision (many people cannot) which means decision in planning and in action, and calmness in crisis. It is vital that a senior commander should keep himself from becoming involved in details.

He must understand men and know what they want, at all stages, in order to maintain their fighting efficiency and their morale at all times. This includes keeping them properly and sufficiently informed.

In the selection of commanders, the sole criteria are merit, leadership and ability to do the job. Anyone who, in battle, falls down on these triple qualifications must not remain in command. Every officer has his 'ceiling' in rank, beyond which he should not be allowed to rise.

My brother's social life, after he was married, probably found its greatest expression while he was at Quetta. He and Betty then had ample opportunity, and the means, to entertain and they lived a full and varied life, apart from Bernard's professional commitments. Betty painted some of her best portraits and landscapes at Quetta, especially paintings of the various Indian classes, Punjabis, Sikhs, Pathans and the local Baluch and Brahui. Both she and Bernard rode and played golf and I remember so well hacking up the Hanna valley with them one summer evening, when I stayed with them at the Staff College. By that time I had transferred to the Indian army and I was stationed with my regiment (the Baluch Regiment) at Karachi which was then only a night's journey by rail from Quetta. Whilst there I attended several of the dinner parties Betty gave in their bungalow, which was of itself an experience. My brother always insisted that no sufficient assessment of an officer could be made without a study of himself, and of his wife if he were married, in his social as well as professional sphere. He therefore made a point of entertaining the students at these dinner parties which were always great fun and most amusing. There were two divisions of students at the Staff College, consisting of both British and Indian army officers, as well as a number of officers from the Dominion forces – Australia, Canada, New Zealand and South Africa – and Betty, under instruction from her husband, always ensured that her guests included some in each of these categories. During dinner, and afterwards over the port and coffee (there was always plenty to drink), Bernard would deliberately introduce a problem for discussion, and, if necessary (which it generally wasn't) follow it up by some perfectly outrageous statement calculated to provoke someone into counter-argument. Betty's own gaiety and charm, and her skill as a hostess, created a relaxed atmosphere and made everyone feel at home.

There were some very colourful personalities at the Quetta Staff College during those three years, so Betty's dinner parties were always stimulating and full of interest. Among the Directing Staff were Frank Messervey (who had been a student under Bernard at Camberley) besides Colonel de Fonblanque,* the artillery officer then so well known as a superb horseman, and Colonel W. L. Fawcett of the 9th Gurkha Rifles who fell in the disastrous Malaya campaign in 1942. Captain George Nangle, the Adjutant and also in the 9th Gurkhas, was often present at these parties. The students included Captain Donald Bateman of the Baluch Regiment who later became a Major-General and Director of Military Training India, and Major L. W. McKay Forbes of the 3rd Gurkha Rifles, perhaps the most colourful character of them all. But looking back at that time, probably two of the most interesting students, in the light of what followed after the war years, were the Sandhurst-trained Indian officers: Captain K. M. Cariappa of that famous regiment the 7th Rajputs, who became the first Commander-in-Chief of the army after India achieved independence, and Captain Kalwant Singh of the 1st Punjab Regiment

* Major-General E. B. de Fonblanque, CB, CBE, DSO.

who was an Army Commander during the same period. One of the officers to reach high rank, among the students, was Lieutenant D. H. Ward* of the Dorsetshire Regiment who eventually became a full General, a Commander-in-Chief and Governor of Gibraltar.

Very early on the morning of Friday 31st May 1935, precisely at three minutes past three o'clock while it was still pitch dark, Quetta city was the scene of an earthquake the like of which had probably never been experienced before in the whole of the Indo-subcontinent. In the space of under one minute the entire town was destroyed, including all the Civil Lines with their police barracks, the large post and telegraph office, the railway station with its extensive installations and marshalling yards, the civil and mission hospitals, and the houses of government officials, British and Indian alike. In the crowded bazaars, where many thousands of Muslim and Hindu shopkeepers and their families lived, virtually every house collapsed burying their inhabitants under tons of rubble and timber. It was in this area that the greatest destruction occurred, so that afterwards it was almost impossible to find where the streets and narrow lanes had been. Much damage was also caused by the fires which broke out, and, in all, thirty thousand people died with many thousands more wounded or maimed for life. The Residency where Sir Norman Cater, the Commissioner General for Baluchistan and Agent to the Governor-General of India, lived was completely demolished, as also was the Quetta Club, the centre of social life in the large British civil and military population. Of course the loss of property, of money, valuables, and goods of every description was prodigious, especially as the banks were all destroyed. In spite of this great destruction however the disaster was not so calamitous as it might have been, and it was certainly not the most appalling of its kind to have occurred in all Asia in this century. (In the earthquake at Tokyo in 1923 over one hundred and fifty thousand people were killed, partly because it occurred at about noon when so many people were cooking their midday meal in houses made of wood, which then promptly caught fire and were burnt to ashes.) Unfortunately

* General Sir Dudley Ward, GCB, KBE, DSO.

Quetta is sited in an earthquake area, derived from being part of the vast mountain chain which stretches from the Alps in the West, through the Caucasus and Iranian mountains, and over the great mass of the Himalaya, to finish in the Indonesian mountain ranges. When the disaster of 1935 occurred the vibration of the earth's solid crust (caused by vast internal pressures which burst their way to the surface) began at the head of the Bolan pass and moved northwards up the Quetta Valley and beyond, for nearly a hundred miles, with a width which varied from fifteen to thirty miles. The quake was therefore generally moving uphill, inside the range of mountains surrounding Quetta, where, very fortunately, it became deflected from the cantonment area by the two very wide and deep *nullah* beds which divide the civil from the military lines. As a result the garrison area, which housed twelve thousand troops composed mainly of the 2nd Indian Division, as well as all the Staff College premises, suffered comparatively small damage compared to the vast destruction in the town and the civil lines.

This comparative immunity from danger, however, in no way applied to the Indian wing of the Royal Air Force whose airfield and hangars, with their barracks, workshops and other installations, were sited in the very path of the earthquake to the west of the cantonments. The officer commanding the R.A.F. was Wing Commander J. Slessor,* who later became famous as an Air Commander-in-Chief and professional head of the R.A.F. Great damage was caused to this R.A.F. station and very heavy casualties, in dead and wounded, were incurred by all ranks; Slessor himself was nearly killed by a head wound from falling timber, and so also was his wife, when their bungalow all but fell apart. Out of twenty-seven aircraft (Wapiti two-seater machines with a top speed, in those days, of just under one hundred miles an hour) only three were left operational, though damaged; yet all three flew reconnaissance that same day.

At the Staff College Bernard had been away from his home for some days engaged on a tour of the North West Frontier, and had only returned to Quetta on 30th May. That evening he and Betty

* Marshal of the Royal Air Force Sir John Slessor GCB, DSO, MC.

entertained a fellow instructor, Lieutenant-Colonel Hawes,* to
dinner, and, years later, Bernard told me of what had transpired.
It had been a hot and sultry day, and on his way home he had seen
many more than usual of those whirling 'dust devils' which are
such a feature of the desert areas in Baluchistan; but normally this
would only presage the advent of a storm, particularly in a mountainous region. It remained hot and sticky that night, though
strangely it suddenly became very cold in the small hours of the
morning. After dinner Bernard wished to continue working in his
study, which led out of the drawing room, and so left his wife and
their guest alone to continue talking. This ability, if that is the
right word, to leave his guests to their own devices, or with his
wife, was merely another facet of my brother's determination that
work came first! As Betty was talking – it was now past eleven
o'clock and four hours before the catastrophe – she noticed that
the silk embroidery on which she was working appeared to be
undergoing an extraordinary transformation; each single thread
was separating and tending to stiffen of itself. The three of them
could only interpret this phenomenon as an excess amount of
static electricity in the atmosphere that night. Later, Bernard also
told me how Hawes' wife, then in England with her two young
children, had a most unusual dream that night with a premonition
of what was to happen – or by then had happened as India's time
is five and a half hours ahead of that in the United Kingdom. In
her dream she was back at the Staff College looking southward
down the Quetta valley when suddenly in the sky she saw groups
of heads with white faces; then these faded and were replaced by
heads with black faces. Finally, before she woke very cold, a voice
said 'He is going to be all right.' In retrospect her dream mirrored
the truth.

The Staff College area is three to four miles from Quetta city,
and though before dawn on 31st May some student officers and
their wives, and servants also, had heard bugles sounding the alarm
call and had seen the glow of fires in the sky to the south, nobody
thought anything much out of the ordinary had occurred. Fires
burning in the bazaar were not so unusual. Some people also, in

* Later, Major-General L. A. Hawes CBE, DSO, MC.

the morning, found their telephone was not working but that again was not uncommon. So, after breakfast Bernard and Colonel de Fonblanque set out with their students for Quetta airfield where the R.A.F. were due to give a demonstration of air support operations. But on arrival they were met by Wing Commander Slessor with his head bandaged, and saw the signs of a major disaster. Barracks and hangars were in ruins, aircraft were smashed, airmen were dead or wounded, as were some of their wives and children. From that moment every officer and employee in the Staff College area was diverted to take part in the relief and rescue operations under the able direction of Major-General Karslake* commanding the 2nd Indian Division, who set up his headquarters on the lawns and tennis courts of the Quetta Club, the buildings of which had been completely destroyed. If the disaster had occurred twenty-four hours later the club would have been packed with members and their guests attending the annual polo ball on the night of Saturday 1st June.

In this brief reference to the great Quetta earthquake of 1935 it would be quite wrong not to mention how all ranks of the garrison, soldiers and airmen both British and Indian, equally with the officers and staff of the civil administration, rose to the occasion in the admirable manner only to be expected of their traditions and training. With thirty thousand corpses lying buried under the ruins of the city the imminent dangers of disease were clear to all, and made more so by the foul smell from so many human bodies rotting in the hot sun. Under Karslake's orders therefore the whole city area was sealed off by a high wire fence and no person was allowed in or out under any circumstances except those on duty. To make matters worse there were more earth tremors in the Quetta valley two days after the initial outbreak, during which the summit of Chiltan, an eight thousand feet high mountain, was seen to burst into flames. Many stories of the disaster† have been told including the record of how men like Major-General Vyvyan, Lieutenant-Colonel Martin, Sir John Cowley and the late Sir

---

* Lieutenant-General Sir Henry Karslake KCB, KCSI, CMG, DSO.
† The best account is in Robert Jackson's well-named book *Thirty Seconds at Quetta*.

Henry Holland so quickly restored the city's communications; power, light and water supplies, hospital and medical services – with the help of course of many others far too numerous to mention. One of the greatest achievements was the fact that amidst all the chaos the staff of the North Western railway kept their main line to Karachi working. In all those activities Bernard played a leading part in the organisation and maintenance of the refugee camp, for the many thousands of homeless, which was set up on Quetta racecourse. Meanwhile orders were issued that no person was to live, and particularly not to sleep, within four walls in case of further earthquakes. A P & O liner was therefore chartered to make a special voyage to England for the evacuation of all women and children from any part of the region in Baluchistan still considered unsafe. Betty and her young son David, then six years old, were thus sent home for some months, but were able to rejoin Bernard at the Staff College well before the year was out. In their ten years of married life this was the only time, apart from a few weeks in 1931 when Bernard preceded her to Palestine, that Betty was separated from her husband.

In May 1937 Bernard returned from India to the United Kingdom. Having completed six years in appointments overseas he was now due for a period of home service and, to his great delight, he was to be promoted to Brigadier and given command of the 9th Infantry Brigade at Portsmouth. He and Betty sailed from Karachi in a City line passenger ship, and I remember passing their vessel in the Red Sea in the old trooper *S.S. Neuralia*, in which I was returning to Bombay with the Indian Coronation Contingent. Of course that summer they were united again with John and Dick Carver, and life seemed to offer everything they could wish for. The Portsmouth Brigade was in the 3rd Infantry Division, commanded by Major-General Denys Bernard, and was included in the formations selected to form part of the British Expeditionary Force for service overseas in the event of war. The Army Commander, whose Headquarters were on Salisbury Plain, was General Sir Archibald Wavell* who had asked that Bernard, on return

* The late Field-Marshal Earl Wavell of Winchester and Cyrenaica PC, GCB, GCSI, GCIE, CMG, MC.

from India, should be given command of the 9th Infantry Brigade. Wavell had done this because he was himself just as keen and well-informed on training matters as Bernard, of whom he thought very highly; above all, he shared my brother's views on the need to rethink both policy and methods, and was in no doubt that it was unorthodoxy that brought victory, rather than just spit and polish and ceremonial drill. When therefore Betty and Bernard first occupied their official quarters in Ravelin House, as Brigade Commander Portsmouth, they were extremely happy. It was not their first home in England but it was the largest they had had so far, and an ideal setting for Betty's paintings together with all their other possessions, furniture, silver and the like. In particular Ravelin House was just what they wanted as a home for David when he was not at his preparatory school at Hindhead, and for John and Dick Carver who were now both officers in the Royal Engineers. Then suddenly fate struck her cruellest blow – there could be none worse – for Betty Montgomery died on 19th October 1937, just ten years after their marriage, and when David their son was only nine years old.

Betty had not been quite her usual self, physically, since their return from Quetta. Perhaps all the strain of the earthquake period, coming at the end of living for six years in a hot and often trying climate, with many worries, had taken its toll of her physique, for she seemed to tire easily though her consistent gaiety and charm were never diminished. From this beginning what followed has often been told. My brother had to take his brigade into camp for late summer manoeuvres on Salisbury Plain, and Betty and David therefore went to Burnham-on-Sea in Somerset for the remainder of the school holidays. One day there, while David was bathing, Betty was stung on the foot by some strange insect whose bite was extremely poisonous. Normally there would have been no need for any great concern, but in this instance the poison spread very rapidly and the condition did not respond to any customary treatment; Bernard was sent for and came at once from Salisbury Plain, returning there after two days when there seemed to be an improvement. By now it was September, and then suddenly reaction set in. The condition instead of improving got worse so that eventually amputation became the last resort in a final endeavour to halt the spread of septicaemia. But it was all of no avail and she died.

It is not for me to dwell upon my brother's personal grief in the awful situation that faced him in that October of 1937. It is all in his *Memoirs*, and in other books about him, for those who wish to read of it. It is better to remember with gratitude the many friends who rallied round him and tried so hard to help. Always prominent among these was a Sapper Officer, Major F. E. W. Simpson, who was Bernard's Brigade-Major at Portsmouth, and who now proved his worth, already firmly established in his work, as a friend and counsellor also. In later years Simpson* rose to high rank and distinction as one of the great team of senior staff officers under Lord Alanbrooke. When that war was over and Bernard became CIGS, he made 'Simbo' his VICS. Probably nothing reveals better my brother's indomitable will and determination than his words to his Brigade-Major (Simpson) immediately he returned to the Salisbury Plain manoeuvres from his first visit to Betty at Burnham, following the mishap to her foot. When he left the Plain he had said to Simpson: 'You must carry on now. My wife is ill and I have to go . . .', or words to that effect. On his return he said to the Brigade-Major, 'Forgive these human failings of mine. I have been away two whole days. Now let's get down to training.'

I have often been asked what would have been the effect, if any, on my brother's personal life and career if his wife had survived that insect bite, or if it had never been. The question is a natural one to put, but very difficult to answer, if only because of the possibilities it raises in terms of the likely influence, or otherwise, of a man's wife on so many great events that have occurred. To attempt an answer one must go back to the time before Bernard married. Until then there is no doubt he was irrevocably married to his profession; he had virtually no other interests. But Betty changed all that and introduced into his life not only new interests, but also, in varying degrees and directions, new standards and values. The overall effect on himself was gradual and probably not visible to those outside his immediate circle of close friends and

* General Sir Frank Simpson GBE, KCB, DSO.

relatives, but it was there. It was noticeable in what can best be described as the rubbing off of corners and sharp edges in his approach to problems, particularly the personal problems of other people when they came his way. But after the awful tragedy of Betty's death my brother without doubt went back, as it were, to his first love and – I can think of no other way to express it – remarried his profession. From that time there followed that grim determination, so often publicised in the various media after he became famous, to pursue and achieve his aims, which happened to coincide with the nation's aims, against all opposition or distraction. That is not to say though, that if Betty had lived the course of his campaigns and their always successful outcome might have been changed – far from it. Nor does it mean that his thoughts on leadership, as briefly outlined earlier in this chapter, might not have been the same, particularly the last one on the selection of commanders. It will be remembered that when he first began to shape those ideas in his mind he was with Betty at Quetta, in the high noon of his marriage years. But it does mean that after 1937 a certain streak of intolerance in him was liable to appear, and sometimes found its expression in altogether unreasonable attitudes. His ban on married officers seeing their wives, during his command of V and XII Corps and South-Eastern army (U.K. 1940–2) is a case in point. Some may not agree with this, or with my view that its background stemmed, at any rate in part, from his anger with fate, call it a form of jealousy if you like, that had suddenly and brutally deprived him of the wonderful happiness and partnership he had so enjoyed during his marriage years. If this view is accepted it may also, again partly, account for his edict, in pursuit of physical fitness, that at every headquarters the whole staff, officers and men, must each week turn out and do a seven-mile cross-country run. In retrospect it can well be asked if in practice this achieved much – except perhaps to decrease the availability of some of the older, but unquestionably very able, officers! Finally there have been, though much later, those occasions when, for no apparently understandable reason, my brother was wont to reject and even turn against certain close relatives and friends of very long standing. In the judgement of those closest to Bernard none of that could have happened if Betty had lived beyond those ten happy years.

After the awful shock of October 1937 my brother devoted all his energy and determination to the training of the 9th Infantry Brigade, which soon became as well known as its commander in terms of enterprise and activity.

Chapter 8

THE EVE OF WAR

It was fortunate for our country that when Hitler's war began, in 1939, the organisational capacity of the regular armies of the British Empire, in terms solely of the numbers and availability of the infantry battalions, was still comparatively large. There were very considerable and widespread deficiencies, in transport, signals and in war material generally; but all battalions, whether British army, Dominion forces, Colonial or Indian units, were armed, equipped and trained in the same way. A certain numerical base was therefore provided by the presence of active units without which any rapid expansion was quite impossible. The British infantry of the line alone consisted of some one hundred and twenty regular battalions, as well as the ten battalions of the Brigade of Guards, whilst the Indian army could muster up to one hundred in addition to the twenty battalions of Gurkha infantry. Apart from these there were the regular colonial forces, which included the equivalent of seven battalions in the King's African Rifles and as many in the West African Frontier Force. All these units and formations were dependent ultimately on the War Office in Whitehall, where the work load involved was considerable. It was therefore with some dismay, mixed with irritation, in the summer of 1938 during the leave season when the majority of the staff at the War Office wished to be on leave, that reports began to arrive indicating that something very irregular was going on at the headquarters of an infantry brigade in the Portsmouth area. It was said that the Commander, one Brigadier B. L. Montgomery, without reference even to the Command Secretary let alone the War Office, had taken it upon himself to negotiate with an un-known circus promoter for the lease of some War Department land at Southsea; it was apparently proposed to hold a Fair on the Common for a week in August. Worse still this Brigadier, when faced with opposition to his scheme by the local City Council, had given five hundred pounds to the Lord Mayor of Portsmouth on condition that the latter 'squared' his Council and got their agree-ment to the proposed lease. This evidently the Lord Mayor had been successful in doing as he needed the five hundred pounds for some other Council project. When the matter was investigated it transpired that the Brigadier considered he urgently needed one thousand pounds for his garrison (married families) welfare fund. He had therefore devised a scheme whereby he would lease the main Brigade football field on Southsea Common for one thousand five hundred pounds, for the whole of the August bank holiday week when the majority of his troops would be on leave. This would then enable him to provide one thousand pounds immedi-ately for his welfare project, and at the same time make the five hundred pounds' conditional payment to the Lord Mayor's fund. However this explanation cut no ice with the military authorities who took the view that the Brigade Commander had acted in a wholly improper manner, and in a way which could under no circumstances be justified; in so doing he had been guilty of a flagrant breach of army regulations and procedure. The production of all the necessary receipts and correspondence arising out of the various transactions, including the welcome increase and benefit to the local army welfare funds, could not be regarded as any mitiga-tion of this most serious offence. In the opinion of the War Office it would now be necessary to take this matter into account when reviewing the Brigadier's promotion prospects. This would shortly occur anyway as it was the time of year when the annual confiden-tial reports on all regular officers had to be submitted.

The incident described in the preceding paragraph may already be known to many, as may its outcome and the action taken by

General Wavell. The latter recognised that Bernard had in him a force similar to the one in him, which drove them both to resist outworn policies and methods, especially where training and leadership, which must always include welfare, are concerned. Wavell also, like my brother, abhorred red tape and doubted the value of parade ground drill which he regarded as time-wasting activity; for him the drill that really mattered was 'battle drill'. There the similarity between the two great commanders ended, except on the plane of professional knowledge and ability and a common regard for the soldiers in the ranks, on whom, ultimately, everything depends. For Wavell was a Wykehamist scholar and poet, with a considerable literary reputation and a linguist in Russian, given to long periods of silence and certainly not prone to self publicity, who always avoided personal interviews and press conferences – it would surely be difficult to find any other distinguished commander of our times more disparate from my brother. Yet one characteristic perhaps they share: in giving judgement they both preferred the short and pithy comment to any long and erudite summing up. On one occasion during the 1939–45 war, after dinner in an officers' mess at which Wavell was present, the conversation turned to the vexed subject of the annual confidential reports on officers. The Commander-in-Chief, as he then was, had been silent for a long while and taken no part in the discussion. Suddenly Wavell came to life. 'The best confidential report I ever heard of,' he said, 'was also the shortest. It was by one Horse Gunner of another and ran – "Personally I would not breed from this officer"!'*

The case of the improper lease of the Garrison football field on Southsea Common had of course been reported to General Wavell. But the latter's predecessor at Southern Command Headquarters had been General Sir John Burnett-Stuart who had been my brother's army commander in Egypt. It seems certain therefore that Wavell would have known about Bernard's other unauthorised action of abolishing the ceremonial church parade without waiting for permission to do so. It was due to Wavell's influence that the matter of the football field was allowed to linger on, without any

* Quoted from *Lord Wavell* by Major-General R. J. Collins.

formal decision, until finally the incident was overtaken by events when Bernard was promoted Major-General. The incident itself however is important in my brother's life story. For it calls to mind how very often in his career he found himself in direct opposition to authority, in the form of his superior officer, for the quite simple reason that he chose to ignore rules and regulations, or equally orders given to himself. This happened when he felt strongly that to implement such orders would prejudice the successful outcome of his own ideas and plans for the common aim. In retrospect this line of conduct began at Sandhurst where he nearly failed to get his commission, continued at Bombay where he deliberately ignored his Commanding Officer's instructions about the football team to play against the Germans, was reflected in his attitude to the Directing Staff at Camberley in 1920, and in his ideas for revising *Infantry Training*, and appeared again at Alexandria and then at Portsmouth. Readers will see this same intolerance of authority, borne of conviction that he was right, appear again and again in his career. The fact that in the light of later events his thinking was generally shown to have been right is a tribute to his courage and determination, especially the courage of his convictions. To this must be added the undoubted fact that he was generally fortunate in the level of his immediately superior commanders. Men like Burnett-Stuart, Pile, Wavell and later Lord Alanbrooke all had the vision and foresight to recognise and support military genius when they found it, even when overlaid by eccentricity and sometimes against the opposition of their contemporaries.

That summer of 1938 provided virtually the first occasion, since the First World War, when any large-scale manoeuvres involving naval, land and air forces were carried out. It had been decided to hold an advanced training exercise to simulate an infantry brigade making an opposed landing on an enemy's coastline. The 9th Brigade was selected as the infantry formation for the exercise in co-operation with a naval task force provided by the then Commander-in-Chief at Portsmouth, Admiral of the Fleet The Earl of Cork and Orrery. This landing exercise, on the Dorset coast, attracted much attention at the time in service circles, chiefly because it showed clearly how totally unprepared our armed forces then were for combined operations, on even a small scale and particularly in equipment. There were no proper landing craft and the infantry disembarked on the beaches from open rowing boats manned by the navy, with air support provided by only a dozen Royal Navy (Swordfish) aircraft. Perhaps, after this lapse of time, two of the most interesting features of the exercise were that the Force Commander was the future Field-Marshal Montgomery, and that also present was the GSO1 of the 3rd Division, then Colonel Frederick Morgan. In the war that began little over one year later, Lieutenant-General Sir Frederick Morgan, KCB, as he became, was the architect of the original planning for Operation Overlord, the campaign for the invasion by Allied forces of North-West Europe. It took just under six years to move from the landing exercise of 1938, with its one infantry brigade, a dozen or so naval aircraft, and a few warships, to the million or more troops, over ten thousand aircraft and the fleets of two nations, assembled for an opposed landing on the French coast. On both occasions the commander of all the land forces was the same man, Bernard Montgomery.

In October of that year my brother was promoted Major-General and appointed to command the 8th Infantry Division in Palestine. The Arab rebellion there was getting out of hand, particularly in the northern part of the territory, for the whole of which the British Government was still responsible under mandate from the League of Nations. Lieutenant-General Haining was then General Officer Commanding the forces in Palestine which up till now had one infantry division only, the 7th, commanded by Major-General O'Connor in the southern part of the country. Haining had therefore asked for an extra division, the 8th, to be formed which, with its headquarters at Haifa, would be responsible for control in Northern Palestine, an area my brother knew well from his previous service there seven years earlier. This new command set-up brought together three officers, Haining, O'Connor and Montgomery, who had all been instructors together at Camberley in the late 1920s; it was perhaps just as well that they had this previous experience of joint working, for the military and political situation in the country generally was very bad. Due to the virtual disintegration of the Arab section of the Palestine police force law and order over most of the mandated territory had broken down. Arab terrorist activity was very great and, worse still, there were rumours of the start of a *jehad*, or holy war, by the Muslim population. Followers of the Grand Mufti of Jerusalem, religious head of the Sunni sect of Islam in Palestine, were encouraging the population to rise against government and kill all unbelievers; the Mufti himself had escaped into Syria from where he continued to incite the Palestinian Arabs to intensify their campaign of murder and destruction. By September the situation had become so bad, especially the need to maintain authority and control over the one thousand five hundred men of the Arab constabulary, that it became necessary to place the whole Palestine police force under command of the army; operational control of police forces was thus delegated to the commanders of the 7th and 8th Infantry Divisions in their respective areas.

When Bernard arrived at Haifa early in October 1938 to take command of the 8th Division he was quite unknown to any of his subordinate commanders. In fact, except for a few of the very senior officers no one had heard of him; he was just a newly pro-moted major-general come to take over the division. It was not long however before all that was changed, in a very decisive way, and his name, appearance and method of working became well known throughout the divisional area. The story of the circumstances in which one army officer then stationed at Haifa, a Lieutenant William Brown of the Royal Artillery, first met Major-General B. L. Montgomery, and of what transpired, will serve to show not only the kind of situation which faced the new Divisional Com-mander but how he dealt with it. At the time Lieutenant Brown, who had about four years' commissioned service and was twenty-four years old, was attached to the staff of the Haifa Town Military Commander, whose headquarters were in the main police barracks. Brown had then been in Palestine for about a year and a half. It was my brother's first week in Palestine and he had only just arrived in Haifa after visiting General Haining at Force Head-quarters in Jerusalem. One morning when Brown was in the Town

Bernard Montgomery
Commanding Officer,
1st Royal Warwickshire
Regiment, 1931

Mrs Bernard Montgomery

General Commanding the 8th Army, Italy, 1943

Commander's office a report was received indicating that some fracas had started in the *Suk* (Arab market). There were ominous signs that trouble was afoot and would develop into a serious situation unless action was taken as a matter of urgency. The Town Commander therefore rang up the army detachment located nearest to the *Suk*, which was standing by against any such emergency, and ordered it to proceed to the scene of the trouble immediately. He then turned to Brown and said, 'Brown, you'd better go down there at once and see what's happening. Take charge and deal with the matter in the way you think best. The emergency detachment is quartered in the Home for British Sailors, right by the *Suk*, and is a mixed bunch, half Royal Irish Fusiliers and half Coast Artillerymen. Get moving.'

When Brown arrived at the scene of the trouble the emergency duty detachment was already there and clearly a grave situation was developing. There was a very large crowd of Arabs who were blocking the street and would not disperse. Furthermore they had started looting shops and breaking windows, and were now stoning the detachment itself; some of them had firearms and others weapons and it all looked most sinister and dangerous. Brown could never be sure who started the shooting. He only knew for certain that it began just after he arrived on the scene and that a little later there were fourteen Arabs lying dead in the street. The only other certainty, beyond all doubt, was that the casualties among the Arabs resulted in an immediate end to the trouble in the *Suk*. The crowds dispersed at once and normal trading was soon resumed as if nothing had occurred. But whether it was the Irish Fusiliers, or the Coast Artillerymen or the Arabs, who fired first he would never know; because of course the troops were emphatic that it was the Arabs who had first opened fire, and equally the Arabs swore by Allah that the wicked British soldiers had begun the shooting and murdered innocent Muslims.

So Brown returned to the Town Commander and reported what had occurred. Later that day he was told to report to his own battery commander. The latter said that the new Divisional Commander had given orders for Brown to report at Divisional Headquarters at 8 a.m. the next morning; apparently the General wanted

9

to have a personal report, and explanation, from Brown of what had occurred, and in particular how it came about that fourteen Arabs had been shot dead. On hearing this Brown asked his battery commander who this new General was. The latter replied: 'He's Major-General Montgomery but I'm afraid I can't tell you any more. I've never heard of him until now. But it might be a good thing to stick to your guns as it were. Take the offensive and justify what occurred.' Brown thought about all this a lot that night.

The next morning Lieutenant Brown duly reported at Divisional Headquarters at 8 a.m. and was shown into the General's office. No one else was present and the conversation that followed, according to Brown, ran on the following lines.

Montgomery: Your name is Brown, isn't it, Lieutenant Brown?
Brown: Yes sir.
Montgomery: What's all this I hear? That you are responsible for all that shooting yesterday, and that you've killed fourteen Arabs.
Brown: No sir, that's quite wrong. The Arabs started the trouble.

Brown then gave the General an account of what had occurred, and finished by saying:

Look here, sir, I've been here now for eighteen months, and I know personally what the situation is. You have only just arrived and you may not be aware that all British other ranks are fed up with being bombed and shot at, and yet not be able to take any retaliation. Not to fire back in the circumstances I have described would have been madness, sir. Besides look at the salutary effect it had . . .
Montgomery: (*Breaking in*) Wait a minute, Brown. Your name is Brown isn't it? What I want to know is: who is interviewing who? you or me? Now, listen to me. It is possible you didn't kill enough Arabs, though the result appears to have been good. On the other hand you may have been most unwise and acted very foolishly. I shall have to decide. That's all.

Brown saluted and went out. He never again heard any more about the incident and there was no report in the press, or elsewhere, of what had occurred in the *Suk* at Haifa that October morning. Looking back at this incident it would appear hard to find a better example of the exercise of discretion by a divisional commander in support of a very junior officer and the men under his command. It would have been so easy just to read the reports, order a formal inquiry and accept the result. But there was a sequel. In the Western Desert in late August of 1942, just before the battle of Alam Halfa, Brown, who by this time was Major Brown and Brigade-Major Royal Artillery of 50 (Northumbrian) Division, was waiting with his Commander for the arrival of the new GOC Eighth Army (General B. L. Montgomery) who was paying his first visit to the artillery units of the Division. When Bernard arrived the Commander introduced Brown to him saying: 'This is my Brigade-Major, Sir, Major Brown. I don't think you know him.' Bernard's reply was instant: 'Indeed I know him. He once gave me a severe rocket! I shall never forget him.' Brown is now Major-General W. D. E. Brown, CB, CBE, DSO, and it is certain he too will never forget his first meeting with Field-Marshal Montgomery, and its sequel.

By April 1939 the operational situation in Palestine had much improved. From Dan in the far north of the country to Beersheba in the south, law and order was on its way to being fully restored, and General Haining reported on the situation to the War Office in the following terms:

PALESTINE
1 Nov. 38 – 31 Mar. 39

The best efforts of units would have availed little had the planning and general staff direction been found wanting. I would mention in this connection the energetic, loyal, and continuous guidance and good work displayed by the two Divisional Commanders, Major General R. N. O'Connor, DSO, MC, 7 DIV and Major General B. L. Montgomery, DSO, 8 DIV, whom I specially wish to bring to notice.

During that winter of 1938 Bernard was informed officially that he had been selected to command the 3rd Division on Salisbury Plain, and would be required to take up his post there the following August. This pleased him very much. He had already commanded a brigade in that division which he knew would mobilise, in the event of war, as one of the two infantry divisions in the II Corps of the British Expeditionary Force; the remaining division, the 4th, would come from the troops of the Eastern Command in England. However an unfortunate mishap now occurred.

The fact of my brother's unexpected and serious illness in the summer of 1939 is possibly not known to many outside army circles. In Palestine he suddenly developed a patch on his lung; this was regarded with some anxiety lest it developed into tuberculosis, having regard especially to his war wound of 1914 which had permanently affected his right lung. In the military hospital in Haifa his condition did not improve, and finally he had to be evacuated by sea, from Port Said to England, in the charge of R.A.M.C. orderlies and nurses. For some reason, never properly understood, this sea voyage had an astonishing effect and he walked off the P & O liner at Tilbury completely cured. Nevertheless he had to enter the Military Hospital at Millbank in London for a thorough inspection, and be passed by a medical board, before he was declared fit to resume normal duty. At this stage, while he was still in Millbank, he realised that the fact of his illness might well hamper his next appointment. It was now past mid-August and Hitler's war was near its beginning. In the War Office mobilisation was plainly seen as in the offing, and already plans were being made accordingly. These plans included a stop on notified appointments so that all officers remained in their present stations and jobs, in order to carry out and complete the complex task of mobilising for war. But Bernard was still a hospital case. He had vacated his appointment as GOC 8th Division, on evacuation as a casualty to the United Kingdom, and was therefore currently unposted without any formal appointment. In all such cases officers of the rank of General were placed on a waiting list, in which they were held pending the availability of suitable employment for them. This is in fact what happened; so my brother found himself without any appointment, unable to take command of the 3rd Division where Major-General D. K. Bernard* was to remain instead of going to Bermuda as Governor and Commander-in-Chief, and equally debarred from returning to the 8th Division where a new commander had been appointed.

Anyone with the slightest knowledge of my brother's character will appreciate how very galling he must have found it to be placed, as it were, in baulk at the very moment when the army was about to mobilise. That he, the very architect of training for war, the writer of *Infantry Training*, should now be set aside by the formality of regulations was intolerable. I so well remember visiting him in hospital at Millbank one fine summer afternoon about this time. I was then in the middle of my final (second) year as a Staff College student and he had asked me to come and see him and tell him 'all about it'. He was always interested in the Staff College training course and he now asked me many questions. What were the students like? Were they any good? Did the Directing Staff know their stuff? (The Commandant was his old friend General Sir Bernard Paget.) Who had come down to Camberley to lecture? I was in the middle of attempting to answer such questions when 'Simbo' (who had been his Brigade-Major at Portsmouth and was now Brevet Lieutenant-Colonel Simpson) arrived, and I recall I left at once – perhaps somewhat relieved at not, as a student, having to pass comment on my instructors to a major general! I do not know what transpired after I had left but Simpson was then at the War Office, as an Assistant Military Secretary, and I have always thought it likely that their conversation led to the decision, taken later officially, that the mobilisation regulations should not prevent my brother from assuming the appointment for which he had previously been chosen. It is only a coincidence that at this time de Guingand was also at the War Office, as Military Assistant to Hore-Belisha, the Secretary of State for War. On 28th August Bernard took command of the 3rd Infantry Division just six days before Hitler's war began.

On leaving hospital my brother's first concern was to make provision for a home for David as he could no longer foresee his own

* The late Lieutenant-General Sir Denis Bernard, KCB, CMG, DSO.

movements once war was declared. Since Bernard's move to
Palestine David's home had been with some kind friends of his
father at Portsmouth, who had looked after him especially during
his school holidays. These arrangements continued until eventually David's home in England was firmly established with Major
and Mrs Reynolds at Hindhead in Surrey. Major Reynolds was a
very old friend of my brother from pre-1914 days. He had been a
regular officer in the Kings Own Yorkshire Light Infantry who had
early abandoned a military career for the profession of school
master. He had been a master at Beachborough Park near Shorncliffe when Bernard rejoined his regiment there in 1925, and the
two had thus met again. Reynolds was now headmaster of David's
preparatory school and he and his wife provided a home for David
during the whole time he was at Winchester also. In his *Memoirs*
my brother wrote of the Reynolds:

> 'Major Reynolds was an old and valued friend of many years'
> standing and from 1942 to 1948 that school building became
> David's home, and mine. Major Reynolds died in 1953 – he and
> his wife were responsible for developing the character of many
> boys on the right lines and the nation lost in him a man of
> sterling character. I owe them much.'

Hitler's War Begins

When I reached this stage in my story I had to decide how to treat
the whole period of the six years of Hitler's war. My Field-Marshal
brother's part in it was so large and so vital that there is scarcely
any account of those years, yet written, in which he does not
figure very prominently in one way or another. Furthermore the
majority of those accounts have given, broadly, the same facts and
details of his actions, though in varying terms, with a very similar
analysis of his character and personality. It therefore seemed to me
important to avoid any such repetition, by confining my own
account to those major and more controversial issues and decisions
in which he became involved, not infrequently, during all the war
years. This will be more relevant to my theme, particularly in the

light of what he has told me personally and, perhaps equally important, of the fact that for the first time the official documents and papers in the Public Record Office, dealing with the war period, have become open to inspection.

The so-called phoney period of the war lasted from September 1939, when the British Expeditionary Force under General Gort* landed in France, until 10th May 1940 when the German armies invaded Holland and Belgium and began their great offensive against the French and British forces. That virtually no fighting between the opposing sides, on any large scale, took place during those eight months was one of the factors that contributed to the successful evacuation of the B.E.F. from the beaches in the last week of May, though at a very heavy cost in arms and war material of every kind. During this relatively quiet time, free from active operations, the formations of the British force, consisting of the I and II Corps commanded by Sir John Dill and Alan Brooke respectively, were able to carry out that intensive training, which they had not done in the United Kingdom. The divisions in each corps, and III Corps was formed early in 1940, were still lacking in tanks, anti-tank guns, anti-aircraft artillery, signal facilities and equipment; but at least they were well trained in the use of what they had, before the German offensive began. Two other factors also contributed to the successful withdrawal of the B.E.F. First, the extremely bitter winter conditions in Northern France and the Low countries, which began before 1939 was ended, adversely affected the timing of Hitler's offensive by delaying it until the spring of 1940. Next, and conversely, it was the fine summer weather conditions at the end of May, especially the flat calm sea in the English Channel, that very largely made possible the escape of thousands of British soldiers from La Panne and Dunkirk.

By now it goes without saying that Major-General Montgomery's 3rd Infantry Division, in II Corps, was trained well and ceaselessly all through that winter of the phoney war period in France. My brother concentrated in particular on training his

* The late Field-Marshal Viscount Gort, VC, GCB, CBE, DSO, MVO, MC.

division for motorised movement by night. He fully appreciated
that the need for this would arise, as it did, and that it would come
suddenly without warning and would have to be carried out over
roads already congested with refugee traffic. This meant very careful staff training at all levels, with of course equivalent preparation
in every unit for movement in the dark without vehicle lights,
except for a dim tail-lamp under the differential, and probably not
even that. Every soldier knows how difficult a complicated night
manoeuvre can be without constant practice; particularly if it
involves lateral movement across the axis of the main traffic flow,
followed by occupation of a defensive position in readiness for a
dawn attack by the enemy. Such practice the troops of the 3rd
Division certainly got, as Alan Brooke well knew when he wrote of
this time in his diary.*

> 'All three (divisions) were commanded by fine soldiers and
> one – the 3rd – by a trainer of genius, Major General Bernard
> Montgomery. It was a matter of the greatest interest watching
> Monty improving every day as he began to find his feet as a
> Divisional Commander. . . . These exercises, all of them admir-
> ably run were an eye-opener to me as to his ability as a trainer.
> Their value was more than proved when we finally carried out
> our advance, as his 3rd Division worked like clockwork.'

Meanwhile, in November 1939 during the course of all this
training, there occurred another of those unfortunate incidents in
my brother's career which nearly removed him from the military
scene. He had long been aware of the incidence of venereal
disease in his division, which, as in other divisions, continued to
cause unacceptable levels of absence from duty in spite of the most
energetic administrative action. He had had similar trouble with
his regiment at Alexandria eight years before, where he had
adopted unorthodox methods, and he now decided to issue an
order to his subordinate commanders on the subject, outlining his
views on how the problem should be tackled afresh. When however
this order, signed personally by himself, came to the notice of his

* Extract from *The Turn of the Tide* by Sir Arthur Bryant.

superior commanders there was very great indignation, particularly by the senior chaplain at GHQ. Lord Gort was informed and much trouble ensued as the Commander-in-Chief took the view that the order was of a most undesirable and improper character and ought therefore to be withdrawn by its originator. Nevertheless the fact remained that to compel any commander to withdraw an order issued personally by himself must result in undermining his whole authority, and cast grave doubts on his capacity to maintain discipline. So here was a pretty kettle of fish, appearing at a most awkward moment for everyone. The story of the issue of this divisional order (3 Div Order 179/A dated 15 Nov. 1939) and of how Brooke successfully intervened to prevent irreparable damage to Bernard, is probably known to many. But to the best of my knowledge the actual order has never since seen the light of day, neither, as far as I am aware, is there a copy of it in the Public Record Office. For several reasons therefore I have thought it right and proper that the document should appear in this book.

Subject: Prevention of Venereal Disease.

Div. 179/A
15 Nov. 39.

List "A"

1.   I am not happy about the situation regarding venereal disease in the Division.

   Since the 18 October the number of cases admitted to Field Ambulances in the Divisional area totals 44.

2.   I consider that the whole question of women, V.D., and so on is one which must be handled by the regimental officer, and in particular by the C.O. The men must be spoken to quite openly and frankly, and the more senior the officer who speaks to them the better.

   My view is that if a man wants to have a woman, let him do so by all means: but he must use his common sense and take the necessary precautions against infection – otherwise he becomes a casualty by his own neglect, and this is helping the enemy.

   Our job is to help him by providing the necessary means:

9*

he should be able to buy French Letters in the unit shop, and
E.T. rooms must be available for his use.

As regards the E.T. rooms – it is no use having one room
in the battalion area: there should be one room in each coy.
area: the man who has a woman in a beetroot field near his
coy. billet will not walk a mile to the battalion E.T. room.

If a man desires to buy his French Letter in a civil shop he
should be instructed to go to a chemist shop and ask for a
"Capote Anglaise".

3.   I know quite well that the cases of V.D. we are getting are
from local "pick ups": hence the need for French Letters and
E.T. rooms.

There are in Lille a number of brothels, which are properly
inspected and where the risk of infection is practically nil.
These are known to the military police, and any soldier who
is in need of horizontal refreshment would be well advised to
ask a policeman for a suitable address.

4.   The soldier on his part must clearly understand the penal-
ties that are attached to V.D., and the reasons.

5.   Finally, then, I wish all unit commanders to keep in touch
with the V.D. problem and handle it in the way they think
best.

We must face up to the problem, be perfectly frank about
it, and do all we can to help the soldier in this very difficult
matter.   (Signed). . .

MARS AMATORIA*

The General was worried and was very ill at ease,
He was haunted by the subject of venereal disease;
For four and forty soldiers was the tale he had to tell
Had lain among the beets and loved not wisely but too well.
It was plain that copulation was a tonic for the bored,
But the gallant British Soldier was an Innocent Abroad;
So ere he takes his pleasure with an amateur or whore,
He must learn the way from officers who've trod that path
    before.

* The Royal Corps of Signals reacted to the order as follows.

No kind of doubt existed in the Major-General's head
That the men who really knew the game of Love from A to Z
Were his Colonels and his Adjutants and those above the ruck,
For the higher up an officer the better he can f—k.
The Colonels and the Majors were not a bit dismayed,
They gave orders for the holding of a Unit Love Parade,
And the Adjutants by numbers showed exactly how it's done,
How not to be a casualty and still have lots of fun.
The Adjutants explained that "capote" did not mean a cup,
That refreshment horizontal must be taken standing up,
They told the troops to work at Love according to the rules,
And after digging in to take precautions with their tools.
Now the General is happy and perfectly at ease,
No longer is he troubled with venereal disease,
His problem solved, his soldiers clean (their badge is now a
    dove)
He has earned the cross of Venus, our General of Love.

"CUPID"

R. Signals.

In this day and age everyone is aware of the vast changes that
have taken place, and are still continuing, in nearly every field of
our social life. These changes include decisions which have revolu-
tionised our thinking as to what is proper, or improper, in literature
to be read by both young and old of our generation. It follows
then that the document I have included should no longer necessarily cause offence to those who see it. Furthermore, readers will
be able to judge for themselves on which side they stand, in these
more permissive days, in the matter of the wisdom, or otherwise,
of the issue of such an order to troops on active service. There will
be many who will see in it not only its logic and clarity (it is not
open to any misunderstanding) but also the very serious intention
underlying it, namely, to come to grips with the problem by fresh
thinking on the part of officers and men alike. There may also be
those who will see the order as still in bad taste, if not more
objectionable, and therefore regret its publication at any time.
Nevertheless readers will I hope enjoy reading it – equally with the

verses preceding which certainly show that the Royal Corps
of Signals were in no doubt about their appreciation! And
above all readers will see in the incident yet one more manifestation
of my brother's unfailing habit of bringing humour into every
facet of his work. There is in him an imp of mischief which has
been with him all his life, which he cannot control, and which
beyond question deserves its place in the pages of this book; perhaps never more so than in this account of 3rd Divisional Order
179/A. Of course General Alan Brooke, as Corps Commander,
left my brother in no doubt of the error of his ways. He made it
quite clear that it was touch and go whether a new commander
would not be required for the 3rd Infantry Division. Bernard fully
accepted all that was said to him, for, as he has told me recently,
'Both as a commander and staff officer Brooke was by far the
greatest soldier of the war.' For his part Brooke wrote in his diary
at the time: 'I never ceased to thank Heaven that I saved Monty
at this danger point in his career.'

Looking at the scene as a whole, provided by the retreat to the
sea at Dunkirk of the British army in May 1940, there was one
most fortunate event to lighten an otherwise wholly black picture.
This was the bringing together, under Brooke's command, of the
two Divisional Commanders, Major-Generals Alexander and
Montgomery. It began on the 18th May when the overall situation
facing the B.E.F. was extremely bad. The French air force had
virtually ceased to operate, and the very small Royal Air Force
contingent was already reduced to half strength, so the Germans
had overall air control. With this great advantage their tanks were
sweeping across Northern France and Belgium. Holland had
already collapsed, the French armies were beginning to totter, and
the Belgian army was clearly not in a position to make any serious
resistance. In these circumstances the immense superiority of the
German armies, particularly in armoured divisions, could not fail
to bring them success. Seven armoured divisions had crossed the
Meuse and were heading for the English Channel, whilst in one
army group alone (Von Rundstedt's) no less than thirty-seven
infantry divisions were available to support their armoured thrust.
At this time there were still only eleven infantry divisions all told

in the B.E.F., and one of these, the ill-fated 51st Highland Division, had been diverted to assist the French in the Maginot Line; the only British armoured division, the 1st, was not yet complete. It was in these dreadful circumstances that Alexander's 1st Infantry Division was transferred by Lord Gort from I Corps to the command of Brooke in II Corps, where for the first time the latter had both Alexander and Montgomery working under him. The two men, 'Alex' then forty-eight years of age and 'Monty' four years older, were clearly totally different characters, though Brooke with his keen perception noted nevertheless the example of calm efficiency that each presented at a time of great peril. For Bernard any emergency served merely to stimulate his senses, so that he positively thrived on crisis. Alexander appeared to react in a quite different way and was described by Brooke in his diary in the following terms:

> 'Alex, on the other hand, gave me the impression of never fully realising all the very unpleasant potentialities of our predicament. He remained entirely unaffected by it, completely composed and appeared never to have the slightest doubt that all would come right in the end.'

The impression made on Brooke by these two commanders in those early days of the war, and the appreciation he made of each, had its lasting effect; for it was Brooke who, later on when he became CIGS, was ultimately responsible for bringing them together again in the Middle East.

It is perhaps not generally known that only an astonishing piece of good luck, in the early months of 1942, prevented Field-Marshal Alexander from being killed by the Japanese in Burma, or made their prisoner until the Far Eastern war ended more than three years later, in either of which cases the Alexander and Montgomery partnership in the desert campaign would not have come about. Burma was invaded by the Japanese late in 1941 and Alexander had been flown to Rangoon in the first week of March 1942 to take command of the hard-pressed and outnumbered army in Burma. Singapore had fallen on 15th February and now it seemed that

Rangoon must suffer a similar fate unless the garrison could be evacuated before the city was surrounded by the Japanese army. After the invasion had begun the troops left in the capital consisted only of one British regiment, the 1st Gloucesters, and one battalion of Burma Rifles, less two companies, together with Burma Army Headquarters. Alexander arrived on 5th March and by the following day he had informed Wavell (then Commander-in-Chief India) and Brooke, the CIGS, of his final decision to abandon Rangoon forthwith. He hoped there was still time to control and co-ordinate the withdrawal of the 17th Indian Division and the 1st Burma Division to Upper Burma, where, with the aid of two Chinese armies promised by General Chiang Kai-Shek, it was the intention to defend the important oilfields. Large fires were burning in Rangoon, which had been looted extensively, when the garrison withdrew at dawn on 7th March, but by the time they had reached the Taukkyan road junction the Japanese 33rd Division had forestalled them and their way was blocked. Two attacks, one by the Gloucesters and another by a battalion of the 63rd Brigade from the 17th Division, both failed utterly so that by nightfall the position was very serious. The 63rd Infantry Brigade had suffered grievously; they had only just arrived from India, partially trained for jungle warfare and without their transport, and on their very first day in action their Commander, Brigadier John Wickham, and all three battalion commanders, had been killed. At sunset that day Alexander, his Chief of Staff Tom Hutton,* the Brigadier-General Staff 'Taffy' Davies,† and the small Army Headquarters staff gathered in a little Burmese hut within less than eight hundred yards of the Japanese road block. It was a scene not easily forgotten: the sky was almost obscured by a dense pall of black smoke from the ninety million gallons of petrol and fuel oil in the Syriam refinery which, with the electric power station and the railway and harbour installations, had been set on fire to prevent their falling into the hands of the enemy. It was clear to all that the Japanese had only to maintain their road block, and then attack in flank or rear, in order to repeat at Rangoon what had happened at Singa-

---

* Lieutenant-General Sir Thomas Hutton, KCIE, CB, MC.
† Major-General H. L. Davies, CB, CBE, DSO, MC.

pore; two Japanese infantry divisions, the 33rd and 35th, were closing in on the city. That night Alexander, imperturbable as ever and still very well turned out, issued his orders for one final all-out attack against the road block at dawn the following morning. I recall that as GSO2 it fell to me to record the orders and ensure they reached all addressees. In the event what transpired was wholly unexpected and quite astonishing. The attack duly took place, but it was then found that the Japanese had vacated the road block and our force was therefore able to continue their withdrawal north as planned. The enemy's objective had been to encircle and capture the city from the north-west, and this they did; they could not have known then what they had missed. So in reality it was due to a serious error of judgment by a Japanese commander that made Alexander available for the tasks he was to accomplish during the rest of those war years, and thereafter.

I shall pass quickly over the events, so often told, of the withdrawal of the British Expeditionary Force from Dunkirk to the English Channel ports, and of how Alexander was in charge for the final stage of the evacuation, having handed over command of II Corps to my brother. When the British army was reconstituted in the United Kingdom Bernard resumed command of his 3rd Division, but was soon appointed to command of the V Corps in the area of Hampshire and Dorset. It was during this time that he first met Auchinleck who was then in charge of Southern Command. Unfortunately from the outset the two men never got on well, and their enmity was to have very considerable repercussions later on. In the circumstances prevailing in the United Kingdom immediately after Dunkirk, with its serious risk of invasion, Auchinleck had seen fit to issue a general order in Southern Command that until further notice no soldier was to be parted from his rifle or revolver, or whatever his personal fire-arm might be, at any time. Bernard disagreed entirely with this precaution; he thought it would be entirely impracticable for day-to-day working and used to say: 'But what happens when a soldier goes to bathe in the sea (by now it was August 1940), or when he is with his girl friend in the dark in the back row of the cinema? What does he do with his rifle then?' He accordingly gave orders that in V Corps area the

order was not to be obeyed by anyone. Of course this set the scene
for a most appalling row and yet another hazard for my brother's
career! However, luckily for him, about this time Auchinleck
returned to India as Commander-in-Chief, so the affair was
allowed to blow itself out.

During this period also my brother resumed his acquaintance
with another future field-marshal; this was Brigadier G. W. R.
Templer* who had been a student under Bernard at Camberley
and was now appointed BGS (Ops) at Headquarters V Corps.
Templer always remembers his manner of arrival at the Corps
Headquarters. He had travelled by car straight from the beach
defences on the south coast where he was a brigade commander.
It was raining heavily when he arrived and as his staff car drew up
at the entrance Bernard was waiting for him. Templer, who always
appreciated the good things of life, had a bottle in each hand when
he got out of the car, gin in his right hand and vermouth in his left.
Thus encumbered he found shaking hands with the Corps Commander somewhat complicated, and also wondered whether his
new general might not comment adversely on his belongings! But
he survived all right and was not long in obtaining Bernard's trust
and confidence. Templer recalls that it was during this period in
the United Kingdom, first with V Corps, then from April 1941
with XII Corps in Kent, and lastly as GOC South-East Army in
Kent, Surrey and Sussex, that my brother began to develop and
put into practice his ideas on self-publicity as an essential element
in leadership and command. He held strongly, as indeed events
showed later, that in time of war senior military commanders had a
duty to become well known, not only to the troops under their
command, the vast majority of whom were not professional soldiers, but also to the thousands of civilians working in the factories,
on the land, as air raid wardens, and elsewhere. This was something he felt had to be taken very seriously, particularly at a time
of great national danger. He used to say to Templer: 'Remember,
you must – however much you may dislike it – put yourself across
to your public as well, in a big way. You must inspire them by

* Field-Marshal Sir Gerald Templer, KG, GCB, GCMG, KBE,
DSO.

talking to them frankly and frequently and so manage to jolly them along. To do this you will generally need to hire a large hall or cinema with a platform for yourself. There you will have to speak to them in words which will gain their loyalty and respect by identifying yourself with each one of them, such as :"You and I have it in us to save the nation. We must do it".' All this happened during those anxious days in 1940–41, and beyond that into 1942, whilst the threat of invasion remained a serious danger for our country and was not lifted until the tide turned in Africa, by which time the United States had entered the war. My brother was clearly influenced at this time, in his thinking on the need for self-publicity, by his experiences in the 1914–18 war when few men in the ranks of the British armies in France had ever heard of General Sir Douglas Haig, let alone seen their Commander-in-Chief. Now Bernard felt strongly that an officer who aspires to be a leader of men, in peace or war, must not rely merely on the fact that he holds a commission which entitles him to give orders and to expect, and if necessary exact, obedience. On the contrary he must first of all create enthusiasm and confidence, in himself, so that the men under his command have a positive wish to follow and obey him. In this connection there is no doubt that my brother much enjoyed this sort of task and that perhaps is one reason why he became so good at it. Some commanders utterly reject any thought of public presentation of themselves by themselves, but for Bernard it was second nature to do so, and there is equally no doubt that he derived this in large measure from our mother. She loved to hold the stage, and, particularly in her old age, much enjoyed basking in reflected glory as 'the Field-Marshal's mother'. This indeed led to most bitter recrimination between them and was the cause of much genuine unhappiness. Mother was not deterred – on the contrary she enjoyed it all – but the rest of us found it rather embarrassing.

During 1941 my brother suffered another heavy loss, this time of all his belongings of every sort. When he had left Portsmouth to command the 8th Division in Palestine he had vacated Ravelin House and stored all his possessions in a local warehouse. There they had remained, as he had left them, until he took his 3rd

Division to France in September 1939 and it seemed right, at that time, to continue to leave them there. Then one night in January 1941 when he was with V Corps in Dorset, German bombers raided Portsmouth and took their toll of many houses including that warehouse. The building was set on fire and completely demolished so that its entire contents were utterly destroyed and nothing could be recovered. All his possessions, which included Betty's, with their furniture, silver and plate, linen, and, perhaps worst of all many of her paintings, were lost for ever. Fortunately three of them – they were portraits in water colour she had done at Quetta of a Sikh, a Punjabi Musulman and a local Brahui – survived. I liked them so much that she had very kindly given them to me. David Montgomery has them now and they are hung in his house in London.

So my brother was left owning literally nothing except his clothing and personal belongings. He was still in this state when his campaign in Egypt began.

Biographers of the future will probably agree that in all the life of Field-Marshal Montgomery the most testing time for him was that period of nearly three years, from August 1942 until the war with Germany ended officially on 8th May 1945. Within these limits it is not difficult to identify those occasions, some of them long in time, when all that he did, particularly the decisions he made and the plans and actions that followed, came under the closest scrutiny and comment, some of it very adverse. The first of these occasions concerned the manner of my brother's assumption of command of the Eighth Army in the Western Desert of Egypt on 13th August 1942. The background to his appointment has been fully described in his *Memoirs*, and in other books, and therefore needs only brief mention here. After the capitulation on 21st June of the garrison at Tobruk with all its great store of war material, particularly petrol and transport of which Rommel stood much in need, Auchinleck had himself relieved General Ritchie* as Army Commander. He had taken with him Dorman-Smith,†

---

* General Sir Neil Ritchie, GCB, KCB, DSO, MC.
† The late Major-General E. E. Dorman O'Gowan, MC. (He had assumed the surname O'Gowan in 1949.)

his Deputy Chief of General Staff, leaving General Corbett, his CGS, to act as Commander-in-Chief at Cairo. Unfortunately none of these measures brought improvement in the overall strategic and tactical situation in the Western Desert; so that towards the end of July the Eighth Army was forced back on a general line running from El Alamein on the Mediterranean coast to the southern edge of the Qattara Depression. This was indeed a serious situation. Coming on top of the heavy losses at Tobruk the subsequent retreat meant that the Eighth Army's resources in tanks were now extremely slender, added to which there was undoubtedly a feeling of unease amongst the troops of all arms generally; they were no longer happy and there had been considerable casualties, particularly in the early June fighting around Gazala where some whole units had been overrun. In Tobruk no less than four brigade groups including the South African Division had been compelled to surrender, after the Germans had succeeded in forcing their way through the perimeter defences, and had destroyed the majority of our tanks and much of the artillery. The overall result was that Cairo was now within range of enemy fighter aircraft, in Alexandria the population could hear the sound of German artillery bombardment, and the Royal Navy had had to withdraw its main base from the port. It was against this background that Churchill had arrived in Cairo with Brooke, who was now CIGS, and had visited Eighth Army Headquarters for breakfast on 5th August. It is on record that the Prime Minister did not enjoy the meal which was eaten, according to him, in heat and discomfort in a fly-blown tent. As a result of this visit decisions were taken to appoint Alexander Commander-in-Chief Middle East and Bernard the GOC Eighth Army, in place of General Gott who had been shot down in an aircraft and killed on 7th August. All along Brooke had pressed for Bernard to take over the Eighth Army.

It had been late in July, not long before these momentous decisions were announced, that de Guingand had been appointed Brigadier-General Staff (BGS) at Headquarters Eighth Army. He had been a member of the Joint Planning Staff in Cairo since January 1941, until, one year later, Auchinleck had made him his

Director of Military Intelligence. Now Auchinleck had brought him forward again into another key appointment. Two men, each of whom in his own way has earned much distinction, had served as junior intelligence officers on de Guingand's staff in Cairo. Captain E. T. Williams,* already a graduate with First Class Honours at Oxford and later a Fellow of Balliol College with many other academic awards, had been spotted by de Guingand as an unusual asset in any intelligence organisation. Later Bill Williams joined Intelligence in Eighth Army and accompanied my brother throughout his campaigns as his Chief of Intelligence, from El Alamein until the final surrender at Luneberg Heath in 1945. He is now Warden, The Rhodes Trust. The other officer, Major J. E. Powell, had originally joined up in 1939 in the ranks of my brother's regiment (the Royal Warwickshire) with which he continued to serve until he was commissioned and appointed an intelligence officer. He is now The Right Honourable Enoch Powell, MBE, MA, MP.

My Field-Marshal brother arrived in Cairo early on the morning of 12th August, Alexander having got there three days earlier. After he had breakfasted at the Mena House Hotel, on the outskirts of the city, Bernard's first act was to visit Auchinleck at the Middle East Command Headquarters. Much has been written about their meeting that morning in Auchinleck's map room. Bernard has always emphasised, particularly in his *Memoirs*, that the Commander-in-Chief, assuming Rommel would attack soon in force, had been planning for a complete withdrawal of the Eighth Army into the Delta, and if necessary further south up the Nile, or even into Palestine. In short plans were afoot, in the event of a serious enemy offensive in the near future, to abandon Cairo altogether if that was essential in order to keep the Eighth Army intact. This assertion has been challenged by many people, particularly of course by Auchinleck and Dorman-Smith, and brought much trouble for my brother including accusations of total inaccuracy and irresponsible conduct. The only certainty about this particular issue is that it will for ever generate controversy, as none of the protagonists on either side, nor equally their supporters past,

* Brigadier E. T. Williams, CB, CBE, DSO, DL.

present and future, will admit the other was right. But over thirty years have passed since Auchinleck and Montgomery talked alone together in a locked room (no one else was allowed to be present) at Middle East Command Headquarters in Cairo on 12th August 1942. Surely after this long lapse of time it should be possible to review the matter again, wholly impartially and particularly in the light of official documents recently released, and reach a balanced conclusion. In the first place one should recognise the atmosphere in which Auchinleck had moved, and which surrounded him since the disastrous fall of Tobruk. He had been barely a year in Egypt and, like his predecessor Wavell, had met in the first place with considerable success only to be followed by a most unfortunate retreat with very great loss. Now he had just been informed that he was to be relieved of his command and could take no future part in the steps which would have to be taken, and which he wished to take, to retrieve the position. Could any commander find himself in a more depressing situation, or one more likely to colour his outlook, especially in discussion with an officer with whose opinion he had already disagreed and who was now to take command of his Eighth Army? Furthermore Auchinleck will have been aware of the view of the situation taken in the War Office, as shown in the documents quoted in the following paragraphs, including the contingency plans which were being considered, both at his own Headquarters and in Whitehall.

In London the situation had been regarded as very serious for some time; so much so that by 7th July the Chiefs of Staff had already been informed by their Joint Planning Staff that the position in Libya was such that our ability to hold lower Egypt and the Suez Canal was in serious doubt. A report on the 'worst case', which might arise if the enemy gained possession of the Nile Delta and Cairo, had been prepared. This clearly showed that the possibility of having to withdraw from the El Alamein position was not excluded from contingency planning. Meanwhile on 31st July Auchinleck sent the following telegram to the War Office in London:

PUBLIC RECORD OFFICE DOCUMENT NO. CAB 56/92

From:—C.in.C. Middle East Desp. 1030 31 Jul 42.
To:— War Office. Recd. 1415 31 Jul 42.

MOST IMMEDIATE

30295 cipher 31 Jul. MOST SECRET

Following received from T.A.C. 8 Army No. CST/123 TOO 0835 date 31/7. Begins. Personal and most secret for C.G.S. for C.I.G.S. from Gen. Auchinleck Adv H.Q. 8 Army 0445 hours G.M.T. 31st July.

One. Situation unchanged.

Two. Held exhaustive conference on tactical situation yesterday with Corps Commanders. Reluctantly concluded that in present circumstances renewal of our efforts to break enemy front or turn his southern flank not feasible owing to lack of resources and effective consolidation of his positions by enemy. Opportunity for resumption of offensive operations unlikely to arise before middle September depending on enemy's ability to build up his tank force. Policy therefore will be temporarily defensive including thorough preparations and consolidation whole defensive area El Alamein – Burg El Arab, and ground to south. Rear Defences along the edge of Delta and round Wadi Natrun will also be developed fully. Meanwhile should chance offer of taking the offensive suddenly and surprising the enemy owing to some lapse on his part it will be seized at once. C.in.C's now considering effect of this tactical situation on general strategical situation and will submit appreciation as soon as possible to Chief of Staff.

Finally on 5th August the War Cabinet recorded their view of the situation in the Middle East in a Minute from which the following is an extract. By this time Sir Winston Churchill had left for Cairo with the CIGS.

PUBLIC RECORD OFFICE DOCUMENT NO. CAB 65/66
W.M. (42) 104TH CONCLUSIONS, MINUTE 2.

Confidential Annex.

(5th August 1942 – 6.30 p.m.)

The War Cabinet had under consideration a Report by the

Chiefs of Staff Committee on the situation which might arise in the Middle East in the event of Germany obtaining a major success against Russia (W.P.(42)335) and a Report by the Oil Control Board on the effect that the loss of the Abadan oil supplies would have on our war effort.

THE DEPUTY PRIME MINISTER said that in giving instructions that the Chiefs of Staff Report should be circulated to, and considered by, the War Cabinet, in his absence, the Prime Minister had had it in mind that his colleagues should be aware of the issues at stake and the main considerations affecting these issues, and thus be in a position to take decisions when the time came. It was clearly undesirable to come to any hard and fast conclusion on this problem while it was under discussion by the Prime Minister and Commanders-in-Chief in the Middle East.

THE CHIEF OF THE AIR STAFF explained that the Report had been prepared in response to a telegram from the Middle East Defence Committee drawing attention to the grave issues with which we might be faced, and propounding the choice which might have to be made if the campaign in Russia went very badly for the Russians. We might, in that event, find that we had insufficient forces to hold the Northern Front and to defend Egypt from the threat from Libya. We should then have to choose between deploying our resources so as to secure the Persian oil field with the consequential loss of Egypt, or concentrating on the defence of Egypt with the risk that we should lose the Persian oil.

For the reasons given in their Report, the Chiefs of Staff had come to the conclusion that, should the worst arise, every effort should be made to hold on to the Abadan area, even at the risk of losing the Nile Delta. The problem was mainly one of oil. The loss of the Persian Gulf oil facilities could only be made good by the services of an additional 270 tankers. Without these, a drop of up to 25% in our war effort would become inevitable. The loss of Abadan would probably result in the eventual loss of Egypt and the grave weakening of our position in the whole of the Indian Ocean area.

The extracts from these official documents surely make it entirely clear that Auchinleck, having stabilised his position on the Alamein line, was determined to resume the offensive, but did not feel able to do so before the middle of September at the earliest; and that meanwhile both he and his fellow Commanders-in-Chief in the Middle East, *and the Chiefs of Staff in London*, appreciated that the one really vital issue, of paramount importance and transcending all else, was our continued possession of Middle East oil. We should be prepared to defend the Abadan area, with the South Persian oil fields, if necessary at the risk of losing the Nile Delta, including Cairo. It follows, from this, that detailed contingency plans had to be made, and were being made, to cover any such eventuality. Furthermore these plans necessarily included details of a Denial Scheme, designed to ensure that the enemy derived the minimum possible economic advantage from any territory he might temporarily occupy. The following extract from the record of a War Cabinet meeting of that time speaks for itself in this respect.

PUBLIC RECORD OFFICE DOCUMENT NO. CAB 65/27
W.M.(42) 85th CONCLUSIONS, MINUTE 3.
 Confidential Record.
(3rd July, 1942 – 12 Noon).
THE CHIEF OF THE IMPERIAL GENERAL STAFF then explained the general scheme of demolitions if the worst came to the worst. A comprehensive list had been prepared in the Middle East and this had been checked with a similar list which had been put together by the Chiefs of Staff. The lists corresponded closely except on two points. The Middle East put the destruction of irrigation plants, including the Aswan Dam in Category 'A', whereas the demolition of cotton was placed in Category 'B'. The Chiefs of Staff considered that the destruction of dams should not be entertained at present, but that the ginning factories should receive the highest priority. They proposed to instruct the Commanders-in-Chief accordingly.
Great George Street, S.W.1.

However it is very important, in this context, to remember that contingency planning does not include actual decisions for either present or future action. No decision to demolish the Aswan Dam was ever made but such action, in war, could have become necessary in circumstances which fortunately never arose. Indeed as early as 24th July instructions to Auchinleck had included the view that large-scale withdrawal of forces and installations from Egypt, including abandonment of that country, were not likely to arise, and that meanwhile he should make every effort towards defeating Rommel and driving him to the limits of Italian Africa.

This access to official papers provides the new setting in which to review the controversial issue of that first interview in Cairo between Auchinleck and the new Eighth Army Commander, about which Ronald Lewin in his admirable book *Montgomery as a Military Commander* wrote, 'No one knows exactly what Auchinleck said to Montgomery on that morning of 12 August. . . .' But now we can be certain that Auchinleck felt it his duty to include, in his briefing of the new Commander, the facts of the official contingency plans as well as his own plans to resume the offensive; in doing this he may well, in the circumstances of his mood, have over-emphasised the·former. My brother did not see Auchinleck again for the rest of the war, though the two men met again briefly in Delhi in June 1946 when Bernard was on tour immediately before becoming CIGS. But the evidence which I have seen and quoted confirms me in the view I have always held that Bernard's condemnation of Auchinleck on this particular point (his allegation that the latter was planning for nothing except a future withdrawal) was most unfair and wholly unjustified. Of course their two personalities, both so different in every way, had much to do with it. Bernard has always been completely intolerant of failure, for which in his view there can be no excuse. So often has he said to me: 'A commander who has failed must go.' In this case Auchinleck had failed and so for him nothing good could be said, so much so that the contingency plans, and nothing else, remained in Bernard's memory of their meeting. To know both these men supports the view that they could never agree on any issue, large or small. Bernard was the absolute professional soldier, quick in decision and action and never at a loss as to what step to take next, demanding absolute obedience and competence in those under his command who were never left in doubt as to what was required of them. Auchinleck, on the other hand, was a very friendly and charming person, always ready to listen to anyone else's opinion, and indeed to seek it, a man who was a natural leader in the sense that he seemed to find no difficulty in attracting the loyalty and devotion of those who worked for him. With it all he was a most competent soldier with a wide knowledge of his profession and particularly popular with all ranks of the Indian army of whose history, traditions and class composition he had an unrivalled knowledge. He was also a painter of some merit. Unfortunately he had the unhappy knack, which has often been referred to, of unsuccessfully selecting his staff. Corbett was clearly the wrong choice for his CGS, and Dorman-Smith probably not the best selection as DCGS; the latter was undoubtedly very clever and highly intelligent, though many officers would agree that his feet were not always on the ground. In this connection one is led to wonder why Auchinleck did not, for his senior staff officer, select 'Gertie' Tuker who was widely known as one of the most able and highly professional officers in the Indian army; Tuker was already in the Middle East commanding 4th Indian Division. It may not come amiss also to speculate that 'the Auk' probably preferred to have an Indian army man as his Chief of Staff in preference to a British service officer; there was always, unfortunately, some lack of rapport, professionally, between the British officers of the Indian army and their colleagues in the British service. Be all that as it may, Auchinleck, an Indian army General, was appointed an Army Commander in the United Kingdom in time of war and later Commander-in-Chief in a vital theatre overseas; no officer could ask for better testimony.

Auchinleck does not appear again in this story so I think it right to emphasise how much he is liked and respected by all British officers of the Indian army. The British service officers probably did not have sufficient opportunity to know him, with the exception of de Guingand who has so ably described his merits, and weaknesses, in his book *Generals at War*. One of 'the Auk's' outstanding characteristics was that he did not have it in him to bear any grudge, no matter what the circumstances. At no time did he show this better than after leaving Cairo in August 1942 when he behaved with extreme dignity and restraint, even though my brother took it upon himself to assume command of the Eighth Army on 13th August, forty-eight hours before he should have done. Four years later when 'the Auk' was Commander-in-Chief in India (he was the last British officer to hold that appointment and the last British officer of the Indian army to be made a Field-Marshal) he very kindly invited my wife and me to visit him in his charming house in Delhi, which later became Nehru's official residence. We had a most memorable stay there, which we shall never forget, in company with Walter Monckton and the distinguished historian Desmond Young. 'The Auk' had been to Rawalpindi to attend the centenary celebrations of the 4th Battalion Baluch Regiment of which I was the last British Commanding Officer. This being relatively so soon after the events and circumstances in which he had had to leave Cairo in that August month of 1942, few men could have been expected to adopt such a magnanimous attitude – especially to another Montgomery!

It was from that time onwards that the partnership between Alexander and my brother grew and developed with very fruitful results in the military field. Bernard has so often maintained that he could not have had a better superior commander, because, he said, 'He always gave me what I wanted and did for me what I asked.' Then he would add: 'In our whole time in Africa Alexander only gave me one order, from Cairo to Tunis, and that was: "Go down to the desert and defeat Rommel", which I did.' Looking back at that whole time when the two worked together it was clearly most fortunate that Alexander possessed in good measure, and was able to exercise with his Eighth Army Commander, those qualities of tact and tolerance which are sometimes so lacking in people in all walks of life. He probably appreciated that his own standard of military knowledge and professional ability, as an Army Commander in the field, could never match my brother's, and reacted accordingly; had this not been the case the relationship between the two commanders would doubtless have come under severe strain – in my view it would have snapped very quickly! For his part my brother never quite forgot, and this again is a personal view, that when he was an instructor at the Staff College at Camberley in the late 1920s Alexander had been a student working under him. Now the roles were reversed. Alexander was the superior officer and Montgomery his subordinate commander; it says much for both of them that the partnership was so successful. Also in this context of relationship with military commanders, history will I hope recognise the most unusual manner in which Bernard succeeded, on occasions, in handling Sir Winston Churchill. He had first met the great man near Brighton when he was commanding the 3rd Division after Dunkirk. As is well known the Prime Minister was a 'thruster' and always avid for quick results on the field of battle, derived no doubt from his military upbringing as a cavalry officer; for him any period of forced inaction, as a precaution or otherwise in battle, was distasteful. So occasions were not wanting, from the Battle of Alam Halfa onwards, when Bernard was urged, in conversation with the Prime Minister personally, to advance and attack the Germans and Italians before he was convinced he was ready; he would not do so unless and until he knew in his own mind that the time was ripe in the fullest sense of the word. It must take a lot of determination to resist such urging by a particularly forceful British Prime Minister, against one's better judgment. But my brother was fortunate in that he possessed supreme confidence in his own knowledge and ability and, furthermore, he did not care what people thought or said about him. He used to recall his own words to the Prime Minister, when the latter urged him to take what he thought was an unsound course. 'Prime Minister, you are telling me how to fight in battle in a way which I know is quite wrong. You are not a professional soldier. I am. You do not know how to fight this battle, or when. I do know. If you wish to replace me, I will go – at once.' Of course he always got his way, and had no further trouble.

Of all those controversial issues that have been provoked by my brother's actions, particularly his tactical control once battle had been joined, perhaps the foremost and certainly one which generated much comment, was the query about his pursuit, or lack of it, immediately after the battle of El Alamein. Briefly his critics have maintained that, having defeated Rommel, he failed to pursue him with sufficient energy and purpose. They might have added that it was Napoleon who, in his War Maxim No. VI, wrote: 'At the commencement of a campaign thought should be expended as to whether an advance should be made or not, but when once the offensive has been assumed it should be maintained to the last extremity.' Of course in any comment on this particular issue the background of the battle itself has to be kept in mind, especially its timing and duration. My brother was determined that he would not assume the offensive until mid-October at the earliest, for two main reasons. First, the Eighth Army needed much new war material, particularly tanks and their associated equipment, and secondly, time was essential in order to train the troops to use so much new equipment. Furthermore as he considered a full, or nearly full, moon was essential (to ensure visibility for mine-clearing operations) it followed that the September waxing moon period would be too early. This insistence on delay until October provoked his first great tussle with Churchill who in the event accepted the October timing. The battle itself lasted a full thirteen days from 23rd October to 4th November. Without over-simplification, and of course without prejudice to the mammoth preparations including the successful deception operation planned by Colonel C. L. Richardson,* and above all the courage and tenacity of the troops and airmen, it is possible to see three main elements in this great British victory. In tabular form these were:

a. The intelligence provided by Bill Williams which showed that the whole of Rommel's German forces, especially his panzer army, were grouped in the north on or about the axis of the coast road.

b. The consequential decision by Eighth Army Commander — a vital one taken in mid-battle on 29th October — to change his plan by directing his main and final offensive blow at the enemy's exposed weak spot, i.e. the junction of the German and Italian forces. This involved switching the preplanned

* Now General Sir Charles Richardson, GCB, CBE, DSO.

break-out operation from the axis of the coast road southward to a central axis, and it was highly successful.

c. Operation SUPERCHARGE, the final thrust through the centre on Monday 2nd November, the result of which ensured the victory, aided of course by the magnificent operations of the Desert Air Force.

For a long time comment on the battle, as a great British achievement, was almost always highly complimentary, particularly to the Eighth Army Commander. However in 1960, eighteen years after the battle, Correlli Barnett, a well-known writer and historian, published his book *The Desert Generals* in which he took an altogether different line, appearing to denigrate Bernard as a military commander, and making many unflattering comments on his character and personality. Of course this raised a considerable storm with many letters in the national press contesting, or supporting, the pros and cons of the case put forward by Correlli Barnett. Looking back at that time and always accepting that it would be a dull world if we all thought alike, I have never been able to understand Mr Barnett's main argument, which appeared to be that El Alamein was an unnecessary battle and should never have been fought. This view appears to ignore completely the very grave strategic situation which faced the Allies at that time. The German threat on the Northern (Russian) Front, on the defence of which our continued possession of the vital Middle East oil supplies depended, was still extremely grave, and remained so until December 1942 when the German armies on the Stalingrad Front began to give way under the stupendous Russian offensive. If meanwhile therefore Rommel had kept the Eighth Army pinned down so close to the Nile Delta and Cairo, or even, worse still, had destroyed it, the whole Allied war effort would indeed have suffered a grievous blow, perhaps beyond repair. We thus had to obtain success in the Desert as quickly as possible and this explains Sir Winston Churchill's urge to expedite the timing. Furthermore it is this question of timing, so often so vital, that disposes of Correlli Barnett's argument that in any case Rommel would have been forced to retreat by the Allied landings in North West Africa

(Operation Torch) in November. Who could justifiably foresee an Allied success for Torch with all its difficult and complicated political and strategic background? There were nearly one hundred and twenty thousand French troops in North Africa who could have resisted the Allies. The late Sir Basil Liddell Hart made this very clear in his book *History of the Second World War*.

For many commentators however Correlli Barnett was on much surer ground when he castigated the great victor of El Alamein for lack of vigour in pursuit after the battle. In an earlier chapter I wrote: 'There may even be some who wonder why, on 4th November 1942, at the close of El Alamein, he [my brother] did not immediately employ the 4th Indian Division, under its very able Commander 'Gertie' Tuker, in an active pursuit role.' Ronald Lewin in his book *Montgomery as Military Commander* wrote in this context:

> 'Tuker, perhaps the most intelligent and percipient of Eighth Army's divisional commanders, had already, on the 3rd, instructed his two uncommitted brigades of the Indian Division to be ready for pursuit as soon as a break occurred, "for we knew we were the only fresh, desert-worthy, troops now left".'

Even more significant perhaps, de Guingand recalls how, ever mindful of this very need to be ready for unrelenting pursuit immediately after the break-out, he had for long been trying to keep in hand the necessary resources for it, particularly in tanks and aircraft. But as time passed the inexorable pressure of events, including his Chief's insistence on superior force for the battle, had compelled him by degrees to thin down the resources, and thus reduced their effectiveness. Even so critics are not wanting who maintain that immediately following the decisive blow the Eighth Army still had sufficient troops, particularly tank regiments and motorised infantry, which, flushed with success and enthusiasm, might have been employed in an all-out pursuit of Rommel. That is the nub of this case against the Eighth Army Commander, and it looks to be a strong one; so much so that it becomes an interesting thought to speculate what might have happened if, say, General Patton, not Montgomery, had been the Army Commander at El Alamein. Would 'Blood-and-Guts' Patton have gone flat out after the battle with everything he had, and if so might he not have continued the pursuit as far as Tobruk or perhaps even further? However any such speculation is probably quite illogical because it postulates that Patton could equally have been the victor of El Alamein. But quite definitely he could never have won that battle! The set piece, the master plan, was not for him.

In due time history will record its verdict on this issue, but not without giving proper weight to the other side of the coin. For the battle had lasted thirteen days continuously and had cost the Eighth Army 13,500 casualties; averaged at one thousand (killed, wounded or missing) per day this was a very high price in any view. Surely then there was an overwhelming need to reduce further loss, and therefore not to take any uncalculated risk? Flat-out pursuit could not in the circumstances be a calculated risk. Above all there had to be no repetition of what had already happened twice in the Western Desert under Wavell and Auchinleck respectively, namely, a rapid advance without sufficient resources or proper tactical training, followed inevitably by near-disastrous retreat. Furthermore the weather had turned against us with very heavy rain which could not fail to hamper an all-out pursuit, and exacerbate the administrative difficulties which were bound to increase if we rushed forward into that 'Cyrenaica Bulge' four hundred miles ahead. No doubt this is what Patton would have done, and yet Eisenhower is on record, more than once, as expressing his anger at the disregard of logistics in Patton's Third U.S. Army when their lines of communication became stretched to near breaking point. Equally important, the Eighth Army training programme, initiated by its Commander, was by no means complete. Enough has been said already to show my brother's constant endeavour to avoid committing troops to a battle role for which he knew they were not as yet properly trained, particularly after thirteen days of continuous and exhausting combat conditions. Meanwhile when all has been said and done the final result is what ultimately matters, not so much what might have happened if some other course had been taken. I began reference to this most con-

With Bernard Shaw in Augustus John's studio, a sketch by James Gunn. The caption reads: 'Conversation piece, suggested on a notable occasion, 9.ii.44. Vain attempt to persuade the unwilling soldier of the importance of the beard as an attribute of greatness.'

To F.M. B.L.M.   J.G

General Montgomery visits a Ministry of Supply arms factory, May 1944

troversial issue with a quotation from Napoleon's War Maxims, so it seems appropriate to conclude with another – Napoleon's Maxim LXXIII:

The first quality of a commander is a personal knowledge of war; this is acquired by experience, and is not natural; for a captain is not born, but made. Not to worry, to have an open mind, to show no change in countenance, to give orders in the midst of fight with as much coolness as when perfectly at rest, are the tests of worth in a general. To exhort the timid, to augment the small number of the brave, to stir up the fight when it grows slack, to rally the troops when broken, to bring back fortune at a desperate crisis, to give one's life if necessary to save the state, are actions pre-eminently suitable to the warrior.

To the above qualities we should add the talent of picking out men and of employing each at the post to which his character calls him. 'My great attention,' says Marshal de Villars, 'was given to knowing the character of my junior general officers. This one, by his boldness of sprit, was suited to lead an attacking column, that one because the natural bend of his mind was rather to caution, without however wanting in courage, would more easily defend a country.' It is only by applying such knowledge at the proper season that we can obtain, and almost make certain, great success.

No doubt many of those who served with the Eighth Army in the Western Desert and Italy, or later with 21 Army Group, will see mirrored in this definition of leadership, for that is what it is, the image of all that Field-Marshal Montgomery so often practised and taught, and urged others to follow.

Chapter 9

MARETH TO THE SANGRO

In his *Memoirs* my brother wrote this of his wartime service during the years 1939–45:

'Probably a third of my working hours were spent in the consideration of personalities. In dealing with subordinates, justice, and a keen sense of fairness are essential – as also is a full measure of human consideration. I kept command appointments in my own hand, right down to and including the battalion or regimental level.'

This insistence on being the final arbiter for appointments as far down the scale as unit commanders was not new for him, but it only became generally known from the time he took over Eighth Army. He always used to carry his 'little black book', a plain pocket note book in which, with meticulous care, he kept his own personal record of the performance and conduct of officers, usually writing it up nightly in his caravan. Of course this record paid him handsome dividends, though some critics maintain that in making it he risked violating his own dictum that a senior commander should never allow himself to become immersed in details. But this charge cannot be valid because he never took part in the actual steps necessary to make any change on which he had decided, except to tell de Guingand, or in 21 Army Group his Deputy Military

Secretary, to take action; when a general officer was involved he invariably told him personally that he was to be replaced. In this context it has been said by others that his replacement of Ramsden* as Commander XXX Corps was most unfair to the latter, in that there was no good reason for it. But that is to ignore the true fact which, put simply, was that Ramsden was doomed from the start. He was acting Commander of the Eighth Army (having been appointed by Auchinleck) when Bernard arrived in Egypt so that, inevitably in the eyes of the new Army Commander, he had on him the taint of failure; he had to go, and if one accepts the wisdom of Napoleon's Maxim which I have quoted ('My great attention was given to knowing the character of my junior general officers') who can blame my brother? But in the event Ramsden made good for he became a General Officer Commanding-in-Chief and was highly decorated. Another Corps Commander, Lumsden,† was also, as it were, the victim of Napoleon's Maxim. The truth is that even before Bernard arrived in Egypt, during his flight there from England, he had been thinking hard about the need to have staff and commanders of his own choosing and by the morning of 13th August, only twenty-four hours after his arrival, his mind was made up. One sentence in his *Memoirs* is the key to this fact. Having recorded his satisfaction at having Alexander as his firm friend and ally, and with de Guingand as his trusted Chief of Staff, he wrote: 'What was necessary next was to get good and reliable subordinate commanders below me.'

This intention underlay all my brother's subsequent moves in personnel changes and led finally to his decision, and action, to have Oliver Leese, Miles Dempsey and Brian Horrocks as his three Corps Commanders.‡ The two former officers had been students under Bernard at the Staff College, and Horrocks had been in his 3rd Division as a battalion commander and had later commanded a division in South East Army. But there was an added

* The late Major-General W. H. Chaplin Ramsden, CB, CBE, DSO, MC.

† The late Major-General H. Lumsden, CB, DSO, MC.

‡ Lieutenant-General Sir Oliver Leese, Bt, KCB, CBE, DSO. The late General Sir Miles Dempsey, GBE, KCB, DSO, MC. Lieutenant-General Sir Brian Horrocks, KCB, KBE, DSO, MC.

reason for these changes. When he took over from Auchinleck there were plenty of officers serving in Eighth Army, at all levels including General Officers, who had been in Egypt a long time and considered themselves well versed in all the special skills required for the proper conduct of battle in the Western Desert. Now, suddenly, these officers had to deal with a new Army Commander who, though he had had no previous active service in the desert, very quickly left them in no doubt that it was he who had all the answers; furthermore their own pre-conceived ideas were no good if they did not conform with the new Army Commander's thinking. This was certainly an explosive situation particularly as, under the previous command system, it had been the custom to allow commanders a great deal of independence of decision and action once battle was joined. This delegation of authority had grown and developed, and had become generally accepted, so long as it was part and parcel of the tactical doctrine prevalent during Auchinleck's time. This doctrine favoured a degree of dispersion of force, based on the concept of fighting in independent brigade groups each with its own artillery, engineers, signals and other supporting arms, or even in smaller formations – 'Jock' columns as they were called. Inevitably, in these circumstances, commanders below divisional level had often to make their own tactical decisions, particularly if there was a signal failure, which could not be co-ordinated with those of similar formations. The short point was that divisional command and control of the battle tended to lapse, and, worse still, this led either to wrong orders being issued, or even to disobedience of orders by independent-minded officers operating in dispersed conditions, with the justification of being the man on the spot. Of course all this was complete anathema to the new Army Commander. His whole concept of battle lay in concentration of maximum force at the right time and place, and in complete accord with the overall plan of the commander who had to keep a firm grip on operations from above, and so ensure that the master plan (which he would amend if necessary) achieved success. For my brother a tactical doctrine which involved any dispersion of force in penny packets, particularly fragmentation of the artillery, was 'quite hopeless' and he would have none of it. So it was after his arrival that the artillery commanders, for example, became so jubilant; for now their regimental picture changed. Instead of having their batteries often allotted under command, or in support, of independent columns they were able to concentrate their action by regiments. The massed artillery fire of the Eighth Army became a legend for all its men to remember, and the thunder of the many hundreds of guns, of all calibres, a sound which no one who heard it will ever forget.

In this story the scene now moves forward in time and place; past the Libyan frontier about Sollum and over the great bulge of Cyrenaica for hundreds of miles of desert country, until Tripoli is finally captured and left behind and the Eighth Army enters Tunisia. It is now the spring of 1943 and the stage is set for the vital battle for the Mareth Line, which began at 2230 hours on 20th March and lasted for fully nine days; it was the final large-scale action in the long desert campaign and the prelude to the end of the war in Africa. Of course a very great deal has happened since the break-out after El Alamein, quite apart from the frequent and arduous engagements with the enemy during the long pursuit of the German and Italian armies through Cyrenaica and Tripolitania. The ports of Benghazi and Tripoli had been completely wrecked and put out of action during Rommel's retreat. But they had now been repaired after prodigious efforts by the Royal Navy and were operating again, so the army no longer had to depend for its maintenance on a system of road communications covering many hundreds of miles. Benghazi to Tripoli is nearly seven hundred miles and it is true to say that if Tripoli had not been taken when it was (23rd January), and the Royal Navy had not so quickly repaired the harbours and port installations, the sheer logistics of the situation would probably have saved Rommel, or at any rate caused serious delay to expulsion of the enemy from Africa. For this great administrative success full credit must be given to two officers, Brian Robertson, then a Brigadier, and his assistant Lieutenant-Colonel Graham.* These two men were the administrative experts at Headquarters Eighth Army, responsible for all the complex and difficult staff work of the A and Q branches

* Major-General Sir Miles Graham, KBE, CB, MC.

and the services (RASC, RAOC, RAMC, RAPC, Provost and the Chaplaincy services). There can be no doubt whatever that without the administrative skill, including a great capacity for improvisation when necessary, of these two men and their staffs, the army could not possibly have reached Tripoli three months, to a day, after the start of the Battle of El Alamein on 23rd October 1942. After Robertson had left Eighth Army on promotion Miles Graham became Bernard's Chief Administrative Officer and remained with him in that capacity until the end of the war in 1945. It is very easy to write in these terms but not easy, unless one has been an administrative staff officer in war, to appreciate the magnitude and variety of the tasks which confronted Graham. For example, the Eighth Army was a multi-national organisation composed of British, Australian, New Zealand, South African, Greek, Free French and Indian troops, each with their own special administrative needs including different ration systems; at one stage in Italy, after the Italian surrender, it was necessary to add a whole corps of Italian troops to the Eighth Army ration list. In this context it was very fortunate that de Guingand, with his wide experience of service with African troops and in India, was a great friend of Graham; so that the two of them (Chief of Staff and Chief of Administration) became the team which contributed so much to the victories of Eighth Army and 21 Army Group.

Miles Graham was one of the very few senior staff officers whom my brother did not personally select to fill a key appointment in his Headquarters. After leaving Eton, where he was a scholar, Graham had graduated at Trinity College Cambridge and thereafter, in 1914, had been granted a regular commission in the 2nd Life Guards. At the end of the 1914–18 war, in which he was twice wounded, he had left the regular army but rejoined his regiment, from the reserve, in September 1939. In August 1942 he was already serving on the administrative staff of Eighth Army when Bernard arrived from England. The story of Graham's first meeting with the new Army Commander, soon after the latter's arrival in the desert, is worth telling as it undoubtedly set the seal on his retention in the Army Headquarters' administrative staff. Bernard was making his first tour of the location, to meet all the staff, when he came across Graham who was busy putting flags on to a large map of Africa. When asked what he was doing Graham replied that he was marking up the map to show the new administrative lay-out in case it was necessary to get the army out of Egypt in a hurry. The ensuing conversation went as follows:

> *Army Commander:* And why are you doing that?
> *Graham:* I don't really know, Sir. I think it's pretty good balls myself.
> *Army Commander:* That's no way to speak to a general; and if I hear any more about a retreat you're sacked. Is that clear? Sacked.

Graham certainly made no further mention of a retreat, and he was not sacked! In after years he said that the arrival of the future Field-Marshal in the Headquarters was like a breath of fresh air for everyone.

The very strong defences of the Mareth position were originally constructed by the French before the war, as an insurance against the possibility of an attempted invasion of Tunisia by Mussolini, who at that stage appeared so intent on increasing his African empire. As at El Alamein topography governed the defence lay-out. About one hundred miles from Tripoli the main road to Tunis traversed a coastal plain stretching inland from the sea for twenty-two miles up to the line of the Matmata hills. The latter were generally impassable for vehicles, except for some narrow and winding routes through the Hallouf pass, but to the west there was an open desert flank, though this had been described by the French as a sand-sea and was regarded as impassable. Across the width of the coastal plain ran a natural obstacle, the Wadi Zigzaou, a water-course two hundred feet wide and generally twenty feet deep, beyond which was an anti-tank ditch sown with mines. This combination of the Wadi Zigzaou, the Matmata hills, and the so-called sand-sea, presented a very formidable and naturally strong defensive position more than forty miles in length; it was defended in depth by nine German and Italian divisions, including the 10th, 15th and 21st Panzer Divisions. The difficulty of finding practicable routes across the Zigzaou, filled as it was with up to three feet of water, had been exploited by the enemy who, on their side, had installed miles of barbed wire with machine guns sited for enfilade fire on fixed lines. However the defenders appeared to have made one serious misjudgment for the sand-sea on the left flank was not impassable. Previous reconnaissance, begun by the Long Range Desert Group as early as January and confirmed by the Desert Air Force, showed that a passable route for tracked vehicles existed and could be improved by bull-dozing methods.

The Eighth Army Commander's plan for the battle, in brief outline, provided for two thrusts against the Mareth Line. XXX Corps (Oliver Leese) was to make a frontal attack across the Zigzaou with the aim of drawing the enemy reserves on to that part of the position. Meanwhile the New Zealand Division under Freyberg,★ strongly reinforced by other units, was to pass round the western flank, via the sand-sea, and envelop the enemy's rear behind the Matmata hills. X Corps (Horrocks) with its armoured divisions was held in reserve to exploit success on whichever flank it appeared. The whole operation was supported by the Desert Air Force. The result of this plan, when put into action, was dramatic and, according to the critics, not unexpected. The main frontal attack across the Zigzaou was unquestionably a failure. Despite most valiant efforts, including attempts by the Royal Engineers to provide crossing places, considerable casualties were incurred from enemy artillery, mortar and machine-gun fire. By the night of the 22nd March XXX Corps had had to fall back to their original start lines; infantry tanks had been lost and no progress had been made. Johnnie Henderson, my brother's ADC and then a Captain in the 12th Lancers, recalls Oliver Leese coming to see Bernard at 2 a.m. on 23rd March, and, the situation being so serious, he (Henderson) woke up the Army Commander; it was the only occasion from August 1942 to June 1945 that he felt justified in rousing his General in the middle of the night. My brother's reaction was immediate and characteristic. He at once gave orders to switch all the main effort from the frontal attack, which had failed, to his left flank, by heavily re-inforcing the New Zealanders

★ The late General Lord Freyberg, VC, GCMG, KCB, KBE, DSO.

in the sand-sea; there the outflanking move had started well but had later been held up. It had involved moving 27,000 men and 200 tanks. At the same time he opened a new thrust by the 4th Indian Division against the enemy held positions in the Matmata hills, with the aim of securing a new supply line via the Hallouf pass. Meanwhile he told Leese, 'You must keep the German reserves tied to your corps front.' This switch of effort was the key to success, so that by 28th March the Eighth Army was in full possession of the famous Mareth Line.

The critics have taken my brother to task on three main aspects of the Mareth battle. Why did he launch XXX Corps in a frontal attack against such an obviously strong natural defence position as the Zigzaou? The attack failed utterly so why did he not see that earlier, and therefore make the famous switch to his left flank earlier, thus expediting the left hook? Finally why did he not launch the 4th Indian Division attack earlier than he did? In short his timing was slow and the critics pointed to this as a reaction similar to his alleged delay in pursuit after El Alamein.

Liddell Hart on the other hand acclaimed the battle as a fine conception. According to him it showed the Eighth Army Commander's 'capacity for flexibility in varying his thrust point, and creating fresh leverage when checked, even better than at El Alamein'. He added that Mareth was my brother's finest battle performance in the war, in spite of the trouble he incurred at the outset by trying to force a breakthrough on a narrow front over the Zigzaou. Liddell Hart's history was published in 1970 so there are still two completely different views as to the merits, or otherwise, of the British plan for Mareth and the subsequent conduct of the battle by my brother; though no one can dispute that the final outcome was again complete success. Future historians however will perhaps invite attention to the great similarity in the tactical concept of both the El Alamein and Mareth battles, and also of the land battle in Normandy in the Caen sector immediately following D-Day in June 1944. In all three battles the same tactical design (the master plan) can be clearly seen. Briefly, this was to fight the battle with the aim, in each case, of deliberately drawing the main enemy strength on to one flank in order (at the right moment) to

10*

stage a massive break-out, either on the other flank or in the centre.
On all three occasions the plan worked, and in each success was
due to maintenance of the one great principle of war – the application of superior force at the decisive point and moment. Put in
even more simple terms, the essence in each of the three battle
plans was compounded of superior strength, applied at the right
place, and timing. Of course none of the plans would have worked
without staff officers of high ability, well trained in Bernard's own
recipe for staff duties – Foresight, Accuracy and Speed.

By the time Tunis was captured on 12th May 1943, with nearly
a quarter of a million of the enemy taken prisoner and the war in
Africa ended, my brother had completed the shaping of his Headquarters to his own personal design. It had taken him a long time
to get what he called the 'right structure' with all its component
parts working correctly, but now he had done it, though, as he so
often told me, 'I could not have done it without de Guingand, my
Chief of Staff, whom I had personally selected.' He had also got the
three officers he wanted as his Corps Commanders and had disposed of other officers who he did not think were up to the mark;
the little black book was showing results. Dempsey had arrived
just before Mareth, but had not taken any part in the actual battle
as he had been engaged on planning the next one – the invasion of
Sicily. Ramsden and Lumsden had gone; also Gatehouse* who
had commanded the 10th Armoured Division at El Alamein.
Above all the chief-of-staff system, of which my brother was the
architect, was in full operation under the able direction of de
Guingand. This system was designed to fulfil three aims, all equally
essential in Bernard's view. In the first place it enabled him to
exercise personal command and control of the battle at all times.
Next it included adequate machinery for timely decision making
at the highest level, with of course necessary consultation with the
staff officers concerned. Finally the system ensured that my brother
personally was protected from too many visitors, including high-
ranking personages, and thereby given time to think with of course
the corollary that he did not risk becoming immersed in detail –
one of his main obsessions. His method of achieving these three

* The late Major-General A. H. Gatehouse, DSO, MC.

aims was as usual simplicity itself, and consisted merely of dividing the Army Headquarters into three echelons, thus:

> Tactical Headquarters   (Tac HQ)
> Main Headquarters   (Main HQ)
> Rear Headquarters   (Rear HQ)

Tac HQ was the site from where the Commander, both in Eighth Army and in 21 Army Group, exercised his personal command and control of the battle. It was always small in size, completely mobile, and sited well forward in the battle area; it included the Commander's caravans, signals and cipher staff, the Military Assistant (MA), liaison officers, Defence Platoon, an ADC, and sometimes an officer from General Staff Branch. A landing strip for light aircraft was generally sited nearby, especially in 21 Army Group days.

It was from Tac HQ that Bernard himself went still further forward towards the front line, in order, as he said, 'to keep a firm hand on the battle in order to ensure that the master plan was not "mucked about" by subordinate commanders having ideas inconsistent with it'. Otherwise my brother issued his orders, to his commanders, orally at Tac HQ. In 21 Army Group days especially, when the forces engaged became so large and the subordinate commanders were not divisional and corps commanders, but full generals commanding armies, the liaison officers were sent out with instructions to report back to their Commander on battle progress. Of course there was always much traffic into and out of Tac HQ, and very senior officers like Freddie de Guingand, who was also a member of Tac, Bill Williams, and Miles Graham spent much time there. In due course to have been an officer of Field-Marshal Montgomery's Tac HQ became a significant appointment and its members developed a great *esprit de corps* for it; so much so that to this day an annual Tac HQ dinner is held in London, attended by all officers who over the years served formally in it. In 1972 more than twenty officers attended the dinner and their names are listed in an Appendix to this book. Naturally the officers who were on the immediate personal staff of their Commander saw more of him at Tac than some others did. Among those who saw most of him were the Military Assistant Kit Dawnay,* the ADCs Johnnie Henderson and Noel Chavasse, the doctor Major Hunter, now Vice Chancellor of Birmingham University, and the Camp Commandant Captain Woodward. My brother, even at times of great stress and battle strain, almost invariably returned to Tac HQ in time for dinner each night. One wonders whether Major Haylock, who ran the Signals Detachment at Tac, and the liaison officers, were aware that their task was the outcome of an experiment begun some twenty-five years ago by the GSOI of the 47th (London) Infantry Division, as related in an earlier chapter of this story.

All the detailed planning and staff work was done at Main HQ under the direction of the Chief of Staff, with the General Staff Branch, the Chief Administrative Officer, the Head of the Intelligence and the commanders of the artillery, the engineers and signals. The staff representatives of the Royal Navy and the Royal Air Force were also at Main being integrated with the army or Army Group Headquarters. There were many distinguished officers at Main HQ Eighth Army some of whom, later on, were transferred to 21 Army Group and remained with my brother until the war ended in 1945. In addition to de Guingand, Williams and Graham, these included David Belchem,† a brilliant young officer on the General Staff, Charles Richardson, 'Slap' White‡ the Chief Signal Officer, Dennis§ the artilleryman, Drummond Inglis¶ the Chief Engineer, and Richards‖ the tank expert. Finally there was Jack Gannon,** the Deputy Military Secretary, who joined Main HQ 21 Army Group on its formation in 1943. Gannon must have been by far the oldest officer in the Army Group for he was over sixty when he joined and yet was tremendously active in every way, besides being extremely popular and well liked by all. He was an Indian army officer of a famous regiment, the P.A.V.O. Cavalry,

---

* Lieutenant-Colonel C. P. Dawnay, CBE, MVO.
† Major-General R. F. K. Belcham, CB, CBE, DSO.
‡ Major-General C. M. F. White, CB, CBE, DSO.
§ The late Major-General M. E. Dennis, CB, CBE, DSO, MC.
¶ Major-General Sir Drummond Inglis, KBE, CB, MC.
‖ Major-General G. W. Richards, CB, CBE, DSO, MC.
** Brigadier J. R. C. Gannon, CBE, MVO.

and was himself a well-known horseman and polo player. For five years before the war he was Manager of Hurlingham Club, and also Honorary Secretary of the Hurlingham Polo Association with which he is still closely associated – he was a very gallant officer and a great warrior.

The majority of the officers and staff of the A and Q branches, and all the staff personnel of the various services and departments, were located at Rear HQ. It was here that the careful and detailed work of maintaining the army went on, and this meant that Rear HQ had to be kept fully in the operational picture. Otherwise the troops in the many units of all arms could not have been supplied with their rations, clothing, vehicles, petrol and weapons of all kinds with their ammunition, varying from the largest artillery shells to small arms ammunition; in fact everything that the soldier needed wherever he might be, from boots and bootlaces to NAAFI stores or bayonets, kilts for Highland regiments or the differing rations needed by Hindu and Muslim soldiers. To all this of course has to be added the vital work of the medical services, from the equipment needed by regimental stretcher bearers in the battle areas, to the staffing and maintenance of the field hospitals and dressing stations with medical equipment and stores. It was in this specialised field that as time went on my brother made his own contribution. He came to realise that when a soldier is wounded and, in the process of evacuation, is passed through many hands, from the regimental aid post back through the field ambulances and casualty clearing stations (CCS) to the field hospitals on the lines of communication, the benefit he may need most, but does not normally get, is the care and attention of women. This was particularly desirable, he thought, at the time and place when a wounded man is coming round from an anaesthetic after an operation, probably an urgent and serious one. The place nearest to the actual front-line fighting where surgical operations can be performed is the casualty clearing station in the divisional area. So he arranged with the RAMC that whenever possible the staff at the CCS should include female nurses from the QAIMNS, or other nursing service. This innovation was very much appreciated by all ranks and was yet further evidence of my brother's determination to maintain morale in all circumstances. Furthermore there was the added dividend that his staff, including all administrative services and departments, not forgetting the chaplains, knew they had one hundred per cent support from their Army Commander personally.

As time passed the size of my brother's Headquarters, particularly in 21 Army Group, naturally tended to increase so that by the time the war in Europe ended there were probably up to a thousand officers in all working at the Main and Rear Headquarters. But from the outset Tac HQ was never allowed to include officers other than those whose functions I have described, so it was always kept small and compact. There remained however the visitor problem for so many people, particularly 'the great ones' (including those who held high-ranking appointments but were not great), wished to see the Army Commander. At Tac HQ this difficulty was overcome by the formation of a visitors' mess where normally all non-members were accommodated, unless of very exceptional importance. It is necessary actually to have stayed at Tac HQ, for a night or more, in order to be able to appreciate the atmosphere there. Informal it certainly was, though this was never stretched beyond the bounds of decorum, and one sensed the great sense of purpose which permeated all ranks serving at Tac, together with their utter loyalty to the Army Commander; it was always calm there, no one ever 'flapped'. In my brother's own mess there was a great deal of humour – particularly at meal times, and, no matter what your rank was, you were encouraged to speak your mind. On one occasion in the desert my brother had told his two ADCs (John Poston* and Johnnie Henderson) to write a paper for him on the concept of the firm base – a subject dear to his heart. Henderson's paper was not, in Bernard's view, at all good and he said so in most uncompromising terms: 'I can't imagine how it is that anyone, such as yourself, who has been with me for so long, could write such unmitigated rubbish.' To this Henderson replied, 'You may have your own ideas on the firm base, General, but these happen to be mine.' The Army Commander was delighted with this reply and roared with laughter.

* Major John Poston, 11th Hussars. He was killed in Germany in the last week of the war.

By his insistence on keeping his Tac HQ small, and indeed in fighting his battles from there, as Rommel did from his 'Battle Headquarters', my brother was able to evolve his own machinery for decision-making. He did not favour the large pre-battle conference at which senior officers present could speak and give their views – his staff would do that, but not he; and this must not be confused with the addresses he was fond of giving to large audiences when he gave out his own reasons or conclusions but did not ask for those of others. The system he favoured is best described by de Guingand.

'I gradually realised that once again Montgomery was absolutely right. He would certainly have gone mad if he had been surrounded by the activities of a Main Headquarters. He would never have been able to exercise such intimate tactical command over his forces. At Tac HQ he was far less accessible and so avoided some visitors who would otherwise have imposed an extreme strain on him. We, the staff, used to carry out staff duties dealing with all possible eventualities. I would normally have discussed the matter generally with my Commander in the first place . . . and I would then either go myself or more usually when dealing with future plans take a team with me, and give him a presentation. All maps would be produced and the particular experts in the Plans, Operations, or Intelligence, branches would say their piece.

'After hearing the exposé of the particular problem, Montgomery would give his views and his decision, or order another line of investigation. The drill went well and everything went along quite smoothly. When a battle was on my Chief would visit the Commanders concerned each day.'

During the last six months of the long desert campaign, before it ended in May 1943, my brother had some new experiences. One of these was his first close contact with the United States armed forces and their commanders, including General Dwight D. Eisenhower. The two men had met briefly for the first time on 27th May 1942 when Bernard was commanding 'Invasion Corner' in

England, but their meeting in Tunisia on 31st March 1943 marked the first occasion when they met each other as Field Commanders of large armies, fighting a war on soil alien to both of them. A first impression has always had great influence on my brother, including information given him by a reliable witness, and particularly if the evidence has pointed to a failure or shortcoming of some kind. I have always thought therefore how unfortunate it perhaps was that, a month or more prior to his meeting with Eisenhower in Tunisia, my brother had received such a bad report of how affairs were conducted at Algiers where Eisenhower had his Headquarters. At the Allied Conference in Casablanca the previous January it had been decided that Eisenhower should become Supreme Allied Commander for the battle for Tunisia, and for the subsequent invasion of Sicily, with both the First and Eighth Armies under his command. Alexander, as his deputy, was to command all the land forces, whilst Tedder had command of all the Allied air forces in the Mediterranean with Coningham* in command of the Tactical Air Force. It is appropriate to note here that these decisions — no doubt primarily the work of the British CIGS Alanbrooke — made three British officers, Alexander, Tedder and Coningham, responsible for Anglo-American co-operation in the land, sea and air battles which had to be won in order to expel the enemy from Africa, and then invade Sicily. That renowned British naval officer, the late Admiral of the Fleet Viscount Cunningham, KT, GCB, DSO, was already in command of the Allied naval forces; another British officer, Broadhurst,† had command of the Desert Air Force in support of the Eighth Army operations. As a result of this new command set-up Alexander went to Algiers, and not long after he had arrived there he gave my brother a very adverse report of the conditions, as he saw them, at the Supreme Commander's Headquarters. In his *Memoirs* Bernard wrote as follows of what Alexander had told him:

* The late Air Marshal Sir Arthur Coningham, KBE, DSO, MC, AFC.
† Air Chief Marshal Sir Henry Broadhurst, GCB, KBE, DSO, DFC, AFC.

'Alexander told me he had found things in a terrible mess when he went over to join General Eisenhower. The First Army was being heavily attacked on the southern part of its front and looked like sliding there. Generally, he found stagnation: no policy, no plan, the front all mixed up, no reserves, no training anywhere, no building up for the future, so-called re-inforcement camps in a disgraceful state, and so on. He found the American troops disappointing; they were mentally and physically soft, and very "green". It was the old story: lack of proper training allied to no experience of war, and linked with too high a standard of living. They were going through their early days, just as we had had to go through ours. We had been at war a long time and our mistakes lay mostly behind us.'

Looking back there is no doubt in my mind it was the receipt of this first report that sowed the seeds of discord, and led progressively to so much trouble between my brother and his American colleagues for the rest of the war. The passage from the *Memoirs* which I have quoted, whether read in or out of context, makes a terrible indictment and it is therefore ironic to add that Alexander's report was in the circumstances only a transient one; it was not of a permanent nature and it was never intended to be such. Furthermore both Commanders, Alexander and Montgomery, realized this and very soon after were not slow to recognise the outstanding military qualities of the American soldier. Bernard wrote in his *Memoirs*, on the same page as his indictment, 'When the Americans had learnt their lesson, and had gained in experience, they proved themselves to be first-class troops. It took time; but they did it *more quickly than we did.*' (The italics are mine.)

Nevertheless, when all is said and done, it has to be recognised that during the war my brother never gave sufficient credit, for being a hard professional soldier, to any of the American generals he met. This is not to say however that he did not believe in them; far from it. It means only that he was never prepared *in public*, at the time, to acclaim their true worth as first-class professional soldiers in every way, and equally, if not more, important, to tell them so personally himself. The evidence for this view lies in a careful reading between the lines of two passages in his *Memoirs*.

During the Battle of the Ardennes, the so-called Battle of the Bulge which lasted from approximately 16th December 1944 to 16th January 1945, Eisenhower placed two American armies temporarily under command of 21 Army Group. Both these armies (the First under General Hodges and the Ninth under General Simpson) formed part of General Bradley's 12 Army Group but were now temporarily diverted to British command under Bernard. After the battle had been fought and won Bernard wrote to General Bradley, on 14th January:

> *My dear Brad,*
>
> It does seem as if the battle of the 'Salient' will shortly be drawing to a close, and when it is all clean and tidy I imagine that your armies will be returning to your operational command. I would like to say two things:
>
> First: What a great honour it has been for me to command such fine troops.
> Second: How well they have all done.
>
> It has been a great pleasure to work with Hodges and Simpson; both have done very well. And the Corps Commanders in the First Army (Gerow, Collins, Ridgway) have been quite magnificent; it must be most exceptional to find such a good lot of Corps Commanders gathered together in one Army.

The reader will be quick to see the lack of any real, unstinted, recognition of the personal performance of both the American army commanders, and, even more obvious, the absence of any reference to Ninth Army Corps commanders. The truth of course was that both Hodges and Simpson were first-class professional soldiers, deserving of the highest praise. However that was not the end of the matter for prior to this, on 7th January, Bernard had held his by now, well-known conference about the battle. It was this unfortunate press conference, unfortunate more in its results which were so skilfully exploited and distorted by the Germans than in what was actually said, that caused such great trouble, politically and otherwise. The full text of the talk my brother gave to his audience of journalists has been reproduced in Chapter 18 of his *Memoirs*; but the main point his listeners drew from it was that victory in the battle was due to himself, and his own command and handling of both British and American troops! This naturally led to a tremendous uproar, to put it mildly, so that even Eisenhower himself, that most generous-hearted of men, felt bound to record his dismay. In his book *Crusade in Europe* he wrote this of the press conference:

'Unfortunately, after the battle was over a press conference held by Montgomery created the impression among Americans that Montgomery was claiming he had moved in as the saviour of the Americans. I do not believe that Montgomery meant his words as they sounded, but the mischief was not lessened thereby. This incident caused me more distress and worry than did any similar one of the war. I doubt that Montgomery ever came to realize how deeply resentful some American commanders were. They believed that he had deliberately belittled them — and they were not slow to voice reciprocal scorn and contempt. ... It was a pity that such an incident had to mar the universal satisfaction in final success.'

In the event my brother fully accepted that he should never have held that press conference and said so in his *Memoirs*, which again was unfortunate because it was too late to say so. Eisenhower's *Crusade in Europe* was published in 1948 and the *Memoirs* ten years later in 1958, so by the time the latter had appeared the damage had been caused, and was virtually beyond repair. Meanwhile, after this long lapse of time, it still remains to seek the real cause underlying my brother's, on the face of it, wholly unreasonable and quite definitely factually incorrect assessment and criticism of American commanders. For unreasonable, above all, it must be as he is second to none in his admiration for the efficiency and great fighting qualities of the United States soldier in the ranks — of all arms — and is on record as having said so; he will never deny that. Furthermore he will always fully agree that the soldier in the ranks, in all armies, has to be properly led, otherwise his efforts will be of no avail, and I have often heard him quote Field-Marshal Slim* (for whom he had unbounded admiration) who once said, 'There are no bad regiments, there are only bad officers.' On this premise then, to which he himself subscribes, it is quite unreasonable to continue to equate magnificent fighting soldiers, in the ranks, with lack of professional expertise at the top level, particularly in view of the outstanding success of the U.S. armies. Furthermore my brother does not maintain that the American armies failed completely to produce any great commanders in the 1939–45 war. For instance he has always emphasised his tremendous admiration for General Douglas MacArthur, both as a leader of troops and a very able professional soldier, second to none in his view in the United States Army. Nevertheless, when my brother gave me this view, I could not help recalling that it was MacArthur who, in 1951, had been relieved of all his commands by the late President Truman for failing to comply with directives forbidding him to make pronouncements on political matters – and that it was Bernard who on many occasions, particularly after he became CIGS and later went to NATO, had also got into serious trouble for speaking his mind on political matters!

It may seem strange in view of what has been said, but the other American general for whom my brother had such regard was General Dwight D. Eisenhower himself. He never agrees that Ike was a hard professional soldier, with personal experience as a leader of troops in battle and a field commander possessing unusual military knowledge and ability. In his view Ike was ideal as a 'political' soldier, a supreme commander equipped to handle all the complex and inter-related political and strategic issues which necessarily beset an international force drawn from several countries. This included handling the diverse and frequently very difficult characters and personalities of the national leaders involved – both military and political – and Bernard is the first to agree that he himself proved to be one of Ike's greatest problems in that sense! In this context it is not over-simplifying the matter to say that to a large extent Eisenhower and Alanbrooke faced a common

* The late Viscount Slim, KG, GCB, GCMG, GCVO, GBE, DSO, MC.

problem in their need to handle Montgomery in such a way that the application of all his outstanding military genius and ability, particularly his power to lead and inspire his armies, was in no sense curtailed. That they succeeded so well is now part of history, and is certainly recognised by my brother. For even in this story enough has been told to show how both Eisenhower and Alanbrooke, each on at least one separate occasion, either had to act, or perhaps more accurately refrain from taking certain action, in order to save Bernard's career. It is necessary to have served at, or visited, Eisenhower's Headquarters to be able to appreciate the extent to which, at one time, an adverse view of my brother developed. For instance at Allied Force Headquarters (AFHQ) during the Italian campaign resentment grew when it became known that the cigarettes which the Eighth Army Commander, himself an ardent non-smoker, used to hand out freely to his troops* were sometimes those he had been given personally by Eisenhower – worse still he had actually asked his Supremo to supply them! Only those who know Bernard really well will be able to appreciate the delight he would take in being told of this reaction in AFHQ! It was all of a piece with his pleasure when he won the bet made with General Bedell-Smith in Tripoli in February 1943. Eisenhower's Chief of Staff had been discussing with de Guingand the timing of the day when General Anderson's First Army would be able to join up with Eighth Army. At one point my brother intervened to say his army would be in Sfax by 15th April, which Bedell-Smith firmly believed was impossible. A bet was accordingly made, the stake being a United States aircraft for Eighth Army Commander's personal use should he reach Sfax by the due date. In fact he got there on 10th April and on 16th a Flying Fortress aircraft (B.17) arrived from Eisenhower; it is a tribute to the latter's breadth of view that apparently no stake was ever mentioned as a requirement from the British should they have failed to reach Sfax by 16th April; perhaps it was appreciated, by both sides, that H.M. Treasury would not have been amused by any suggestion to incur national expenditure by laying odds on the outcome of success or otherwise in war.

* See account in Chapter 1.

Against this background of the major events which became so liable to hamper Anglo-American co-operation at Army Commander level, it is possible to attempt an assessment of the root cause of the trouble. My brother had been through the First World War and had seen the United States enter the conflict in 1917, too late in his view to gain worthwhile experience as professional soldiers at high command level. Between the wars the Americans did not, as the British did, have further comparable war experience, and certainly in his opinion no American commander, by December 1941 when the United States entered the war, could claim to match his own standard of practical experience and knowledge. In the Desert campaign only Alexander was superior, as Commander-in-Chief on the battlefield, to himself. Then, after Casablanca, Alexander becomes Land Forces Commander and Eisenhower appears on the scene as Supreme Commander, remaining in that capacity *vis à vis* Bernard until the war is over. The effect of this development on my brother has to be seen not as a petty reaction to the impact of an additional authority, but in terms of his sincerely held conviction that the supreme commander, in any Anglo-American theatre of war, did not necessarily have to be an American. This is the nub of the whole matter stemming from his equally strong conviction that the criteria for supreme military command must be, primarily, the possession of the highest possible standards of professional knowledge and ability allied to practical experience of high command on the battlefield.

The flaw in this argument, clearly seen, is of course that it ignores the political factor, not the need for the incumbent to observe it (that is always fully accepted by Bernard) but that the selection of the incumbent depends so much upon it, particularly where national force levels are concerned. From the invasion of Europe onwards the vast size of the United States' contribution to the Allied forces made it imperative that the Supreme Commander should be an American. Furthermore, Eisenhower's reputation for complete impartiality unquestionably pointed to him as the ideal choice for the highest appointment in an international force in war. Who but Eisenhower could have issued an order to his Headquarters Staff in the following words?

'If I hear of a dispute at a high staff level, between, say, three-
or even four-star generals which cannot be resolved, then both
men, irrespective of nationality, will be replaced immediately.'

In this connection time has wrought a great change in my brother
for as I write these words he has told me that in his view Bradley
was a first-class professional soldier, and it was very fortunate he
was available to command 12 Army Group. Two of General
Bradley's subordinate commanders, Hodges and Simpson, whose
armies were placed temporarily under 21 Army Group, 'were in
the same class as professionals, possessing much military knowledge and ability and made first-class army commanders'. Perhaps
however there is one short point, in this context, which I should
emphasise. My brother himself would not have made a good
Supreme Commander! This view in no way detracts from his
reputation and superb performance as a Commander-in-Chief at
army and army group level, or his unrivalled capacity for leadership. However there will probably be general agreement that his
talents are not those best suited to deal with complex political
issues on an international scale. Besides as a supremo it is more
than likely he would not have been able to resist the need, in his
view, to be well forward so that he 'kept a firm hand on the battle
in order to ensure the master plan was not mucked about by
subordinate commanders having ideas inconsistent with it'! In this
he would probably have been right, but would it have worked? In
this connection also I am conscious of a gap in my story which
time and opportunity prevent me from filling. It would have been
fascinating, and certainly most rewarding, to have been able to
talk with some of the United States and Canadian generals whose
names have been seen by my readers. If, for instance, General of
the Army Omar Bradley, General Mark Clark or Lieutenant-
General Granville Simonds had commented on certain passages,
the result could not have failed to make this book more interesting.
That great soldier General Walter Bedell Smith died in 1961, and
the Army Commanders General Courtenay Hodges and General
Henry Crerar a few years later.

Long before the total expulsion of the Axis forces from Africa

had been completed the Western Allies had decided to attack what
Churchill described as the soft under-belly of Europe, by an
invasion of Sicily and Southern Italy, with the ultimate aim of
knocking the Italians out of the war. Planning for these difficult
operations, which would inevitably involve a sea-borne assault
against an opposed landing, had begun very early in 1943, though
Bernard, preoccupied as he was with the Desert campaign, did not
take any part in the matter until April. The Sicilian invasion began
on 10th July and was followed by the attack on Southern Italy on
3rd September, on which day also, four years exactly after Hitler's
war began, the Italian Government signed an Instrument of Surrender at Syracuse in Sicily. In the event however that was by no
means the end of the war in Italy, for Hitler very quickly occupied
and took control of all the Italian mainland, with very strong
reinforcements of German forces, and a long and arduous campaign
ensued with much bitter fighting, on land in particular. Bernard as
Commander of the Eighth Army played a major part in all these
operations, together with two very famous American generals,
General George S. Patton who commanded the Seventh U.S.
Army in Sicily, and General Mark Clark, Commander of the Fifth
U.S. Army on the Italian mainland. Then, very early on the morning of Christmas Eve 1943, by which time Naples had been regained though much fighting in Italy still lay ahead, my brother
received a telegram from the War Office instructing him to return
to London in order to take command of 21 Army Group for the
invasion of North West Europe across the English Channel.

Those nine months, from April to December, during which
Bernard was either preparing for, or actively engaged in, the
Italian operations were possibly the most frustrating for him of all
the war years. For the campaign was neither planned nor conducted in accordance with the principles which he thought it
essential to apply when land operations by joint British and
American forces were involved. This led to some trouble which,
with the benefit of hindsight, can now be seen as almost identical
with the difficulties that followed during the campaign in North
West Europe. The plan prepared at Eisenhower's Headquarters
envisaged the Eighth Army with two Corps (Leese and Dempsey)

landing on the south east coast of Sicily from just south of Syracuse, round the Pachino peninsula, as far west as Gela. The Seventh U.S. Army would land some one hundred and twenty miles further west astride Trapani. Of course this concept was complete anathema to Bernard for apparently from the outset it meant there would be dispersion, not concentration, of force. Any plan so based was doomed to failure in his view; a 'dog's dinner' he called it though not officially in those terms! However he signalled to Alexander (the Land Forces Commander) in words which left no doubt as to his meaning:

'I am prepared to carry the war into Sicily with the Eighth Army but must really ask to be allowed to make my own army plan. . . . Time is pressing. If we delay while the toss is being argued in London and Washington the operation will never be launched. All planning is suffering because everyone is trying to make something of a plan which they know can never succeed.'

Of course this reaction in Eighth Army to the AFHQ plan raised a great storm, especially as Bernard was strongly supported by Admiral Ramsay,* the naval commander responsible for landing Eighth Army in Sicily; on the other hand Ramsay's views were not shared by Admiral Cunningham (Naval C-in-C in the Mediterranean) or by Tedder, the Air C-in-C. Matters were not made any easier by a signal which Admiral Cunningham sent to the First Sea Lord in Whitehall on 28th April in which he said, 'I am afraid Montgomery is a bit of a nuisance; he seems to think that all he has to do is to say what is to be done and everyone will dance to the tune of his piping. Alexander appears quite unable to keep him in order. Tedder is also absolutely opposed to his new plan.'

I have included the quotation from Admiral Cunningham's signal as it appears to show so well the degree of antipathy which my brother's reaction to the plans of higher authority was sometimes liable to create. Equally important this sort of situation underlines the high quality, and the success, of the joint efforts of

---

* The late Admiral Sir Bertram Ramsay, KCB, KBE, MVO. He was killed on active service in France in January 1945.

the two Chiefs of Staff, Generals Bedell Smith and de Guingand, at their respective Headquarters (AFHQ and Eighth Army), without which vital planning would have been still further delayed. At Algiers on 2nd May there was still no final decision as to how the Sicily invasion should be conducted. Bernard wanted to shift the U.S. Seventh Army landing from the Palermo area to the Gulf of Gela, so that both armies (British and American) landed side by side, *concentrated*, and thus well placed to capture the vital airfields in the centre of the island. In the event the Eighth Army plan was adopted, in circumstances which are worth recording and which reflect great credit on Bedell Smith. My brother arrived at Algiers on 2nd May and went immediately to Bedell Smith's office, but did not find him there. Eventually he found the Chief of Staff in the lavatory, whereupon he at once put the Eighth Army plan to him and the two men discussed it at length, following which Bedell Smith said there would be no difficulty in adopting the plan; he would see Eisenhower about it at once. This he did and Eisenhower agreed. In retrospect it seems curious that the agreed plan for the invasion of Sicily was finalised in an Algerian loo; miraculous also that apparently the plan was not compromised for lack of security! However unfortunately that was not the end of the matter. Bernard's next step, having got agreement to his plan, was to propose that the co-ordination, direction and control of the assault landings, and the subsequent operations on the island, should be the responsibility of one army commander, with a joint Anglo-American staff – by inference this would have to be himself! But Eisenhower would have none of that and insisted on a two-army command structure, one British and one American, under Alexander as Land Forces Commander. Readers will see in this incident an almost exact parallel with the controversy provoked by my brother over the question of one Allied Land Forces Commander in North West Europe at the end of 1944.* In his *Memoirs* Bernard recorded sadly that although the original plan for the Sicily invasion was sound, the campaign itself was not conducted on sound lines. As a result some forty thousand German, and sixty thousand Italian troops withdrew safely to the mainland.

* See account in Chapter 6.

The Allied invasion of the Italian mainland has been described in books by a number of writers. All these admirable accounts, whether by Alan Moorehead, Lord Tedder, Eisenhower, Sir Arthur Bryant (*The Alanbrooke Diaries*), Ronald Lewin, Field-Marshal Montgomery, Sir Francis de Guingand and Sir Basil Liddell Hart, resemble each other to a large extent and understandably so. Of these eight writers however only two, de Guingand and Liddell Hart, drew particular attention to the opportunities which, according to them, were lost by the Allies in the original planning of the invasion. It was their contention that when the Allies decided to make two assault landings, one in Calabria (at the toe of Italy) on 3rd September and the other at Salerno south of Naples, ten days later, they failed to make sufficient use of their command of sea power in the Mediterranean. This of course is an unusual charge to make in view of our traditional use of, and reliance on, naval power throughout our history. But in their view it would have been better to use Allied amphibious power in order to land the Eighth Army in the Taranto-Brindisi area where excellent port facilities existed. This would have provided a firm base for an advance along the Adriatic coast, where incidentally the topography would have provided an easier route, less mountainous than the Tyrrhenian sea coast, and thereby considerably eased the logistical problem; the latter was made more difficult by the torrential winter rains which broke late in October. Liddell Hart backed this argument by quoting from the papers of the German Commander-in-Chief Field-Marshal Kesselring, and his Chief of Staff General Westphal, both of whom expressed their surprise that the Allies had not followed this course. In short the Germans felt strongly that the Allies would have had better success prospects by landing on the exposed heel of Italy, where, they claimed, the garrison at Taranto consisted of only one parachute division with three batteries of artillery.

The argument against the views quoted in the preceding paragraph rested primarily on the undeniable fact that assault landings by the Allies in the Taranto-Brindisi-Bari area could not have been supported by shore-based fighter aircraft operating from Sicily; owing to shortage of aircraft carriers the limit of range for Allied fighters was about Salerno, where the U.S. landings in fact took place. No doubt history will record its verdict on this issue in due time, weighing in the balance the pros and cons of using sea power to secure a firm base on the Adriatic coast, against the more cautious method of ensuring support, with fighter cover, for the land battle including the sea-borne assault. As for the Commander Eighth Army he was in no doubt that all was not right with the strategic concept for the mainland campaign. According to him no attempt was made to co-ordinate Eighth Army operations with those of the Fifth Army landing at Salerno; he was therefore in no way surprised when the Salerno assault very soon encountered grave difficulties. Although he does not mention it in the *Memoirs*, one can discern, reading between the lines, what his own preference would have been. He would have liked a concept more in his own classic tradition, with one Allied army deliberately drawing the main enemy strength, with their reserves, to its own front, whilst the other army is poised for the decisive blow against the enemy's exposed weak point; both operations controlled and co-ordinated by a master plan which ensured concentration of force, not dispersal, at the right time and place.

My brother's last problem in Italy was how to say good-bye to the officers and men of the Eighth Army. In just sixteen months he had fashioned an instrument, perhaps team is a better word, which functioned like clockwork and responded to his will and control in a manner not often seen in any walk of life. He had gained their loyalty, trust and affection, not least because they knew he would never let them down; a large number of them had been with him all the way from El Alamein to the Sangro river in Italy where he was now to leave them. Characteristically his timing for the occasion of his farewell address was superb – the evening of 30th December 1943 and the day before he was to leave for England. As usual he left all the details to his Chief of Staff who, with his customary skill, arranged for a great gathering to attend at the Opera House in the town of Vasto on the Adriatic. It was a most moving occasion, so well described by de Guingand in *Operation Victory* that it needs only a short extract from that account to portray the feelings of all those who were present:

'He started very quietly, apologising in case his voice might let him down for, as he said: "This is not going to be easy, but I shall do my best. If I happen to find difficulty in speaking on occasions, I hope you will understand." I felt a lump coming in my throat, and one could feel every one of his audience was perfectly tuned into his mood. . . .'

Oliver Leese arrived at Vasto that night to take over command of the Eighth Army, and the following morning Bernard flew to Morocco, en route for London, taking with him de Guingand, Graham and Williams, and others of his staff who were to take part in his next venture. Winston Churchill was at Marrakesh, recovering from a recent illness, and had invited my brother to stay with him for New Year's Eve and the following day, before leaving for London.

Chapter 10

NORMANDY TO NATO

By the time the new Commander of 21 Army Group arrived in London he had already been told by Eisenhower that, for the invasion of France, he was to command all the ground forces involved in the sea and airborne assault on the coast, and the subsequent operations in the land battle. This meant that as Land Forces Commander he would, in the first place, have operational control of the First U.S. Army (Bradley), the Second British Army (Dempsey), two U.S. Airborne Divisions (82nd and 101st) and the 6th British Airborne Division. Later on, in France, his army group was increased by the addition of the Third U.S. Army (Patton) and the First Canadian Army (General H. D. G. Crerar). This command organisation continued until Eisenhower transferred SHAEF (Supreme Headquarters Allied Expeditionary Force) to France and himself assumed field command of all the armed forces, with Bradley appointed to command 12 Army Group comprising all the American ground forces, and my brother remaining as 21 Army Group Commander. Before the European war ended Ike was commanding three army groups composed in all of nine armies, including one French army and the First Allied Airborne Army with very powerful air forces. No other general in history can have commanded so many men, and women, on the battlefield; their numbers were counted in millions.

As I wrote in Chapter 5 my brother was allotted St Paul's

School as his official Headquarters for the five months he was in the United Kingdom before the invasion took place, and during that time he lived at Latymer Court, a block of flats just opposite the school buildings. It was from St Paul's that he made extensive tours of the United Kingdom in order to visit every formation that was to take part in the initial assault, including the majority of regiments and units of all arms. He did most of this touring in a special train which he had been allotted, named 'Rapier', which was very comfortably fitted out in every possible way; and by so doing he was also able to be seen by many of the thousands of men and women working in the factories, on the railways, and in other essential war work. In his book *The Desert Generals* Correlli Barnett has strongly criticised my brother for making so many visits of this particular kind, to his army in the Middle East, on the grounds that 'Wellington and Marlborough would have found a calculated personal appeal to the army inconsistent with their personal rank'. I have never been able to reconcile this view with either common sense or sound reasoning, and certainly Eisenhower could not, for in *Crusade in Europe* he wrote, 'Soldiers like to see the men who are directing operations; they properly resent any indication of neglect or indifference to them on the part of their commanders and invariably interpret a visit, even a brief one, as evidence of the commander's concern for them.'

It needs no imagination to appreciate the prodigious amount of staff work, at all levels, that was required before the mammoth preparations for the invasion could be regarded as complete. It was for this reason that Bernard had insisted on bringing with him from Italy senior officers who already had practical experience in landing operations and had also seen much active service. So it was while he was touring the United Kingdom, as I have described, that men like de Guingand, Williams, Graham, Herbert,* Charles Richardson, 'Hobo' and others too numerous to mention, were coping with many difficult and complex problems. These varied from preparation of the staff studies, which were essential to ensure proper and timely use of completely new features like the 'Mulberry' (artificial) harbours, and Hobo's tanks, to the measures

* Lieutenant-General Sir Otway Herbert, KBE, CB, DSO.

needed to maintain armies composed of British, Canadian, American, Belgian, Polish, Free French and Dutch troops. By the end of August Bernard's command in France amounted to twenty American divisions, twelve British divisions, three Canadian divisions, one French and one Polish division. For many of the officers and men working at St Paul's School, including senior officers from other headquarters of the Allied invasion force, 7th April and 15th May were notable occasions. On the 7th my brother held a conference for all the senior naval, army and air force commanders of the invasion force, including all officers of the rank of general or equivalent in other services, as well as certain very senior staff officers. This meeting in the Great Hall where, as a schoolboy the Commander 21 Army Group had gone every morning for four years to hear prayers read in Latin by the High Master, the great Doctor Walker, was also attended by the Prime Minister and the British Chiefs of Staff. Bernard opened the conference by explaining its purpose which, put simply, was to present the plan for the invasion so that all commanders had a similar view of what was required of all ranks. Army commanders and commanders-in-chief of naval and air forces followed with an exposé of their own plans. In his account of this meeting de Guingand wrote 'Montgomery made a big impression that day, especially amongst some who were still not quite convinced of his true ability.'

On 15th May the final conference for *Overlord* was held in the same place. This meeting was convened by Eisenhower and was attended by H.M. the King, the Prime Minister with the principal members of his War Cabinet, the British Chiefs of Staff, and Field-Marshal Smuts, besides all the Commanders-in-Chief involved in the invasion. Ike wrote of this gathering that during the whole war he attended no other conference so packed with rank as this one. It was about the end of April when Tac and Main HQ of 21 Army Group moved to Portsmouth, which was one of the chief embarkation areas and where Admiral Ramsay had his Naval Invasion Command Headquarters. Rear HQ of the Army Group remained in London. At Portsmouth both Tac and Main HQ now reverted as close as possible to battlefield conditions. Vehicles had to be made waterproof and all messes and officers were accommodated

Planning D-day at St Paul's School, London, 1944. *Left to right:* Gen. Bradley, Admiral Ramsay, Air Marshal Tedder, Gen. Eisenhower, Gen. Montgomery, Air Marshal Leigh-Mallory, Gen. Bedell Smith

Senior officers at S.H.A.P.E., 23 October 1956. *Back row* (l to r): Air Marshal
H. A. Constantine; General C. V. Schuyler; Lieut-General P. Brisac; Air Vice
Marshal H. Campbell. *Front row* (l to r): General L. Norstad; General A. M.

in caravans, tents or huts. Bernard and his personal staff, including his Chief of Staff and Chief of Administration, lived at Broomfield House, a small but comfortable country house with a garden. The time was the prelude to Overlord, and there was still ceaseless work to do preparing for it in these conditions. It was also early summer and many distinguished people came to lunch or dine at Tac HQ; they included H.M. the King, the Prime Minister and some of the Commonwealth Premiers, and one night Eisenhower came to dine alone with Bernard. Of course there was frequent contact with the two army commanders, Dempsey and Bradley, and with the naval and air commanders involved. So the month of May passed and by the time June began the stage for Overlord was set. It still remained to decide the actual date of D-Day, but now, as is well known, the weather turned against us, and to resolve the problem was not easy. On 5th June my brother went to Hindhead to see his old friends the Reynolds about their arrangements for the care of David who was now at Winchester, and whom he had already seen. It was Bernard's last commitment before the invasion began. Some of the many ship convoys involved were already at sea when Eisenhower decided D-Day was to be the 6th June.

I do not propose to describe all the hazards and perils of the assault on the beaches, by both British and American armies, and the course of the battle that followed until a firm lodgement on the mainland of France had been achieved. It has all been well told by others including the great success of Hobo's 79th Armoured Division, composed of his wonderful, and almost weird machines. These varied from tanks which could swim in the sea, to 'flail' tanks which literally flailed enemy minefields and so exploded them, to tanks carrying flickering searchlights which blinded the opposition, or plain heavily armoured bulldozer tanks. The upshot of it all was that by 7th June the Allied troops had reached Bayeux, the beach heads were cleared, and a partial link up obtained with the airborne troops who had been dropped ahead of the beaches. By 10th June a firm base had been obtained on French soil some sixty miles long and varying in depth from eight to twelve miles. It is against this background, of results achieved in the first five days of the invasion, that my brother's master plan has to be seen

including all the controversy that arose from its execution. Briefly
it was his intention that, following the landings in Baie de la Seine,
every effort should be made in the Caen sector (Second British
Army) to entice the main enemy strength, particularly in armour,
to that flank. If the Germans reacted accordingly then, once Caen
with its vital road and rail communications centre was captured,
Second Army, reinforced by First Canadian Army, would contain
and pin down the bulk of the German armies. This would enable
two very powerful American armies (Bradley's First and Patton's
Third Army) to break out on the western flank south of Falaise,
and continue on to the Loire River past Angers, Tours and Orleans,
and then swing north to Paris and the Seine. By this device the
greater part of the German forces would be encircled and destroyed. It was the master plan, the grand design, which in its concept so resembles the Montgomery pattern in his other campaigns
– to fight the battle with the aim of deliberately drawing the main
enemy strength on to one flank in order (at the right moment) to
stage a massive break out on the other flank, or in the centre.

In the event the master plan succeeded and the enemy was
encircled and destroyed, but many difficulties and much trouble
arose before that time came, because, as so often happens, the
timing of the plan did not work out as hoped. To begin with First
U.S. Army had to clear the Cotentin peninsula and capture the
port of Cherbourg; but it was not possible to complete those tasks
until 26th June, and Caen was not taken by the British and
Canadian armies until 9th July. Caen was the vital strategic target,
the hinge on which all else depended, and until it had been taken
the right hook (the final break-out) certainly could not begin. It
was from about this time that impatience, with what was called
'Monty's caution', grew and developed and was featured quite
largely in the national newspapers. The public expected and longed
to have news of a great Allied offensive and they were worried that
perhaps something had gone wrong. Even Eisenhower, that generally calm and unruffled person, expressed anxiety and said at the
time,* though strictly off the record, never in public: 'Why doesn't
Monty get going? What's the matter with him? Why doesn't he

* Quotation from *Eisenhower was My Boss* by Kay Summersby.

get going?' But Bernard was not to be deterred by any of this, nor even by the disquiet expressed very forcibly by both Churchill and Eisenhower. He knew the moment was not ripe for the break out until enough German armour had been attracted to, and been pinned down by the British and Canadian armies. So, as before El Alamein, he insisted that the timing should be his responsibility and of his choosing, and once again events proved him right. On 27th July U.S. troops broke out west of St Lo and by the 31st they were through Avranches; the great offensive was in full flood. By 11th August the Americans were across the Loire and Patton was racing for the Seine which he reached on 19th August. Paris fell on 25th August. Meanwhile the enemy was retreating from Normandy and the Allied forces, in co-operation with the British and Canadian armies, had begun the destruction of the German armour caught in the Argentan-Falaise trap. In this trap, set and sprung by the British master plan, at least six hundred and fifty enemy tanks were destroyed and the German Seventh Army virtually annihilated; there was great slaughter. On 1st September H.M. The King approved the promotion of General Montgomery to the rank of Field-Marshal.

It is perhaps not yet generally known that not long hence our nation will have a permanent record of this great Anglo-American victory and war effort, culminating in Overlord, on public view in the Imperial War Museum. As long ago as 1967 Lord Dulverton commissioned the Royal School of Needlework to make, as it were, a Bayeux Tapestry in reverse. It will be another record of an armed invasion made across the English Channel, but nearly nine centuries later and culminating this time in a defeat on Norman soil. The great work – the Overlord Embroidery – will consist of thirty-three panels 264 feet in length (64 feet longer than Bayeux) and by the generosity of Lord Dulverton is, when finished, to be presented to the nation, on whose behalf it will be displayed at the Imperial War Museum. The Embroidery will depict and commemorate the war effort of the people of Great Britain, from Dunkirk to Overlord and the liberation of France.

During the early months of 1944 my brother had sat for his portrait to be painted by Augustus John. Kit Dawnay who had been instructed to make all the arrangements with the distinguished artist, addressed this minute to his General:

Dear General Monty,

I have seen Augustus John today and he is delighted with the idea of painting your picture. However he is asking £500 for a picture. It is a stiff price, but I understand that he is getting that and more for portraits at the moment. Will you let me know what you feel about this? I will in any event return to the charge and see if I can get him to make some reduction. He will want about half a dozen sittings, provided the light is good; this is apparently most important.

Yours ever,
Kit Dawnay

Bernard minuted back:

This is OK, and you can proceed with the arrangements.
Jan. 15   BLM

A week later Augustus John wrote to Dawnay in the following terms which indicate he was apparently not unwilling to consider reducing his price:

Fryern Court
Fordingbridge
Hants
Jan. 22 1944

Dear Colonel Dawnay,

Good, I will be ready Thursday afternoon at 3 o'clock – and any other day which suits the General.

I quoted the price I would ordinarily ask but if General Montgomery finds it stiff I will of course reduce it. How about £400?

Yours sincerely
Augustus John

Bernard Shaw happened to be in the studio when my brother

arrived for one of the sittings, and subsequently wrote to Augustus John giving his impressions of both the painting and the sitter; these two letters of G.B.S. appear in full in the *Memoirs*. Bernard never liked the portrait, perhaps because he was never really *en rapport* with the great artist. For immediately following the first sitting he said to Dawnay, 'Who is this chap? He drinks, he's dirty, and I know there are women in the background!'

That distinguished portrait painter, the late Sir James Gunn, RA, who has painted my brother on several occasions, left a charming impression, in the form of a pencil drawing, of the scene in the studio when Bernard Shaw was present. In the drawing Augustus John is shown palette in hand, with Bernard as his sitter, and the portrait standing on its easel. In the background Bernard Shaw sits, watching. Gunn wrote these words underneath his drawing:

Conversation piece, suggested on a notable occasion, 9.2.44. Vain attempt to persuade the unwilling soldier of the importance of the beard as an attribute of greatness.

To FM, BLM.
JG

After that great Allied victory in Normandy with the subsequent advance to the Seine and beyond through eastern France into Belgium, where Brussels was liberated on 3rd September and Antwerp was taken the following day, Bernard became involved in further controversy, at a high level, about future strategy in Europe, Eisenhower had taken personal command of both army groups on 1st September so my brother took the opportunity to put to him an outline strategy, which, if adopted, was in his view the quickest way of smashing Germany and so ending the war in Europe. Very briefly this plan, known as the Single Thrust strategy, had three main elements:

a. 21 Army Group, heavily reinforced by at least twelve American divisions from Bradley's Group, would move with its right flank on the Ardennes, advance into the Ruhr across the Rhine, and then sweep on through the North German plain into the heart of

Germany. This would mean also providing 21 Army Group with great strength in armour, including all the necessary logistical support on a massive scale.

b. 12 Army Group meanwhile would contain and pin down [note the same wording as in his Overlord plan] the German armies south of the Ardennes, whilst the Seventh US Army, which by this time had landed in the South of France, would move north west towards the Saar. The main point to note here was that the Allies did not possess sufficient logistical strength to support two main offensives.

c. Finally to change the system of command now would mean losing cohesion in the control of the ground operations. 21 Army Group Commander should therefore continue to have tactical control and direction of all the land operations; this policy was vital in order to ensure tactical success.

It needs no imagination to appreciate the great storm that arose when Bernard presented this plan! For in broad terms he was proposing, in the American view, to allot the greater part of the Allied resources in military and logistical effort to the northern front, leaving the United States forces an unspectacular holding role; worse still, if possible, he was proposing to remain himself in command of all the land forces.

In the event, as was inevitable in the political circumstances, my brother's plan was not accepted and Eisenhower's Broad Front strategy was adopted; this meant an advance, as it were in line, towards the Saar, the Frankfurt region, the Ruhr and the west bank of the Rhine. But would Bernard's Single Thrust have worked in practice, however impracticable it may have appeared on political grounds? The case has already been hotly debated but the following points stand out:

1. A glance at *a.* and *b.* in the preceding paragraph clearly shows this plan as, in essence, very similar to the plan for the Overlord landings, but in reverse internationally with the Americans given the holding role, though 'holding' by no means implied a defensive role; on the contrary it meant strong offensive action.

2. De Guingand opposed this plan – it was the only major issue on which he ever failed to agree entirely with his Chief. He thought the risks, in case for any reason the Single Thrust failed, could not be calculated, though the results of failure would be quite unacceptable. There remained the possibility that the Germans might succeed in striking a critical blow at the right flank of the Single Thrust, and so perhaps cut off 21 Army Group from its crossings over the Rhine; this fearsome hazard looked particularly dangerous as long as we could not depend on the port of Antwerp for maintenance.

In the matter of command organisation Bernard did not in fact insist that he himself should be the Land Forces Commander; on the contrary he offered to serve under General Bradley if the latter was appointed as such. Personally I have always felt that, in the strictly military sense, only one person could have made a success of such an immense task, and that would have been my brother – as indeed he succeeded with the Overlord landings. But I make one very strong proviso with this supposition; the Single Thrust strategy could not in any event have worked until Antwerp became available as the maintenance port for 21 Army Group. Antwerp at that stage was the Achilles heel of the Allied effort in North West Europe. Although the port itself had been liberated on 4th September it could have no practical value, as a base port, until the River Scheldt and its wide estuary leading to the coast at Flushing, including Walcheren Island and the sea approaches, had been cleared of the enemy. This complex and dangerous task had been allotted to the First Canadian Army under that great soldier General Simonds,* (General Crerar was sick, temporarily, in England) and it was not until 3rd November that it was completed, after much hard fighting. Even then the Royal Navy had an immense salvage operation in clearing the river and its approaches of all obstacles and mines, so it was 26th November before the port was finally opened for shipping.

When I had reached this point in my story I recalled that in the last paragraph of the Introduction I had originally referred to my

* Lieutenant-General Granville Simonds, CB, CBE, DSO.

brother as 'a Field-Marshal who had never lost a battle'. Now I had to consider whether I was fully justified in describing him in those terms. Had he never lost a battle? For I was on the point of writing about the Battle of Arnhem, and, after my reading on the subject it seemed clear that we had lost it. Furthermore it was my brother's battle, there could be no doubt about that; it was fought by the Second British Army with an Allied airborne corps under command (1st British Airborne Division, two US airborne divisions and the Polish Parachute Brigade). My research showed that no British writer had described the battle as a victory, and the Daily Record in the Cabinet Office War Room was extremely sparse on the subject. The battle lasted from 17th to 25th September 1944 and the following entries from the Cabinet papers tell a depressing story:

PUBLIC RECORD OFFICE DOCUMENT   CAB 100/12
18 SEP 44
Airborne landings have taken place in the ARNHEM-NIJMEGEN area. The landings have been a success and only 40 aircraft are reported missing, which represents $2\frac{1}{2}\%$ of the total landed.
20 SEP 44
Airborne Tps in the ARNHEM area are engaged in intense fighting against strong opposition to secure the main road bridge over the Lower Rhine at that point.
25 SEP 44
1st Airborne Division is still isolated on the North of the Lower Rhine.
26 SEP 44
It proved impossible to get sufficiently strong reinforcements across the Lower Rhine to relieve 1st Airborne Division and an attempt to withdraw remnants of the Division was to have been made last night. Only 1,200 fit men of the Division are believed to remain.
28 SEP 44
About 2800 officers and men have been evacuated from the Arnhem Bridgehead.

All the evidence (and in *Operation Victory* de Guingand had written of Arnhem 'The three main reasons for failure . . .') showed the need to excise that description in the Introduction. Here, fortunately for me, Bill Williams came to my rescue; clearly it is not for nothing he is Editor of the *Dictionary of National Biography* for he proposed the simple solution of substituting for 'battle' the word 'campaign', which I promptly did.

In one sense even Arnhem could show some very positive gains; for it is true to say of this battle that although it has to be described as an operational defeat, it was nevertheless an administrative victory. A brief description should justify this view. Operation Market Garden, the code name for the battle, had as its aim the seizure of the crossings over the Rhine, with a bridgehead beyond the river, in the general area of Arnhem-Nijmegen. Once the river crossings had been secured it would be far easier to strike at the great industrial area of the Ruhr, from its north flank, whilst the American Army Group, having crossed the Rhine between Bonn and Cologne advanced eastwards round its south flank. That was Eisenhower's broad strategy, and for 21 Army Group the main objective was undoubtedly the vital Arnhem bridge over the Rhine. They did not get it, but they did capture the Nijmegen bridge over the Lower Rhine (called the Waal river in Holland), and, once gained, they never lost it. It was possession of this bridge that was an administrative advantage, without which the eventual crossing of the main Rhine by 21 Army Group, in March 1945, would have been immeasurably delayed. Most writers have agreed there were faults in the tactical plan for the battle, including the unfortunate fact that the airdrop of 1st Airborne Division was made too far from the main objective – the Arnhem bridge – so that the German II S.S. Panzer Corps was able to intervene before the bridge could be seized. In retrospect it looks much as if Market Garden should not have been allowed to take place until Antwerp was open for shipping. Again the port was our Achilles heel, for if logistic support for Arnhem had been easier and on a larger scale the result might have been different. In his *Memoirs* Bernard admits all this, and his views were later supported by Chester Wilmot in that significant study of the war years *The Struggle for Europe*.

There was also one other important factor which counted much in the balance and had to be kept in mind by all British commanders, particularly my brother. Our country had now been fighting for four years so inevitably his resources in manpower, especially experienced officers and NCOs, were growing less. Nobody knew better than he did what lack of reinforcements could mean in battle.

The last great controversial issue, during the course of the war, in which my brother became involved was the Ardennes Battle (the Battle of the Bulge in December 1944). But I have already written of that in this chapter, and also in Chapter 6. I shall therefore pass swiftly over the great events of the first four months of 1945, which saw not only the last battles but also the Germans coming to surrender at 21 Army Group Tactical Headquarters on 3rd May. They returned again on 4th May to hear, and to sign, the terms of unconditional surrender read to them by Field-Marshal Montgomery. Those first four months of the year were notable for many reasons. Much publicity was given to the discovery and liberation of the many thousands of Jews, and other Displaced Persons (DPs), who under the Hitler regime had been incarcerated in prison camps for racial, religious or political reasons. In these concentration camps many of the wretched victims had been murdered in the gas ovens, or had suffered barbaric cruelties and were then just left to die of disease or malnutrition. During the Burma campaigns I myself saw the atrocities committed by Japanese troops, and after their surrender I twice travelled the length of the notorious Burma-Siam railway, from the Thai frontier through the dense jungle of the Three Pagodas pass to its terminal in Burmese territory. I had seen all the conditions of the prison camps, in which the Allied prisoners of war of the Japanese had been kept whilst they built the railway line. But nothing in my memory can surpass the horrors of Belsen, the concentration camp near Hanover in my brother's army group area. There I saw all the evidence of the gas ovens with the corpses of men and women lying rotting in the streets of the camp, or resting quietly where they had just died whilst their contemporaries who remained alive, awaited a similar end.

Against this background of a defeated nation, in an area which contained a million and a half German prisoners-of-war, with a further million civilian refugees (including the DPs) my brother was made Commander-in-Chief and Military Governor of the British Zone of Germany. Of course the problems were tremendous, especially with the approach of winter. Food was very short, there was little fuel available for domestic use, medical equipment and supplies for the civilian population were very difficult to come by, and there was a grave risk of serious epidemics occurring. Bernard tackled all these immense tasks with his customary zeal and energy and of course his first move was to obtain a deputy selected by himself. He therefore asked the War Office to appoint Lieutenant-General Sir Ronald Weeks,* then DCIGS, as his Chief of Staff, to deal specifically with the divisions of the Control Commission for Germany which eventually assumed responsibility for all the civil administration. My brother remained in Germany for just a year and has written a most detailed account of his activities and the views he formed during that time in his *Memoirs*. He was at great pains to draw attention to the difficulties and dangers, which he foresaw would almost certainly grow worse during the Allies' negotiations with the Russians. In his dealings with Control Commission Officials, and his own subordinate military commanders, he generally began his remarks by saying, 'What you've got to do is to save Germany from Communism; it is part and parcel of our struggle to rehabilitate Germany.'

On 27th June 1946 Bernard arrived at the War Office to begin his appointment as Chief of the Imperial General Staff. He had reached the peak of his profession, having become the professional head of his service and holding the highest rank in the British army. My brother served more than two years at the War Office during the greater part of which time he lived in a very comfortable flat in Westminster Gardens, opposite Marsham Court. As a prelude to becoming CIGS he had made quite an extensive overseas tour, visiting many countries in the Middle East including India. He did this, as he said, 'to give myself time to think', and, he added: 'The British Army must not, as after World War I, be allowed to drift aimlessly without a policy or doctrine.'

* The late Lord Weeks, KCB, CBE, DSO, MC.

There was no doubt at all that after his arrival in Whitehall no one in the War Office was allowed to drift aimlessly! In an earlier chapter of this story I referred to a period in my brother's life when, strangely and very regrettably for all those who know him well, he was seen to reject (perhaps repudiate is not too strong a word) not only his own kith and kin but also some of his best friends – including those who had served him so well and for so long. Astonishingly, the latest victim now turned out to be none other than his trusted Chief of Staff de Guingand. It may be extraordinary to record, but de Guingand had not been allowed to witness the surrender ceremony at Tac HQ 21 Army Group on 4th May 1945; his Chief had told him not to attend! Later de Guingand was not detailed to appear at all on the great victory parade held in London, in the presence of H.M. The King and Sir Winston Churchill, in which my brother took a most prominent part; just as curiously, de Guingand was not allotted a front seat on any of the stands on the route of the procession, and in the end had to buy a back seat (all he could get) for himself and his wife. But that was not the end of this affair. Six months before he became CIGS Bernard sent for de Guingand, then on sick leave, and asked him if he would accept the appointment of VCIGS when he (Bernard) arrived at the War Office. (VCIGS was a prize appointment and one that almost certainly led to further advancement.) But in June 1946, in the War Office, my brother informed Sir Francis that he was selecting another officer as his VCIGS! Admittedly there were other factors which intervened and, looking back, Sir Francis will probably agree that the cards fell right for him when he did not become VCIGS. After all, he was definitely not what Bernard called 'a Whitehall soldier', and, in the event, he has prospered exceedingly in his new and present sphere of life. But that does not account for why it all happened, and I must venture an explanation. It was all part and parcel of what in our family we all came to know and recognise so well, though our mother never did, for reasons that will be clear. Increasingly during his official life, though chiefly from the time he became famous, my brother developed an absolute fixation not to allow any person, no matter who it might be, and including members of his own family, to appear as though he or she should have the main credit (on occasions it would be any credit) for the achievements attributed to himself. Be that as it may, he never, in his true self, wavered in the slightest in his genuine gratitude and regard for those, such as Sir Francis, who did so much for him; the *Memoirs* make this very clear. It is however this trait in his character which has brought some people to say he suffers from megalomania. Equally it accounts for his strange treatment of our mother at what is known in the family as 'the great Monmouth Scandal'! Bernard was to become an Honorary Freeman of Newport (Monmouthshire) and was to visit that famous industrial port in order to have the honour conferred upon him by the Mayor and Council in their Town Hall; it was to be a notable civic occasion followed by a formal lunch party to which the local dignitaries in all walks of life were invited. Mother knew about this intention and determined to be present herself also. She therefore wrote to the Council, without telling Bernard, asking that she might be invited to attend and of course received a warm invitation to do so; disaster followed, for when my brother was told of it he intervened, and insisted that she should not be allowed into the luncheon room. It needs no imagination to appreciate the distress and sorrow that ensued, though in due time our mother fully recovered and was none the worse for it!

Bernard has always been the first to admit that, during the time he was CIGS at the War Office not only did he encounter many difficulties, but frequently they were of his own making. Chapter XXX of his *Memoirs* is entitled 'I Make Myself a Nuisance in Whitehall'. In it he described his efforts to persuade the Government of the day (it was Mr Attlee's post-war Labour administration) to remedy what he thought was the parlous state of the army by introducing national service in peacetime. The late Sir Stafford Cripps was a foremost opponent of any such idea and at one meeting criticised a War Office paper on the subject, saying it was sketchy and prepared without sufficient thought. That any paper sponsored by himself (the master of clarity and accuracy) should be described in such terms was something quite new to Bernard and he was not taking it lying down! So he wrote of that particular meeting: 'I attacked and routed him, with the help of the Prime Minister with whom I had had several private talks on the subject.' He was afterwards advised by his Secretary of State for War to leave the handling of Ministers to others, the inference being that he (Bernard) did not know how to do it! Clearly he did not always find it easy to get on with the senior members of the civilian element at the War Office, perhaps because, during the war years, he had become a close friend of the late Sir James Grigg, KCB, KCSI (who was first Permanent Under Secretary of State, and then Secretary of State for War) and he did not come across his like again. The exception was Lord Shinwell who was his Secretary of State when he left the War Office and of whom he wrote: 'Shinwell had a quick and clear brain . . . he and I became great friends.'

It has always been a habit of my brother to avoid going to large staff meetings if he possibly could, particularly if he knew he would be bound to meet there some individual he heartily disliked or with whom he strongly disagreed. It has to be said that as CIGS he sometimes allowed this habit to outweigh the need for him to attend very important meetings in London, such as those of the Chiefs of Staff (COS); at those meetings it was normal for the professional heads of the three armed forces to be present, unless for some pressing reason it was impossible. During his time in Whitehall the Chief of the Air Staff, in the Air Ministry, was Marshal of the Royal Air Force Lord Tedder, but it was Bernard's invariable custom not to attend any COS meeting if he knew Tedder was to be there. He therefore invariably took steps, before each meeting, to ascertain if the Chief of the Air Staff would be present. If Tedder was going then Bernard would be represented by his VCIGS, at that time Sir Gerald Templer. If Tedder's deputy was to attend the meeting then the CIGS would be there; but it was extremely rare for any COS meeting to be held with both Tedder and Montgomery present. The fact is that even before the plans for the Sicily invasion were being made, when Tedder was Commander-in-Chief of the Allied Air Forces in the Mediterranean, the two men had not got on well together. Then Tedder became Eisenhower's deputy in Europe and matters grew worse, so that any agreement between the two was virtually impossible. It was clear that in their thinking on the course and conduct of the war their views were totally incompatible and could never be resolved.

The first indication of this state of affairs had come as early as November 1942 when the Eighth Army had regained Tobruk at the Eastern edge of the Cyrenaica bulge. Tedder, then the Air Commander-in-Chief in Cairo, had sent Bernard a signal supporting a proposal that the Eighth Army should send a force across the Bulge in order to cut off Rommel's forces as they withdrew south from Benghazi. This signal caused trouble; for Bernard already regarded any such proposal as unsound strategically and impracticable in logistic terms. To have the project put to him now, 'by some airman sitting back amongst the flesh pots of Cairo and not knowing the facts of the case', was not good enough. But that was only the beginning of the affair, and the degree of antipathy that eventually developed between the two men is plainly seen in those passages in Tedder's book, *With Prejudice*, which deal with two vital periods following the Normandy Landings: first, after very severe gales in mid-June 1944 had destroyed one of the two artificial harbours and interrupted the disembarkation of men and supplies for four days; and again on 23rd July, just two days before the break out from the bridgehead and the beginning of the Great Allied offensive. In his description of the first of these dangerous periods Tedder wrote:

'As the days slipped by, I could not help being worried about Montgomery's method of conducting the battle. . . . Because we had not secured the areas south and south-east of Caen, whose airfields could speedily be used, our air forces were still largely based in Great Britain. I also feared that our delay in attacking, for whatever reason, would allow the enemy to assemble a reserve.'

Clearly Tedder's main bone of contention with Bernard was the former's opinion that 21 Army Group had been dilatory in obtaining the use of airfields for the R.A.F. Bernard on the other hand took an entirely opposite view and, in the *Memoirs*, wrote of this particular issue: 'They [the airfields] were not all-important to me. If we won the battle of Normandy, everything else would follow, airfields and all. I wasn't fighting to capture airfields; I was fighting to defeat Rommel in Normandy.' But of course there was more to it than the issue of airfields. In Bernard's view it was intolerable that an 'airman' should venture to question his professional ability, and then go on to suggest he lacked a sense of timing in his conduct of the battle. However the trouble did not end there. On 22nd July Bernard had issued a directive to his army commanders about which Tedder wrote:

'I told Eisenhower in a letter of 23rd July that I could see in the new directive little indication that Montgomery appreciated the vital importance of time, which Eisenhower had emphasised in his letter of 21st. Nor could I see any indication of the bold offensive action which the time factor demanded and our strength justified. I was shocked by the satisfaction with the situation which the directive expressed. For weeks after the landings, while our build-up proceeded, the enemy struggled from hand to mouth with inadequate forces, split up in bits and pieces along the line, disorganised in command and short of material and weapons. . . . I therefore urged again that Eisenhower himself should form a Tactical Headquarters in France, and take control of the two Army Groups, thus putting an end to an arrangement by which 21 Army Group had operational control over General Bradley's forces.'

Of course this open invitation to Eisenhower to remove Bernard from his operational command of the British and American armies in Northern France became known to my brother; the fact that two days later his conduct of the battle from its outset, and especially his sense of timing, were seen to have been completely right, and fully justified by events, made no difference. It was not possible for Tedder and Montgomery to work together in harmony again.

The sequel to this was on the face of it surprising; for some seven months later, in February 1945, when in both London and Washington discussions were taking place with a view to Field-Marshal Alexander replacing Tedder as Eisenhower's Deputy (Tedder was then to become deputy to the Chief of the Air Staff, Lord Portal) Bernard went out of his way to ensure that Tedder did not leave SHAEF. In the *Memoirs* Bernard says that he strongly advised Eisenhower to retain Tedder, mainly for political reasons *vis à vis* the Americans. The latter might think that Alexander had been brought in, in order to strengthen the support for British policy. Reading between the lines however I have always thought it likely that Bernard, notwithstanding his antipathy to Tedder, preferred to see him remain at SHAEF rather than have to deal with a British army officer as Eisenhower's deputy. Tedder was an RAF officer and his primary role was to co-ordinate the Allied air operations. Eisenhower had said that Alexander, if he came to SHAEF, would under no circumstances be allowed to act as a land forces commander, and thus come between himself and his army group commanders. But Bernard, in spite of his always harmonious and friendly relations with Alexander, probably saw it as inevitable that if the latter came to SHAEF he (Bernard) might find his right of direct access to Eisenhower in some way curtailed, or at any rate made more difficult. After all, Alexander was a very distinguished soldier and also a Field-Marshal who was, incidentally, three months senior to Bernard on the British Field-Marshal List.

During his time as CIGS my brother made a point of visiting as many as possible of the countries which had sent contingents from their armies to serve under his command during the war just ended. The list of the territories concerned was a long one as it included all the countries of the British Commonwealth, the governments of which were not slow to invite the CIGS to be their guest, and many of the Colonies. His tours included a visit to the U.S.S.R., and also to the United States where he was the guest of General Eisenhower and the American army, and had a meeting with President Truman at the White House. At that time, it was the late summer of 1946, his *Memoirs*, which were the main source of his subsequent unpopularity with many Americans, had not been published so his trip to the U.S.A., and also to Canada, was a great success. But there were already reservations: this was the first occasion on which my brother allowed himself to become seriously involved in political affairs. (How often have I heard him say, 'A soldier should not meddle in politics'!) In his telegrams to London, reporting on his talks with President Truman and the American Chiefs of Staff, he had asked that 'the Prime Minister be informed', but this did not meet with the approval of Ministers in Whitehall. Of course he realised this for in the *Memoirs* he wrote of this tour, clearly with some relish, 'It was obvious to me from the many telegrams which had passed, that I had stepped into the middle of the political stage, and there was apprehension in the Chiefs of Staff Committee, in the War Office, in the Foreign Office and at No. 10 Downing Street, about what I was doing and what I would do next.' That this did not deter him from making similar forays into the political arena will be apparent later.

It is likely that no previous CIGS had spent so much of his time out of the United Kingdom, and my brother was almost certainly the first holder of that office to make an officially approved visit to the Soviet Union, at the invitation of Marshal Stalin and the Russian Chiefs of Staff. During all those extensive visits overseas in 1946–8 Bernard was accompanied by his Military Assistant Lieutenant-Colonel G. S. Cole,* who certainly found that appointment no sinecure. My brother had a great liking for sea travel, and whenever he had to cross the Atlantic, if time permitted always chose to make the journey in one of the large trans-ocean liners, rather than go by air. During one such voyage, when he and George Cole were returning from New York to Southampton in the Cunard Liner *Mauretania*, he found that a fellow-passenger was the distinguished Russian statesman M. Gromyko. The latter was then Soviet Representative on the United Nations Security Council and Deputy Foreign Minister of his Government at Moscow. Bernard was particularly keen on meeting Gromyko and having a chat with him, though, apart from the political wisdom or otherwise of doing so, it was clearly going to be a very difficult matter to arrange. Soviet Ministers when travelling outside the U.S.S.R. do not appear anxious to meet, let alone have friendly chats with, foreigners however distinguished they may be; further-

* The Late Lieutenant-General Sir George Cole, KCB, CBE.

more very important and senior Ministers, such as Gromyko, were always surrounded by strong-looking body-guards, and in other ways prevented direct access to themselves by strangers. Bernard knew all this and, with his Military Assistant, made his master plan. Phase I was to be a preliminary approach, through an intermediary, to the Soviet statesman to let him know that Field-Marshal Montgomery was on board and would much welcome an opportunity to meet M. Gromyko, at a time and place convenient to the latter. If this method of approach failed then it would be necessary to implement Phase II; this was a very simple plan but it had an important clandestine element which needed careful preparation, so George Cole had been instructed to carry out certain reconnaissance and report the results to his chief. M. Gromyko lost no time in sending his reply which, perhaps not unexpectedly, was a polite but definite 'No'. The stage was now set for Phase II.

The reconnaissance had shown that it was Gromyko's habit to take a walk on deck, accompanied by two body-guards, every morning about the time when the majority of passengers were either at breakfast or still in their cabins. The decks were then comparatively deserted and Gromyko almost invariably followed the same route. Starting from well forward on the starboard side of the promenade deck the three men used to walk aft as far as possible, then turn right-handed past the bar entrance and climb the far side, port, ladder to the boat deck, from where they continued their way forward. At the head of this port, boat deck, ladder there were large ventilators, behind which two men could remain effectively concealed from the eyes of anyone climbing the ladder from below. The CIGS and his Military Assistant therefore planned to waylay Gromyko by hiding behind the ventilators before he started to climb the ladder. As he set foot on the deck Bernard would suddenly emerge from behind a ventilator and confront him; at the same time the MA would step from behind the other ventilator in such a manner that, accidentally and with many apologies, he distracted the attention of the body-guard who had preceded Gromyko up the ladder. Some of my readers may regard the action I have described as a planned antic, or at best a boy-scout episode, but undignified and therefore inappropriate for the professional head of the British army and his staff officer, particularly when the other party involved was a high-ranking Soviet diplomat. Be that as it may, the sequel will surely show the affair in a different light. For the plan worked in all respects! Gromyko was confronted exactly as intended, without any mishap, and then immediately afterwards any passengers about were no doubt astonished to see the Soviet Deputy Foreign Minister and Field-Marshal Montgomery walking round the deck arm-in-arm, both apparently in very good humour. There is no record of how they conversed, or what was said by either of them. Looking again at the previous chapters of this story I cannot but see this incident as further evidence, not only of that imp of mischief in my brother, but also of his resolution never to accept defeat. On one other such voyage, however he did not win.

It was late autumn when the Field-Marshal and his MA were returning from the United States by sea in the liner *Queen Mary*. The voyage coincided with the anniversary of my brother's birthday on 17th November, and this fact was known to some people on the ship including the Chief Steward. A very large and special birthday cake had been made and duly presented to the Field-Marshal with appropriate celebration; but it would of course take time to finish it all, so my brother was in the habit of asking those few passengers he knew and liked to join him for tea, when the cake would be produced; this fact also became known. One of the passengers on this voyage was a very charming lady who was travelling alone; she was well known in America for her wealth and influence and, understandably perhaps, thought she would like to meet Field-Marshal Montgomery at one of his tea parties. She therefore had a message sent to him to that effect. Bernard had heard of this lady's generosity, and, as she had made the approach, decided it would be in order to make her presence at his tea table conditional on her subscribing liberally to one of the charitable institutions of which he was patron. He therefore had her informed that she would be very welcome to come to tea with him, but that at the same time he would expect her to contribute to the charity concerned – a four-figure sum in dollars was mentioned. The lady was delighted and agreed, but Bernard was not yet wholly satisfied with the bargain and decided he must have the cheque in the first place. As he said: 'It must be on the basis of pay now, and tea and cake later, or not at all!' However this was not acceptable to the other party, and as neither side would give in the CIGS did not get his cheque and the lady did not get her tea party.

It was my brother's invariable custom to have his report of each tour covering all the countries visited completed, typed and ready for issue in all respects, by the time his aircraft had landed at the airfield in England where he was due to return. This was no light task, either for his staff officer or the secretarial staff, who went with him, for it generally entailed typing the report in the aircraft up to the moment of touchdown, on account of some last-minute addition or correction. There was always a staff car waiting at the airfield in readiness to take the Sergeant Clerk who had typed the paper direct to the War Office; this made sure that the CIGS could table a complete report of his tour to his colleagues in Whitehall the day following his return. Towards the end of his time as CIGS Bernard's MA reported to him that the Sergeant Clerk who had accompanied him on every tour had unexpectedly fallen very ill. After treatment he had recovered, but he could not now expect to remain in the army, on the active list, with the promotion and career prospects he had always had. He would therefore have to retire prematurely as his medical category was too low, though his ability was in no way impaired. My brother's reaction to this news was immediate. 'Telephone to Mr X,' he said. 'Tell him I want to see him at once, here.' Mr X had been on Bernard's staff in 21 Army Group; when the war ended he went back to his pre-war professional life and, by 1948, had attained a position of considerable influence. Mr X duly arrived and saw Bernard in the War Office, as a result of which the Sergeant Clerk, when he retired, was given the opportunity to start a new professional life but in an altogether different setting. He eventually became the deputy head of a very important department in a major business undertaking. This incident underlines, not only the sense of gratitude my brother felt towards a non-commissioned officer of his personal staff who had experienced great misfortune, but also his talent of being able to pick the right man for the job – and if necessary gamble on his judgement. The little black note book did not refer only to officers.

In 1947, after he had been less than a year at the War Office, Bernard began to realise he could not continue to live in his flat at Westminster Gardens. The accommodation there was neither suitable nor large enough for David, who was just completing his national service prior to going to Trinity College Cambridge. It so happened that his old friends the Reynolds were then living in Hampshire in the village of Isington. Their beautiful house stood on the bank of the River Wey and had originally been the home of the local miller. The mill itself was immediately opposite, just beyond the old stone bridge which carried the road over the water rushing from the sluices at the side of the Reynolds' garden. The mill building, part of which dated from the seventeenth century, looked very dilapidated and still contained all its old machinery; but it was uniquely situated as it stood on a triangle of land, with the main stream of the River Wey on one side and the mill stream, which flowed under the building, on the other. In front a meadow ran down to form an apex of land where the mill water rejoined the river about a hundred yards or so from the building. From its upper floors there were fine views, both up and down stream, over the fields and meadows of the valley of the Wey, with the dark outline of Alice Holt forest just visible to the south east. There were trout in the river, which was about six yards wide at this point on its long journey to join the Thames. From the start Bernard liked this old mill and when the Reynolds told him it might be possible to buy it, with the adjoining meadows, he took to the idea at once. So eventually he bought the property and it became his home.

Of course there was a great deal of work to be done before the water mill could become a habitable residence. The main structure was sound, but it was now necessary to redesign the interior completely as the building had never been lived in. So architects and masons were consulted, and in due course given 'the master plan' for the home that was to be made out of Isington Mill. It took a long time to complete all the work and it was not until the early 1950s that everything was ready. The house now has two floors above ground level with three large reception rooms, five bedrooms and three bathrooms, apart from attractive and very comfortable accommodation for servants in the old cottage at the south end of the building. My brother was fortunate in one respect, for the Governments and various organisations in Australia, Tasmania and Canada, had generously presented him with timber for the reconstruction, including the building of a large barn that was needed to house his three wartime caravans, in which he had lived during his campaigns from El Alamein until the war in Europe ended. So all the floors in the house are Tasmanian oak, while the stairways, doors, bookcases and built-in cupboards are made of mountain ash from Victoria. The Government of Canada provided cedar shingles for the roof of the caravan shed, which was otherwise a gift from the Australian Government. The New Zealand Government, knowing he had lost all his belongings during the war, gave him some most useful furniture. His friend Sir William Mallinson arranged for the importation of all the timber involved.

There had never been a garden at the old mill, so Bernard now had to plan and supervise the considerable work needed to create the type of garden he wanted. For the meadows were overgrown with thistles and weeds and the river and the mill stream were full of mud and slime which concealed the pebbles beneath. My brother planted an apple orchard at the end of his garden, on the apex of land where the river and the mill stream join one another, with a lawn and beds for roses and flowering shrubs between the orchard and the house. He had the river and the mill stream completely cleaned out; all the mud and weeds were removed so now the water in both runs clear and swift, and the bed of pebbles and gravel is clean and tidy. Both streams are kept in perfect order and any stones that look dirty or unsightly have to be removed. Whether the trout, or other fish in the river, look with favour on this frequent tidying-up of their environment is another matter; certainly there is no evidence that Bernard's stretch of the river has ever been fished. It has taken many years to produce the garden in its present state, but the result is very satisfying with colours mainly of gold, yellow and red, derived from the rose bushes and flowering shrubs of which he is so fond. No flowers are grown except the roses, as he relies on the many species of shrubs he has planted to give him what is virtually an all-the-year-round colour scheme. No weeds are allowed on the lawn or anywhere else, and worms and moles are forbidden and certainly never appear. Bernard is happy in the setting of his garden of which he is very proud, and rightly so for its design is pleasing to the eye and, equally important, it has an atmosphere all its own; very peaceful and quiet it is and even the wartime caravans, still with their original maps marked with troop dispositions and the photograph of Rommel in one corner, do not look out of place.

Inside the house the dining-room is on the ground floor, on one wall of which my brother has hung the family portraits which used to be at New Park. The pictures of six generations of our family hang there now, including a portrait of Bernard by James Gunn, showing him wearing a uniform jersey with no medal ribbons except that of the American DSM. A portrait of David was added after Bernard came to the Mill, and a photograph of Henry Montgomery, David's son, completes the generations. A main feature in the design of the house is the large room, of similar dimensions, on each floor. These rooms stretch the length of the building, from east to west, with windows running the full width on both sides giving plenty of light and air at all times. My brother has his study in one of these large rooms, on the first floor, where he now spends much of his time and in which he keeps his favourite paintings, pictures, books and other possessions. It was here that he wrote his *Memoirs* and the books that followed. His favourite painting hangs over the chimney piece. It was given to him by Sir Winston Churchill, and is a Churchill picture painted by Sir Winston during one of his wartime visits to Marrakesh. In the foreground is the Moroccan plain across which a wide river runs fast, and is interrupted in its course by shallow rapids, beyond which it flows on over rocky ground. In the background is the great range of the Atlas mountains showing the valleys which run down to the plain. Sir Winston has most effectively portrayed the varied colours of this Moroccan scene, especially the reddish brown of the soil with the grey stones in the river-bed and the backdrop of high mountains which dominate the scene. One day Bernard told Sir Winston how much he liked the painting, whereupon the Prime Minister said he would present it to him; before doing so however Churchill took brush and palette and painted in on the canvas, in the middle distance, the figure of an Arab crossing the plain on a donkey.

My brother's bedroom leads out of the room just described. I have always found it surprising that over his bed he has hung two photographs. One, naturally enough, is of father, but the other is of Pope Pius XII. Both my parents, with their very strong prejudice against the Roman Catholic Church, would have been horrified even to contemplate one of us owning the Pope's picture! But Bernard had several audiences of Pope Pius XII during his NATO appointment, and always held him in high regard.

In September 1948 my brother was appointed permanent Chairman of the Land, Naval and Air Commanders-in-Chief Committee of the Western Union, with headquarters at Fontainebleau. The short name for this cumbersome title was Chairman of UNIFORCE. It was the beginning of the defence set-up which came into being on 4th April 1949 as part of the North Atlantic Treaty Organisation (NATO), and which later became the Supreme Headquarters Allied Powers Europe (SHAPE) in Paris. Bernard remained with this organisation for a long time, including the period he spent at UNIFORCE. His first Supreme Commander was his old chief General Eisenhower, and he then served in succession under General Matthew Ridgeway, General Alfred Gruenther and General Lauris Norstad.

My brother very much enjoyed his time at NATO largely because he travelled so extensively, visiting all the fifteen NATO countries and inspecting their armies and defence establishments. His Supreme Commanders were happy that he should do this for his prestige as an international soldier was enormous, and his reputation as a high-ranking officer, able to advise on every aspect of a country's defence needs, was equally high. So he was not often in Paris, where for a long time he lived outside the city in the Trianon Palace Hotel at Versailles. As was perhaps to be expected he took no part in the social life of SHAPE and very seldom, if ever, attended any of the official entertainments. But he liked to go from time to time to the British Embassy, where it was said that the only woman he cared to be put next to at dinner was Nancy

Mitford, who had settled in France. In these circumstances, especially his long absences from Paris, it was only natural that he never really understood and certainly never liked the formalities by which SHAPE business was conducted. It was primarily an International Headquarters, and essentially American in character and practice. This my brother could never really bring himself to admit and he therefore felt very frustrated when, on return from some inspection visit, he suddenly came up against routine and procedure which he did not appreciate. The office minutes he wrote from SHAPE on such occasions well illustrate his reactions, and are so typical of his style, that I have thought it appropriate to reproduce three examples. I am sure my readers will appreciate them.

The first example is a minute he sent to a senior British officer at SHAPE Headquarters:

SACEUR's Wartime Responsibilities

1. I have just seen a letter to Staff Division signed by you directing ACOS PANDP to assemble a working group of interested SHAPE Divisions 'to examine and recommend what action, if any, should now be taken within SHAPE to enable the staff divisions best to assist SACEUR in the discharge of his responsibilities short of general war and Phase II of an all out conflict'.

2. To assemble such a working party is a complete waste of time and effort. It represents the negation of all principles of command. It can only result in more paper, more committees, and less decision.

3. The answer is quite simple. It is to ascertain from SACEUR what he wants, and how he wishes to command the forces given him. The Staff must then organise themselves to carry out his orders. This principle applies in all the work that is done at SHAPE – but is never carried out. Until SHAPE get this principle right, its staff will continue to increase in size and inefficiency.

4. The paper attached to your letter is a dreadful one. It is a mass of quotations and platitudes. How can the staff plan to

assist SACEUR in war if they do not know how he proposes to exercise his functions of command?

5. I recommend that you cancel your letter, and that no further action is taken in this matter until SACEUR has given a clear lead as to how he proposes to command in war.

Montgomery of Alamein
Field Marshal

Copy to: Chief of Staff

There follow two minutes my brother addressed to the Chief of Staff at SHAPE. Both are self-explanatory:

Chief of Staff
1. Have you read the attached?
   If we have a Prize List at SHAPE, I would give it 1st Prize, and an Olympic Gold Medal, for the maximum number of:
   Platitudes
   Cliches
   Long-winded sentences
   Unusual words, which many will not understand
   Verboseness
2. Surely in a paper for the NATO Council we must go for clarity of expression, conciseness, and keep strictly to the point. We must marshal the facts, and prove something from them. It is quality of contents of the paper that will count – not quantity of paper.
3. I hope The Almighty will attend the Council Meeting when this paper is discussed. Especially if the rest of the 465 pages are like this 35. His help will certainly be needed.

Montgomery of Alamein
Field Marshal

Chief of Staff
1. I have seen a Memorandum you have sent to certain NMR's regarding 'General Personnel Policy at the Fontainebleau Headquarters' – dated 6 August, 1957. It must be clear to all that Valluy is trying to blow up his HQ so that he becomes a

minor Supreme Commander in Central Europe. It is not the job of the two Deputy COS to deal with National Governments; it is our job. Their job is to get on with the war.
I utterly disagree with his proposals.

2. I have also seen a draft letter, which SACEUR is being asked to sign, to certain National Chiefs of Staff about the Command Structure in the Centre. I hope he will NOT sign it. Why do we refer to others a disagreement between SHAPE and C-in-C Centre? And if we *must* do so, why do we not say what *we* think is the right answer? And what is our view as to the right answer?

3. In a previous minute I recommended that The Almighty be asked to attend the next meeting of the NATO Council – to help in explaining a SHAPE memorandum – because it seems that we have no officer at SHAPE who can write clearly. It would seem that we ought to ask Him to call in at SHAPE, on His way to the Council.

Montgomery of Alamein
Field Marshal

Reading between the lines it seems likely that my brother's minutes, written on his return from a lengthy absence, probably provoked some adverse reaction at SHAPE Headquarters. For he was referring to plans and projects which had been prepared and accepted at all staff levels so it was too late now to seek any substantial changes. The British representatives at SHAPE no doubt agreed that he was completely right, judged from the standpoint of an efficient National Headquarters. But he was dealing with, and was indeed part of, an International Organisation where, *inter alia*, sensitive political considerations had to be given their due weight. This Bernard could not stomach. On one occasion indeed it was the political considerations that brought him into conflict, and caused him some trouble, not with the NATO authorities, but with the British Government. Towards the end of his time at SHAPE my brother, who had already been to most of the capitals of Europe including Moscow, decided he would much like to visit General Franco in Madrid, and he made plans accordingly. But

Spain is not a member of the North Atlantic Treaty Organisation, and clearly there would be considerable repercussions, both military and political, if a British Field-Marshal, holding the appointment of Deputy Supreme Commander of NATO armed forces, were to pay an official visit to the Head of the Spanish Government. So Bernard was told that his proposed visit to Madrid was not approved and could not be made, and some very acrimonious telegrams were written and dispatched before the last was heard of this issue. On the other hand on any purely military occasion my brother was always very much in his element at SHAPE. At the end of each calendar year he personally conducted a training exercise, on an international scale, and attended by high ranking officers from all the NATO nations. It was invariably an outstanding success.

Chapter 11

THE LAST CHAPTER

On 1st August 1968 the Field-Marshal wrote to me about his last book *A History of Warfare* which had just been published. He had presented a signed copy to my wife and myself and in his accompanying letter had said:

'I suggest the best way to study the book is to read the first two chapters and the last four, first. Actually the last chapter, *Epilogue – The Ideal of Peace* was written by me before I began any work on the book at all. I find it is always best to write the last chapter first, so as to understand what you are working towards. As a matter of fact I wrote the last chapter four years ago, late in 1964, when I was in King Edward VII Hospital for Officers recovering from an operation!'

In writing this book I followed my brother's advice and wrote this last chapter before any other.

The Field-Marshal flew from Paris to London on 18th September 1958 having served for ten years as Deputy Supreme Commander of the armed forces of NATO. This was a record never likely to be equalled, and he was now to revert to the unemployed register though not to retire; Field-Marshals remain on the active list for life. As he landed at Northolt from his private R.A.F. Dakota aircraft, immaculate in service dress with ten rows of medal ribbons, he could look back on an astonishing career; a success story indeed. But it is unlikely anyone present on that occasion will have recalled how, fifty-one years earlier when a cadet at Sandhurst, everything had pointed to his inability to follow a military career.* My brother himself has often said how fortunate it was that these early setbacks occurred, and channelled his career into the path it was to take. When he returned to England on this occasion it was difficult to recall all the details of his success. Apart from his well-known military record he had become a Knight of the Garter and of the Order of the Bath, a peer of the realm, and an Honorary Freeman of the City of London and of forty-three other major cities and towns at home and abroad. He was also a Freeman of three of the City of London Livery Companies and held honorary degrees at thirteen universities in England and other countries. He was already the author of five books, and was now about to publish his *Memoirs* which were to become world famous and were translated for sale in the languages of the fifteen NATO countries. It was at the Wimbledon Lawn Tennis Championships some years earlier that, for the first time and quite unexpectedly, he had happened to meet his publisher and discussed with him the writing of his *Memoirs* and their publication, on his own terms. The resulting book, including serialisation rights in a London newspaper and an American magazine, earned him personally a sum expressed in six figures, not a bad record for a Sandhurst cadet who had been reduced to the ranks for misdemeanour. Meanwhile his list of official farewell engagements appeared very formidable. He had already lunched with the President of France (de Gaulle) and his Ministers and dined with the British army officers of SHAPE. At a farewell ceremonial parade in Paris he had been decorated by General de Gaulle with the Médaille Militaire; this is the highest French military decoration, given very seldom to French soldiers and only exceptionally to foreigners. He had also dined with his Supreme Commander General Norstad and the officers of Supreme Headquarters and with the Secretary General M. Spaak and the Council of NATO. He had previously paid farewell visits to the NATO Governments

* See page 134.

and also to Marshal Tito, whom he described as 'a proper chap'. For his final farewell in London he was entertained by Ministers at a Government luncheon in Lancaster House and by the Army Council at the Royal Hospital, Chelsea. A week later he flew to Nice to attend Sir Winston and Lady Churchill's Golden Wedding celebrations.

In the ten years that followed up to 1968 my brother systematically developed his own, and for him a new, way of life. He based himself at the Mill to which he had become so attached, and loved to entertain his many friends and acquaintances in all walks of life. Distinguished soldiers, sailors and airmen, ministers of government and politicians all came to see him, to consult him and seek his advice; he was very proud of these visits. He did not go a great deal to London which he increasingly disliked, but he always attended important debates in the House of Lords which he described as 'the best club in London'. His life in other respects was an extremely active one, particularly in three fields – travel, writing and broadcasting. The list below of the journeys he made shows what an astonishing constitution the Field-Marshal had. He was always able to travel in comfort but the frequency and length of his journeys between 1958 and 1962 were enough to tax the strength of a far younger man. His long tour in South Africa in 1962 occupied several months and he was then seventy-five years of age. Thereafter his trips to South Africa were mainly for recreation, though on one occasion he advised the Government of the Union on defence matters.

May	1959	Russia
November	1959	South Africa
January	1960	India
April	1960	Canada
May	1960	China
September	1961	China
October	1961	Canada
December	1961	Central America (Honduras, El Salvador, Guatemala, Nicaragua)

Arrival in China, 1960

In Johannesburg, 1962

January	1962	South Africa
Early	1963	,, ,,
Early	1964	,, ,,
January	1965	,, ,,
Early	1966	,, ,,
May	1967	Egypt – 10 days

My brother recorded the details of all his major journeys, in considerable detail, in his book *Three Continents* published in 1962. Inevitably he met and had long talks with the heads of state and of governments in all the countries he visited. In so doing it has to be said that he sometimes tended to look upon himself in the guise of a roving ambassador, and forwarded his reports on certain countries direct to the Secretary of State at the Foreign Office. Rather naturally this did not always endear him to the officially appointed British heads of mission in the territories concerned. A little earlier than this the Field-Marshal had again run into trouble with the Americans because of his forthright comment on United States policy and leadership during the 1939–45 war. He had added his own personal view of General Eisenhower's capacity as a professional soldier. This, he was the first to admit, lost him Eisenhower's friendship, though, as he claimed, for the wrong reasons, and he certainly regretted it very much. There are some people no doubt who will say that it was *folie de grandeur* which caused him all these troubles. But those who take that view seem to forget that for more than twenty years, from 1946, he travelled the world and wherever he was attracted wide publicity. More important, whatever he wrote or said was invariably based on his own personal experience and was the complete truth as he knew it. There was one occasion however when his speeches brought him serious trouble, at any rate potentially. Early in May 1962 he sent me the following letter, enclosing evidence of a threat to kill him:

Isington Mill
4-4-62

Dear Brian,
  Enclosed seems to be up your street. It may have some connection with my speech in the Foreign Affairs Debate, when I

12

said there cannot be ONE Germany. And that we should give
de facto recognition to East Germany. Or it may have some
connection with the "weed killer" remark.

Yrs. ever,
Bernard

30th March 1962

Field Marshal Montgomery
London
Dirty Bastard,

We come over soon. We spit you in your face.
We bomb you with shit. You shithead.
You are a war criminal and a criminal gangster.
Attention: Plastic bombs will make an end to your life.
Your house will burn down soon.
You are the most miserable creature living in Britain,
you must be killed soon. And you will be.

The German A O S
Executive

Above is the copy of a letter received at the Mill on 4th May
1962. The envelope was franked on the reverse as sent by 'F. M.
Douglas, Park Hotel, Düsseldorf'.

The 'weed-killer' remark referred to by the Field-Marshal was
a statement by him in an address which he had been invited to give
to the officers attending a course at the Royal Military College of
Science at Shrivenham in March 1962. In this address he had
reviewed the European politico-military scene, and at one point
had seen fit to refer to Adenauer, the Chancellor of the West
German Republic, in the following terms: 'Dr Adenauer needs a
dose of weed-killer. He's an old man and over-sensitive. A small
dose would do.' Of course my brother had in mind that Adenauer,
then aged eighty-six, had been Chancellor for the past thirteen
years, and he knew that his audience of regular British army
would not fail to see the humour of his remark. However, he had
previously warned them that his address was confidential and that

care must be taken not to repeat outside anything he said. Unfortunately his trust was misplaced, or more likely gossip was overheard, for the 'weed-killer' remark was quoted verbatim in the British national press a few days later. As a result of the threatening letter the security authorities and the Chief Constable of Hampshire were alerted, and appropriate precautions were taken, but nothing untoward occurred. Later the German AOS were reported as a dissident and subversive organisation on the Continent, though the actual originator of the letter was never identified.

Bernard's last tour abroad in 1967, apart from short trips to the Continent, deserves especial mention. He had long wished to re-visit the site of the Battle of El Alamein, and a quarter of a century after that world-famous event was an appropriate time. Towards the end of 1966 therefore he wrote privately to Gamel Abdel Nasser, President of the United Arab Republic, and asked if it could be arranged. He planned to take with him two of his Eighth Army comrades, Lieutenant-General Sir Oliver Leese and Brigadier H.S. H.Mainwaring, and four press representatives including two photographers all from the *Sunday Times*, which had offered to defray the whole cost of the journey by air to Egypt and return to London for the entire party of seven. In due course President Nasser replied and said that his Government would very much welcome the visit as planned. Furthermore the Government of the U.A.R. was prepared to pay all the cost of accommodation, travel and maintenance incurred by the party during their stay in Egypt. This was a remarkable gesture to come from a foreign country whose relations with the British Government at that time were particularly delicate; the seven day Israeli-Egyptian war of June 1967 began just over one month after the Field-Marshal and his party arrived at Cairo airport on 3rd of May. It was for this reason, and particularly because Bernard had made all the arrangements with the President of the U.A.R. personally, without bothering to inform any British official, that his journey was not exactly looked on with favour in Whitehall. The first thing the Foreign Office in London, and the British chargé d'affaires in Cairo, knew about it was the receipt of a letter from the Field-Marshal to say that he was leaving for Cairo by air on 3rd May. In the circumstances the concern in London is not difficult to appreciate, more especially perhaps in view of what followed.

When he landed at Heliopolis the Field-Marshal was given a most elaborate military reception. There to meet him was the Chief of Staff of the U.A.R. Armed Forces, together with the Commanders-in-Chief of the Army and the Air Force, some three dozen generals and other celebrities, a band and a guard of honour. He then drove through Cairo in state in a car flying the Union Jack – in itself a most unusual distinction at this time of strained diplomatic relations – to the Mena House Hotel near the Pyramids. It was there he had stayed on his first arrival in Cairo to take command of the Eighth Army on 12th August 1942. The highlights of the ten-day visit that followed were his lecture to the officers attending the Egyptian staff college, and his appearance at the El Alamein war memorial at the scene of the battle. What was not reported however was his two-hour talk alone with President Nasser and General Mahomed Fawzi (the Chief of Staff who asked for his advice on how to conduct war against Israel! Later, at a hotel outside Cairo, he spent two days as the personal guest of Muhammad Hassanein Heykal, editor of the influential newspaper *Al Ahram* and regarded as Nasser's closest friend and adviser. He even requested the British chargé d'affaires in Cairo to send a cipher telegram to the Secretary of State at the Foreign Office in London giving his views on how the Egyptian problem should be handled. He added the name of the only British Minister in the then Labour administration with whom, he said, Nasser had told him he was prepared to negotiate. There is no doubt that this kind of action did not improve the Field-Marshal's standing in the eyes of the British Government. After all no other Englishman, and certainly no official, had been able so far to obtain the access and private interviews which he had had. At the same time there must also have been the presumption, amounting to certainty, that during all those controversial tours – whether to meet Khruschev, Mao Tse Tung, President Nasser, Marshal Tito or Dr Verwoerd in South Africa – the Field-Marshal would only have been allowed to see what his hosts wished him to see. Furthermore it would also have been appreciated that his hosts might well view his arrival as an opportunity to put across their own particular propaganda line to a person of undoubted distinction and standing in all countries – and hence see some potential gain in his visit. No doubt it was thoughts such as these that conditioned the British Government's attitude to some of the Field-Marshal's journeys.

In between his travels throughout the 1960s my brother occupied some of his time by broadcasting, both on television and sound radio. In the event he became quite expert and the B.B.C. made occasional use of his services, with Jack de Manio and other celebrities interviewing him. The Americans also sent Ed Murrow to interview him after completion of his travels in Asia, Africa and the Americas. His talks were not confined to military topics and he achieved quite considerable popularity in programmes such as Desert Island Discs and a Christmas broadcast on the B.B.C. light programme. For the Desert Island Discs programme, which was broadcast on 20th December 1969, the book he chose to take with him, other than the Bible and Shakespeare, was his own *History of Warfare*. There is no doubt his voice was popular and people in all walks of life liked to listen to him, and he, it is only fair to say, also liked to listen to his own voice. Probably his most famous broadcast was on a B.B.C. sound radio programme, just before his eighty-third birthday, entitled *The Human Factor in My Life*. In it my brother talked about the broad philosophy which has influenced him from the time when he was a young boy until the evening of his life. This was greatly applauded and was later reproduced in full in *The Listener*. More recently, on the night before his eighty-fifth birthday, B.B.C. radio repeated a previous broadcast of his entitled *Music in My Life*. I should perhaps add that Bernard is not really musical in the true sense!

After his memoirs, my brother wrote four more books: *An Approach to Sanity* (a study in East-West relations) in 1959; *The Path to Leadership*, 1961; *Three Continents*, 1962; and his last book *A History of Warfare* in 1968. *An Approach to Sanity* included an account of his personal interview with M. Khruschev in the Kremlin during his visit to Russia in 1959, where he also met again that great soldier Marshal Sokolovsky. In the same year he gave two Chichele lectures at Oxford University taking for his subject the

Conflict between East and West. The text of both these lectures, and of articles he wrote on international affairs, was later published in the *Sunday Times*. Since the end of the war, and particularly from the time he became CIGS, my brother's close friendship with Denis Hamilton* has developed considerably. It was Hamilton who appreciated that after he had left NATO Bernard might find it difficult to accept the sudden change from high office, with all the facilities that went with it. Clearly he would need some new outlet for his still undiminished energy and initiative. So it was this friend, with his keen insight into new circumstances, who first gave Bernard the idea that he should consider his future in terms of writing, with foreign travel, and the knowledge it brings, as the platform from which to develop his thoughts and the manner of expressing them. In this climate the friendship between the two men lives on, with much mutual appreciation.

My brother made quite a lot of money from all these activities including the profits derived from his writing. He himself has never been a great spender, but on the other hand he has a great admiration for money and for people who possess it. Indeed it is a curious trait in his character that he tends to regard professional achievement, in any walk of life, as synonymous with the possession of financial wealth. But he is generous by any standards in his charity lists. On more than one occasion he was presented by an admirer with large sums of money, all of which he donated immediately to St John's School, Leatherhead, of which he was a governor. Nevertheless, and this appears strange by contrast, when a very near relative of his was left widowed and extremely hard up he gave her £5 saying, 'I hope you will find this a help.' He really meant it too, and fortunately her sense of humour enabled her to see the funny side of it! All this only goes to demonstrate the truth that all great men have their eccentricities, and certainly the Field-Marshal is not without his. He has always loved success, and this has led, there is no doubt, to an enormous admiration for himself and his own influence. A letter he sent me, shortly after his visit to Khrushchev, speaks for itself in that sense:

---

* Now Chairman and Editor-in-Chief TIMES NEWSPAPERS LTD.

> *Isington Mill*
> 29-5-59

My dear Brian,

You may like to know that Hoyer-Millar* is coming here tomorrow, Saturday, at 4.30 to have tea with me. He is coming alone!!

> *Yrs. ever*
> *Bernard*

Some ten years later, in 1968, he sent me a copy of *Hansard* with a letter in which he wrote:

> *Isington Mill*

Dear Brian,

You may like to read in Hansard my speech in the Defence Debate in the House of Lords on Wednesday last. The house was full; members from the Commons crowded their place at the Bar of the House, and the steps of the Throne were filled with Privy Councillors!

> *Yrs. ever*
> *Bernard*

Critics of the Field-Marshal will say that letters such as these are evidence of overwhelming conceit and arrogance; but in reality they serve to show his supreme confidence and judgement in his own ability and opinions. Without this confidence, and the courage that goes with it, he could not have become one of the greatest commanders in our history, who, at El Alamein, symbolised the turning point in our fortunes. Modesty is not perhaps his strong point but military genius certainly is. It was genius in that sense that gave him the flair to adopt the beret, with its two cap badges, in those critical days in the desert. In all our military history no soldier, with the exception of the Gloucestershire Regiment who wear the 'Back Badge', has worn more than one badge on his

---

* Sir Frederick Hoyer-Millar, then Permanent Under Secretary of State at the Foreign Office.

head dress. His two-badge head dress became therefore a symbol of recognition of himself, and of his leadership, to the many hundreds of thousands of all ranks who served in his Eighth Army, and later in 21 Army Group.

In the mid 1960s Bernard encountered family troubles which for a time saddened his life considerably. David Montgomery divorced his wife, who had left him, and this was a very great blow to my brother for several reasons. In the first place his strong religious convictions compelled him to regard marriage as indissoluble, no matter what the circumstances might be. In his description of our family in his *Memoirs* he had written, 'None of us has been through the divorce courts.' Now this had happened to his son. But, more than that, Bernard had always claimed to have 'fashioned' the marriage, which he had very much welcomed, and he was proud of it. He was a close friend of David's parents-in-law, the late Sir Charles Connell and Lady Connell, and took great delight in his two grandchildren. For a long time he was not able to adjust his outlook to the circumstances of a broken marriage, and the legal consequences that followed. In particular he could see no distinction in the divorce proceedings between the admission of the 'guilty party', in an undefended case, and the customary request by the other party for the exercise of the court's descretion. It needs no imagination to appreciate the misunderstandings and difficulties that this caused. It is sufficient to say that much unhappiness ensued, including a period during which there was a break in the friendly relationship between the Field-Marshal and my wife and myself. Fortunately this came to an end late in 1967, and then, early in 1970, my nephew's second marriage, to Tessa Zulueta, daughter of the late Lieutenant-General Sir Frederick Browning and Lady Browning (Daphne du Maurier) finally healed the family wounds.

Sir Winston Churchill's death on 24th January 1965 greatly affected my brother. His high regard for Churchill is well known and was described in great detail in *The Path to Leadership*. He was in South Africa when Churchill died and Lady Spencer-Churchill telegraphed to him asking if he would agree to be one of the distinguished personages who were to act as pall bearers at the state funeral in St Paul's Cathedral. I have always been somewhat at a loss to understand why he did not come home to attend the funeral of his old friend, whom he had known for nearly a quarter of a century. On the face of it the explanation lies in the fact that less than six months earlier he had had a serious operation, for prostate gland, so that his trip to South Africa, by sea, was mainly to recoup his strength and avoid the English winter. But he could have returned to London by air, without much trouble and if necessary for little more than one day, and then resumed his interrupted convalescence. But there is another reason which may explain why he did not come home immediately. As long as I can remember Bernard has always disliked attending funerals, and has avoided doing so whenever possible. For instance when our mother died at New Park in 1949, aged eighty-five, he was living near Paris, within easy reach of Ireland; however he did not go to her funeral in Moville. This, it has to be said, caused considerable offence to the local country people who were so fond of our parents. Nevertheless looking back I cannot recall ever feeling really disappointed by Bernard's conduct at an important time – except on this occasion of Sir Winston's state funeral. Perhaps however there is one other. During the war he had promised to attend the reception in the Savoy after my wife and I were married. He was in England and of course all appropriate preparations were made, but at the last moment he went to a football match instead. The Field-Marshal's Christmas card in the year that Churchill died had two photographs; one of himself taken with Sir Winston, and the other of himself standing beside the great man's grave. He was often asked to stay at Chartwell with the Churchills, particularly after Sir Winston's second term as Prime Minister (he is a very great admirer of Lady Spencer-Churchill) and he has always particularly enjoyed the best, though perhaps not so widely known, of all the 'Churchill stories'. When Winston was Prime Minister there occurred one of those unfortunate, but much-publicised, incidents in Hyde Park in which a man, very prominent in political and social life, was discovered by the police with a girl *in flagranti delicto*, and was charged in the courts with an act of public indecency. It was winter at the time, and when the Prime Minister was told about it he immediately said: 'Man, woman; winter's night, raining, grass all wet, very cold. Makes you proud to be an Englishman!'

In 1966 my brother received Her Majesty the Queen's command to carry the Sword of State at her State Opening of Parliament on 21st April. The event was televised for the first time that year. The duty is an onerous one as the sword is heavy. It has to be carried in front of the Queen during her procession and entry into the House of Lords, held upright whilst she is reading her speech, and carried again in procession during her departure from the Palace of Westminster. The Field-Marshal was then in his seventy-ninth year and it says much for his vigour and constitution that he completed the duty, not only in that year but also in 1967. Then in 1968 when he was rising eighty-one he asked that he should again be given the honour of carrying this sword at the State Opening of Parliament. In doing so he would be completing the hat-trick for this duty. The Queen agreed. It is probable that he made a mistake in attempting this task for the third time. A peer's robes are heavy to wear and in a crowded chamber the temperature is certainly high. Added to this there was the effort of carrying the sword in procession, and standing with it motionless for up to half an hour. As a result whilst the Peers were awaiting the arrival of the Commons, and before the Queen had begun to read her speech, my brother realised he was swaying and could not continue. He therefore signalled to his neighbour that he could not carry on and someone must relieve him. This was clearly the right decision and Lord Tryon, Keeper of the Privy Purse and Treasurer to H.M. The Queen, immediately took his place, while he was escorted from the chamber. The Field-Marshal said afterwards how amused he was that the only member of the House of Lords to follow him out was Baroness Summerskill, a member of the Labour party to which he did not subscribe. She revived him with champagne and sandwiches in the library for which he felt much better. Later he received a letter from the Queen's private secretary saying how sorry she was he had had to leave the ceremony and thanking him for his services in that duty.

Saturday 17th November 1967 was my brother's eightieth birthday. To mark the occasion his old friend 'Simbo', who was then Governor of the Royal Hospital Chelsea, gave a dinner party at the Governor's House. A dozen or so of my brother's closest friends were present and the Field-Marshal motored that afternoon to Chelsea where he was to stay with the Governor and Lady Simpson. That night burglars came to the Mill. The fact of the birthday was no doubt well known and his intended absence might have been assumed, if not already known, and plans could be made in advance accordingly. The thieves broke in through the double garage which adjoins the house, and from which an unlocked door leads into the entrance hall. The three female members of the domestic staff live in a servants' wing which is separated from the rest of the house by a passageway and a stout wooden door. They heard nothing. The thieves were evidently experts and were intent on taking silver and jewellery, nothing else. They made no disturbance or noise and they left no mess. But they took every item of silver, gold and jewellery in the house, for which they evidently made a detailed and careful search. Their loot included silver cigar boxes presented with the scrolls declaring the grant of the Freedom of the Cities of Belfast and Portsmouth, and gold cufflinks and pencil presented by the Mayor of New York. Also taken was the star of the Order of the Garter which shows the figure of St George, in gold and enamel, killing the dragon. The thieves however, for reasons unknown, did not take all the Garter insignia, leaving behind the riband of the Order, a heavy gold collar from which the star is suspended. The most important item stolen, of intrinsic value, was the emblem of Knighthood of the Order of the Elephant presented to the Field-Marshal by the King of Denmark; this is the highest State honour of Denmark which, since the 1939–45 war, has only been awarded to three foreigners (Churchill, Eisenhower and Montgomery). The emblem consists of an elephant in gold and enamel, about the size of a match box, studded with rubies and diamonds, and worth thousands of pounds. But the most serious loss, and a grievous one as it was quite irreplaceable, was the Field-Marshal's baton covered in crimson velvet with gold mountings. This had been presented to my brother personally, and signed, by H.M. King George VI at a private ceremony at

Buckingham Palace in 1944. Very fortunately the thieves did not touch, presumably because they could not find it, what was then probably my brother's most prized possession, and certainly a document of the highest national and international significance. This was the historic Instrument of Unconditional Surrender of all the German armed forces in Holland, Denmark and North West Germany signed at the Field-Marshal's headquarters on Luneberg Heath on 4th May 1945. When my brother first disclosed his possession of this document, publicly in the House of Lords, there was a considerable parliamentary storm – which he survived! Later on in 1969 he presented the document to the Imperial War Museum where it remains on display in perpetuity.

When the housekeeper entered the dining room on the ground floor, before 8 a.m. on Sunday 18th November, she saw at once what had occurred and telephoned immediately to the Royal Hospital at Chelsea, and to the police. The Field-Marshal was at breakfast when he heard the news and returned to his home as soon as possible. In spite of intense police efforts nothing has ever been recovered. In their view the thieves will almost certainly have broken down most of the items in order to realise the cash value of the silver, gold and precious stones. This theory seems most likely as virtually no item could have been disposed of intact without considerable risk of recognition; this would be particularly so in the case of the Field-Marshal's baton, though one day perhaps, say half a century or more hence, it may turn up in some remote part of the world for sale as a souvenir. Of course the Field-Marshal received the insurance value but that naturally could not compensate for all this grievous loss which he felt deeply. The numerous public appeals, in the press and elsewhere, and the offer of substantial rewards, for information leading to the recovery of the stolen property have never had any results. Additional burglar alarms were installed and other precautions were taken at the Mill. And about a month later, the Field Marshal wrote me the following letter, enclosing the photograph which is reproduced as the frontispiece of this book:

> Isington Mill
> 12-12-67

My dear Brian,
    You and Bunty may care to have this coloured photograph, taken in my dining-room alongside the painting of our father — on the morning of my birthday and before the burglary. It is my Christmas present to you both.

> Yrs. ever
> Bernard

In retrospect the decline in the Field-Marshal's astonishing constitution, with all its vigour and energy, clearly followed his operation for prostate gland in 1964. Physically he has never been quite the same again. This was accentuated by a series of heart attacks for which he went into King Edward VII Hospital, for treatment by his friend, the distinguished surgeon and former Olympic athlete, Sir Arthur Porritt.* The latter had been a Brigadier R.A.M.C. under the Field-Marshal in 21 Army Group, and was well aware that my brother had been shot through the lungs in the First World War. As related earlier the wound left him with only one and a half lungs and it was remarkable that he had continued to play in the British Army Lawn Tennis Championships after the 1914–18 war. But the cumulative effects of his operation in 1964, and the subsequent heart trouble, meant that in 1968 he had to cancel a planned trip round the world. This was to have included visits to Newfoundland, where he was to receive an honorary degree at the University, and to Sydney to attend the New South Wales El Alamein reunion. Nevertheless his love of travel still prevailed and he had planned another tour in the winter of 1969, to Australia and New Zealand and then across the Pacific to Vancouver, all by sea. From Vancouver, where he was to have met Donald, our then eldest surviving brother, and his family, he would have flown back to England. However early in 1969 he wrote to me saying:

* Now Lord Porritt, GCMG, KCVO, CBE.

'I went out in the garden today for the first time for many weeks. I have had a very unpleasant winter which has pulled me down a good bit; some days I feel well, some days I do not. I have had to cancel my visit to New Zealand and Canada next winter. The doctors say I must not make the journey with all the changes of temperature involved. Maybe they are right.'

This setback in my brother's health in no way affected his mental agility, or his sense of humour, which still showed very clearly in the letters he wrote. Some people may think his words outrageous but to those close to him they merely exemplify his ability always to see the funny side of life. I wonder if many people, in their eighty-first year, will have written, as he did, in the letters quoted below:

My dear Brian,

You are both coming here to lunch on Sunday next, September 1.

May I suggest (with due respect!) that you allow plenty of time for a long cross-country journey on a Sunday. You can arrive here *as early as you like*; but not as late as you like.

Lunch is at 1 p.m. It irritates my staff to put it back – and me too.

> *Yrs. ever*
> *Bernard*

Dear Brian,

You may be interested in the enclosed. Your Aunt C., a dreadful female, has passed over Jordan. I doubt if she will meet her ghastly husband; he is more likely to be in a pretty hot climate!

I do not want any of it back.

I expect you both to lunch here on Sunday July 7 – 12.30 p.m.

> *Yrs. ever*
> *Bernard*

My dear Brian,

Very many thanks for the birthday gift from you and Bunty. The small mats are exactly what is needed in my home to stop people who are uncivilised, and not trained to the house, from ruining my furniture with spilling alchohol over it. Born 1887. Still going strong!

Would you and Bunty care to come to lunch here on Sunday 1st December?

Yrs. ever
Bernard

Since he left his last NATO appointment my brother has been as zealous as ever in providing himself with all the means needed for his material comfort, with his domestic staff as his main concern. For some years he had relied on European servants but he was never really content until, early in 1968, he obtained the services of one family, all of whom live locally in his village. There is no doubt that the members of this family give him most selfless and devoted service at all times, and without doubt ensure his physical well-being in his old age. Indeed without them we, as a family, would have found it very difficult to feel happy about his comfort at the Mill, living, as he does, so completely alone. The letter below shows his appreciation of his staff — six in all:

Isington Mill
16-2-68

Dear Bunty,

Certainly come to lunch on Saturday February 24 — you, Brian, Tom.*

Arrive 12.30 p.m.

Domestic problem solved.

New car, Triumph 1300, is superb.

Three unmarried Cox girls live in the house; Michael Cox is my chauffeur, since I have given up driving; Peter Cox is the gardener; Mrs. Cox, the mother, is the daily. So I am now in the

---

* Tom is my step-son, T. D. G. Mac Neece.

hands of the Cox family, and all foreigners are "out". Weekly
wage bill is enormous, but anything for a quiet life.

Yrs. ever

Bernard

It is in this quiet setting that he is enjoying his retirement from
public life, with very few visitors except for members of his family
and his close friends and companions from his wartime days. He
still gets a large fan mail which he much appreciates, and he is
delighted when he is sometimes sent luxurious presents by friends
such as Mr Garfield Weston. Where his present health is concerned
he is still, as an officer on the active list of the army, in the care of
the Royal Army Medical Corps and is attended, when necessary,
by Colonel J. Webb MC, MD, FRCP, Senior Consultant Physi-
cian at the Cambridge Military Hospital, Aldershot.

In 1969 two events occurred which gave my brother much
pleasure. These were the Silver Wedding of my wife and myself,
and the visit to England at the same time of our Canadian nephew
and his wife with two of their children, whom he liked enormously.
It was most unusual for him to attend and enjoy family parties and
he was certainly never slow to make this clear. A year later, after he
had entertained five of us he wrote to my wife: 'I don't care about
these family parties, with five people round my table. There will be
no more; they tire me. When would you and Brian like to come
and lunch here alone?'

After the Field-Marshal realised that his days of travel were at
an end, he used to spend a fortnight or so every January at the
Carlton Hotel in Bournemouth, going there in the New Year.
Some of his closest friends were always invited to join him including Sir Basil and Lady Liddell Hart who went several years running. My brother regarded Sir Basil as the greatest military
historian of his generation, though he argued fiercely with him out
of sheer delight in provocation. It was not all enjoyment staying
with him at the Carlton, as my wife and I found to our cost. His
penchant for publicity could sometimes be embarrassing as, for
instance, when he turned to a German waiter in the restaurant and
remarked, 'I killed Germans, you ought to be damn lucky to be

alive'! It was during one of these visits to Bournemouth that he summoned his research team, which he had employed in writing *A History of Warfare*, to join him at the Carlton Hotel for his final reading of the book in draft. In December 1970 my sister Winsome astounded our family, and most of all the Field-Marshal. At the age of seventy-six and a widow for the past twelve years she became engaged to Sir Godwin Michelmore,★ a widower aged seventy-seven, and a former Mayor of Exeter. Of course the whole family were delighted and no one more so than my brother. He attended the wedding, in Exeter early in the New Year of 1971 when he was staying at Bournemouth, and thoroughly enjoyed it.

Since the time of my sister's wedding the Field-Marshal has left the Mill to attend one more formal event. This was the occasion, on 12th May 1972, when he motored to the Staff College at Camberley to unveil a portrait of himself, which had been painted by the distinguished artist Terence Cuneo. It was a year or so earlier that Mr Cuneo had been commissioned by the then Commandant of the College, now Lieutenant-General Sir Allan Taylor, KBE, MC, to paint the picture. The latter had felt for some time that Camberley ought to have a permanent and fitting memento of the Field-Marshal's long association with the Staff Colleges, first as a student and later as an instructor at both Camberley and Quetta. When General Taylor left the Staff College to become the GOC South Eastern District he was succeeded as Commandant by Major-General P. H. Howard-Dobson, CB, to whom it fell to make all the arrangements for the unveiling of the portrait. In the painting Mr Cuneo has depicted the Field-Marshal clad in the informal uniform of his own choosing which he always wore in the desert, an open khaki shirt and loosely tied silk neck scarf under a sleeveless leather jacket, with for head dress the famous two-badge beret. He is standing half turned towards the viewer with his left hand on his hip and that well-known determined look on his face, mingled with a glint of humour in his eyes. It is the sort of stance I have seen him adopt so often when sizing up a problem, or judging a subordinate's capacity, and the painter has done well in portraying him in that very mood; the famous Montgomery nose

★ Major-General Sir Godwin Michelmore, KBE, CB, DSO, MC.

is unmistakable and clear for all to see. In the background of the picture is the desert, with all its dun colours lit up by the glow in the sky from the bright light of flames, shown with the smoke pouring from the tanks which have been set on fire in the battle. The portrait hangs above the fireplace in the ante-room of the officers' mess, and there could be no place more appropriate for this painting. Looking at it from the bar in the ante-room one seems almost to hear my brother, with that expression on his face, repeating to the students of the generations that come after him, his well-known doctrine for staff officers: 'Foresight, Accuracy, and Speed'.

The ceremony of the unveiling was a very simple but none the less memorable occasion. It was a fine summer afternoon when the Field-Marshal arrived at the Staff College on that Wednesday in May. Some officers, their wives and girl friends, were playing tennis on the courts below the terrace in front of the College and there was nothing unusual to be seen, except the number of motors in the car park, each bearing the stars which identify the occupant as a high-ranking service officer. It had been decided to limit the numbers attending the ceremony to a comparatively few senior serving officers, otherwise it would have been quite impossible to accommodate all those who might wish to be there. Apart therefore from the Commandant and his deputy, Brigadier P. R. Leuchars, CBE, the officers attending on this basis included:

The Chief of the General Staff	Gen. Sir Michael Carver, GCB, CBE, DSO, MC
The Adjutant General	Gen. Sir John Mogg, GCB, CBE, DSO
The Military Secretary	Lt.-Gen. Sir John Sharp, KCB, MC, MA
The GOC S.E. District	Lt.-Gen. Sir Allan Taylor, KBE, MC
The Director of Army Training	Maj.-Gen. A. G. Patterson, CB, DSO, OBE, MC
The Director, Royal Armoured Corps	Maj.-Gen. P. R. C. Hobart, CB, DSO, OBE, MC (Nephew of 'Hobo', Bernard's brother-in-law.)

David Montgomery and my brother's doctor, Colonel J. F. Webb, MC, RAMC, were also present, as well of course as Mr Terence Cuneo himself. After the unveiling of the portrait, and a brief speech by the Commandant, there were no more formalities, so my brother was able to converse as he wished with those present, in the setting and atmosphere of the College which he had known so well and where he had begun his married life. Then, after tea, the gathering broke up and the Field-Marshal returned to the Mill. It had been a very moving occasion and one which none of us present are likely to forget.

The last chapter is approaching its ending, though this is clearly not the end of the family that produced this very great soldier. My brother often used to say, 'To find out about a man, his performance and record, you must find out what makes him tick.' Enough has now been said, not only in this book but in many others, to answer this question about himself. In particular how much does he owe, in his make-up and character, to our Montgomery blood and how much to our mother who was a Farrar? In this matter we, as a family, can draw conclusions without we hope risk of over-simplification. So far all those who have written about him, and they are not a few, have pronounced him unreservedly a Montgomery who owed little to his maternal ancestry. As related in an earlier chapter he himself has often said to me, 'I do not care for the Farrar blood.' Be that as it may the truth is that in his make-up, overall, he drew his strength, and much of his very strong character and tenacity, largely from our mother. He fought with her, frequently and for long, as has been told, and neither ever gave way. The reason is clear to see. They were both remarkably alike in character and personality, so obviously neither *could* give way. This is not to say that he was not fundamentally an Irishman like his father before him. But the Bishop, in addition to all his charm and sense of humour, was a mystic and seer as well as a scholar and a great evangelical churchman. It is to our mother that the Field-Marshal owed his iron will and determination, his complete self-confidence in the rightness of his cause and his own ability to attain it. He has been likened in character to Cromwell but the only resemblance there is his strong religious convictions which he drew jointly from both our parents. Finally I am led to say, does it really matter from what origin he drew his greatness? It is more important to ask will his ending necessarily mark the end of an era? Will there be another like him? Surely the answer is 'Yes'. As he himself said, 'Marlborough and Wellington were two of the finest soldiers ever produced by our nation, and, indeed, possibly by any nation.' The Field-Marshal completes the hat-trick, and there will certainly be another when the time comes for us to need such a man. From what family he will come is another matter.

APPENDIX

OFFICERS WHO ATTENDED TAC HQ DINNER (EIGHTH ARMY AND 21 ARMY GROUP) 1972

Maj.-Gen. R. F. K. Belchem, CB, CBE
T. S. Bigland, Esq., DSO, MBE, TD
G. Butterworth, Esq.
Capt. N. V. Chavasse, MC, MBE
Maj. T. G. Coverdale
Lt.-Col. C. P. Dawnay, CBE, MVO
Maj.-Gen. Sir Francis de Guingand
Lt.-Col. P. Earle, MC
Capt. J. R. E. Harden, DSO, MC
Maj. D. W. J. Haylock
J. Henderson, Esq., MBE
Maj. T. E. B. Howarth, MC
Maj. R. B. Hunter, MBE, MC, Ch. B. Hon. LL.D
Maj. F. S. Lawrence
F./Lt. T. Martin
Maj. D. C. M. Mather, MC, MP
Richard O'Brien, Esq.
Capt. H. Oddy
Maj. P. R. Odgers, MBE
Lt.-Gen. Sir John Sharp, KCB, MC
Capt. J. F. Stafford
Maj. H. Wake, MC
Capt. W. H. Woodward, MBE

INDEX

Photographs are to be found facing
the pages listed in bold type.